Crisis, Chaos, and Organizations

A volume in
Research in Organizational Science
Daniel J. Svyantek, *Series Editor*

Research in Organizational Science

Daniel J. Svyantek, *Series Editor*

Organizations Behaving Badly: Destructive Behavior and Corrective Responses (2021)
Daniel J. Svyantek

Sports and Understanding Organizations (2017)
Daniel J. Svyantek

Organizational Processes and Received Wisdom (2014)
Daniel J. Svyantek and Kevin T. Mahoney

Received Wisdom, Kernels of Truth, and Boundary: Conditions in Organizational Studies (2013)
Daniel J. Svyantek and Kevin T. Mahoney

Emerging Themes in International Management of Human Resources (2010)
Philip Benson

Refining Familiar Constructs: Alternative Views in OB, HR, and I/O (2007)
Daniel J. Svyantek and Elizabeth McChrystal

A Closer Examination of Applicant Faking Behavior (2006)
Mitchell H. Peterson and Richard L. Griffith

Crisis, Chaos, and Organizations

The Coronavirus and Lessons for Organizational Theory

edited by

Daniel J. Svyantek

Auburn University

IAP

INFORMATION AGE PUBLISHING, INC.

Charlotte, NC • www.infoagepub.com

Library of Congress Cataloging-in-Publication Data

A CIP record for this book is available from the Library of Congress
http://www.loc.gov

ISBN: 978-1-64802-779-6 (Paperback)
978-1-64802-780-2 (Hardcover)
978-1-64802-781-9 (E-Book)

Printed and bound by CPI Group (UK) Ltd, Croydon, CR0 4YY

y effect in complex systems theory ent was the initial case(s) of CO- ng point for the pandemic, there s of lives lost and trillions of dollars ne COVID-19 pandemic. World gov- ving to deal with this pandemic, but precedented strategies (e.g., the U.S. ulus package[s]) have been used to important thing to remember about hat there are no dominant responses ge. As the event cascades throughout n only be tried out to see if they work. here is no way, however, to predict the ist be made and implemented to see e.

uations where old approaches do not what must be done in the future. Tush- e two types of changes that may occur These are competence-enhancing and ompetence-enhancing changes are ini- nd do not lead to great changes in the d. These changes are incremental. Com- rastic changes in the industrial system. old technologies and old companies. This ne current dominant organizations in an arise and take over the industry.

old as more and more organizations are n of when they will open again. Individual own responses to the situation. All of these ng-term impact on the nature of work and tual or psychological) that exists between both small and large companies.

expand Tushman and Anderson's (1986) f competence-enhancing and competence- nportant organizational constructs (e.g., or- posal that Svyantek and Brown (2000) make t during competence-enhancing and compe- hange is very different. During competence- are able to predict the future fairly well and, to improve effectiveness or efficiency in the here are more concerned with how the orga- vironment. However, during competence-de- effects of decisions are not foreseeable before

CONTENTS

their implementation, the role of the manager is to provide social support for the employees. Here the manager's role becomes one on maintaining worker motivation and morale. The manager's decisions and communication are directed within the organization towards employees. In the midst of this pandemic, it is impossible to know if the changes being made in organizations are competence-enhancing or competence-destroying.This volume provides 12 interesting views on the nature of changes being made by organizations during the COVID-19 pandemic.

The first chapter addresses the nature of science and the role of theory in interpreting data during the COVID-19 pandemic. We have been told, during the past year, to follow the science to deal with COVID-19 by politicians and talking heads during the past year. However, science uses different theories to interpret data. Spector's chapter describes the effects of using two different lenses to interpret the same data. He uses frames based on epidemiological theory and public health theory to show how these frames affect decisions made. He notes that during a crisis such as COVID-19, responses being made are not the only responses that are legitimate. These responses, and differences in these responses, are based on the different frames being used. This chapter is particularly relevant today as we begin to see the effects of decisions made based on epidemiological theory have ramifications in the public health sector. The epidemiological interpretation may have lowered the death rate slightly. However, we are beginning to see the impact of these epidemiological decisions on public health issues. For example, Christakis et al., (2020) discuss how the life expectancy of children may have been impacted negatively by the decisions made based on the epidemiological frame. Similarly, Engzell et al. (2021) have shown that in the Netherlands, during a very short lockdown period in comparison to other countries, school children learning from home made little or no progress. This chapter clearly illustrates the dilemma that may occur when "the facts and the science" are based more on a political decision-making process in which power and non-health issues affect how the potential consequences of the decisions being made are predicted.

The next three chapters describe the impact of COVID-19 on employees in organizations below managerial levels. Each of these provides insight into how the COVID-19 pandemic has affected workers.

DiStaso et al. introduce the concept of "disruptive workload change," defined as workload change that is the consequence of disruptive contexts external to the organization, and distinguish this concept from other forms of workload change. They look at this issue with both essential and non-essential workers. They discuss both antecedents and consequences of this disruptive workload change. Their discussion of this issue illustrates the problems faced by organizations during a competence-destroying change period. They recommend that managers identify the aspects of the

COVID-19 work environment that may be most disruptive for employees and determine whether these distressing aspects of work are only temporary. Even though the COVID-19 pandemic is continuing to unfold and leaves the future ambiguous, there may be some aspects of the work environment that managers should make a deliberate effort to communicate potential end points for stressful aspects of work may help by allowing employees to look forward to those end points. This communication is directed internally and helps maintain employee morale during the crisis.

Cubrich et al. investigate the impact of the COVID-19 on first responders. They describe how the COVID-19 pandemic had increased the risk and stress faced by public safety employees (e.g., police, firefighters, emergency medical service [EMS] personnel, and 911 dispatchers). They describe the unique sets of risks and stresses imposed on different public safety workers (e.g., police officers versus EMS personnel). Their chapter identifies the key challenges and factors at multiple levels of analysis (i.e., individual, group, organizational, national) facing public safety organizations. A multilevel approach is adopted to understand the pressures faced by these individuals. They propose a conceptual model to organize, inform, organize, guide, and advance research on potential challenges for public safety organizations due to crises such as COVID-19. They differentiate between top–down and bottom–up approaches to change in this crisis and the interactions between these approaches. One important consideration in their discussion is the effect of the changes on the organization. Their chapter takes an interesting perspective on the competence-enhancing versus competence-destroying distinction for the changes being made. They note that flexibility in agility in public sector organizations right after a crisis increases significantly but this flexibility reduces over time. They proposed that during a crisis strict rules and hierarchy are relatively relaxed, encouraging personnel at different levels to look for solutions and act fast. However, once the initial shock of a crisis passes, old rules and hierarchies are reinforced leading to a reduction in agility and quick action. This is especially dangerous in the case of a pandemic because it usually lasts a relatively long time and is often unpredictable. Therefore, one of the issues that organizations face during an extended crisis is this return to the old normal before the crisis has ended means the organization has interpreted the change as competence-enhancing. Cubrich et al. note, however, that the environment is still unpredictable and chaotic and change may be competence-destroying. Cubrich et al. provide recommendations for public safety organizations to deal with this issue. All organizations with strong cultures may face this issue during the pandemic. Their recommendations are relevant for many organizations other than the public safety organization.

Svyantek and Williams' chapter deals with the impact of the COVID-19 pandemic on academic environments. They note that crisis healthcare policies instituted in academic environments may disproportionately devalue and endanger the lives of disabled people during a pandemic and produce more vulnerable and disabled lives. Therefore, when imagining the "new normal," the authors look to disability communities for guidance in forging just communal practices of work, sociality, and care for working from home. This chapter describes changes in policies and practices that are more bottom–up (derived from employees' needs) but requiring top management support. The authors propose that framing work from home initiatives based on the views of disability advocates will have benefits for all employees facing work from home situations. This chapter echoes the "return to old ways" issue seen in Cubrich et al. They note that institutions of higher education have a tendency to return to old practices as the pandemic extends in time. Similarly, this chapter provides an example of the issue described in Spector's chapter. Different frames of reference for the change, held by administrative personnel in higher education, affects the institutionalization of practices developed during the pandemic. They offer recommendations for improving work from home practices in higher education. These practices, as for Cubrich's et al. recommendations, have generalizable applications to many organizations.

The fifth chapter by Neale is the first of four chapters that investigate the role of the leader in crisis situations. Neale's chapter provides an interesting discussion of how successful adaptations to the pandemic crisis occur from the bottom–up. However, this chapter also describes the role of management in supporting their employees and the changes being made by the employees. The chapter investigates the experience of elementary teachers as they abruptly moved from brick-and-mortar classrooms into their digital classrooms resulting from the COVID-19 global pandemic. Neale discusses the feelings of the teachers facing these changes. These changes were stressful and instituted by directives from above without the teachers' inputs. As a result, there was a need for the development of communities of support among the teachers. The chapter describes these communities and the bottom–up process which developed these communities. An important insight in the chapter is that the role of managers (e.g., principals of schools) changed. The manager could not provide information on how to do teaching in a distance learning environment because they had never done this. However, principals providing comfort and understanding to the teachers were important in keeping morale up. This supports the views proposed earlier for managers in competence-destroying change. Neale offers recommendations for organizations in such situations with generalizability beyond the academic organization.

Cannon and Middleton-House's chapter investigates crisis decision-making and leadership needs during times of crisis in organizations. They describe these crisis situations as those where the environment is volatile, of leadership (collaborative, consultative, directive, and coercive) have impacts on both acceptance of, and resistance to change. The author's make a critical distinction between crisis and chaos. This distinction provides insight into what leaders can do in such situations. Crisis may support competency-enhancing changes that improve the organization's functioning. Chaos, however, is more clearly linked to competence-destroying change and the need to influence employee morale to maintain the organization through these times. The authors provided recommendations for leaders based on three change themes. These three themes relate to the role of the leader in leading change by understanding the organizational culture and its employees and then creating the behaviors that will improve acceptance of change.

The last two chapters provide insight into how large, multinational companies and industries are dealing with the COVID-19 pandemic. Moi et al.'s chapter deals with the role of social media and digital communications for organizations seeking to successfully navigate a crisis. They deal with the communication strategies used by Amazon.com to deal with customers during the COVID-19 pandemic. The authors' finding provided insight into how social media communication strategies take place during a pandemic crisis. They show using current knowledge on crisis communication strategies in a social media context how, during a global pandemic crisis, organizations can learn about users and customers to develop digital communication strategies that will increase corporate reputation. They show important ways to limit the effects of negative comments by small sub-groups. The chapter provides managers some means of creating effective and suitable communication strategies. Considering the pivotal role of social media in people's lives, the authors' propose it is critical to show managers implementing corrective actions how to more effectively deal with customers. These corrective actions reflect changes in practice and tone of messages to customers during such a crisis.

Ajami et al.'s chapter describes the ways in which crises provide potential opportunities for new practices in large, multinational industries. The industry being investigated is the oil industry. The authors describe how global economic challenges such as COVID-19 may create opportunities to develop new organizational linkages and configurations that could lead to greater sustainability in the oil industry. The world was on its way to becoming a transnational market for goods, capital, and economic services prior to the COVID-19 crisis according to the authors. However, the coronavirus has altered the international markets' configurations of assets and capabilities. These changes have altered established global supply chains that benefited both global producers and consumers. A reconfigured, seamless global economy would allow for a better fit for both customers and suppliers. Through technological linkages and configurations, these companies could allow enterprises to capture economies of scale and scope, and address organizational efficiencies and effectiveness in the new environment created by COVID-19. COVID-19 is likely to impact organizational structures and make cross-country alliances in the international oil industry desirable. In this new environment, each organizational participant can be encouraged to leverage its most valuable assets and exchanges of resources and capabilities to generate revenue for both state-owned oil organizational entities, as well as the publicly traded multinational organizations.

The effects of the pandemic on organizations are still occurring as this volume goes to print. These chapters, however, provide important insights for all organizations during this time of crisis. This volume's chapters all provide views on the breadth of change in organizational environments created by the COVID-19 pandemic and the forms of organizational responses developed to meet the challenge of these changes. The chapters express bottom–up and top–down approaches to environmental change. The chapters provide insight into the way organizations perceive the effect of COVID-19 as (a) a permanent or transitory change in the organization's environment and (b) as a crisis or opportunity. Taken together, the chapters provide both scientists and practitioners with a starting point for understanding the impact of COVID-19 on organizational theory and on management practice for readers.

—Daniel J. Svyantek

REFERENCES

Abraham, F. D., Abraham, R. H., & Shaw, C. D. (1990). *A visual introduction to dynamic systems theory for psychology.* Aerial Press.

Christakis, D. A., van Cleve, W., & Zimmerman, F. J. (2020). Estimation of US children's educational attainment and years of life lost associated with primary school closures during the Coronavirus disease 2019 pandemic. *JAMA Network Open, 3*(11), e2028786. https://doi.org/10.1001/jamanetworkopen.2020.28786

Engzell, P., Frey, A., & Verhagen, M. D. (2021). Learning loss due to school closures during the COVID-19 pandemic. *Proceedings of the National Academy of Sciences of the United States of America, 118*(17), 1–7.

Liebovitch, L. S. (1998). *Fractals and chaos simplified for the life science.* Oxford University.

Svyantek, D. J., & Brown, L. L. (2000). A complex systems approach to organizations. *Current Directions in Psychological Science, 9*(2), 69–74.

Tushman, M. L., & Anderson, P. (1986). Technological discontinuities and organizational environments. *Administrative Science Quarterly, 31*(3), 439–465.

CHAPTER 1

A CRITICAL APPRAISAL OF THE DOMINANT PANDEMIC NARRATIVE

Bert Spector
Northeastern University

> If the system fails
> the broken bodies
> become invisible and/or hyper-visible
> —Daniel Borzutzky (2020), "Systemic Risk"

This chapter offers a critical examination of what I have labeled the dominant pandemic narrative; the story that came to dominate much of the COVID-19 discourse in the early months of the pandemic. I come to this project with three underlying assumptions that I can make immediately explicit. I believe that

- critique during times of crisis is essential;
- no response to a crisis, no matter how legitimate, is the only legitimate response; and
- all responses, no matter how legitimate, reflect a particular view of the world.

Crisis, Chaos, and Organizations, pages 1–31

All narratives exist as human constructions by which the narrative author forges the ambiguously complex dynamics of the world into a clear sequence of well-defined events, an unambiguous delineation of protagonists and antagonists, and a self-assured assertion of cause-and-effect. No narrative can tell the "whole story" or include every contingency, so the narrative author must engage in "selective appropriation" in order to mold a coherent story (Ewick & Sibley, 1995, p. 200). Authors make choices about what to leave in and what to omit.

When a particular narrative becomes widely promoted and generally adopted—that is, a dominant narrative—what is selectively excluded can become at best tangential and at worst invisible (Minichin, 2006). The process of selective appropriation, so vital to the construction of a coherent narrative, can be problematic, even dangerous, when that narrative is constructed for the purpose of communicating what is claimed to be a real-world crisis.

Crisis Narratives

Narrative theory most typically focuses on stories set in an explicitly imagined world; one that unfolds through children's stories, screenplays, folktales, novels, and so on (e.g., Cadden , 2011; Propp, 1968; Varotsis, 2015; Walsh, 2007). These studies are foundational to the development of narrative theory. Issues of accuracy particularly are replaced by an appreciation of the mechanics upon which a narrative is built and the ways in which narratives attract and appeal. A make-believe narrative operates in a made-up world, but the story proceeds in a coherent way, true to its own internal logic (Fisher, 1987).

But when narrative authors seek to tell a story about real-world contingencies, their intent is different than make-believe. Now, the narrative author is seeking to communicate what is taken to be an actual event, not a fairy tale. A real-world narrative can take many forms: from a personal memoir to a national history. These narratives represent themselves as offering an accurate correspondence with the external world. Crisis narratives, a subset of real-world narratives, insist that the contingencies contained in the story pose an immediate and urgent threat to a valued social unit (Spector, 2019). Crisis narratives embed their core claim of urgency within an overarching narrative structure.

The power of the crisis narrative author is considerable. The creators of a crisis narrative, often people in leadership and other influential positions, make choices about how to define the contours of the event they are describing. In making that decision, they are exercising the power to circumscribe the event. Keep that in mind: the exercise of power built into the process of constructing a crisis narrative. When a particular narrative becomes dominant, it asserts itself as the controlling frame for any and all subsequent consideration and responses. The inevitable narrative construction process of selective appropriation now becomes controlling. Dominance results in the invisibility of some contingencies and the hyper-visibility of others.

Crisis narratives gain particular import as a way of communicating and understanding the dynamics of an apparently disruptive and threatening situation (Seeger & Sellnow, 2016; Spector, 2019). Authors of a crisis narrative invite their audience into a shared understanding of patterns, of how *A* influences *B* and then shapes *C*. That invitation comes in the form of a compelling story that acts as a carrier of the core claim; their objective descriptions and subjective ascriptions. Through the act of constructing a story, the narrative author asserts cause-and-effect to make a case for a particular point of view regarding the urgent contingencies and the appropriate response (Abbott, 2008; Patterson & Monroe, 1998; Shenhav et al., 2014).

The world does not come prepackaged with a single, objectively "true" narrative. The SARS-CoV-2 pathogen does not sport a "global pandemic" name tag or tell people to wear masks or keep schools open or crowd into local bars on Saturday night. The virus simply seeks host environments that allow it to replicate. The same is true of all events we label as crises; they await human attribution of meaning, and that attribution unfolds in the form of a narrative.

We cannot expect any narrative author to tell the "whole story" or include every contingency. What we can and should do is be aware of the choices the authors are making about what to leave in and what to omit. Some contingencies are rendered hyper-visible. Others become invisible by virtue of omission. Cuomo (2020), for instance, brought hyper-visibility to coronavirus-related infections and deaths in his May 1 briefing. As indicated by his deployment of the term "ancillary" (12:08) his narrative did not provide equal weight to all outcomes.

That decision—what to leave in, what to leave out—makes the role of the narrative author quite powerful. That power is amplified if the narrative author has access to a national or international pulpit. What presidents say, for example, becomes front page news, so their own version of the story gets amplified. But no matter how commanding or authoritative narrative authors may be, no matter how many times we are exposed to their story, we need to remember: It is still a constructed story (Fisher, 1987).

We can ask of Cuomo's story—as we can and should ask of any and every narrative (Frank, 2012)—what "truth" is being asserted? What alternative narratives existed? Cuomo was reflecting and advancing what had come to be the dominant narrative of the pandemic, the version of the story that had come to be accepted by most constituents. The process of fact curation, a process inherent in the construction of a coherent narrative, can be problematic, even dangerous (Minichin, 2006). That is not to imply that there is no such thing as verifiable realities.

Building on Brute Facts

Legitimate crisis narratives build on what Searle (1995) called "brute facts": realities that cannot legitimately be wished away or denied. The story then unfolds with plausible logic as a way of ordering, presenting, and explaining those facts. Our knowledge of brute facts is provisional—we often learn tomorrow that we were wrong yesterday—and not always easily attained. Nevertheless, they amount to actual contingencies capable of being verified or discredited. They cannot be lied away, denied away, or wished away, which is not to say, there haven't been leaders who have attempted all three.

The brute facts of the pandemic remained "maddeningly unclear in these early months" (Yong, 2020). This "is a *novel* virus," noted a UCLA-based epidemiologist, "new to humanity, and nobody knows what will happen" (Kristof, 2020, para. 2, emphasis added). We are, after all, still learning more about the 1919 influenza epidemic. Still any legitimate narrative of a crisis is obliged to seek a knowledge of reality to the best of the narrative author's ability.

The basic brute facts of the pandemic as they were known at the point of Cuomo's briefing are laid out in Exhibit 2.1. Any and all legitimate pandemic narratives must start here. That does not ensure that there will be only one legitimate narrative. There are often multiple, even contradictory, narratives that can be considered as legitimate. It is common, particularly in reaction to highly complex contingencies, that there will be different, even competing crises narratives. You may not agree with a particular narrative. It may not be right. But a narrative based on brute facts and plausibly argued is legitimate. And in the case of pandemic, one particular legitimate narrative emerged as the dominant pandemic narrative.

EXHIBIT 2.1 The Brute Facts of the Coronavirus Pandemic (Based on Doctors Without Borders, 2020)

A new coronavirus was first reported in Wuhan, China, on December 31, 2019. There was no known human pre-immunity, no vaccine, and no specific treatment. The virus is contagious, and everyone is presumed to be susceptible.

Coronaviruses are a large family of viruses, most of which are harmless for humans. Four types are known to cause colds, and two other types can cause severe lung infections: Severe Acute Respiratory Syndrome (SARS) and Middle East Respiratory Syndrome (MERS). The novel coronavirus was named SARS-CoV-2, because of its similarities to the virus that causes SARS.

SARS-CoV-2 seemed to target cells in the lungs, and possibly elsewhere in the respiratory system. Cells infected by the virus produce more virus particles, which can then spread to other people.

Understanding of this new coronavirus and the resulting disease—known as COVID-19 as a shortening of COronaVIrus Disease-2019—was still evolving. The airborne virus mainly spreads from person to person, including from people who appear to have no symptoms. SARS-CoV-2 can be transmitted through small particals from the nose or mouth which are spread when an infected person coughs or exhales. People can contract COVID by touching objects or surfaces contaminated with the virus, and then touching their eyes, nose, or mouth, although they are far more likely to be infected by breathing in droplets from a person with coronavirus who coughs out or exhales droplets.

THE EMERGENCE OF A DOMINANT NARRATIVE

In the history of medical responses to pandemic outbreaks, scientific researchers regularly, even predictably, become "prisoners of particular paradigms and theories of disease causation" (Honigsbaum, 2019, p. 7). The effect of such unconscious imprisonment was that the scientists were blinded "to the threats posed by pathogens both known and unknown." That problem—we can think of it as the problem of paradigms—is unsurprising to anyone familiar with Kuhn's (1962) historical study of scientific revolutions.

Paradigms are comprised of a distinct set of concepts, theories, and methods of inquiry and investigation. They define a particular way of thinking about the world and determine what questions to ask, what facts to look at, and how to interpret what is learned.[2] Through their dominance, paradigms define "normal science" and encourage knowledge advancement within those boundaries. But that dominance also constricts learning, particularly learning that might occur, to use a contemporary idiom, "out of the box."

By defining what questions to ask, a scientific paradigm also shapes what questions *not* to ask. And therein lies the limitations of dominance. The underlying assumptions of a paradigm are not on the table for consideration. Critique of the paradigm's parameters falls outside the realm of "normal science." Stay within the paradigm and advance knowledge about the

2020). These were insights unavailable to decision makers in the early months. However, even when those data became known, many schools remained physically closed.

The second set of risks—how many children would permanently drop out of school, how many would be endangered by staying home, and so on—posed an even greater measurement challenge. There was data available. The Boston public school system, for instance, found that 20% of its students failed to log in to a class in May even once. In Philadelphia, only 53% of elementary school children were making daily contact. Officials in East St. Louis, Illinois, one of the poorest communities in the United States, reported that 35% of school students had "internet access challenges." In a national survey, the majority of responding teachers said that less than half of their students were showing up for remote classes (Associated Press, 2020; Graham et al., 2020; Toness, 2020).

Models pointed to rising childhood hunger and suggested the extent of lasting developmental harm.[5] Those statistics *were* reported, as was the dramatic rise in poverty particularly among minority children (Bauer, 2020; DeParle, 2020; Goldstein, 2020). None, however, made their way to the omnipresent scroll on cable news or attracted the label "tragedy" in *Times'* headlines. They were all ancillary to the dominant narrative's relentless emphasis on infection rates and death. The first set of risks loomed more immediately and frightfully. Hyper-visible. The second set of risks lingered on the periphery, as an ancillary outcome.

Flatten the curve, in fact, became the virtual motto of the response and the organizing construct of the dominant narrative. Any and all action designed first to contain—keep the disease local—and then, once the disease spread, to mitigate against the damage caused by that spread. Ninety percent of the world's school aged population was sent home. That was standard pandemic protocol, according to epidemiologists (Walensky & del Rio, 2020).

Stay-at-home orders came from state and local officials, while Fauci made clear, in opposition to the president's stated position, that every state should shut down: "I don't understand why that's not happening" (Strauss, 2020, para. 7).[6] By the dynamics of N_E—minimize the spread of and the damage caused by the coronavirus—this was the way to achieve optimal outcomes. Many people would still get infected, sick, and die, but the numbers would be far less than otherwise.

Social distancing, isolation, quarantining, and, in a very real sense, shutting down society would, "without a doubt" save lives that would otherwise be lost to COVID. During the shutdown, researchers could "seek treatments and develop vaccines" while public health institutions and hospitals could "build up the testing and treatment capacity that must be in place before any 'return to normal'" (Branswell & Jospeh, 2020; Gavin, 2020; S. Roberts,

2020; Sailor, 2020; Specktor, 2020). And what about the all-important question of when and how to reopen?

The "Science" of Reopening

"Science" would be the guide to matters involving reopening. The governor of Michigan said so when she insisted that the state would make decisions depending on a "data-driven approach based on facts, based on science, based on recommendations from experts" (Elassar, 2020). California's governor agreed. "Science, not politics must be the guide" (Almasy et al., 2020, para. 2). That appeal to science as a unitary construct is highly problematic.

Because "science" never speaks in a single, unequivocal, authoritative voice, and scientists are no more immune to selectivity biases and the construction of interpretative narratives than any other group, "following the science" can mean almost anything (Leng & Leng, 2020). That is especially true in regard to topics characterized by high complexity and great uncertainty.

Underlying the stated determination to "follow the science" was an insistence that decisions concerning a pandemic response should not be responsive to political self-interest. Follow-the-science decision makers would take a full accounting of the brute facts. That's a desirable goal. It would have been more accurate, however, if governors had announced their intention to follow a particular version of science as articulated by a particularly prominent group of scientists while ignoring some scientific outliers. More accurate, perhaps, but far less reassuring.

The dominant narrative led these governors to conflate "the science" with "the science of epidemiology." *That* was the science they intended to follow. That conflation makes some sense. A pandemic, after all, is a widespread epidemic. But it also leads to a belief that there is no science other than the science of epidemiology.

Epidemiologists prepare for epidemics and do their best, once an outbreak has occurred, to mitigate, contain, and prevent future epidemics. N_E grew from that commitment and would prove its effectiveness largely on the dual metric of infection rates and COVID-19 deaths. National responses—by the United States, Sweden, Germany, and so on—were judged to be better or worse based on those numbers.

Accurate numbers were admittedly tough to come by: spotty testing results, possible manipulation by national governments, and so on, hindered clarity of statistics. Still, these were the metrics N_E relied on. Denmark's response was more effective than that of their neighbor Sweden, because Denmark reported a death rate of 9.7 people per 100,000 inhabitants while Sweden reported 39.57. Infection rates per 1 million inhabitants told a somewhat different story, with Sweden reporting a significantly lower rate

(3,591) than other countries, including the United States (4,544). Even though the causes of infection and death rates are multifactorial, the figures became the primary metric of the pandemic. How many people have been tested for COVID. How many have died of COVID-19? (Armstrong, 2020a, 2020b; N. McCarthy, 2020; Sung & Kaplan, 2020).

N_E offered its own heroes and villains. There was, through a process of anthropomorphism, the coronavirus itself, depicted as a ball, often green, with irregularly spaced protrusions, pocked with lunar craters, and offering eyes and an expressive, often sneering mouth (Cavna, 2020). Heroes? They were plentiful: Dr. Fauci, certainly; for many, Governor Cuomo; front-line health care workers; first responders, even package and grocery-delivery people. *Newsweek* even populated a special page of "Pandemic Heroes" (https://www.newsweek.com/pandemicheroes). Those heroes and villains often came packaged by the mass media, which emphasized and amplified N_E, helping to ensure its dominance. The role of the mass media in promoting N_E deserves special attention.

Circulating and Reinforcing N_E

"A 'tragedy' is unfolding." That *Times* headline from April 9th deployed a brutally emotional term to characterize New York City's emergence as the "epicenter" of COVID (Correal & Jacobs, 2020). With a cluster of abutting city neighborhoods—Corona, Elmhurst, East Elmhurst, and Jackson Heights with a combined population of 600,000—reporting over 7,260 coronavirus cases, the term was legitimately applied. But there was no such emotion attached to any reporting on the dire situation of the city's youth population exacerbated by school closings. When that situation was reported—and it was—the language was factual, a matter-of-fact assessment:

- "The Pandemic Sent 1.5 Billion Children Home From School [Globally]: Many Might Not Return" (Stancati et al., 2020).
- "New York Parents Are Stressed Out About Their Children Falling Behind, Survey" (Grosserode, 2020).
- "Research Shows Students Falling Months Behind During Virus Disruptions" (Goldstein, 2020).

Where was the "tragedy"? It is possible, of course, that readers might see these headlines and think to themselves: That *is* a "tragedy." But the coverage did not convey that emotion. For NE, the tragedy grew from the spread of the disease. All other consequences, as disturbing as they might be, are unfortunate and unintended but necessary outcomes. They are ancillary to the main task of controlling the spread of the coronavirus.

The dramatic arc of N_E remained focused on disease prevention and control. Media outlets reinforced that plot with a steady deluge of data presented on cable news. Two cable news stations visually framed their broadcasts with an ever-present red banner—CNN ran their banner across the bottom while MSNBC preferred the right-hand side of the screen.

Visual framing is a form of argument; it positions images in a way that influences the audience to adopt a particular point of view (Lorenzo-Dus & Smith, 2018; Pandey et al., 2014). Reliance on numbers offers reassurance that what matters is being counted and thus counts. The converse is also communicated: What is not being counted does not count (Stone, 2020). That reassurance is misleading, of course. What is being counted in the visual framing and what is left out? The patina of scientific objectivity renders uncounted matters less consequential.

The staggering economic "cost" was calculated in terms of lives lost, and models suggested how many lives could have been saved if social distancing rules had been imposed just a week sooner if the president had not downplayed the seriousness of the epidemic or the benefits of wearing masks. On Memorial Day weekend, the *Times* highlighted, in a heartbreaking illustration, the 100,000 lost lives (Darcy, 2020; Frakt, 2020; Glanz & Robertson, 2020; Staff, 2020b). The deadly toll exceeded 200,000 in mid-September. Children excluded from virtual classrooms or residing in food insecure homes were nowhere to be seen or counted.

The number of deaths was indeed staggering, exceeding, it was reported, the combined U.S. death toll in the Korean and Vietnam wars.[7] Those wars spanned 23 years. The 100,000 number had been reached in 3 months and continued to grow into the summer, fall, and winter.[8]

To personalize those statistics, *Times*' stories focused on individual tragedies. The same day *The New York Times* covered Cuomo's (2020) May 1st press briefing, "Grandma Rocket, the Virus and a Family Whose Love Bridged 2,500 Miles" (Fink, 2020) and "After a Lifetime Together, Coronavirus Takes Them Both" (Rosman, 2020), appeared on the front page. MSNBC and CNN regularly ran profiles of individuals who had died of COVID.[9]

The press reported on the counterexamples of countries that chose not to respond initially with a sweeping shutdown of society. Sweden, for example, avoided lockdowns, kept schools open, and generally relied on voluntary compliance with guidelines for mask wearing and social distancing (Davies & Roeber, 2020; Gudbjartsson et al., 2020). The coverage was not positive, insisting that N_E was the *only* legitimate narrative. Sweden's deathrate was too high compared with Denmark (even though Denmark opened schools quickly and Sweden had a significantly lower infection rate than the United States). Another article quoted an economist as concluding, "They literally gained nothing. It's a self-inflicted wound, and they have no economic gains." Sweden's economy had suffered its own decline (Goodman, 2020, para. 3).

Many of the negative stories focusing on Sweden's alternative narrative condemned the approach for being "lax":

- "Grim Coronavirus Death Toll Projected in Sweden After Lax Approach to Pandemic" (CBS News, 2020).
- "Is Sweden's Lax Approach to the Coronavirus Backfiring?" (Neuding & Sanandaji, 2020).
- "Sweden Can't Explain Away the Fact That Its Lax Coronavirus Approach Is Killing People" (Winant, 2020).

"Lax" is not a descriptive term, not a usage of reportage. It is, rather, an expression of judgement, of *negative* judgment. Its deployment assumes a deficient deviance from a standard. In this case, Sweden's approach was evaluated not as an alternative narrative but rather vilified as a deviation from the dominant narrative, N_E, that was asserted to be the standard.

As COVID cases surged again in late Summer 2020 across Europe, Sweden escaped with very low numbers (Keyton, 2020). A *The New York Times* article took note of the phenomenon under the headline, "Vilified Early Over Lax Virus Strategy, Sweden Seems to Have Scourge Controlled" (Erdbrink, 2020). No mention was made of the paper's own role in conducting that admitted vilification. Whatever may be said about the efficacy of Sweden's response, and no response should be above criticism, to label it as "lax" was a dismissive over-simplification.

Like any narrative, N_E was a human construction built around an argument of how to view the pandemic. And like any dominant narrative, it worked to marginalize and discount an alternative narrative. No agency in the United States, including the *The New York Times*, tallied the number of student in-person school days lost (the number of students out of school times the number of days schools were operating remotely). A study reported by the *Journal of the American Medical Association Network* found that school shutdowns would lead to reduced educational attainment, which, in turn, would shorten the life expectancy of publicly educated primary-school aged children by an estimated 5.53 million years of life lost (Christakis et al., 2020). That staggering finding failed to earn a headline from *The New York Times.*

Articles in *The New York Times* and elsewhere recognized the developmental damage caused by school closings and the particular hardships imposed on young and disadvantaged children. They did not, however, tally those lost days or display them visually on the front page. No article referred to those lost school days and resulting harm as a "self-inflicted wound." Saying Sweden "literally gained nothing" made those outcomes invisible.[10]

Adding "they have no economic gains" (Goodman, 2020, para. 3) justified that invisibility.

In its starkest form, N_E offered a binary choice: Stay home or die. Or, as the *The New York Times* phrased it in a front-page headline, "Your Life of Your Livelihood" (Tavernise et al., 2020). Of course it was an impossible choice, especially when livelihood meant capacity to feed one's family and pay for housing.

When a single narrative comes to dominate media coverage, alternatives become marginalized, dismissed by the logic of that dominant narrative. That does not mean there wasn't one. The science of epidemiology shaped the dominant narrative. Other sciences had a say in a differing story.

THE POSSIBILITY OF A COUNTER NARRATIVE

There was an important counter-pandemic narrative available alongside N_E. I am not referring to the science deniers or those who saw political/cultural gain from fighting science and denying reality, but from conscientious leaders attempting to address the public health and well-being needs of their communities. The most significant counter narrative built from public health experts and is thus labeled N_{PH}.

The two fields—epidemiology and public health—are distinct, a distinction often elided in the mass media. A *Washington Post* video, for instance, correctly identified Anthony Fauci as an infectious disease expert, but posted the video under the misleading headline, "Fauci Is the Public Health Expert Leading Us Through the Coronavirus Crisis" (https://www.youtube.com/watch?v=t-sy2IMCX9w). He was not, nor did he ever claim to be a "public health expert."

Epidemiology is a biomedical science focusing on the study of disease (Morrison, 1984). It is a data-driven science that "relies on a systematic and unbiased approach to the collection, analysis, and interpretation of data" (www.cdc.gov/csels/dsepd/ss1978/index.html, para. 3). The intention of epidemiological scientists is to be politically neutral and ideologically uncommitted. "The way you can survive and maintain the integrity of science as well as your personal integrity," Fauci explained, "is that you cannot be ideological" (as quoted in Warraich, 2020, para. 9). Science, in the stated position of epidemiology, can and should remain neutral.[11]

Public health and epidemiology are related disciplines, which is different than saying they are interchangeable. At universities, departments of epistemology are typically found within schools of public health, residing alongside environmental health sciences, nutritional sciences, health management and policy, and so on (e.g., https://sph.umich.edu/directory).

By providing scientific input to public health approaches, epidemiology is structured to serve public health but not to dominate it.

The fields are far from being identical or interchangeable. Public health assumes a broad, multi-disciplinary "beyond biomedical science" perspective (Brown, 2019, p. 4). It is not *a* science, but rather an integration of multiple sciences.

While epidemiology rests entirely within the biomedical sciences, public health calls on a wide array of social sciences—sociology, psychology, anthropology, political science, and economics mainly but not exclusively—to analyze the "relationships between health and society" (Dew, 2014, p. 2). By scanning a single issue of the *American Journal of Public Health* released in August 2020, the breadth of interests and expertise in the field becomes almost startlingly apparent (Table 1.1). The goal of epidemiology is to understand the origins, composition, and spread of a disease; public health promotes social wellness (https://www.apha.org/what-is-public-health).

While epidemiology claims non-ideology as its sine qua non, public health embraces ideology (King, 2002). The ideology of public health has evolved over time, starting with a colonialist conception of caring for subjugated populations out of a combination of paternalism and the concern for the health of occupying troops and the economic interests of the colonial power (e.g., Curtin, 1998; Seth, 2018). Emerging in the 1990s, public health experts came to be identified largely with a social justice and human rights ideology that committed the field to the belief "that everyone has the right to a standard of living adequate for the health and well-being of him or herself and of his or her family. These rights include food, clothing, housing, medical care, necessary social services, and the right to security in the event of unemployment, sickness, disability, widowhood, old age or in circumstances beyond control" (Unite for Sight, 2000, para. 13). Social justice and human rights are now taken to be cornerstones of a healthy community and thus legitimate concerns of public health.

TABLE 1.1 Public Health Concerns Addressed in August 2020 Issue of *American Journal of Public Health*

• Sexual orientation and gender identity	• Prescription drug monitoring
• Climate silence	• Consumer product safety
• Internet access for children	• Food security
• Health of incarcerated populations	• Health among immigrant populations
• Dangers of wildfires	• Lessons of history
• Health and safety of voting	• Codes of ethics
• Inequalities in women's health care	• Firearms
• Bike helmet laws	• Health insurance coverage
• Work conditions	• Community-based syringe exchanges
• Access to contraception	• Youth suicide

The fields of epidemiology and public health often offer different narratives to chart divergent responses to the same conditions. A policy choice that appears perfectly rational from an epidemiological perspective might appear to be "unwise" when considered through the comprehensive lens of public health (Savitz et al., 1999). During the pandemic, for instance, the invigoration of a social protest movement associated with #BlackLivesMatter evoked warnings for epidemiologists concerning the spread of the disease. A number of public health experts embraced a different idea, that a mass movement aimed at promoting racial justice was a way to promote social wellness (Warraich, 2020).

As epidemiologists promoted lockdowns and quarantines to flatten the curve, the broader focus of public health science warned of a robust catalogue of consequent ill health that would include:

- poor indoor air quality said by the WHO to be responsible for 3.8 million premature deaths worldwide in 2016 (Ansari & Yousefabad, 2020),[12]
- negative mental health comes related to implementing quarantine orders (Dubey et al., 2020),
- a rise in instances of domestic abuse (Mohan & Le Poidevin, 2020),
- increasing childhood malnutrition and hunger (Husain, 2020),
- an estimated 80 million babies worldwide missing regular vaccinations (Fox, 2020),
- the possibility of long-dormant diseases breeding in unused office buildings (Horberry, 2020),
- a sharp rise in global hunger due to loss of income (Dahir, 2020),
- a sharp rise in childhood diseases around the world—diphtheria, cholera, measles, a mutated strain of poliovirus—due to interruptions in inoculation projects (Hoffman & Maclean, 2020), and
- an "epidemic" of lost learning and developmental opportunities as a result of school shutdown (Saldaña, 2020).

As the human toll accumulated, newscasts paid attention. The drastic rise of hunger that resulted from the economic shutdown amounted to "a human crisis equal to the public health crisis of the disease," suggested an MSNBC commentator on August 3. To public health experts, however, no such bifurcation existed. Hunger *was* a public health crisis.

There were also more systemic effects of lockdowns that significantly impacted social wellness. Lockdowns and school closures exacerbated existing racial and class divides, and inconsistent enforcement and exemptions for particular classes of workers added to the cleavage. Racism and poverty are, it is acknowledged but not fully appreciated, leading causes of poor health (Gill & Bhopal, 2003; Honan & Chapman, 2020; Pinkster, 2020; Southall, 2020).

Decision-science, also excluded from the popular mandate to "follow the science," raised concerns about the efficacy of strict lockdown preferred by N_E. Perhaps strict stay-at-home behavior would work to flatten the curve if people actually did stay at home. But the order itself was bound to fail. Enough was known about how people make decisions to suggest a more effective approach: eschew absolutes in favor of a "more balanced public health approach"; one, say, that emphasized, "Stay close to home, keep your distance, wash your hands," rather than "Shut down and stay at home, or get sick." Thinking in terms of decision science, Oster (2020) noted, "When people are advised that one very difficult behavior is safe, and (implicitly or not) that everything else is risky, they may crack under the pressure, or throw up their hands" (para. 7). Just as a policy of abstinence was an ineffective response to unwanted teen pregnancies (as compared with information about and access to effective birth control), a stay-at-home policy invited resistance. "If people think all activities (other than staying home) are equally risky, they figure they might as well do those that are more fun" (para. 3).

N_{PH} accepted the utility of lockdowns, but only temporarily and under specific conditions. "Lockdowns alone are generally insufficient to stop viral spread," argued Marcus (2020, p. 10). They served a purpose: to prevent the health system from being overwhelmed by COVID cases and to buy time to scale up coronavirus testing, contact tracing, and personal protective equipment (PPE). Unless a lockdown of the population was accompanied by an intense buildup in public health infrastructure, the country would be "back to where we started, only now with a population that's no longer willing or able to continue these drastic measures, which were never intended to be a long-term solution anyway" (Marcus, personal correspondence, June 30, 2020).

N_{PH} focused on that infrastructure: "systems to produce diagnostic tests fast and in great abundance; better surge capacity of health-care providers; smart supply chains for PPE and ventilators, and coordinated plans for moving them from one jurisdiction to another; coordinated planning among cities, states, provinces, nations, and international agencies for containing infectious disaster; public education to stiffen willingness to endure social distancing and quarantine monitoring; better public-health leadership and reliable funding cycles; and, most critically, the political will to risk paying for preparedness that might not be needed" (Khan, 2016; as quoted in Quammen, 2020, para. 42).[13]

There seemed little question that America's public health system was in disarray in 2020, unable to cope with an epidemic that was both novel in its particulars and perfectly predictable, even expected, in a general sense. Decades of neglect, exacerbated by an explicit gutting under Trump led to a "diminished capacity to predict, detect, and respond to an emerging infectious disease" (Specter, 2020, para. 7). N_{PH} aimed at addressing not only the urgency of the coronavirus but also preparing for what was sure to be future dangerous viral epidemics. There were other countries where the public health infrastructure was considerably more robust.

N_E was the dominant response in most of the world. It was not, however, the only legitimate response. Iceland, led by a team consisting of the country's director of emergency management, its chief epidemiologist, and its director of health, followed N_{PH}. There was to be no general lockdown. Primary schools were kept open, after only a 1-day closure for preparation. Most businesses remained open as well. Headlines suggesting that Iceland had somehow "beat" the coronavirus were exaggerated and did not reflect the more cautious language of the country's leaders (Kolbert, 2020). Residential care facilities were hit particularly hard and the economy sagged, mainly from lack of tourists. There was understandable reluctance to dub Iceland, a small country without the hyper-density of cities such as New York or London, as the "model" for the world.[14]

The point of highlighting Iceland, and considering Denmark, Sweden, and a small number of other countries, is *not* to suggest that their approach was superior to the path urged by N_E. Evidence suggested that New Zealand and Germany were able to navigate successful N_E interventions (Lauterbach, 2020; A. Roberts, 2020). Still, there remains far too little that is known and far too much that is unknown to offer any confident final assessment. What the path followed by these countries suggests is that N_E did not represent the inevitable response to the pandemic, just the most widely articulated one.

In the United States, pediatricians lent their voice in endorsement of N_{PH}. In June 2020, with no vaccine or medical treatment on the immediate horizon and the impossibility of guaranteeing school "safety," there was talk about keeping schools closed even in the fall. The Southern California chapter of the American Academy of Pediatrics, representing about 1,500 doctors, pushed back. "Prolonging a meaningful return to in-person education would result in hundreds of thousands of children in Los Angeles County being at risk for worsening academic, developmental, and health outcomes," the statement said (Kohlia, 2020, para 3). Educators, often represented through various union spokespeople, took issue with suggestions of openings, concerned with the wellness of teachers and staff (Will, 2020).

N_{PH} emerged as a counter narrative not in hindsight but concurrently with the dominance of N_E. The two narratives are delineated in Table 1.2 as a way to highlight their occasional overlaps and significant distinctions. My intent is not to suggest that one narrative was more correct or in any way superior to the other. That is a determination that requires time, perspective, and wide-ranging expertise, and one that may never be fully settled. What the existence of a counter narrative demonstrates in that N_E did not represent the inevitable response to the pandemic, just the most widely articulated one.

TABLE 1.2 Contrasting Narratives

	N_E	N_{PH}
Initiating Event	**Outbreak of SARS-CoV-2 in Wuhan**	
Role of Biomedical Science	Central	Informational
Role of Social Sciences	Ancillary	Central
Goal of Intervention	Flatten the curve	Care for societal wellness
Chief Spokesperson	Epidemiologist as "explainer-in-chief"	Public health advocate/ (ideally) president as explainers in chief
Guiding Decision Principle	Follow the (epidemiological) science	Follow the (public health) sciences
General Response	Shutdown society	Quarantine virus, not country
Personal Responsibility	Wear face mask, wash hands, watch distance	
Schools	Closed	Closed briefly or not at all
Measures of Effectiveness	Quantitative presentations of numbers of infected, hospitalized, deaths	Qualitative assessments of public health/wellness outcomes
Unintended Outcomes	Unfortunate but necessary; ancillary to main epidemiological purpose	All public health outcomes share equal priority

THE DOWNSIDE OF A DOMINANT NARRATIVE

This chapter has offered a critical appraisal of the dominant pandemic narrative. There is no intention to pass judgment of the efficacy of either the dominant N_E or the counter N_{PH}. Any attempt to do so would quickly bog down in measurement questions: Not just *how* to measure efficacy but *what* to measure. These are vital matters, well worth the time and expertise required to undertake such an appraisal, but they are matters that reside beyond the scope of my consideration here.

Likewise, other than in passing, the chapter has averted its analytic gaze from the actual approach taken by the U.S. president and most, but not all, Republican state governors. The outcomes of that approach, regardless of the metrics used to evaluate efficacy, have been disastrous. The president abided by neither N_E nor N_{PH}, adhering instead to a toxic compound of lies, wishful thinking, denial, and conspiracy thinking. That narrative was never legitimate and cost tens of thousands of unnecessary deaths.[15]

The point of the chapter, rather, is the degree to which a narrative became dominant and the impact of that dominance. As was noted, the dominant narrative of the pandemic, N_E, quickly became self-sealing. If other countries could not measure up according to the metrics that N_E posed as vital, then their narrative could not be right. Certainly, these counter narratives should not be considered to be legitimate alternatives worthy of consideration. When a narrative becomes dominant, it claims the attendant authority of asserted "rightness." This is the only possible interpretation of reality. The fact of domination privileges the perspective offered by the narrative of its own particular interpretation of reality. As the mass media circulates meaning, their favored narratives take on the character of general understanding even as their underlying assumptions and claims go either marginalized or unchallenged.

Constructionist crises studies focus on claims of crisis as human-authored narratives. It is the narrative that adds coherence and consistency to a set of only partially understood, complex, and ever-shifting dynamics. *This* is the proper way to understand those contingencies. There were several legitimate narratives—narratives that presented facts accurately and built on plausible logic—available for framing a response to the rapid, horrifying spread of the novel coronavirus that unfolded in the first half of 2020. With the encouragement of experts and amplification by the media, one particular narrative came to dominate. It was an epidemiological narrative based on biomedical science and focusing on minimizing the damage of the virus and "flattening the curve"; that is, containing and reducing its spread.

Coalescing around N_E had important consequences. It bound people together in a common—which is not to say universal—commitment. At the same time, having a dominant narrative worked, inadvertently but powerfully, to marginalize the many alternative views of how to think about and act upon the situation that were available.

All narratives, whether dominant or counter dominant, are human constructions. If and when they are fact-based and plausibly argued, they represent legitimate responses to a particular situation. And as human constructions, they reflect a point of view, a perspective on what is right and wrong, good and bad, desirable or undesirable. When a narrative becomes dominant, it is tempting to think that it is the only legitimate way of viewing the world. It isn't. It never is. No response, no matter how legitimate, is the only legitimate response.

That's why critical thinking is so essential, even—especially—in times of extreme urgency. Watch for the underlying assumptions of the dominant narrative. Ask: Who and what does it favor and who/what is put at a disadvantage. Wonder if the media is offering legitimate alternatives. If not, why not? For a single, guiding question to frame critical thinking, we can all ask: Why this, not that?

This is not the first time a dominant narrative has prevented alternatives from being considered, although it may well be the most significant instance in our lifetimes. It won't be the last. The explicit goal of this chapter was to offer a heads-up: Don't be too quick to decide what is true. Claims of truth can and should *always* be contested. Critical thinking is *always* advised.

ENDNOTES

1. That initial U.S. case occurred in Washington State. New York infections, subsequent studies found, entered the state largely through Europe (Harcourt et al., 2020; Zimmer, 2020).
2. I take Kuhn's use of paradigm to assume dominance.
3. The Trump administration worked actively to marginalize and discredit Fauci, to little effect (Ledderman & O'Donnell, 2020).
4. Who was and was not designated an essential worker? Across the United States, a patchwork of state-by-state pronouncements occurred, embracing the following categories: energy, childcare, water and wastewater, agriculture and food production, critical retail (i.e., grocery stores, hardware stores, mechanics), critical trades (construction workers, electricians, plumbers, etc.), transportation, nonprofits, and social service organizations (National Conference of State Legislatures, 2020). Teachers were not included until late August 2020, when the Department of Homeland Security issued a guideline that teachers be considered essential. At this point, the question of school reopening for Fall 2020 was considered so political that teachers' unions refused to endorse such a designation. The president of the American Federation of Teachers argued that the critical worker designation could be used to "threaten, bully, and coerce" teachers into classrooms without the proper safety considerations (Westwood, 2020).
5. As many school districts remained closed to in-class learning in Fall 2020, preliminary surveys suggested that this high level of "lost" students persisted (Goodnough, 2020).
6. By late fall, Fauci was insisting that schools should be open and bars closed, not the other way around (Fowler, 2020). I would *never* want to leave the impression in this piece that Fauci was anything less than a caring, dedicated, brilliant scientist with a robust view of public well-being.
7. I don't want to slight this point. The count being used in news stories for war fatalities in Korea (33,686) and Vietnam (58,220) was for *United States* fatalities only. Total casualties in Korea reached nearly five million, and in Vietnam over one million. These numbers included all combatants from all sides as well as civilian fatalities. A headline from the April 28 *National Geographic* that declared, "U.S. Coronavirus Deaths Now Surpass Fatalities in the Vietnam War," should have read "Now Surpass *U.S.* Fatalities in the Vietnam War." Has a modern pandemic ever outpaced war in terms of fatalities? Yes. Deaths from the 1919 flu epidemic were about 25% higher than total fatalities in World War I.
8. With Thanksgiving 2020, the spread of COVID matched and in many cases exceeded the initial outbreak.
9. When Donald Trump told a September 2020 rally that COVID "affects virtually nobody," the toll had just reached 200,000 (quoted in Rupar, 2020). He was engaging in a different narrative altogether, unhinged from reality. Two

weeks later, Trump tested positive for COVID, as did the first lady, the White House press secretary, two senior advisors, two former advisors, two Republican senators, and the Republican National Party chairwoman.

10. As coronavirus cases surged across the United States in mid-summer and early Fall 2020, the phrase "literally gained nothing" seemed more apropos to the United States than to Sweden. That is not necessarily a reflection on the efficacy of N_E, given how sporadically it was adhered to across the country.
11. Can science ever be non-ideological? That's a great debate, but one that resides beyond the scope of this chapter. The important point here is the way Fauci thought about and characterized science.
12. According to the U.S. Environmental Protection Agency, indoor air is typically 2.5 times more polluted than ambient air and sometimes 100 times more (Ansari & Yousefabad, 2020).
13. There is no reason to think that Fauci opposed that agenda. I am simply stating that, as an epidemiologist, it was not his main focus.
14. For all its vastness, the United States contains 92.9 people per square mile compared to 39 in the United Kingdom and 9 in Iceland (https://www.infoplease.com/world/population-statistics/population-density-square-mile-countries).
15. There is no way of calculating the precise numbers of deaths caused by the incompetent, counterproductive approach taken by the president, but an Oxford study noted a 28% lower excess death rate (the number of deaths above what would be expected) in Europe than in the United States. If the United States had managed to respond as effectively as Europe, there would have been 57,800 fewer deaths ("Research Finds," 2020). The numbers become even more stark when compared with the particular response in Germany.

REFERENCES

Abbott, H. P. (2008). *The Cambridge introduction to narrative.* Cambridge University Press.

Almasy, E. S., Hanna, J., Maxouris, C., & Mossburg, C. (2020, April 14). *California Gov. Gavin Newsom says science, not political will, dictates when state can reopen.* CNN. https://www.cnn.com/2020/04/14/us/us-coronavirus-reopening-tuesday/index.html

Ansari, M., & Yousefabad, S. A. (2020). Potential threats of COVID-19 on quarantined families. *Public Health, 183*, 1.

Armstrong, M. (2020a, May 18). *COVID-19 cases per million inhabitants: A comparison.* Statista. https://www.statista.com/chart/21176/covid-19-infection-density-in-countries-most-total-cases

Armstrong, M. (2020b, June 8). *The best and worst-rated national COVID-19 responses.* Statista. https://www.statista.com/chart/21928/approval-ratings-national-covid-19-responses

Associated Press. (2020, October 11). *East St. Louis students lacking internet for remote learning.* https://apnews.com/article/melissa-lawson-il-state-wire-internet-access-technology-mo-state-wire-6d2fd04f21d371f829b2408c4dfe8219

Bartesaghi, M. (2015). Intertextuality. In K. Tracy (Ed.), *The international encyclopedia of language and social interaction* (pp. 1–6). John Wiley.

Bauer, L. (2020, May 6). The COVID-19 crisis has already left too many children hungry in America. *Brookings.* https://www.brookings.edu/blog/up-front/2020/05/06/the-covid-19-crisis-has-already-left-too-many-children-hungry-in-america

Borzutzky, D. (2020). Systemic risk. *Critical Quarterly, 62*(1), 29.

Branswell, H. (2020, March 11). *Why 'flattening the curve' may be the world's best bet to slow the coronavirus.* STAT. https://www.statnews.com/2020/03/11/flattening-curve-coronavirus/

Branswell, H., & Joseph, A. W. (2020, March 11). *WHO declares the coronavirus outbreak a pandemic.* STAT. https://www.statnews.com/2020/03/11/who-declares-the-coronavirus-outbreak-a-pandemic

Brown, A. E. C. (2019). *Bioethics, public health, and the social sciences for the medical professions: An integrated case-based approach.* Springer.

Bruner, J. (2002). *Making stories: Law, literature, life.* Farrar, Straus and Giroux.

Cadden, M. (2011). *Telling children's stories: Narrative theory and children's literature.* University of Nebraska Press.

Cavna, M. (2020, March 18). How the world's political artists are depicting the covid-19 pandemic. *Washington Post.* https://www.washingtonpost.com/arts-entertainment/2020/03/18/coronavirus-political-cartoons

CBS News. (2020, July 22). Grim coronavirus death toll projected in Sweden after lax approach to pandemic. https://www.cbsnews.com/news/sweden-coronavirus-death-toll-projections

Christakis, D. A., Van Cleve, W., & Zimmerman, F. J. (2020). Estimation of US children's educational attainment and years of life lost associated with primary school closures during the coronavirus disease 2019 pandemic. *JAMA Network, 3*(11), e2028786. https://jamanetwork.com/journals/jamanetworkopen/fullarticle/10.1001/jamanetworkopen.2020.28786?utm_source=For_The_Media&utm_medium=referral&utm_campaign=ftm_links&utm_term=111220

Correal, A., & Jacobs, A. (2020, April 9). A 'tragedy' is unfolding: Inside New York's virus epicenter. *The New York Times.* https://www.nytimes.com/2020/04/09/nyregion/coronavirus-queens-corona-jackson-heights-elmhurst.html

Cuomo, A. (2020, May 1). *New York COVID-19 briefing transcript.* Rev. https://www.rev.com/blog/transcripts/andrew-cuomo-new-york-covid-19-briefing-transcript-may-1

Curtin, P. D. (1998). *Disease and empire: The health of European troops in the conquest of Africa.* Cambridge University Press.

Dahir, A. L. (2020, May 13). 'Instead of coronavirus, the hunger will kill us.' A global food crisis looms. *The New York Times.* https://www.nytimes.com/2020/04/22/world/africa/coronavirus-hunger-crisis.html.

Darcy, O. (2020, May 28). *Fox News looks the other way as U.S. passes grim 100,000 death milestone.* CNN. https://www.cnn.com/2020/05/28/media/fox-news-coronavirus-deaths-reliable-sources/index.html

Davies, G., & Roeber, B. (2020, May 27). *Sweden stayed open during the coronavirus pandemic: Is it a model for the future?* ABC News. https://abcnews.go.com/

International/sweden-stayed-open-coronavirus-pandemic-model-future/story?id=70666450

DeParle, J. (2020, October 15). 8 million have slipped into poverty since May as federal aid has dried up. *The New York Times.* https://www.nytimes.com/2020/10/15/us/politics/federal-aid-poverty-levels.html?action=click&module=Top%20Stories&pgtype=Homepage

Dew, K. (2014). *The cult and science of public health: A sociological investigation.* Berghahn Books.

Dubey, S., Biswas, P., Ghosh, R., Chatterjee, S., Dubey, M. J., Chatterjee, S., Lahiri, D., & Lavie, C. L. (2020). Psychosocial impact of COVID-19. *Diabetes and Metabolic Syndrome Clinical Research and Reviews, 14*(5), 779–788.

Editorial Board. (2020, October 20). Fauci is an American hero trying to save lives – Everything that Trump is not. *Houston Chronicle.* https://www.houstonchronicle.com/opinion/editorials/article/Editorial-Fauci-is-an-American-hero-trying-to-15662717.php

Elassar, A. (2020, April 15). *Governors across the U.S. are emphasizing science, not politics, to decide when to reopen: Here's where all 50 states stand on reopening.* Fox 10. https://www.fox10tv.com/news/coronavirus/governors-across-the-us-are-emphasizing-science-not-politics-to-decide-when-to-reopen-heres/article_56e7bd63-bfda-5322-b823-d585601ec287.html

Erdbrink, T. (2020, September 29). Vilified early over lax virus strategy, Sweden seems to have scourge controlled. *The New York Times.* https://www.nytimes.com/2020/09/29/world/europe/sweden-coronavirus-strategy.html?referringSource=articleShare

Ewick, P., & Sibley, S. S. (1995). Subversive and hegemonic tales: Toward a sociology of narrative. *Law & Society Review, 29*(2), 197–226.

Fink, S. (2020, May 2). Grandma Rocket, the virus and a family whose love bridged 2,500 miles. *The New York Times.* https://www.nytimes.com/2020/05/02/nyregion/hospital-family-coronavirus.html?referringSource=articleShare

Fisher, W. (1987). *Human communication as narration: Toward a philosophy of reason, value, and action.* University of South Carolina Press.

Foucault, M. (1970). *The order of things: An archeology of the human sciences.* Pantheon Books.

Fowler, H. (2020, November 30). Close bars and keep schools open, Fauci says. *Miami Herald.* https://www.miamiherald.com/news/coronavirus/article247504030.html

Fox, M. (2020, May 22). *WHO says 80 million babies are missing out on routine childhood vaccines.* CNN. https://www.cnn.com/2020/05/22/health/vaccine-babies-coronavirus-who-wellness/index.html

Frakt, A. (2020, May 11). Putting a dollar value on life? Governments already do. *The New York Times.* https://www.nytimes.com/2020/05/11/upshot/virus-price-human-life.html

Frank A. W. (2012). *Letting stories breathe: A socio-narratology.* University of Chicago Press.

Gavin, K. (2020, April 15). With the Covid-19 curve flattening, it's time to prevent a second peak. *University of Michigan Health Lab.* https://labblog.uofmhealth.org/industry-dx/covid-19-curve-flattening-its-time-to-prevent-a-second-peak

Gill, P. S., & Bhopal, R. S. (2003). Racism and health: Challenge to racism must continue. *British Medical Journal, 326*(7394), 880–881.

Glanz, J., & Robertson, C. (2020, May 20). Lockdown delays cost at least 36,000 lives, data show. *The New York Times.* https://www.nytimes.com/2020/05/20/us/coronavirus-distancing-deaths.html

Goldstein, D. (2020, June 5). Research shows students falling months behind during virus disruptions. *The New York Times.* https://www.nytimes.com/2020/06/05/us/coronavirus-education-lost-learning.html?referringSource=articleShare

Goodman, P. S. (2020, July 7). Sweden has become the world's cautionary tale. *The New York Times.* https://www.nytimes.com/2020/07/07/business/sweden-economy-coronavirus.html?searchResultPosition=1

Goodnough, A. (2020, September 22). As schools go remote, finding 'lost' students gets harder. *The New York Times.* https://www.nytimes.com/2020/09/22/us/schools-covid-attendance.html?referringSource=articleShare

Grady, D. (2020, March 8). Not his first epidemic: Dr. Anthony Fauci sticks to the facts. *The New York Times.* https://www.nytimes.com/2020/03/08/health/fauci-coronavirus.html

Graham, K. A., Hanna, M., & Correa, J. D. M. (2020, May 24). Why many Philly students aren't logging on for school and what that could mean for September. *Philadelphia Inquirer.* https://www.inquirer.com/news/coronavirus-school-attendance-philadelphia-district-hite-remote-learning-20200524.html

Grosserode, S. (2020, April 17). New York parents are stressed out about their children falling behind, survey finds. *Rockland/Westchester Journal News.* https://www.lohud.com/story/news/education/2020/04/17/new-york-parents-stressed-children-falling-behind-school/5146818002

Gudbjartsson, D. F. Helgason, A., Jonsson, H., Magnusson, O. T., Melsted, P., Norddahl, G. L., Saemundsdottir, J., Sigurdsson, A., Sulem, P., Agustsdottir, A. B., Eiriksdottir, B., Fridriksdottir, R., Gardarsdottir, E. E., Georgsson, G., Gretarsdottir, O. S., Gudmundsson, K. R., Gunnarsdottir, T. R., Gylfason, A., Holm, H., . . . Stefansson. K. (2020). Spread of SARS-CoV-2 in the Icelandic population. *New England Journal of Medicine, 382,* 2302–2315. https://doi.org/10.1056/NEJMoa2006100

Harcourt, J., Tamin, A., Lu, X., Kamili, S., Sakthivel, S. K., Murray, J., Queen, K., Tao, Y., Paden, C. R., Zhang, J., Li, Y., Uehara, A., Wang, H., Goldsmith, C., Bullock, H. A., Wang, L., Whitaker, B., Lynch, B., Gautam, R., . . . Thornburg, N. J. (2020). Severe acute respiratory syndrome coronavirus 2 from patient with coronavirus disease, United States. *Emerging Infectious Diseases, 26*(6). https://wwwnc.cdc.gov/eid/article/26/6/20-0516_article

Herzenberg, M. (2020, May 5). *State confirms another 1,700 coronavirus-related nursing home deaths.* NY 1. https://www.ny1.com/nyc/all-boroughs/news/2020/05/05/state-reports-over-a-thousand-new-coronavirus-related-deaths-in-new-york-nursing-homes-

Hinchey, P. H. (2010). Positivist and constructivist epistemology. *Counterpoints, 24*(1), 33–55.

Hoffman, J., Maclean, R. (2020, June 14). Slowing the coronavirus is speeding the spread of other diseases. *The New York Times.* https://www.nytimes

.com/2020/06/14/health/coronavirus-vaccines-measles.html?referringSource=articleShare

Honan, K., & Chapman, B. (2020, May 6). NYPD data shows racial disparities in social-distancing enforcement. *Wall Street Journal.* https://www.wsj.com/articles/nypd-data-shows-racial-disparities-in-social-distancing-enforcement-11588964081

Honigsbaum, M. (2019). *The pandemic century: One hundred years of panic, hysteria, and hubris.* Norton.

Horberry, M. (2020, May 20). After coronavirus, office workers might face unexpected health threats. *The New York Times.* https://www.nytimes.com/2020/05/20/health/coronavirus-legionnaires-offices.html

Husain, A. (2020, June 12). After the pandemic, a global hunger crisis. *The New York Times.* https://www.nytimes.com/2020/06/12/opinion/coronavirus-global-hunger.html?referringSource=articleShare

Keyton, D. (2020, September 20). *Sweden spared surge of virus cases, but many questions remain.* AP News. https://apnews.com/article/virus-outbreak-sweden-stockholm-death-rates-europe-a01ddfa2e8ef839b2ee05e2cbcd63169

King, N. B. (2002). Security, disease, commerce: Ideologies of postcolonial global health. *Social Studies of Science, 32*(5/6), 763–789.

Kohli, S. (2020, June 3). Pediatricians say kids should be in school despite coronavirus risk. *Los Angeles Times.* https://www.latimes.com/california/story/2020-06-03/coronavirus-school-return-risks

Kolbert, E. (2020, June 1). How Iceland beat the coronavirus. *The New Yorker.* https://www.newyorker.com/magazine/2020/06/08/how-iceland-beat-the-coronavirus?utm_source=onsite-share&utm_medium=email&utm_campaign=onsite-share&utm_brand=the-new-yorker

Kristof, N. (2020, May 20). Let's remember that the coronavirus is still a mystery. *The New York Times.* https://www.nytimes.com/2020/05/20/opinion/us-coronavirus-reopening.html?referringSource=articleShare

Kuhn, T. S. (1962). *The structure of scientific revolutions.* University of Chicago Press.

Lahut, J. (2020, April 2). Inside Gov. Andrew Cuomo's daily coronavirus briefings, and how their contrast to Trump's became must-see TV. *Business Insider.* https://www.businessinsider.com/inside-gov-andrew-cuomos-daily-coronavirus-press-briefings-2020-4

Lauterbach, K. (2020, October 19). Will Germany's effective COVID strategy work again as it enters a second wave? *The Guardian.* https://www.theguardian.com/commentisfree/2020/oct/19/germany-covid-second-wave-virus

LeBlancc, P. (2020, April 3). *Fauci: 'I don't understand why' every state hasn't issued stay-at-home orders.* CNN. https://www.cnn.com/2020/04/02/politics/fauci-stay-home-coronavirus-states-cnntv/index.html

Ledderman, J., & O'Donnell, K. (2020, July 12). *White House seeks to discredit Fauci as coronavirus surges.* NBC News. https://www.nbcnews.com/politics/white-house/white-house-seeks-discredit-fauci-amid-coronavirus-surge-n1233612

Leng, G., & Leng, R. I. (2020). *The matter of facts: Skepticism, persuasion, and evidence in science.* MIT Press.

Lewis, D. (2020, October 29). Why schools probably aren't COVID hotspots. *Nature.* https://www.nature.com/articles/d41586-020-02973-3

Lorenzo-Dus, N., & Smith, P. (2018).The visual construction of political crises: A news values approach. In M. Patrona (Ed.), *Crisis and the media: Narratives of crisis across cultural settings and media genres* (pp. 151–176). John Benjamins Publishing Company.

Lyotard, J.-F. (1984). *The postmodern condition: A report on knowledge.* University of Minnesota Press.

Mansoor, S. (2020, April 5). Data suggests many New York City neighborhoods hardest hit by COVID-19 are also low-income areas. *Time.* https://time.com/5815820/data-new-york-low-income-neighborhoods-coronavirus

Marcus, J. (2020, May 11). Quarantine fatigue is real. *The Atlantic.* https://www.theatlantic.com/ideas/archive/2020/05/quarantine-fatigue-real-and-shaming-people-wont-help/611482/

McCarthy, K. (2020, April 13). *Covid-19 survey: Teachers say less than half of students attending their remote classes.* Fishbowl. https://www.fishbowlapp.com/insights/2020/04/13/covide-19-survey-teachers-say-less-than-half-of-students-attending-their-remote-classes

McCarthy, N. (2020, May 26). *COVID-19 deaths per 100,000 inhabitants: A comparison.* Statista. https://www.statista.com/chart/21170/coronavirus-death-rate-worldwide

Minichin, T. J. (2006). Beyond the dominant narrative: The ongoing struggle for civil rights in the U.S. South, 1968–1980. *Australasian Journal of American Studies, 25*(1), 65–86.

Merriam-Webster. (n.d.). ancillary. In *Merriam-Webster.com dictionary.* Retrieved from https://www.merriam-webster.com/dictionary/ancillary

Mohan, M. (Reporter), & Le Poidevin, O. (Video Journalist). (2020, June 12). *Coronavirus: Domestic violence 'increases globally during lockdown.* BBC. https://www.bbc.com/news/av/world-53014211/coronavirus-domestic-violence-increases-globally-during-lockdown

Morrison, A. B. (1984). Public policy on health and scientific evidence: Is there a link? *Journal of Chronic Diseases, 37*(8), 647–652.

Mumby, D. K. (1993). *Narrative and social control: Critical perspectives.* SAGE Publications.

National Conference of State Legislatures. (2020). *COVID-19: Essential workers in the states.* https://www.ncsl.org/research/labor-and-employment/covid-19-essential-workers-in-the-states.aspx

Neuding, P., & Sanandaji, T. (2020, April 8). Is Sweden's lax approach to the coronavirus backfiring? *Washington Post.* https://www.washingtonpost.com/opinions/2020/04/08/is-swedens-lax-approach-coronavirus-backfiring

Norman, G. (2020, May 13). *New York Gov. Cuomo's press conference pushed back following sign-language order.* Fox News. https://www.foxnews.com/us/cuomos-press-conference-pushed-back

Olmos, O. (2017). *Narration as argument.* Springer.

Onishi, N., Méheut, C., & Francini, A. (2020, November 30). Positive test rate of 11 percent? France's schools remain open. *The New York Times.* https://www.nytimes.com/2020/11/30/world/europe/france-covid-schools.html

Oster, E. (2020, May 14). The 'just stay home' message will backfire. *The Atlantic.* https://www.theatlantic.com/ideas/archive/2020/05/just-stay-home-message-will-backfire/611623/

Pandey, A. V., Manivannan, A., Nov, O., Satterthwaite, M., & Bertini, E. (2014). The persuasive power of data visualization. *IEEE Transactions on Visualization and Computer Graphics, 20*(12), 2211–2220.

Patterson, M., & Monroe, K. R. (1998). Narrative in political science. *Annual Review of Political Science, 1*(1), 315–331.

Pinkster, J. (2020, April 19). The pandemic will cleave America in two. *The Atlantic.* https://www.theatlantic.com/family/archive/2020/04/two-pandemics-us-coronavirus-inequality/609622

Propp, V. (1968). *Morphology of the folktale.* Austin University of Texas Press.

Quammen, D. (2020, May 4). Why weren't we ready for the coronavirus? *The New Yorker.* https://www.newyorker.com/magazine/2020/05/11/why-werent-we-ready-for-the-coronavirus

Research Finds That Inadequate Us Pandemic Response Cost More American Lives Than World War I. (2020, October 1). *Oxford News.* https://www.ox.ac.uk/news/2020-10-01-research-finds-inadequate-us-pandemic-response-cost-more-american-lives-world-war-i

Rorty, R. (1979). *Philosophy and the mirror of nature.* Princeton University Press.

Rosman, K. (2020, May 2). After a lifetime together, coronavirus takes them both. *The New York Times.* https://www.nytimes.com/2020/05/02/us/coronavirus-couples.html?referringSource=articleShare

Rothschild, A. (2020, April 7). Dr. Fauci has been dreading a pandemic like Covid-19 for years. *The New York Times.* https://fivethirtyeight.com/features/dr-fauci-has-been-dreading-a-pandemic-like-covid-19-for-years

Rupar, A. (2020, September). *'It affects virtually nobody': Trump erases coronavirus victims as US death toll hits 200,000.* Vox. https://www.vox.com/2020/9/22/21450772/trump-swanton-ohio-rally-coronavirus-affects-virtually-nobody

Sailor, C. (2020, May 21). Have we flattened the curve? *Washington State News Tribune.* https://www.thenewstribune.com/news/coronavirus/article242762861.html

Saldaña, R. (2020, April 14). After the pandemic comes the epidemic of lost learning and family insecurity. *Education Week.* https://www.edweek.org/ew/articles/2020/04/15/after-the-pandemic-comes-the-epidemic-of.html

Savitz, D. A., Poole, O., & Miller, W. C. (1999). Reassessing the role of epidemiology in public health. *American Journal of Public Health, 89*(8), 1158–1161.

Searle, J. R. (1995). *The construction of social reality.* Free Press.

Seeger, M., & Sellnow, T. (2016). *Narratives of crisis: Telling stories of ruin and renewal.* Stanford University Press.

Seth, S. (2018). *Difference and disease: Medicine, race, and the eighteenth-century British Empire.* Cambridge University Press.

Shenhav, S. R., Oshri, O., Ofek, D., & Sheafer, T. (2014). Story coalitions: Applying narrative theory to the study of coalition formation. *Political Psychology, 35*(5), 661–678.

Southall, A. (2020, May 7). Scrutiny of social-distance policing as 35 of 40 arrested are Black. *The New York Times.* https://www.nytimes.com/2020/05/07/nyregion/nypd-social-distancing-race-coronavirus.html

Specktor, B. (2020, March 16). *Coronavirus: What is 'flattening the curve' and will it work?* Live Science. https://www.livescience.com/coronavirus-flatten-the-curve.html

Specter, M. (2020, March 17). The coronavirus and the gutting of America's public-health system. *The New Yorker.* https://www.newyorker.com/news/daily-comment/coronavirus-and-the-gutting-of-americas-public-health-system

Spector, B. (2019). *Constructing crisis: Leaders, crises, and claims of urgency.* Cambridge University Press.

Staff. (2020a, May 6). Nearly 1 in 5 young children in the U.S. don't get enough to eat, research found. *The New York Times.* https://www.nytimes.com/2020/05/06/us/coronavirus-live-updates.html?action=click&module=Spotlight&pgtype=Homepage

Staff. (2020b, May 24). An incalculable loss. *The New York Times.* https://www.nytimes.com/interactive/2020/05/24/us/us-coronavirus-deaths-100000.html?action=click&module=Top%20Stories&pgtype=Homepage

Stancati, M., Brody, L., & Fontdeglori, X. (2020, June 3). The pandemic sent 1.5 billion children home from school. Many might not return. *The Wall Street Journal.* https://www.wsj.com/articles/the-pandemic-sent-1-5-billion-children-home-from-school-many-might-not-return-11591179919

Stone, D. (2020). *Counting: How we use numbers to decide what matters.* Liveright Publishing.

Strauss, V. (2020, April 6). Schools of more than 90 percent of the world's students closed during this pandemic. *The Washington Post.* https://www.washingtonpost.com/education/2020/04/06/schools-more-than-90-percent-worlds-students-closed-during-this-pandemic-this-graphic-shows-how-fast-it-happened

Sung, W. W. Y., & Kaplan, R. M. (2020, May 15). *Why do countries' COVID-19 death rates vary so much?* MedPage Today. https://www.medpagetoday.com/infectiousdisease/covid19/86527

Tavernise, S., Healy, J., & Bogel-Burroughs, N. (2020, May 1). Your life or your livelihood: Americans wrestle with impossible choice. *The New York Times.* https://www.nytimes.com/2020/05/01/us/coronavirus-reopening-workers.html?referringSource=articleShare

Toness, B. V. (2020, May 23). One in five Boston public school children may be virtual dropouts. *Boston Globe.* https://www.bostonglobe.com/2020/05/23/metro/more-than-one-five-boston-public-school-children-may-be-virtual-dropouts/

Unite for Sight. (2020). *Ideologies of global health.* http://www.uniteforsight.org/global-health-university/ideologies-of-global-health#_ftn2

Varotsis, G. (2015). *Screenplay and narrative theory: The screenplectics model of complex narrative systems.* Lexington Books.

Von Foerster, H. (1973). On constructing a reality. In H. von Foerster (Ed.), *Observing systems* (pp. 288–309). Intersystems.

Walensky, R. P., & del Rio, C. (2020, April 17). From mitigation to containment of the COVID-19: Putting the SARS-CoV-2 genie back in the bottle. *JAMA Network, 323*(19), 1889–1890. https://jamanetwork.com/journals/jama/fullarticle/2764956

Walsh, R. (2007). *The rhetoric of fictionality: Narrative theory and the idea of fiction.* Ohio State University Press.

Warraich, H. J. (2020, July 14). *Fauci's strategy for effective public health advocacy: "You cannot be ideological.'* STAT. https://www.statnews.com/2020/07/14/fauci-advice-public-health-advocacy-you-cannot-be-ideological

Westwood, S. (2020, August 21). *White House formally declaring teachers essential workers.* CNN. https://www.cnn.com/2020/08/20/politics/white-house-teachers-essential-workers/index.html

Will, M. (2020, July 10). Teachers' unions are wary of reopening schools. Here's what they're saying. *Education Week.* https://blogs.edweek.org/teachers/teaching_now/2020/07/teachers_unions_are_wary_of_reopening_schools_heres_what_theyre_saying.html

Winant, C. (2020, May 7). Sweden can't explain away the fact that its lax coronavirus approach is killing people. *Los Angeles Times.* https://www.latimes.com/opinion/story/2020-05-07/sweden-coronavirus-response-killing-people

Yong, E. (2020, April). Why the coronavirus is so confusing. *The Atlantic.* https://www.theatlantic.com/health/archive/2020/04/pandemic-confusing-uncertainty/610819

Zimmer, C. (2020, April 8). Most New York coronavirus cases came from Europe, genomes show. *The New York Times.* https://www.nytimes.com/2020/04/08/science/new-york-coronavirus-cases-europe-genomes.html

CHAPTER 2

THE IMPACT OF WORKLOAD, WORKLOAD CHANGES, AND ANTICIPATED WORKLOAD CHANGES DURING COVID-19 ON WORKER WELL-BEING

Michael DiStaso
University of Central Florida

Kristin Horan
University of Central Florida

Chelsea LeNoble
Embry-Riddle Aeronautical University

Mindy Shoss
University of Central Florida

Zoe Politis
University of Central Florida

Ignacio Azcarate
University of Central Florida

Crisis, Chaos, and Organizations, pages 33–64

The novel coronavirus (COVID-19) pandemic has led to significant changes in most aspects of daily lives, including work (Rudolph et al., 2020). Many employees have lost their jobs, been furloughed, or experienced a reduction in work hours. These effects have been especially pronounced in hospitality and aviation industries, for whom economic demand plummeted virtually overnight (Borden et al., 2020; Josephs, 2020). At the same time, other workers have experienced a direct increase in workload and/or a dramatic change in the settings in which work is completed. For example, Liu, Yang, et al. (2020) reported heavy workload increases among healthcare employees as they worked in new contexts, grappling with an overload of patients and new regulations and protocols. Workload is strongly tied to employee well-being (Bowling & Kirkendall, 2012), and a critical examination of consequences of these disruptive workload changes is therefore warranted.

The purpose of the present chapter is to encourage increased attention to the consequences of disruptive workload changes by organizing the scattered literature on workload change and applying this literature's theory to the COVID-19 workplace. We extend the workload change literature by introducing the concept of disruptive workload change, defined as workload change that is the consequence of disruptive contexts external to the organization, and distinguish this concept from other forms of workload change. Further, as the COVID-19 pandemic represents a threat both to individuals' health and the stability of their work, we explore health/safety and economic perspectives as two theoretical approaches to examine the effects of disruptive workload changes on well-being in the COVID-19 context. Finally, given that the COVID-19 pandemic is a dynamically unfolding event with an unclear and shifting end point, we also consider how people's anticipated workload changes are also relevant to understanding how the pandemic impacts worker well-being.

The chapter is organized as follows. First, the COVID-19 context is described and this COVID-19 context is placed into existing theory on extreme contexts. Second, a typology of types of workload changes is provided and the nature of workload increases and workload decreases that the pandemic has instigated is described. Third, we then present two perspectives about how disruptive workload changes may impact well-being during COVID-19: a health/safety perspective and an economic perspective. Fourth, in considering questions about anticipated workload change, we present survey data from four industry groups (hospitality/service, healthcare, other essential, and other non-essential workers) that showcase the effects of perceived workload and anticipated workload changes on well-being during the COVID-19 pandemic. Finally, implications for research and practice are discussed to aid both researchers and workplaces responding to workload changes during the COVID-19 pandemic and future disruptive events.

THE COVID-19 CONTEXT

As Hällgren et al. (2018) astutely state: "Context matters" (p. 113). Indeed, to understand the impact of COVID-19 on organizations and their members, it is important to examine the nature of COVID-19 as an event system and organizations impacted by COVID-19 as disrupted contexts. Broadly, extreme contexts research is focused on "understanding how organizations avoid, or cope with, extreme or unexpected events" (Hällgren et al., 2018, p. 112). There is inherently a cause-and-effect temporality to understanding these concepts. First, an extreme event occurs or is likely to occur. In general, *events* have been defined as "discrete, discontinuous 'happenings,' which diverge from the stable or routine features of the organizational environment" (Morgeson et al., 2015, p. 519). Hällgren et al. (2018) define *extreme* events as being outside of the organization's ability to control or prevent and severely negatively impacting members of organizations. Importantly, extreme events can severely impact those who experience the event vicariously; direct exposure to the event is not a requirement under this conceptualization. Once the event itself is defined, the event-triggered context becomes relevant. Johns (2006) defines *context* as "situational opportunities and constraints that affect the occurrence and meaning of organizational behavior" (p. 386). As a result of an extreme event, the work context itself becomes extreme to the extent that it affects or has the potential to affect functioning of the organization and its members.

Hällgren et al. (2018) provide a matrix for categorizing extreme contexts in organizations based on the event occurrence (potential vs. actual) and the nature of extreme activities (related vs. unrelated to that work context). Risky contexts are comprised of potential-related activities and are exemplified by work environments in which there is a potential for extreme events to occur related to the nature of the work (e.g., nuclear power plant maintenance). Emergency contexts are comprised of actual-related activities in which the nature of the work is to address or respond to emergencies (e.g., emergency medicine). Disruptive contexts, finally, are characterized by actual-unrelated activities that are outside of the normal or anticipated scope of organizational operations in response to major, unexpected events (e.g., tornado-damaged offices). They "do not usually allow for preparation . . . and catch organizations and/or communities off-guard" (Hällgren et al., 2018, p. 135).

Ascribing to this extreme events and contexts framework, the COVID-19 pandemic involves the actual occurrence of an event and activities that are exogenous to typical organizational functioning. Therefore, the COVID-19 pandemic can be understood as an extreme, *disrupted context* that features numerous co-occurring and inter-related events at multiple levels of analysis. Consistent with the definition of disruptive contexts provided by Hällgren et al. (2018), the onset of COVID-19 was unexpected, unpredictable, and difficult to precisely categorize due to its differential impact across sectors and organizations (U.S. Bureau of Labor Statistics, 2020). Even those organizations (e.g., state department of health; hospital systems) that typically respond to medical or public health events—and might otherwise be conceptualized as emergency contexts—are experiencing significant disruption (Blumenthal et al., 2020).

In their review of 138 extreme context studies, disruptive contexts represented 10.87% of their sample (Hällgren et al., 2018). Within the studies reviewed, the primary foci included sociopolitical and institution-level factors and the primary method of studying disruptive contexts was qualitative designs such as case studies and interviews. Despite the likelihood of disruptive organizational contexts triggering individual-level adversity for employees, research on this is virtually non-existent (represented by there being "nil" for the "behaviors and reactions to extreme events" cell under disruptive contexts; Hällgren et al., 2018, Table 13, p. 143). Together, the importance of this work in practice and the gap of literature in this area highlight the need for more research on the impact of disruptive contexts on levels of analysis within organizations, such as departments, teams, and employees.

WORKLOAD AND WORKLOAD CHANGES DURING THE COVID-19 PANDEMIC

When extreme events trigger disruptive contexts, a number of possible consequences may occur that change the nature of work. One primary consequence is that unexpected, unprecedented events are likely to instigate changes to tasks and activities. As a result, variations in workload are likely to occur when tasks and activities shift from routine to nonroutine (see for instance Jafari et al., 2020). Existing research on extreme contexts has identified some of these consequences, including surges in workload at the initial response stage of disaster management (Rezapour et al., 2018), work intensification and shifts between intensely extreme and mundane work (Wankhade et al., 2020), uneven distributions of workload among employees (Levin et al., 2006), and increased multitasking needs in stressful environments (Driskell et al., 2018).

Workload refers to the volume or difficulty of job-related demands, tasks, and activities that an employee has at a given period of time (Spector & Jex, 1998; Bowling & Kirkendall, 2012). This construct is different from work hours, which refers to the amount of time an employee engaged with their job, regardless of the amount of or difficulty of the job demands. In the occupational stress literature, workload is framed as a stressor that predicts physical and psychological strain (Alarcon, 2011; Bowling et al., 2015;

Ilies et al., 2007; Ilies et al., 2010). Workload has been distinguished along several different dimensions (Bowling & Kirkendall, 2012; Spector & Jex, 1998). First, the subjective-objective distinction concerns how workload is measured: subjective measures ask participants to report their level of job demands while objective measures operationalize workload in terms of the number of tasks to complete. Second, the qualitative-quantitative distinction clarifies whether we are referring to the amount of demands expected of an employee (quantitative workload) or the difficulty of those demands (qualitative workload). Finally, the experienced-anticipated distinction relates to whether workers are reflecting on their current workload or predicting their future workload levels (DiStaso & Shoss, 2020).

Employees' experience of their workload may change based on some feature of the job itself or some external circumstance, and these changes can occur rapidly or gradually. Some jobs feature a workload that varies throughout the day (e.g., firefighters' call volumes can vary, and they expect their workload to increase when emergencies happen; Villeneuve et al., 2020) or across a season (e.g., auditors' workloads grow near fiscal year end; Johnson et al., 2002). We label this type of change *routine workload change*, which we define as intensifications or reductions in workload that are cyclical and expected over time. Routine workload change occurs in jobs that have increased or decreased workload at particular times of the day (e.g., restaurant workers during the dinner rush), particular days of the week (e.g., grocery store workers during the weekend), or particular times of the year (e.g., retail workers during the holiday season). An example of gradual workload change comes from the study of work intensification over time from the field of labor economics (Green, 2001; Green, 2004). In this literature, work intensification refers to increases in the amount of effort required to perform job tasks over time (Green, 2001; Green & McIntosh, 2001). It is attributed to increased expectations to work at a very fast pace and with tight deadlines (Green, 2001; Franke, 2015). It has been measured through hours worked (using previous hours worked as a control variable), perceptions of role overload, and time demands, which refer to the perception that employees must increase work time to meet the expectations of the organization (e.g., Mackey & Boxall, 2008).

In contrast to gradual and routine workload change, this chapter brings attention to a particular type of workload change relevant to the COVID-19 pandemic that we call *disruptive workload change*. Disruptive workload change is rapid workload change that is instigated by extreme contexts external to the organization. Research has illuminated some of the causes and consequences of gradual and routine workload change, but disruptive workload change remains unstudied. The closest analogue to disruptive workload change is the concept of emergent episodic organizational change from the study of organizational change and development (Martins,

2010). According to Martins (2010), theories of emergent episodic change posit that environmental demands external to the organization instigate unplanned changes as organizations adapt to these demands. Similarly, we argue that disruptive workload change occurs as a response to the COVID-19-disrupted environment.

Although not directly addressed in the aforementioned literature, workload changes also vary in the extent to which the change is temporary or permanent. When an employee leaves an organization, team members are sometimes asked to take on the responsibilities of the exiting employee. Such changes are usually believed to be temporary, but length of the workload change depends on the organization's ability or willingness to fill the empty work role. Similarly, there is speculation about the duration of workload changes instigated by the COVID-19 pandemic (Arruda, 2020; Rosenbaum, 2020). It is possible that workload changes will be reverted in the future if the changes have limited utility beyond addressing pandemic-specific disruptions, and they may become permanent if they provide further utility for employees or the organization.

COVID-19 suddenly and drastically changed many aspects of work for most people, including their place of work, work processes, or the workload itself (Rudolph et al., 2020; Sinclair et al., 2020). Work within organizations has been forced to change to adapt to unexpected circumstances (e.g., supply chain disruptions, changes to available services, changes to patronage and customers), comply with safety and virus control guidelines (e.g., social distancing, enhanced sanitation protocols, bans on large gatherings and events), and/or directly respond to the pandemic (e.g., mobilizing of public health and emergency management units for community testing, reallocation of healthcare services to emergency departments and intensive care units). These disruptions happened simultaneously, and individual workers experienced many changes to their work at once. For some workers, this disruptive workload change took the form of workload increases (intensifications). For others, this disruptive workload change took the form of workload decreases (reductions). The following subsections describe some ways that COVID-19 has instigated these two forms of workload change.

We first address examples of disruptive workload intensifications, which have affected workers across industries. These examples are not all inclusive, but rather provide illustrations of affected occupations represented in preliminary COVID-19 research and popular press. Healthcare professionals serving on the frontlines of COVID-19 have encountered more patients requiring more intensive care and more arduous work procedures (Barello et al., 2020). Outside of the direct response to COVID-19 in healthcare, changes to daily life have indirectly led to disruptive workload intensification in other sectors. Postal and delivery personnel experienced increased work hours and number of deliveries (Nawaz, 2020). A poll of information technology (IT) support staff found an increase in workload during COVID-19 due to an increased number of tickets related to transitioning the workforce to remote work (Grajek, 2020). Many employees increased their work hours to accommodate for the lack of a commute, going from 9-hour workdays to 12-hour workdays (Davis & Green, 2020). Even when workers have not experienced a direct increase in the quantity of in-role demands, new and uncertain circumstances may increase the total number of demands that must be balanced. For example, remote workers suddenly face new challenges as previously distinct lines between work and non-work suddenly collapsed (Kang, 2020). Roommates and partners now working in shared spaces faced more interruptions (DeVore, 2020), and parents found themselves playing the roles of both employee and teacher (Burbank, 2020). Indeed, there is some evidence that workload has indirectly increased due to the increased burden of balancing work and family demands (Vaziri et al., 2020). In other words, the tension between work demands and family demands adds pressure to employees with no more hours in the day to assist in meeting these demands.

Many workers have also experienced disruptive workload reductions due to COVID-19 (Gifford, 2020), and many of these reductions in work hours or workload can be traced to social distancing requirements and the allocation of resources toward essential activities (Gooch, 2020; Murphy et al., 2020). Employees experienced a complete, immediate drop in workload in the form of layoff and furlough (U.S. Bureau of Labor Statistics [BLS], 2020), and others have experienced a reduction in work hours or workload. In terms of work hours, exposure to the virus during non-work hours can involve legal requirements to quarantine (Parmet & Sinha, 2020), prohibiting individuals from maintaining their normal work schedules. In addition, many parents (especially mothers) have been forced to leave the workforce or transition to part-time work in order to cope with childcare closures (Collins et al., 2020). In terms of on-the-job workload, some workers have seen workload reductions due to a decreased number of patients or clients. In some areas of healthcare deemed to be non-essential, patient volumes decreased because people were either required to postpone or voluntarily delayed nonurgent medical visits (Murphy et al., 2020; Shi et al., 2020).

IMPLICATIONS OF WORKLOAD AND WORKLOAD CHANGE DURING COVID-19: HEALTH/SAFETY AND ECONOMIC PERSPECTIVES

Thus far, we reviewed this literature and presented evidence of disruptive workload changes that have occurred during COVID-19. However, these bodies of literature do not shed light on the consequences of disruptive workload changes that may occur during a public health disaster, especially one that has both economic and health/safety threatening elements. These elements of the COVID-19 pandemic makes disruptive workload change unique from other forms of workload change. This section considers how the economic and health/safety threatening elements of the COVID-19 pandemic shape the well-being consequences of workload intensifications and reductions during the pandemic. We describe the health/safety perspective, which suggests that elements of pandemic that threaten workers' health influence how they react to workload changes. We then discuss the pandemic's economic threatening elements, such as job insecurity and work hour insecurity, that may also influence the consequences of workload changes. These perspectives challenge existing perspectives on the consequences of workload change by pointing to the important role of context in shaping how individuals react to workload changes. They also suggest that there are paradoxes where both workload intensifications and reductions may have simultaneous positive and negative impacts on well-being. Table 2.1 summarizes these perspectives and theoretical effects on well-being.

Occupational Health Perspective

From an occupational health psychology standpoint, workload is considered to be a stressor that requires physical or mental exertion to address (Bowling & Kirkendall, 2012; Spector & Jex, 1998). A large body of literature links workload to emotional exhaustion, suggesting that the continued exertion of resources to address high workload may lead to experiences of burnout and poor health (Bowling et al., 2015; Nixon et al., 2011). From

TABLE 2.1 Summary of Disruptive Workload Perspectives and Expected Well-Being Effects

Change	Health/Safety	Economic
Intensification	• Fulfill prosocial desires during a time of collective societal struggle (+) • Increase disease exposure risk (–) • Increase in depleting & exhausting job demands (–)	• Security of employment status (+) • Signal of being essential to the organization (+) • Signal of being essential to society (+) • Sense that work is valued & meaningful (+)
Reduction	• Endanger well-being benefits (e.g., structure, identity, meaning, social affiliation) (–) • Fewer stressors & depletion (+) • More time to dedicate to other important life roles (+)	• Not enough work to justify their work role/position (–) • Work is less meaningful to the organization (–) • Work is less critical for functioning of society (–)

this perspective, workload intensifications represent demands placed on employees that must be addressed with additional mental or physical exertion. Further workload intensifications may also signal fewer opportunities for recovery (DiStaso & Shoss, 2020; Fritz & Sonnentag, 2006). Preliminary evidence from data collected during COVID-19 suggests that workload continues to be an occupational stressor in this way (Zhou, Wang, et al., 2020). Consistent with this literature, a national poll conducted in the United States found that burnout has increased throughout the COVID-19 pandemic, and the most common cause attributed to this increase in burnout was workload (Eagle Hill Consulting, 2020).

Although the majority of workload literature typically focuses on the detrimental aspects of increases in workload, there could be situations in which an increase in workload represents a resource for health, safety, or well-being. An employee may view disruptive workload intensification as an opportunity to fulfill prosocial desires during a time of collective societal struggle, even voluntarily increasing their workload (Flynn, 2020), reaping health and well-being benefits of helping during times of crisis (Hällgren et al., 2018, Shoss et al., 2020). Alternatively, a disruptive reduction in workload may endanger the intangible well-being benefits that an individual receives from work, including structure, identity, meaning, and social affiliation (Hulin, 2002). Stories of extraordinary ways that individuals have used their occupation to contribute to COVID-19 control and relief efforts have emerged, such as a news story documenting manufacturing employees who lived in their factory for 28 days working long days to make materials for frontline personal protective equipment. Although some types of strain were mentioned in the employees' adapted work life (e.g., work–family conflict for those missing their family), reflections on their experience were largely positive as they were "happy to be able to help" (Flynn, 2020). Thus, at least in disaster contexts, workload increases could have a diverse impact on health and safety, sometimes resulting in strain and sometimes resulting in more positive outcomes, perhaps in some cases simultaneously. These stories highlight an opportunity for researchers to explore dual processes in which increased workload could have both detrimental and protective factors for worker health and safety.

The COVID-19 pandemic forces researchers to consider workers' health-related concerns when considering the link between workload and psychological strain. Work roles differ considerably in the extent to which they require physical contact with others and exposure to disease/illness. COVID-19 is transmitted through social contact (CDC, 2020), and these risk-enhancing job characteristics may influence how workload changes are perceived. For workers in some occupations (e.g., healthcare, customer service), workload intensifications may represent increased risk of exposure to COVID-19 (and conversely, workload reductions may represent less exposure to COVID-19), particularly in occupations where core job tasks do not support physical distancing or telecommuting (Baker et al., 2020). There is evidence of different rates of potential COVID-19 transmission as a function of occupation and industry, with the highest risk of infection occurring in the healthcare industry (Baker et al., 2020). The vast majority of occupations in the hospitality, food service, and healthcare sectors involve some level of physical proximity with customers/patients and co-workers, putting them at a higher risk of infection (Gamio, 2020; Repko, 2020). Healthcare workers have experienced particularly high levels of burnout, depression, and anxiety, and these increases are partly attributed to increased service demands, changed task content, and concern about infecting others (Denning et al., 2020; Liu, Luo, et al., 2020; Scott et al., 2020). When these employees experience workload intensifications, they may have to perform under the stress of possibly getting sick and bringing illness home to their family members (Zhou, Zhou, et al., 2020). Hence, this would suggest that workload intensifications for individuals in public-facing occupations may be particularly detrimental for well-being.

The health/safety literature generally focuses on workload intensifications as opposed to decreases in workload (e.g., Mariappanadar, 2014), so there is less evidence as to what disruptive workload reductions may represent for employees and organizations. However, the perspectives described above regarding energy exertion and exposure to disease/illness would suggest that workload reductions may be beneficial for well-being. Indeed, research on workload often issues practical recommendations encouraging workload reductions. Workload can also be interpreted through a lens of time limitations, and research shows that employees make tradeoffs when workload in the domains of their life are high and time is limited, and this can have negative implications for health behaviors such as sleep (e.g., Barnes et al., 2012). A reduction in workload could be interpreted as a unique opportunity to dedicate time to other life domains that may have been previously unattended, including life domains that are supportive of well-being such as leisure and health. Despite the numerous health benefits of detachment from work and recovery during non-work hours, it can be particularly challenging in the face of high workload (Sonnentag & Kruel, 2007). During lockdowns, some individuals found time to exercise, walk outdoors, pursue hobbies, and spend time with children, reaping affective benefits (Lades et al., 2020).

In summary, both traditional occupational health perspectives and health threatening elements of COVID-19 would suggest that workload increases are detrimental to employee well-being. These same perspectives would suggest that workload reductions may be beneficial for well-being. However, an alternative perspective is that workload intensifications may be positive when the workload is meaningful and fulfills psychological needs.

Economic Perspective

Recent evidence suggests that perceived financial resources are an important contributor to well-being during COVID-19 (Wanberg et al., 2020). An economic perspective on disruptive workload changes focuses on factors that influence financial resources, including signals about employees' job status and viability. We also focus on the experience of job insecurity, or a perceived threat to one's job as it is currently experienced (Shoss, 2017), and work hours insecurity, or the perceived threat to one's work hours. From an economic perspective, we argue that job insecurity and work hours insecurity are tied to perceptions about the importance or value of one's work role, and that these perceptions are particularly salient during the pandemic.

Signals about work role criticality, we argue, can be derived from numerous sources. Most notably, the concept of work role criticality has come to the forefront during the COVID-19 pandemic because of the distinction between essential and non-essential workers. The U.S. Department of Homeland Security's Cybersecurity and Infrastructure Security Agency (CISA; 2020) uses the term *essential* to describe jobs that "conduct a range of operations and services that are typically essential to continue critical infrastructure operations" (p. 1). Workers who have essential work roles are required to continue working during COVID-19 and other emergencies, implying that these work roles are essential to the functioning of society. There are some nuances behind the essential label, however. First, there is within-industry variability in the types of work roles are considered essential. Some workers in the healthcare sector, for example, have lost their jobs because the medical services that they provided were deemed able to be delayed (Gooch, 2020; Murphy et al., 2020). Second, there is variability in how workers interpret their essential or non-essential status, as recent evidence suggests that even healthcare workers may be skeptical about being labeled "heroes" by the media (Hennekam et al., 2020). These nuances suggest that judgments about the importance of one's work role are inherently subjective, influenced only in part by official essential and non-essential terms.

We argue that perceptions of work role criticality are also partly informed by micro-level experiences in the workplace, including workload and workload changes. For individual employees, workload and workload changes can cue to employees the extent to which their work is important or valued. For example, an employee who is assigned important, meaningful projects may intuit that their contributions to the organization are valued. Similarly, being assigned many tasks (i.e., a high workload) could signify that one's work is critical to the organization's function. Particularly in a COVID-19 context, an individual could interpret their increased workload as indicative of the necessity of their job.

When cues are derived from society (e.g., their work is labeled essential), workers (e.g., emergency department nurses) are expected to experience a higher level of job security. These workers are more likely to feel that society needs them to continue working because the signals suggest that their work is in high demand even when the economy is in jeopardy. Thus, it is possible that the consequences of disruptive workload changes will vary as a function of one's industry, as some industries have fared better during the pandemic than others (BLS, 2020). As noted above, signals can also be derived from a worker's experience of workload or workload intensification. Workload intensifications can communicate that one's work is valued by the organization. This value, in turn, can signal that one's employment is stable during the COVID-19 pandemic. Thus, workers who experience workload intensifications may feel that their job is secure because their organization needs them to continue working. This may particularly be the case for nonessential employees. These workers may find sudden COVID-19-instigated workload reductions to be highly threatening, as these reductions could signal that there is not enough work to justify maintaining their employment. As a result, a workload increase may, in this context, be somewhat beneficial for well-being to the extent that individuals appraise the increase in workload with a positive attitude or gratitude for the stability of their job (e.g., Dang et al., 2020).

In summary, an economic perspective on workload change suggests that workload changes are a signal that individuals use to gauge the continued viability of their industry and their jobs. In particular, workload intensifications would indicate better prospects for current employment and workload reductions would indicate poorer prospects for employment. Given that job insecurity is a major stressor with established longitudinal effects on health and well-being (De Witte et al., 2016), this perspective would suggest that workload intensifications would have a beneficial impact on well-being.

EMPIRICAL STUDY: EFFECTS OF ANTICIPATED WORKLOAD CHANGE

One of the unique elements of the COVID-19 pandemic is that it is ongoing with no clear endpoint, painting an ambiguous picture of the future. Because the COVID-19 pandemic is continually developing, workers not only wrestle with past and present disruptive changes, but also try to predict and prepare for potential future disruptive change. Studies show that employees make predictions about their future workload, and that these predictions affect their well-being in the present (Casper & Sonnentag, 2019). We extrapolate from the present-focused health/safety and economic perspectives described above to argue that workers' anticipation of future disruptive workload changes may also influence their well-being to the extent that future workload changes could threaten their health/safety or financial status. In fact, the very aspect of not knowing what will happen in the future (i.e., uncertainty) is an important factor that contributes negatively to well-being (Elstak et al., 2015; Verkuil et al., 2010) particularly extreme contexts like the COVID-19 pandemic where the future is highly ambiguous. Thus, employees' expectations about workload changes may strongly contribute to their well-being during COVID-19. The primary purpose of the supplemental study, therefore, is to examine whether the logic described about workload changes also apply to anticipated changes.

Our team has been collecting data on anticipated workload change over the course of the pandemic thus far. To supplement the perspectives described above, we present the following analyses to examine how the health/safety and economic perspectives might explain reactions to anticipated workload change. We showcase descriptive statistics from the data we collected, and we test whether levels of health/safety variables (i.e., emotional exhaustion and COVID-19 anxiety) and economic variables (i.e., job insecurity and work hours insecurity) differ across industry types.

From a health/safety perspective, we assess the extent to which workload and anticipated workload change are associated with emotional exhaustion and COVID-19 anxiety. The existing literature has linked workload changes to general emotional strain, and our study extends this by shedding light on the extent to which anticipated workload changes impact strain specific to COVID-19. We also test the extent to which job characteristics such as physical proximity and exposure to disease/illness are associated with emotional exhaustion and COVID-19 anxiety because we argued that workers occupying these higher risk jobs may interpret workload increases as more threatening.

From an economic perspective, we test the extent to which workload and anticipating workload change is associated with job insecurity and work hours insecurity. We do this to test the hypothesis that workload may represent a signal that one's employment is secure. Applying the logic that non-essential workers may derive cues from their work environment even more so than other workers. We test whether industry groups moderates the relationship between anticipated workload change and job insecurity and work hours insecurity.

Data Collection Procedure

We collected survey data between March 2020 and July 2020 to capture workers' experiences at the onset of the COVID-19 pandemic. We aimed to recruit a diverse sample of essential and non-essential employees, with a particular focus on employees in the hospitality and healthcare industries as these industries have been particularly impacted by COVID-19. To obtain this sample, several recruitment strategies were used. First, an e-mail list from a major hospital network in the Southeast United States was used to recruit employees in the healthcare sector. Second, employed adults who were also enrolled in courses were recruited at a large Southeastern university. Finally, a snowball sampling strategy was used to recruit participants through social media. Individuals were eligible for the study if they indicated that they were employed at least part-time, and individuals could participate if they were currently working or if they were recently laid off or furloughed due to the COVID-19 pandemic.

The original sample included 328 employees. After screening out participants who failed attention checks or reported not giving adequate attention to the survey ($N = 50$), 278 participants remained for data analysis. On average, participants were 27.99 years old ($SD = 12.29$) and were mostly female (71.6%). Most participants were White (57.9%) or Hispanic/Latino (20.9%). A small portion of the participants (6.8%) reported being laid off or furloughed, 79 of these participants (28.4%) reported that they were still working at a decreased number of work hours, and 180 participants (64.8%) had no change or an increase in work hours.

Participants provided their primary industry and job title, and briefly described their job responsibilities. The research team used this information to code each participant into one of four industry groups. Participants were coded as "hospitality/service" if they worked in hotels, restaurants, or theme parks; as "healthcare" if the participant identified themselves as physician or nurse or worked in a hospital setting that supports medical personnel; "essential (other)" if the participant held essential jobs (including teachers, information technology workers, and first responders) as identified by U.S. federal guidelines (CISA, 2020). Finally, participants were coded as "non-essential" if they worked in any number of industries not labeled essential by CISA (2020). A summary of the measures of key study variables are described in Table 2.2.

Descriptive Statistics and Industry Group Differences

Descriptive statistics and correlations among study variables are displayed in Table 2.3. The economic and health/safety perspectives suggested that there may be differences in key study variables between groups. We first examined differences in risk-enhancing job characteristics (i.e., physical proximity and exposure to disease/illness). Industry group means of risk-enhancing job characteristics are displayed in Figure 2.1. Healthcare workers differed considerably in their exposure to disease/illness ($M = 70.94$; $SD = 32.16$). Workers in the healthcare and hospitality/service industries

TABLE 2.2 Summary of Study Measures

Variable	Scale	Citation	Notes
Workload	1–5 *(strongly disagree–strongly agree)*	Spector & Jex (1998)	Example item: "My job required me to work fast."
Anticipated Workload Change	1–5 *(decrease a lot–increase a lot)*	Caplan et al. (1980)	Example item: "What changes do you expect in…the amount of work you have to do?"
Emotional Exhaustion	1–5 *(strongly disagree–strongly agree)*	Halbesleben & Demerouti (2005)	Example item: "During my work, I often feel emotionally drained."
COVID-19 Anxiety	1–7 *(strongly disagree–strongly agree)*	Wu et al. (2009)	Example item: "Thinking about coronavirus (COVID-19) makes me feel anxious."
Job Insecurity	1–5 *(strongly disagree–strongly agree)*	Vander Elst et al. (2014)	Example item: "I feel insecure about the future of my job."
Work Hours Insecurity	1–7 *(strongly disagree–strongly agree)*	Van den Broeck et al. (2014)	Example item: "I am worried about whether I will have enough work hours in the future."
Physical Proximity	0–100 *(I don't work near other people–very close)*		O*Net database rated jobs using the item "To what extent does this job require the worker to perform job tasks in close physical proximity to other people?" Participants' jobs were matched to O*Net job codes to derive a physical proximity score.
Exposure to Disease or Infections	0–100 *(never–every day)*		O*Net database rated jobs using the item "How often does this job require exposure to disease/infections?" Participants' jobs were matched to O*Net job codes to derive a physical proximity score.

TABLE 2.3 Descriptive Statistics and Correlations Among Study Variables

Variable	*n*	*M*	*SD*	1	2	3	4	5	6	7	8
1. Workload	258	3.14	0.99	—							
2. AWC	259	3.10	0.83	.42**	—						
3. Emotional Exhaustion	255	3.54	0.97	.42**	.24**	—					
4. COVID-19 Anxiety	259	4.61	1.71	.16**	.12	.27**	—				
5. Job Insecurity	190	1.94	0.95	–.04	–.09	.12	.28**	—			
6. Work Hours Insecurity	259	3.97	1.97	–.01	–.20**	.20**	.33**	.49*	—		
7. Proximity	259	69.50	16.22	.03	.04	.16*	.09	–.03	.20**	—	
8. Exposure to Disease	259	27.57	29.03	.03	.05	.12	.01	–.05	.17**	.54**	—

Note: AWC = Anticipated workload change; * Correlation is significant at the 0.05 level (2-tailed); **Correlation is significant at the 0.01 level (2-tailed).

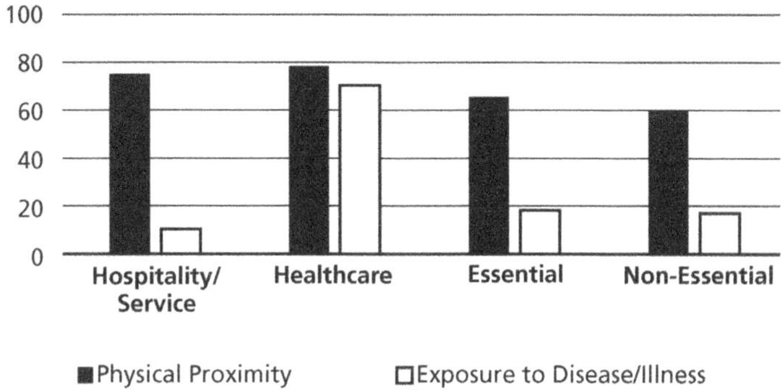

Figure 2.1 Risk-enhancing job characteristics by industry group.

both reported high levels of physical proximity ($M = 78.53$; $SD = 20.94$; $M = 76.00$; $SD = 8.00$) compared to workers in other essential and non-essential occupations.

We also tested whether levels of key study variables differed across industry groups, and Figure 2.2 displays means of each variable by industry group. We conducted one-way analyses of variance to assess industry group differences in the means of workload, anticipated workload change, COVID-19 anxiety, emotional exhaustion, job insecurity,[1] and work hours insecurity. There were no differences by industry group in reported levels of workload ($F[3, 263] = 1.68$, $p = .17$), emotional exhaustion ($F[3, 260] = 0.74$, $p = .53$), or COVID-19 anxiety ($F[3, 255] = 0.33$, $p = .80$). However, there were industry

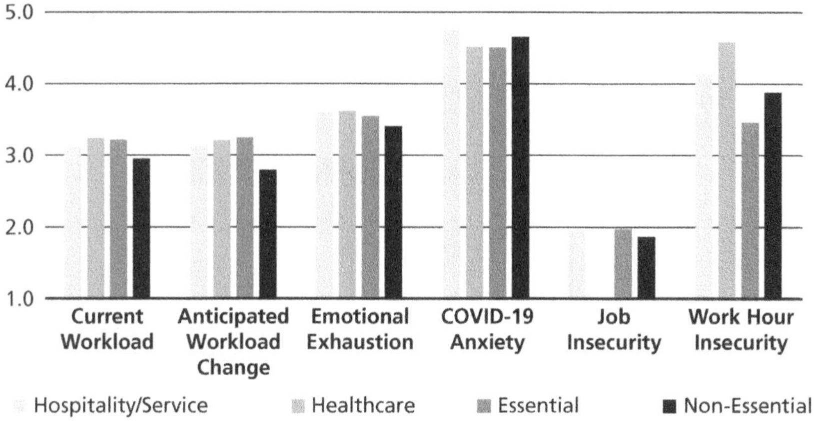

Figure 2.2 Means of main study variables by industry group. *Note:* Sample of healthcare workers reporting job insecurity was insufficient for forming meaningful comparisons.

group differences in anticipated workload change ($F[3, 264] = 4.94$, $p < .01$), such that healthcare ($M = 3.22$, $SD = 0.84$) and essential ($M = 3.23$, $SD = 0.73$) workers tended to expect workload increases compared to non-essential workers, who tended to expect workload decreases ($M = 2.74$, $SD = 0.90$). Job insecurity did not differ between industry groups ($F[2, 178] = 0.19$, $p = .83$). Work hours insecurity, however differed statistically significantly by industry group ($F[3, 264] = 3.86$, $p = .01$), such that healthcare workers ($M = 4.59$, $SD = 1.71$) tended to experience more work hours insecurity than essential workers ($M = 3.49$, $SD = 1.97$).

To examine whether particular industry groups were differentially impacted by changes in work hours, we also examined the impact of COVID-19 on participants' employment stratified by industry groups. Participants reported their employment impact by indicated whether they (a) had been laid off or furloughed, (b) had their work hours reduced, and (c) had their work hours increased or maintained; thus, this analysis provides information regarding participants' changes in work hours at the onset of COVID-19. Figure 2.3 displays the number of participants belonging to each category, stratified by industry group. A chi-square test of independence revealed that employment impacted significantly differed by industry group membership, χ^2 (6, 278) = 33.03, $p < 0.05$. Healthcare workers differed considerably from the other industry groups. No healthcare workers in our sample experienced a layoff or furlough, and only $n = 4$ healthcare workers in the sample (7.54%) reported a workload reduction. Workers in the hospitality/service industry group and the non-essential group tended to have similar employment impact, with a similar distribution of layoffs/furloughs, work hour decreases, and work hours increases. Essential employees reported fewer layoffs/furloughs ($n = 2$) than employees in the non-essential

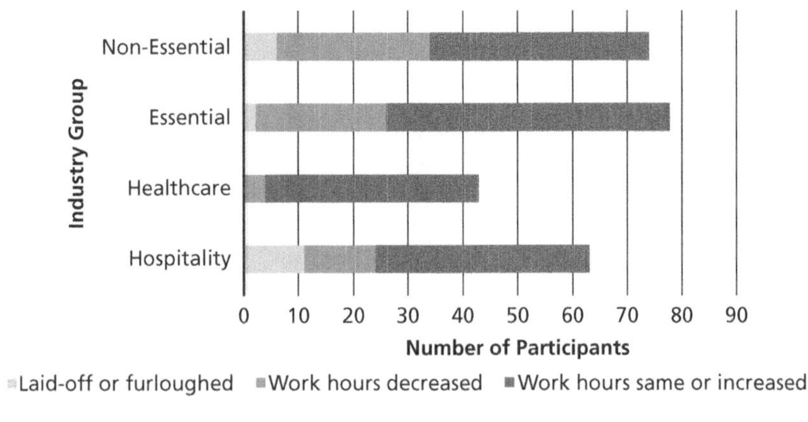

Figure 2.3 Employment impact by industry group. *Note:* χ^2 (6, 278) = 33.303, $p < 0.05$.

and hospitality industry groups, but about one-third of these participants reported a decrease in work hours ($n = 24$; 30.7%). This suggests that many essential employees' work hours were impacted by COVID-19 even when they were able to keep their jobs.

Relationship Between Current and Anticipated Workload and Health/Safety Variables

We then tested the extent to which workload and anticipated workload change related to health/safety variables. Workload was positively associated with emotional exhaustion ($r = .42$, $p < .01$), and anticipated workload change was also positively associated with emotional exhaustion ($r = .24$, $p < .01$). This suggests that employees with high current workloads or who anticipated workload intensifications experience higher emotional strain. We also examined whether workload and anticipated workload change was associated with COVID-19 anxiety, as our discussion earlier suggested that workload could represent exposure to disease/illness for many employees. Workload was positively related to COVID-19 anxiety ($r = .16$, $p < .01$) but anticipated workload change was not related ($r = .12$, $p = 06$).

To test our prediction that particular types of jobs pose a greater risk to workers' health/safety, we also examined the extent to which risk-enhancing job characteristics (physical proximity and exposure to disease/illness, as measured by O*Net) were associated with well-being indicators. Results indicated that physical proximity was associated with emotional exhaustion ($r = .16$, $p < .05$), but not COVID-19 anxiety ($r = .09$, $p = .17$). Exposure to disease/illness was not correlated with emotional exhaustion ($r = .12$, $p = .06$) nor COVID-19 anxiety ($r = .01$, $p = .85$).

Relationship Between Current and Anticipated Workload and Economic Variables

We examined relationships between workload and anticipated workload change and the economic variables (i.e., job insecurity and work hours insecurity). Neither workload nor anticipated workload change correlated with job insecurity (workload $r = -.04$, $p = .59$; anticipated workload change $r = -.09$, $p = .23$). Workload was not associated with work hours insecurity ($r = -.01$, $p = .87$), but anticipated workload change was ($r = -.20$, $p < .01$), suggesting that workers who anticipated decreases in workload were also concerned about loss of work hours. We also examined relationships between economic variables and COVID-19 anxiety. Both job insecurity ($r = .28$, $p < .01$) and work hours insecurity ($r = .33$, $p < .01$) were positively related to COVID-19 anxiety. Inconsistent with existing literature on job insecurity, job insecurity was not related to emotional exhaustion ($r = .12$, $p = .10$), but work hours insecurity was positively related to emotional exhaustion ($r = .20$, $p < 01$). This may indicate that both types of economic insecurity were sources of COVID-19-specific stress, but work hours insecurity was a more salient source of general stress in the present sample.

We proposed that the relationships between anticipated workload change and job insecurity/work hours insecurity may differ as a function of industry group. We reasoned that workers in non-essential work roles are more likely to look to cues in the work environment that signal work role criticality. Therefore, we examined the extent to which industry group membership moderated the relationships between (a) anticipated workload change—job insecurity, and (b) anticipated workload change—work hours insecurity. Industry group was dummy coded such that non-essential employees were used as the referenced group that was compared to hospitality, healthcare, and other essential employees. Regression results are displayed in Table 2.4 and Table 2.5. Regression results indicated that the relationship between current workload and work hours insecurity did not vary by industry group. However, there was a statistically significant difference between essential and non-essential workers in the relationship between anticipated workload change and job insecurity ($B = .52$; $SE = .23$; $p < .05$). Figure 2.4 displays the simple slopes for each industry group. As seen there, the relationship between job insecurity and anticipated workload change was very strong and negative for non-essential employees. In other words, non-essential employees tended to view anticipated workload intensifications positively; if they anticipated a workload increase, they tended to experience less job insecurity.

TABLE 2.4 Regression Results Predicting Job Insecurity

Variable	*B*	*SE*	*p*
Constant	2.02	.071	<.001
AWC	–0.493	.152	<.001
Hospitality Dummy Code	0.281	.183	.127
Essential Other Dummy Code	0.148	.184	.424
AWC × Essential	0.523	.229	.023
AWC × Hospitality	0.200	.213	.348
R^2	0.27		

Note: AWC = Anticipated workload change. The non-essential workers group is the referent group.

TABLE 2.5 Regression Results Predicting Work Hours Insecurity

Variable	*B*	*SE*	*p*
Constant	3.82	.231	<.001
Anticipated Change	–0.496	.251	.049
Hospitality Dummy Code	0.461	.325	.157
Healthcare Dummy Code	0.947	.354	.008
Essential Dummy Code	–0.188	.322	.560
AWC × Essential	–0.066	.388	.864
AWC × Healthcare	–0.289	.400	.471
AWC × Hospitality	–0.069	.361	.848
R^2	.10		

Note: AWC = Anticipated workload change. The non-essential workers group is the referent group.

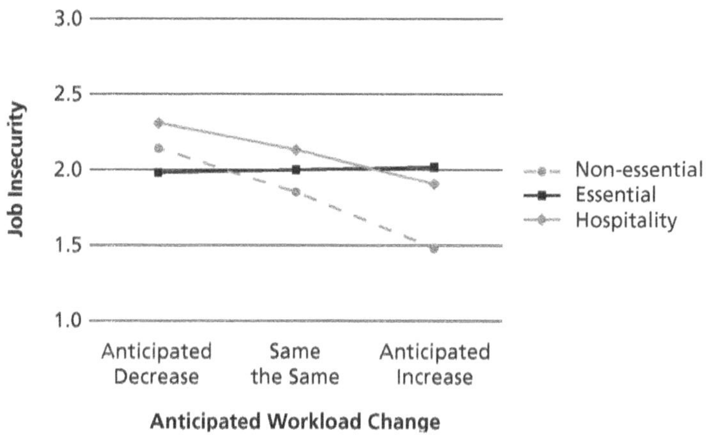

Figure 2.4 Relationships between anticipated workload change and job insecurity as a function of industry group.

Summary of Findings

The present study's findings suggested anticipated workload intensifications were primarily seen as a source of stress. Anticipated workload change predicted emotional exhaustion, consistent with the greater occupational health literature (i.e., workload is a stressor that depletes employees' personal resources). It was not, however, strongly associated with COVID-19 anxiety, though this relationship was trending positive and nearly reached statistical significance. Current workload did positively relate to COVID-19 anxiety, suggesting that workers in our samples may have been more present-focused.

We also found some evidence that relationships among anticipated workload change and economic variables differed as a function of industry group. We argued that workers with work roles that are not seen as essential to society may look for cues in the work environment that signal that their work role is essential to the organization. Consistent with this, workers whose jobs were coded as non-essential demonstrated a stronger, negative relationship between job insecurity and anticipated workload change for non-essential workers in our sample compared to essential workers.

LOOKING FORWARD: IMPLICATIONS AND FUTURE DIRECTIONS

The literature on workload change is small, as occupational stress researchers tend to frame workload as a somewhat static stressor (Bowling & Kirkendall, 2012). We organized the existing literature on workload change as focusing on two forms: routine and gradual workload change. In doing so, we argued that workload changes instigated by COVID-19, categorized under the label "disruptive workload change," are unique in many ways. In addition to being abrupt and initiated outside of organizations, we suggested that the COVID-19 context itself contains both health/safety and economic threatening elements that make this form of workload change different. In the COVID-19 contexts, researchers and practitioners should also consider risk of disease exposure involved in frontline workers as well as employees' perception that one's work is essential or critical.

The supplemental evidence presented in this chapter suggests that disruptive workload intensification contributes to emotional strain. Our results were largely consistent with existing occupational health literature, which frames workload intensification as a stressor (Franke, 2015). However, more work is needed to determine whether negative effects of workload intensifications vary more as a function of increased energy exertion or the disruptiveness of the change. We suggested that disruptive workload intensifications may be viewed positively when they are perceived to signal employment security or when they fulfill one's psychological needs. We found some evidence in favor of the former hypothesis for non-essential workers specifically, but future studies should directly measure perceptions of work role criticality and task meaningfulness to better test these effects.

We encourage future research to further examine disruptive workload change and how it compares to gradual and routine workload change. COVID-19-instigated workload change should share some features with other types of disruptive workload change. We defined disruptive workload change as being initiated outside of the organization by disruptive events. COVID-19 is unique in its health-threatening elements that mandate safety protocols such as physical distancing (CDC, 2020), and this feature may not be shared with disruptive workload changes instigated by other natural disasters that may not share this mandate. However, the element of rapid, unplanned change will accompany disruptive workload changes caused by other extreme contexts. Predictability of change may play an important role in understanding the consequences of workload change, given individuals' motivations to reduce uncertainty (e.g., Elstak et al., 2015). This emphasizes the importance of considering the context of workload change because disruptive, gradual, and routine workload changes all have theoretically important distinguishing features. Beyond simply inserting workload change as a stressor where cumulative workload was previously examined, we encourage future researchers to examine the degree to which these categories of workload changes may be fundamentally different from one another as well as different from the experience of cumulative workload.

Variables such as predictability may play an important role in understanding events that could change workload, given individuals' motivations to reduce uncertainty (e.g., Elstak et al., 2015). COVID-19 represents a large scale event introducing unexpected change and uncertainty (Baker et al., 2020). It could be that anticipated changes in workload bear different implications for employee quality of life. Furthermore, changes in workload can be shared among groups of employees or could be relatively isolated to a single employee. In the case of COVID-19, changes in workload were shared among groups of employees (i.e., many frontline employees experienced a collective increase in workload while masses of laid off and furloughed employees experienced a decrease in workload). This shared experience could influence attributions and coping processes. Future research is encouraged to examine the social influence and processes of shared and isolated changes.

There is variability in how disruptive workload changes have manifested. Some workers have to perform entirely new tasks, some workers have to complete a greater number of tasks, and some workers have to complete tasks in new contexts. For example, due to COVID-19, restaurants now require employees to sanitize frequently touched surfaces more often, suggesting that some tasks are performed more frequently (Romeo, 2020). Employees in many retail stores now have to monitor the number of customers in a store at a given time (i.e., an entirely new task; McNamara; 2020). These are examples of direct changes to workload, but there are also examples of cases where workload has indirectly been affected because of the changed work context. Workers that have transitioned to telework and work interdependently with others may find it easier or more difficult to collaborate with their colleagues, depending on the organization's technological resources. In other words, these employees may have the same quantity of workload and observe differences in how difficult the work is to complete (i.e., quality of workload). Our supplemental analyses did not capture these levels of nuance due to the diversity of changes in work status, workload, work context, and resulting shifts in health or safety that individuals experienced during COVID-19. This presents an opportunity for future research on workload change, and may be relevant to the study of routine, gradual, and disruptive workload change.

Our chapter also has relevance for organizational practice. The supplemental evidence presented in this chapter suggests that disruptive workload changes contribute to emotional strain. Even when disruptions to the nature of work are unavoidable, organizations can implement practices that help people navigate or adjust to workload changes. The literature on recovery shows the importance of encouraging employees to take respite (Hahn et al., 2014; Sonnentag, 2001) and recent research has shown that employees tend to experience less emotional strain when they believe their high workload levels are temporary (DiStaso & Shoss, 2020). In the COVID-19 context, we suggest that managers identify the aspects of the COVID-19 work environment that are most distressing and determine whether these distressing aspects of work are only temporary. Even though the COVID-19 pandemic is continuing to unfold and leaves the future ambiguous, there may be some aspects of the work environment that managers can foresee. Making a deliberate effort to communicate potential end points for stressful aspects of work may help by allowing employees to look forward to those endpoints.

We previously argued that employees may look to current and future workload levels to make judgments about the importance of their work role during COVID-19. Our study suggests that this may be particularly helpful for employees in industries that are not labeled essential. We advise that managers be more proactive in communicating the meaningfulness of employees' work roles. This recommendation is consistent with job characteristics literature that positions experienced meaningfulness as a key link between job characteristics and job attitudes and well-being indicators (Humphrey et al., 2007). Still, more research needs to be done to examine perceived work role criticality and how it interacts with workload changes over time. COVID-19 has disrupted many aspects of work conducted in organizations across industries. This chapter sought to highlight the consequences of disruptive workload changes. We pointed out that the small literature on workload change could not accommodate the disruptive workload changes instigated by COVID-19 because of its unique health/safety and economic threatening elements. Our proposed typology distinguishes the COVID-19-instigated disruptive workload change from other forms of workload change, and we built theory on disruptive workload change specifically by drawing from literature on health/safety and economic vulnerability. Our study of anticipated workload change provided some initial insight into the consequences of anticipating disruptive change, but more work is needed to extend the theoretical perspectives developed in this chapter.

AUTHOR NOTE

This publication was partially supported by grant number T42OH008438, funded by the National Institute Occupational Safety (NIOSH) and Health under the Centers for Disease Control and Prevention (CDC). Its contents are solely the responsibility of the authors and do not necessarily represent the official views of the NIOSH or CDC or the Department of Health and Human Services.

NOTE

1. The job insecurity measure was not administered to one of the samples primarily intended to recruit healthcare employees. Thus, analyses involving job insecurity compare hospitality, essential, and non-essential industry groups.

REFERENCES

Alarcon, G. M. (2011). A meta-analysis of burnout with job demands, resources, and attitudes. *Journal of Vocational Behavior, 79*(2), 549–562. https://doi.org/10.1016/j.jvb.2011.03.007

Arruda, W. (2020, May). 6 ways COVID-19 will change the workplace forever. *Forbes.* https://www.forbes.com/sites/williamarruda/2020/05/07/6-ways-covid-19-will-change-the-workplace-forever/?sh=1fe8a189323e

Baker, M. G., Peckham, T. K., & Seixas, N. S. (2020). Estimating the burden of United States workers exposed to infection or disease: a key factor in containing risk of COVID-19 infection. *PLoS One, 15*(4), e0232452. https://doi.org/10.1371/journal.pone.0232452

Barnes, C. M., Wagner, D. T., & Ghumman, S. (2012). Borrowing from sleep to pay work and family: Expanding time-based conflict to the broader nonwork domain. *Personnel Psychology, 65*(4), 789–819. https://doi.org/10.1111/peps.12002

Barello, S., Palamenghi, L., & Graffigna, G. (2020). Stressors and Resources for healthcare professionals during the Covid-19 pandemic: Lesson learned from Italy. *Frontiers in Psychology, 11*, 2179. https://doi.org/10.3389/fpsyg.2020.02179

Blumenthal, D., Fowler, E. J., Abrams, M., & Collins, S. R. (2020). Covid-19—Implications for the health care system. *New England Journal of Medicine, 383,* 1483–1488. https://doi.org/10.1056/NEJMsb2021088

Borden, T., Akhtar, A., Hadden, J., & Bose, D. (2020, October 8). *The coronavirus outbreak has triggered unprecedented mass layoffs and furloughs: Here are the major companies that have announced they are downsizing their workforces.* Business Insider. https://www.businessinsider.com/coronavirus-layoffs-furloughs-hospitality-service-travel-unemployment-2020

Bowling, N. A., Alarcon, G. M., Bragg, C. B., & Hartman, M. J. (2015). A meta-analytic examination of the potential correlates and consequences of workload. *Work & Stress, 29*(2), 95–113.

Bowling, N. A., & Kirkendall, C. (2012). *Workload: A review of causes, consequences, and potential interventions.* In J. Houdmont, S. Leka, & R. R. Sinclair (Eds.), *Contemporary occupational health psychology: Global perspectives on research and practice, Vol. 2* (p. 221–238). Wiley Blackwell. https://doi.org/10.1002/9781119942849.ch13

Burbank, M. (2020, August 17). COVID-19 pits full-time parenting against full-time work, and women are the hardest hit. *The Seattle Times.* http://www.chronline.com/community/covid-19-pits-full-time-parenting-against-full-time-work-and-women-are-the-hardest/article_ed46610e-e0a8-11ea-baae-03c28dbb5019.html

Caplan, R., Cobb, S., French, J., Jr., Harrison, R., & Pinneau, S. (1980). *Job demands and worker health: Main effects and occupational differences.* Institute for Social Research.

Casper, A., & Sonnentag, S. (2020). Feeling exhausted or vigorous in anticipation of high workload? The role of worry and planning during the evening. *Journal of Occupational and Organizational Psychology, 93*(1), 215–242.

Centers for Disease Control and Prevention. (2020). *How to protect yourself and others.* https://www.cdc.gov/coronavirus/2019-ncov/prevent-getting-sick/prevention.html

Collins, C., Landivar, L. C., Ruppanner, L., & Scarborough, W. J. (2020). COVID-19 and the gender gap in work hours. *Gender, Work & Organization, 28*(S1), 101–112. https://doi.org/10.1111/gwao.12506

Dang, A. K., Le, X. T. T., Le, H. T., Tran, B. X., Do, T. T. T., Phan, H. T. B., Nguyen, T. T., Pham, Q. T., Ta, N. T. K., Nguyen, Q. T., Van Duong, Q., Hoang, M. T., Pham, H. Q., Nguyen, T. H., Vu, L. G., Latkin, C. A., Ho, C. S. H., & Ho, R. C. M. (2020). Evidence of COVID-19 impacts on occupations during the first Vietnamese national lockdown. *Annals of Global Health, 86*(1), 112. https://doi.org/10.5334/aogh.2976

Davis, M. F., & Green, J. (2020, April 23). *Three hours longer, the pandemic workday has obliterated work-life balance.* Bloomberg. https://www.bloomberg.com/news/articles/2020-04-23/working-from-home-in-covid-era-means-three-more-hours-on-the-job

Denning, M., Goh, E. T., Tan, B., Kanneganti, A., Almonte, M., Scott, A., Martin, G., Clarke, J., Sounderajah, V., Markar, S., Przybylowicz, J., Chan, Y. H., Sia, C.-H., Chua, Y. X., Sim, K., Lim, L., Tan, L., Tan, M., Sharma, V., & Ooi, S. (2021). Determinants of burnout and other aspects of psychological well-being in healthcare workers during the Covid-19 pandemic: A multinational cross-sectional study. *PLoS ONE, 16*(4), 1–18. https://doi.org/10.1371/journal.pone.0238666

DeVore, A. (2020). *Guide to working from home with roommates, spouse, kids, or parents.* https://bluesignal.com/2020/08/27/guide-to-working-from-home-with-roommates-spouse-kids-or-parents/

De Witte, H., Pienaar, J., & De Cuyper, N. (2016). Review of 30 years of longitudinal studies on the association between job insecurity and health and well-being: Is there causal evidence? *Australian Psychologist, 51*(1), 18–31.

DiStaso, M., & Shoss, M. K. (2020). Looking forward: How anticipated workload change influences the present workload-emotional strain relationship. *Journal of Occupational Health Psychology, 25*(6), 401–409. https://doi.org/10.1037/ocp0000261

Driskell, T., Salas, E., & Driskell, J. E. (2018). Teams in extreme environments: Alterations in team development and teamwork. *Human Resource Management Review, 28*(4), 434–449. https://doi.org/10.1016/j.hrmr.2017.01.002

Eagle Hill Consulting. (2020). *Employee burnout from COVID-19 on the rise, with 58% of U.S. workers reporting burnout.* https://www.prnewswire.com/news-releases/employee-burnout-from-covid-19-on-the-rise-with-58-of-us-workers-reporting-burnout-301122967.html

Elstak, M. N., Bhatt, M., Van Riel, C. B., Pratt, M. G., & Berens, G. A. (2015). Organizational identification during a merger: The role of self-enhancement and uncertainty reduction motives during a major organizational change. *Journal of Management Studies, 52*(1), 32–62. https://doi.org/10.1111/joms.12105

Flynn, M. (2020, April 23). They lived in a factory for 28 days to make millions of pounds of raw PPE materials to help fight coronavirus. *The Washington Post.* https://www.washingtonpost.com/nation/2020/04/23/factory-masks-coronavirus-ppe/

Franke, F. (2015). Is work intensification extra stress? *Journal of Personnel Psychology, 14*(1), 17–27. https://doi.org/10.1027/1866-5888/a000120

Fritz, C., & Sonnentag, S. (2006). Recovery, well-being, and performance-related outcomes: The role of workload and vacation experiences. *Journal of Applied Psychology, 91*(4), 936–945. https://doi.org/10.1037/0021-9010.91.4.936

Gamio, L. (2020, March 15) The workers who face the greatest coronavirus risk. *The New York Times.* https://www.nytimes.com/interactive/2020/03/15/business/economy/coronavirus-worker-risk.html

Gifford, J. (2020, July 30). *Redundancies vs reduced hours: Juggling workloads through coronavirus.* Personnel Today. https://www.personneltoday.com/hr/redundancies-vs-reduced-hours-juggling-workloads-through-coronavirus/

Grajek, S. (2020, April 24). *EDUCAUSE COVID-19 QuickPoll results: The technology workforce.* Educause. https://er.educause.edu/blogs/2020/4/educause-covid-19-quickpoll-results-the-technology-workforce

Green, F. (2001). It's been a hard day's night: the concentration and intensification of work in late twentieth-century Britain. *British Journal of Industrial Relations, 39*(1), 53–80. https://doi.org/10.1111/1467-8543.00189

Green, F. (2004). Work intensification, discretion, and the decline in well-being at work. *Eastern Economic Journal, 30*(4), 615–625.

Green, F., & McIntosh, S. (2001). The intensification of work in Europe. *Labour Economics, 8*(2), 291–308. https://doi.org/10.1016/s0927-5371(01)00027-6

Gooch, K. (2020, June 5). Record number of healthcare workers laid off, furloughed during pandemic. *Newsweek.* https://www.beckershospitalreview.com/workforce/record-number-of-healthcare-workers-laid-off-furloughed-during-pandemic.html

Hahn, V. C., Binnewies, C., Sonnentag, S., & Mojza, E. J. (2011). Learning how to recover from job stress: Effects of a recovery training program on recovery, recovery-related self-efficacy, and well-being. *Journal of Occupational Health Psychology, 16*(2), 202–216. https://doi.org/10.1037/a0022169

Halbesleben, J. R., & Demerouti, E. (2005). The construct validity of an alternative measure of burnout: Investigating the English translation of the Oldenburg Burnout Inventory. *Work & Stress, 19*(3), 208–220.

Hällgren, M., Rouleau, L., & De Rond, M. (2018). A matter of life or death: How extreme context research matters for management and organization studies. *Academy of Management Annals, 12*(1), 111–153. https://doi.org/10.5465/annals.2016.0017

Hennekam, S., Ladge, J., & Shymko, Y. (2020). From zero to hero: An exploratory study examining sudden hero status among nonphysician health care workers during the COVID-19 pandemic. *Journal of Applied Psychology, 105*(10), 1088–1100. https://doi.org/10.1037/apl0000832

Hulin, C. L. (2002). Lessons from industrial and organizational psychology. In J. M. Brett & F. Drasgow (Eds.), *The psychology of work: Theoretically based empirical research* (pp. 3–22). Lawrence Erlbaum Associates Publishers.

Humphrey, S. E., Nahrgang, J. D., & Morgeson, F. P. (2007). Integrating motivational, social, and contextual work design features: a meta-analytic summary and theoretical extension of the work design literature. *Journal of Applied Psychology, 92*(5), 1332–1356. https://doi.org/10.1037/0021-9010.92.5.1332

Ilies, R., Dimotakis, N., & De Pater, I. E. (2010). Psychological and physiological reactions to high workloads: implications for well-being. *Personnel Psychology, 63*(2), 407–436. https://doi.org/10.1111/j.1744-6570.2010.01175.x

Ilies, R., Schwind, K. M., Wagner, D. T., Johnson, M. D., DeRue, D. S., & Ilgen, D. R. (2007). When can employees have a family life? The effects of daily workload and affect on work-family conflict and social behaviors at home. *Journal of Applied Psychology, 92*(5), 1368–1379. https://doi.org/10.1037/0021-9010.92.5.1368

Jafari, M. J., Zaeri, F., Jafari, A. H., Payandeh Najafabadi, A. T., Al-Qaisi, S., & Hassanzadeh-Rangi, N. (2020). Assessment and monitoring of mental workload in subway train operations using physiological, subjective, and performance measures. *Human Factors and Ergonomics in Manufacturing & Service Industries, 30*(3), 165–175. https://doi.org/10.1002/hfm.20831

Johns, G. (2006). The essential impact of context on organizational behavior. *Academy of Management Review, 31*(2), 386–408. https://doi.org/10.5465/amr.2006.20208687

Johnson, L. E., Davies, S. P., & Freeman, R. J. (2002). The effect of seasonal variations in auditor workload on local government audit fees and audit delay. *Journal of Accounting and Public Policy, 21*(4/5), 395–422.

Josephs, L. (2020, August 16). *A flood of job losses looms as airline industry struggles in pandemic.* CNBC. https://www.cnbc.com/2020/08/16/a-flood-of-job-losses-looms-as-airlines-industry-struggle-in-coronavirus-pandemic.html

Kang. M. (2020, June). *COVID-19 has been both good and bad for work–life balance.* https://www.peoplemattersglobal.com/article/employee-relations/covid-19-has-been-both-good-and-bad-for-work-life-balance-26159

Lades, L., Laffan, K., Daly, M., & Delaney, L. (2020). Daily emotional well-being during the COVID-19 pandemic. *British Journal of Health Psychology, 25*(4), 902–911. https://doi.org/10.1111/bjhp.12450

Levin, S., France, D. J., Hemphill, R., Jones, I., Chen, K. Y., Rickard, D., Makowski, R., & Aronsky, D. (2006). Tracking workload in the emergency department. *Human Factors: The Journal of the Human Factors and Ergonomics Society*, *48*(3), 526–539. https://doi.org/10.1518/001872006778606903

Liu, C. Y., Yang, Y. Z., Zhang, X. M., Xu, X., Dou, Q. L., Zhang, W. W., & Cheng, A. S. (2020a). The prevalence and influencing factors in anxiety in medical workers fighting COVID-19 in China: A cross-sectional survey. *Epidemiology & Infection, 148*, E98. https://doi.org/10.1017/s0950268820001107

Liu, Q., Luo, D., Haase, J. E., Guo, Q., Wang, X. Q., Liu, S., Xia, L., Liu, Z., Yang, J., & Yang, B. X. (2020b). The experiences of health-care providers during the COVID-19 crisis in China: A qualitative study. *The Lancet Global Health, 8*(6), e790–e798. https://doi.org/10.1016/s2214-109x(20)30204-7

Mackey, K., & Boxall, P. (2008). High-involvement work processes, work intensification and employee well-being: A study of New Zealand worker experiences. *Asia Pacific Journal of Human Resources, 46*(1), 38–55. https://doi.org/10.1177/1038411107086542

Mariappanadar, S. (2014). Stakeholder harm index: A framework to review work intensification from the critical HRM perspective. *Human Resource Management Review, 24*(4), 313–329. https://doi.org/10.1016/j.hrmr.2014.03.009

Martins, L. L. (2010). Organizational change and development. In S. Zedeck (Ed.), *APA handbook of industrial and organizational psychology* (pp. 691–728). American Psychological Association. https://doi.org/10.1037/12171-020

McNamara, A. (2020, April 4). Walmart and Target limit number of shoppers in stores amid coronavirus *pandemic.* CBS News. https://www.cbsnews.com/news/walmart-target-limit-number-of-shoppers-in-stores-coronavirus-pandemic/

Morgeson, F. P., Mitchell, T. R., & Liu, D. (2015). Event system theory: An event-oriented approach to the organizational sciences. *Academy of Management Review, 40*(4), 515–537. https://doi.org/10.5465/amr.2012.0099

Murphy, T., Akehurst, H., & Mutimer, J. (2020). Impact of the 2020 COVID-19 pandemic on the workload of the orthopaedic service in a busy UK district general hospital. *Injury, 51*(10), 2142–2147. https://doi.org/10.1016/j.injury.2020.07.001

Nawaz, A. (2020, June 8). *Pandemic increases workload, health risks for postal and delivery employees.* PBS News Hour. https://www.pbs.org/newshour/show/pandemic-increases-workload-health-risks-for-postal-and-delivery-employees

Nixon, A. E., Mazzola, J. J., Bauer, J., Krueger, J. R., & Spector, P. E. (2011). Can work make you sick? A meta-analysis of the relationships between job stressors and physical symptoms. *Work & Stress, 25*(1), 1–22. https://doi.org/10.1080/02678373.2011.569175

Spector, P. E., & Jex, S. M. (1998). Development of four self-report measures of job stressors and strain: Interpersonal conflict at work scale, organizational constraints scale, quantitative workload inventory, and physical symptoms inventory. *Journal of Occupational Health Psychology, 3*(4), 356–367. https://doi.org/10.1037/1076-8998.3.4.356

Parmet, W. E., & Sinha, M. S. (2020). Covid-19—The law and limits of quarantine. *New England Journal of Medicine, 382*(15), e28. https://doi.org/10.1056/nejmp2004211

Repko, M. (2020, March 10). *Walmart, Starbucks and others face a new coronavirus challenge: Sick workers and fearful customers.* CNBC. https://www.cnbc.com/2020/03/10/coronavirus-walmart-and-others-cope-with-sick-workers-fearful-customers.html

Rezapour, S., Naderi, N., Morshedlou, N., & Rezapourbehnagh, S. (2018). Optimal deployment of emergency resources in sudden onset disasters. *International Journal of Production Economics, 204*, 365–382. https://doi.org/10.1016/j.ijpe.2018.08.014

Romeo, P. (2020, May 21). *COVID-19 gives rise to new restaurant jobs.* Restaurant Business. https://www.restaurantbusinessonline.com/workforce/covid-19-gives-rise-new-restaurant-jobs

Rosenbaum, E. (2020, June 18). *6 of the biggest, permanent changes coming to work: Honeywell, Genpact CEOs.* CNBC. https://www.cnbc.com/2020/06/18/6-permanent-changes-coming-to-work-honeywell-genpact-ceos.html

Rudolph, C., Allan, B., Clark, M., Hertel, G., Hirschi, A., Kunze, F., Shockley, K., Shoes, M., Sonnentag, S., & Zacher, H. (2020). Pandemics: Implications for research and practice in industrial and organizational psychology. *Industrial and Organizational Psychology: Perspectives on Science and Practice.* https://doi.org/10.31234/osf.io/k8us2

Scott, A., Tan, B. Y. Q., Huak, C. Y., Sia, C.-H., Xian, C. Y., Goh, E. T., Zbikowska, G., Dykowska, G., Martin, G., Kinross, J., Przbylowicz, J., Fedorowski, J., Beatty, J. W., Clarke, J., Sim, K., Abhiram, K., Flott, K., Lim, L. J. H., Wells, M., . . . Sounderajah, V. (2020). Determinants of burnout and other aspects of psychological well-being in healthcare workers during the COVID-19 pandemic: a multinational cross-sectional study. *MedRxiv.* https://doi.org/10.1101/2020.07.16.20155622

Shi, J., Giess, C. S., Martin, T., Lemaire, K. A., Curley, P. J., Bay, C., Mayo-Smith, W. W., Bolan, G. W., & Khorasani, R. (2020). Radiology workload changes during the COVID-19 pandemic: implications for staff redeployment. *Academic Radiology, 28*(1), 1–7. https://doi.org/10.1016/j.acra.2020.09.008

Shoss, M. K. (2017). Job insecurity: An integrative review and agenda for future research. *Journal of Management, 43*(6), 1911–1939. https://doi.org/10.1177/0149206317691574

Sinclair, R. R., Allen, T., Barber, L., Bergman, M., Britt, T., Butler, A., Ford, M., Hammer, L., Kath, L., Probst, T., & Yuan, Z. (2020). Occupational health science in the time of COVID-19: Now more than ever. *Occupational Health Science, 4*, 1–22. https://doi.org/10.1007/s41542-020-00064-3

Sonnentag, S. (2001). Work, recovery activities, and individual well-being: A diary study. *Journal of Occupational Health Psychology, 6*(3), 196–210. https://doi.org/10.1037/1076-8998.6.3.196

Sonnentag, S., & Kruel, U. (2006). Psychological detachment from work during off-job time: The role of job stressors, job involvement, and recovery-related self-efficacy. *European Journal of Work and Organizational Psychology, 15*(2), 197–217. https://doi.org/10.4324/9781003059714-5

U.S. Bureau of Labor Statistics. (2020). *Supplemental data measuring the effects of the coronavirus pandemic on the labor market.* Labor Force Statistics from the Current Population Survey. https://www.bls.gov/cps/effects-of-the-coronavirus-covid-19-pandemic.htm#highlights.10.37423/200501004

U.S. Department of Homeland Security, Cybersecurity & Infrastructure Security Agency. (2020). *Advisory memorandum on identification of essential critical infrastructure workers during COVID-19 response.* https://www.cisa.gov/sites/default/files/publications/Version_3.0_CISA_Guidance_on_Essential_Critical_Infrastructure_Workers_1.pdf

Van den Broeck, A., Sulea, C., Vander Elst, T., Fischmann, G., Iliescu, D., & De Witte, H. (2014). The mediating role of psychological needs in the relation between qualitative job insecurity and counterproductive work behavior. *Career Development International, 19*(5), 526–547.

Vander Elst, T., De Witte, H., & De Cuyper, N. (2014). The job insecurity scale: A psychometric evaluation across five European countries. *European Journal of Work and Organizational Psychology, 23*(3), 364–380. https://doi.org/10.1080/1359432X.2012.745989

Vaziri, H., Casper, W. J., Wayne, J. H., & Matthews, R. A. (2020). Changes to the work–family interface during the COVID-19 pandemic: Examining predictors and implications using latent transition analysis. *Journal of Applied Psychology, 1059*(10), 1073–1087.

Verkuil, B., Brosschot, J. F., Gebhardt, W. A., & Thayer, J. F. (2010). When worries make you sick: A review of perseverative cognition, the default stress response and somatic health. *Journal of Experimental Psychopathology, 1*(1), 87–118. https://doi.org/10.5127/jep.009110

Villeneuve, M., Fournier, P. S., & Biron, C. (2020). Managing boredom and motivation: The unusual case of stress in firefighting. In R. J. Burke & S. Pignata (Eds.), *Handbook of research on stress and well-being in the public sector* (pp. 74–87). Edward Elgar Publishing.

Wanberg, C. R., Csillag, B., Douglass, R. P., Zhou, L., & Pollard, M. S. (2020). Socioeconomic status and well-being during COVID-19: A resource-based examination. *Journal of Applied Psychology, 105*(12), 1382–1396. http://dx.doi.org/10.1037/apl0000831

Wankhade, P., Stokes, P., Tarba, S., & Rodgers, P. (2020). Work intensification and ambidexterity-the notions of extreme and 'everyday' experiences in emergency contexts: Surfacing dynamics in the ambulance service. *Public Management Review, 22*(1), 48–74. https://doi.org/10.1080/14719037.2019.1642377

Wu, P., Fang, Y., Guan, Z., Fan, B., Kong, J., Yao, Z., Liu, X., Fuller, C. J., Susser, E., Ju, J., & Hoven, C. W. (2009). The psychological impact of the SARS epidemic on hospital employees in China: exposure, risk perception, and altruistic acceptance of risk. *The Canadian Journal of Psychiatry, 54*(5), 302–311. https://doi.org/10.1177/070674370905400504

Zhou, Y., Wang, W., Sun, Y., Qian, W., Liu, Z., Wang, R., Qi, L., Yang, J., Song, X., Zhou, X., Zeng, L., Liu, T., Li, Z., & Zhang, X. (2020). The prevalence and risk factors of psychological disturbances of frontline medical staff in China under the COVID-19 epidemic: Workload should be concerned. *Journal of affective disorders, 277*, 510–514. https://doi.org/10.1016/j.jad.2020.08.059

Zhou, Y., Zhou, Y., Song, Y., Ren, L., Ng, C. H., Xiang, Y. T., & Tang, Y. (2020). Tackling the mental health burden of frontline healthcare staff in the COVID-19 pandemic: China's experiences. *Psychological Medicine, 51*(11), 1955–1956. https://doi.org/10.1017/s0033291720001622

CHAPTER 3

WHO RESCUES THE RESCUERS?

Multilevel Challenges Facing First Responder Organizations

Marc Cubrich
The University of Akron

Ketaki Sodhi
The University of Akron

Allie Pettruzzelli
***APT* Metrics**

Dennis Doverspike
Doverspike Consulting LLC

Even during what may be considered "normal" times, the work of public safety employees (e.g., police, firefighters, emergency medical service [EMS] personnel, and 911 dispatchers) can be categorized as high risk and

Crisis, Chaos, and Organizations, pages 65–96

high stress. When human error is introduced, the services provided by public safety professionals have the potential to result in extremely harmful and fatal outcomes. First responders, or the individuals responsible for immediately going to the scene of an emergency to assist, are often exposed to dangerous situations and required to make rapid, critical decisions. This duty does not rest on a few individuals; it is believed that over three million individuals in the United States alone may be considered first responders, and their employing departments have annual operating budgets of over $181 billion (Department of Homeland Security, 2017).

Due to the high-risk nature of their occupations, public safety personnel face various physical and psychological threats on the job and experience a distinct set of challenges, stressors, and outcomes. Direct physical threats may come in the form of assault, threats of violence, injuries, car accidents, or exposure to harmful pathogens (Donnelly et al., 2015). Furthermore, public safety professionals often face chronic work stressors, including long work hours, inconsistent shift scheduling, sleep restriction, and conflict with coworkers (Blau, 2011; Donnelly & Bennett, 2014; Gevers et al., 2010; Gregov et al., 2011). These chronic stressors, along with higher exposure to traumatic events, place public safety professionals at an increased risk of developing post-traumatic stress disorder (Collins & Gibbs, 2003; Donnelly, 2012), depression (Bennett et al., 2005; Gershon et al., 2009), anxiety (Bennett et al., 2005), substance misuse, and suicidality (Martin et al., 2017). Additionally, this work-related stress has been linked to increased absenteeism (Deery et al., 2014), turnover (Allisey et al., 2014), and burnout (Vettor & Kosinski, 2000).

THE CORONAVIRUS DISEASE (COVID-19) AND UNIQUE FACTORS FOR PUBLIC SAFETY PERSONNEL

With the disruptive impact of the coronavirus disease (COVID-19) pandemic across the United States, many of these stressors have been exacerbated, while other novel stressors have emerged, further impacting public safety employees and their respective organizations. Although many individuals can avoid exposure to the virus by sheltering at home, first responders are considered "essential workers" and must continue working and responding to service calls (Stogner et al., 2020). By continuing to interact with the public during the pandemic, public safety personnel face greater risk of exposure to COVID-19. With a prolonged threat of virus exposure, employees may develop concerns about their personal health or potentially exposing their families to the virus.

Making matters worse, public safety professionals have often lacked the personal protective equipment (PPE) necessary to reduce the likelihood of infection from the virus. As COVID-19 spread across the United States, a variety of factors, including increased demand for PPE and global supply chain issues, led to a national shortage of PPE (Ranney et al., 2020). With public safety agencies struggling to replenish their dwindling PPE, many first responders were forced to make difficult ethical decisions about how to best protect themselves, their families, and the public (Maguire et al., 2020).

Additionally, the COVID-19 pandemic has impacted business for public safety agencies and the workloads of employees. In areas with high rates of COVID-19 infections, agencies are often responding to an increase in calls related to the virus with reduced workforces, as its employees are more likely to be infected by the virus and unable to serve. Consequently, public safety professionals in areas with high rates of COVID-19 infections may experience increased stress from having to carry the burden for their sick peers (Stogner et al., 2020).

Although many public safety professionals have struggled to manage their increased workloads, others have experienced the complete opposite effect of the COVID-19 pandemic on their workload. In general, emergency calls that are unrelated to COVID-19 have decreased during the pandemic (Careless, 2020a). This reduction in call volume is due to a variety of factors, including widespread shelter-in-place guidelines and reduced population activity (Stogner et al., 2020).

Public safety agencies in areas with low rates of COVID-19 infections, especially those in rural, underfunded areas, have had to cut employee hours to save on costs due to low or inconsistent call volumes (Careless, 2020b). Consequently, public safety professionals in these areas experience a completely different set of stressors due to COVID-19, as many struggle to financially support themselves with reduced hours.

Although the COVID-19 pandemic has increased many stressors similarly across public safety professions, there have also been unique effects for specific jobs within these professions. For example, early in the pandemic, police officers were suddenly expected to ensure that citizens followed social distancing guidelines and stay-at-home orders, and experienced anxiety as they enforced these unpopular and highly-debated restrictions on the public they served (Stogner et al., 2020). In fact, some high-level police officials have refused to enforce what they refer to as "unconstitutional" COVID-19 orders (Fowler, 2020). This has created tension between these officials and their respective local and state politicians and within police departments.

For medical first responders, there were unique challenges of EMS that increased the immediate risk of being infected with COVID-19. According to safety guidelines developed by the Centers for Disease Control and Prevention (CDC, 2020a), EMS, and fire personnel providing medical care to patients with COVID-19 were at a greater risk of infection as they transported patients in the small, enclosed space of an ambulance. Although medical first responders faced a greater risk of infection, the smoke that firefighters breathed in as they battled fires increased their risk of developing severe COVID-19 symptoms (Montrose, 2020).

Taken together, it is clear that the current crisis has created a variety of unique challenges for public safety personnel, and these challenges will continue to affect public safety organizations and potentially create long-term organizational changes in the way work is done. In order to address potential changes in basic organizational processes, this chapter identifies the key challenges and factors at multiple levels of analysis (i.e., individual, group, organizational, national) facing public safety organizations. More specifically, we adopt a multilevel approach and propose a conceptual model to organize, inform, organize, guide, and advance research on potential challenges for public safety organizations due to crises such as COVID-19. The benefits of adopting a multilevel approach and proposed conceptual model are discussed hereafter.

BENEFITS OF A MULTILEVEL APPROACH

Most studies in psychology and management focus on either the micro level (e.g., individual well-being) or the macro level (e.g., organizational impact). There is a distinct lack of research considering key constructs as a meso paradigm. The meso paradigm advocates for simultaneous consideration of at least two levels of analysis such that one or more of those include individual or group as well as organizational variables and the process through which these are interlinked. As stated by House et al. (1995), organizational phenomena are inherently present at multiple levels of analysis, and meso paradigms allow researchers to effectively address the relationships that may exist across different levels. Thus, there is a call to better apply multilevel theory when hypothesizing about constructs that may exist at various levels of analysis.

In the context of public safety, the lack of multilevel research is especially glaring because public safety-related work usually involves multiple stakeholders at various levels (e.g., nurses, hospitals, state government, etc.). In other words, public safety personnel are generally nested within the organizations for which they work, which are further nested within their state's government and infrastructure. Moreover, these are nested within and influenced by the general national or societal structure. An implication of this is that individuals can have bottom-up influences on organizations, while organizations can have top–down influences on groups and individuals. A bottom–up influence or effect refers to impacts that units at lower levels of analyses can have on units at higher levels of analyses.

For instance, the effect that interactions between individuals on a team can have on the functioning or performance of a team as a whole can be considered a bottom–up effect. These dynamic, interactive processes involve work-unit members contributing to the overall functioning of the unit (e.g., team or department), which can in turn impact operations at higher levels of analysis (e.g., organizational level, government level). In other words, individual and group behaviors or processes collectively influence and make up organization-level processes, which can then exert an upward influence on the structures set up by governments and related bodies.

On the other hand, a top-down effect refers to the influence that units at higher levels of analyses may exert on individuals or groups that are a part of it. For instance, the impact that organizational policies have on teams or individual employees can be considered a top–down effect. Governments and social structures can influence the processes adopted by public safety organizations, which in turn can set the context, establish boundaries, and determine the constraints within which teams and individual personnel are expected to work.

Since current conceptualizations of challenges within the public safety context generally consider each level of analysis separately, and often ignore the meso context, there is a gap in theory and research surrounding antecedents and consequences of challenges faced by public safety organizations. This gap is further intensified by the fact that the coronavirus is unlike most other emergencies, requiring swift action from not just public safety organizations but also individual personnel, and local and state governments.

Most natural or man-made critical incidents (e.g., earthquakes, floods, epidemics) are generally limited in their impact (geographically and in terms of the populations they affect), as well as their duration (Brito et al., 2009). This allows public safety organizations from unaffected areas to step in and provide assistance. However, the COVID-19 pandemic has not only affected several areas at once but has also lasted for a long time, with unpredictable spikes in activity. This makes it challenging to provide cross-organizational support and requires units at multiple levels of analysis to effectively coordinate, adapt, and ensure public safety. Simply put, in the case of a pandemic, there is an increased need for alignment and collaboration between individual personnel, operational teams, organizational decision makers, and government officials.

This reflects a classic multilevel paradigm, requiring multiple levels within a system to work with and influence each other. Thus, in order to advance theory and research on multilevel responses to the current challenges within public safety systems, this current chapter offers a conceptual model that aims to highlight the myriad of top–down and bottom–up influences that impact public safety outcomes. In short, with the eventual goal of improving coordination and agility within public safety organizations, as well as the lives and mental health of the first responders, this model seeks to hierarchically organize the individual, group, organizational, and societal factors that shape the world of public safety and provide a framework for advanced multilevel research.

PROPOSED CONCEPTUAL MODEL

In an effort to organize, inform, guide, and advance research on potential challenges for public safety organizations as a result of crises such as COVID-19, we present our full conceptual model in Figure 3.1. The proposed conceptual model shown in Figure 3.1 is intended to serve as a heuristic to explore the myriad influences at multiple levels of analysis that affect public safety organizations, their employees, and those they serve. As noted in multilevel theorizing and research, psychological research often ignores macro-level influences, while organizational theory and research

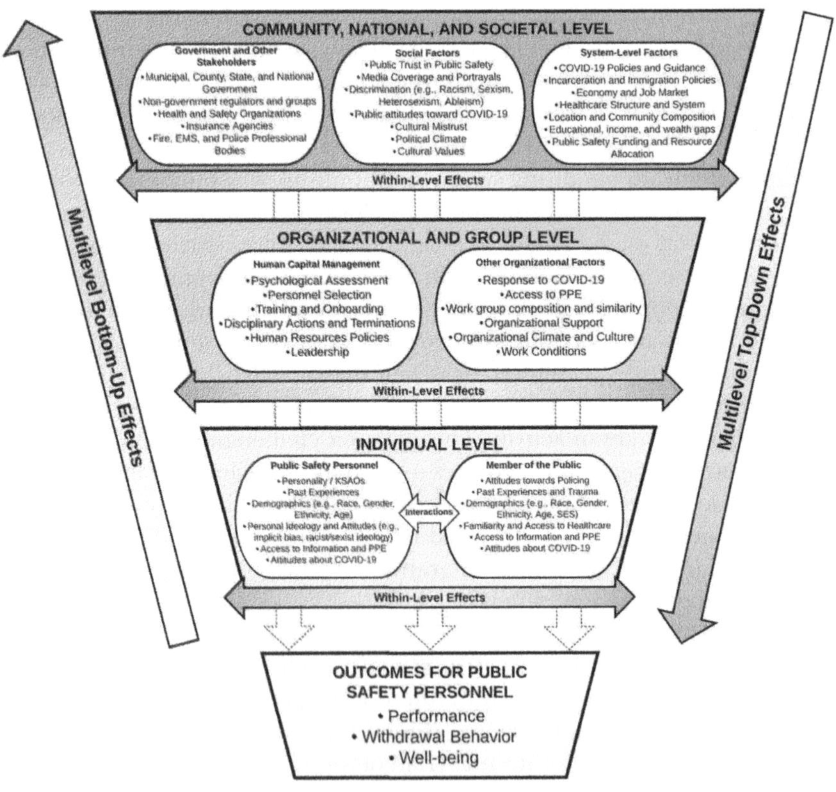

Figure 3.1 Conceptual model of multilevel influences for public safety professions.

may overlook key micro- and individual-level considerations. The conceptual model presented in Figure 3.1 includes factors at the (a) individual level; (b) group and organizational levels; and (c) community, national, and societal levels of analysis. The consideration of critical factors within and across levels of analysis allows researchers to identify potential within-level, top–down, and bottom–up effects and can inform the development of a more replete organizational theory. Eventually, the hope is that such a model can guide and improve applied practices for public safety organizations facing crises such as the COVID-19 pandemic.

With the potential benefits of the proposed model in mind, we also wish to specify the limitations and boundaries of our theoretical framework. First, it is not to say that every factor identified in the conceptual model may directly relate to or influence the other identified factors. Further, we do not intend to suggest that all public safety professions are interchangeable. We acknowledge that there are unique influences and challenges for each public safety profession, but they are united by a common set of influencing factors that are characteristic of public safety organizations and occupations. In addition to the shared influences across public safety professions, the conceptual model in Figure 3.1 identifies the unique factors associated with each profession (e.g., EMS, fire, and law enforcement professional bodies). Although we believe the proposed conceptual model has merit and applicability to public safety organizations globally, it should be acknowledged that much of the described research is largely based on insights from samples in the United States. Moreover, some of the factors identified in the conceptual model are specific to or play a more prominent role in public safety organizations based in the United States. Finally, it should be noted that certain levels of analysis identified in the model (e.g., the organizational and group levels) may be considered theoretically and hierarchically distinct. However, these bands were used to create a parsimonious way to organize multilevel theorizing and propositions.

With the proposed benefits and limitations identified, the following sections delve further into the key factors indicated at each level of analysis, highlighting challenges for public safety organizations, and identifying potential within-level effects and past research to support these claims.

Individual Level

The individual level identifies attributes, behaviors, attitudes, experiences, and other factors associated with individuals. In the present context, we identify these respective factors for individual public safety personnel, with a secondary focus on individual-level considerations for members of the public. Individual public safety personnel interact with each other within

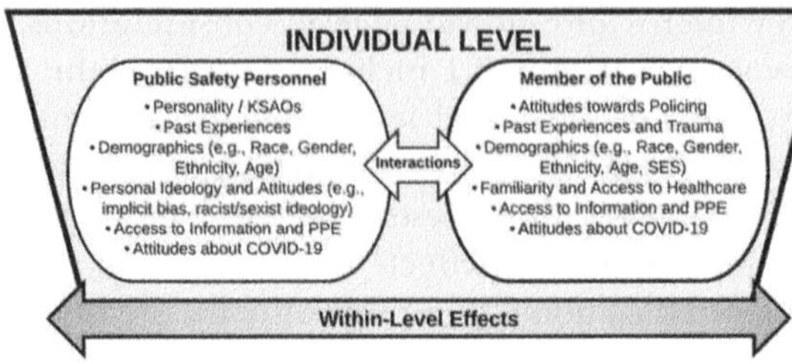

Figure 3.2 Individual-level influences for public safety professions.

an organization, and these factors also influence interactions and outcomes for the individuals they serve (i.e., members of the public). Figure 3.2 highlights key considerations at the individual level. Traditional psychological research has focused on factors at the individual level (e.g., personality, demographics, attitudes), and how they influence the outcomes for public safety personnel, their organizations, and those they serve.

Among the most extensively researched areas, research examining personality and other individual traits has illuminated the critical characteristics of public safety personnel. The psychological assessment of police, in particular, has a long tradition. In fact, one of the first articles in the *Journal of Applied Psychology* was by Terman and associates (1917) on police testing in San Jose, California. Meta-analytic results examining personality traits show that four of the Big Five personality traits (all but agreeableness) significantly predicted police officers' performance (O'Brien, 1996). Similarly, research has found associations between personality and job satisfaction (Meronek & Tan, 2004; Skibba, 2002), job performance (Meronek & Tan, 2004), and burnout (McCall, 2001; Vaulerin et al., 2016) among firefighters. Finally, among EMS personnel, research has found associations between personality and job performance (Fannin & Dabbs, 2003; Niculita, 2013), decision-making (Pilárik & Sarmany-Schuller, 2011), and post-traumatic stress disorder (Sheikhbardsiri et al., 2015).

Clearly, personality has been studied extensively with regard to public safety professions. In the context of COVID-19 and other potential public health crises, personality has the potential to play a critical role as well. Personality can influence the attitudes, behaviors, and outcomes of public safety professionals as it relates to COVID-19 and can also influence these respective factors for members of the public. In the time since the emergence of COVID-19, research has already evinced relationships between personality and compliance with COVID-19 restrictions (Carvalho et al., 2020; Zajenkowski et al., 2020), coping (Prentice et al., 2020; Volk et al., 2020), concerns about the impact of coronavirus on health services and socioeconomic infrastructures, personal safety, and the likelihood of voluntary self-isolation (Bacon & Corr, 2020), to name a few. An understanding of personality differences can inform an understanding of the attitudes, behaviors, and outcomes of public safety personnel, and also sheds light on interpersonal interactions between public safety personnel and members of the public.

Another body of research has identified key sociodemographic characteristics and their associations with various factors relating to public safety personnel. For example, a meta-analysis examining sociodemographic factors associated with burnout among police officers found that younger, female, and those in a serious or marital relationship were more susceptible to certain facets of burnout (Aguayo et al., 2017). Studies have consistently supported the notion that education and police performance are moderately correlated (Hayeslip, 1989). Research on firefighters and EMS personnel has suggested associations between demographic variables and work injury frequency and duration (Liao et al., 2001), work and non-work stressors, negative affective states, and pain complaints (Beaton et al., 1996).

In recent years, increased attention has been given to what many see as an unreasonable use of force by law enforcement against unarmed Black citizens (Ruggs et al., 2016). As a result, a particular focus in demographic research has been on the role that these variables play in use of force decisions and other discriminatory treatment by police officers. While the literature on sociodemographic variables can be characterized by inconsistent findings overall, commonly studied variables include officer sex (i.e., generally, male officers are more likely to use force than females; Bolger, 2015; Johnson, 2011; Kop & Euwema, 2001; Morabito & Doerner, 1997), education (Paoline & Terrill, 2004, 2007; Rydberg & Terrill, 2010; Terrill & Mastrofski, 2002), and experience (Kaminski et al., 2004; Paoline & Terrill, 2007; Rydberg & Terrill, 2010). In terms of the officer's race, the majority of studies have found that officer race has no influence on the officers' decisions to use force (Engel & Calnon, 2004; Lawton, 2007; McCluskey et al., 2005). As with any research on demographic variables, many of these relationships are frequently contingent on a variety of other contextual factors. The consideration of these factors in light of the impact of higher levels of analysis can further illuminate or explain observed associations with demographic variables.

Although the majority of the research examining discriminatory treatment and sociodemographic variables has been on police officers, EMS and firefighting professions are not immune to similar concerns. Implicit class and racial biases are common in the medical field (Green et al., 2007; Teachman & Brownell, 2001). Even when indicating no explicit preference by race, physicians hold unconscious biases against minority patients that impact diagnoses (Stepanikova, 2012) and contribute to disparities in their likelihood of treating disorders (Green et al., 2007). Namely, false beliefs about biological differences between Black and White people continue to shape the perceptions and treatment of Black people in a medical context, leading to racial disparities in pain assessment and treatment (Hoffman et al., 2016).

As indicated by Scarborough (2017), some firefighters harbor individual prejudices, which are in opposition to the institutional culture of egalitarian service that is characteristic of firefighting professions. As part of their work, firefighters are faced with life-or-death decisions that are influenced by shared understandings of whose lives matter (Scarborough, 2017). A qualitative study over 3 years found that prejudices based on age, race, gender, ethnicity, and medical condition shaped some firefighters' individual perceptions of whose lives mattered (Scarborough, 2017). Although the study suggested that the demographics of members of the public did not produce significant variation in actual behavior on the fireground, other characteristics of an emergency contribute to shaping response times and emotional reactions (Scarborough, 2017).

Finally, while the focus of the present chapter is on public safety personnel specifically, it is also worth noting research investigating individual-level characteristics and attributes of civilians. For example, research has investigated how characteristics of members of the public influence interactions or experiences with public safety personnel. Unfortunately, who the person is appears to play a role in use of force decisions among police officers. Suspects who are minorities, males, and/or lower class are more likely to have force used against them (Bolger, 2015; Engel & Calnon, 2004; Leinfelt, 2005; McCluskey & Terrill, 2005; Paoline & Terrill, 2007; Terrill & Mastrofski, 2002; Rydberg & Terrill, 2010; Terrill et al., 2003). These results are in line with Kochel et al.'s (2011) finding that race plays a significant role in officer decision-making (Bolger, 2015).

Taken together, it is clear that demographic variables play a significant role in public safety professions, and these associations have implications in the context of COVID-19 and other potential pandemics. For example, at the time this chapter was being written, in many places in the United States, it was illegal not to wear the proper face covering when in public. As a result, police were asked to intervene or arrest individuals for not following these mandates or laws (Stogner et al., 2020). In light of past research examining demographic variables and policing behavior, there was the potential that minority, male, and/or poor individuals might be disproportionately or more severely targeted by the enforcement of these mandates.

Since the start of the pandemic, EMS and fire personnel have been faced with responding to emergency calls for COVID-19. In line with the aforementioned research, treatment or response to individuals may be influenced by sociodemographic variables of the public safety personnel and members of the public. Given that Wuhan, China was initially seen as the epicenter of COVID-19, many Asians have been scapegoated for the introduction of the virus and have witnessed high levels of discrimination based on race (Kantamneni, 2020). Instances of witnessing employees blame Chinese people for the virus, references to COVID-19 as the "Chinese virus," profiling Asians as disease carriers, and even verbal and physical assaults on Asian people have taken place. Further, given systemic barriers to accessing health resources as well as the historical mistreatment of Black people in the healthcare system, Black people in the United States may have lower access to care or may be more likely to have distrust in the healthcare system (Novacek et al., 2020).

In addition to the potential for sociodemographic variables to influence interactions between public safety personnel and members of the public, these variables also directly influence attitudes toward public safety, access to and familiarity with the healthcare system, attitudes about COVID-19, and susceptibility to the virus itself. As just one example, population-based surveys indicate 33% of African Americans are very concerned they will get COVID-19 and require hospitalization as compared to only 18% of Whites (Pew Research, 2020). A survey on public attitudes, behaviors, and beliefs related to COVID-19 found that among respondents who had been in public areas during the preceding week, significantly more women, older adults, retired persons, and those living in urban areas reported wearing cloth face coverings (Czeisler et al., 2020). In light of their susceptibility to the negative effects of the virus, age in particular seems to shape attitudes toward COVID-19. Results indicate a significant association between age and feeling safe without community mitigation strategies, with younger adults feeling safer than older adults (i.e., individuals older than 65 years), which might relate to perceived risk for infection and severe disease (Czeisler et al., 2020).

Although a full exploration of all potential individual-level factors is beyond the scope of the present discussion, it is clear that past psychological research at the individual level can inform organizational theory and policies. Namely, this research highlights the diversity of attributes, behaviors, attitudes, experiences, and other factors associated with individuals, suggesting a one-size-fits-all approach to addressing the current crisis may fall short. Our review of the current literature base revealed a number of gaps within and across levels of analysis. Our conceptual model may be used as an organizational scheme for meta-analytic research. Organizational theory and policies should carefully consider critical individual-level factors and their implications for the successful implementation of pandemic measures.

Organizational and Group Level

Progressing upward in the hierarchy of the proposed conceptual model, the organizational and group level is composed of higher-level factors that include human capital management processes and broader group or organizational characteristics. Human capital management involves the attraction, assessment, selection, development, and compensation of personnel in order to create and maintain a skilled, committed, and well-motivated workforce (Baron & Armstrong, 2007). As noted by multilevel theory, researchers explicitly recognize that lower-level entities such as individuals are nested within higher-level collectives such as groups and organizations (Aguinis et al., 2013). With that said, lower-level entities do not necessarily have to be individuals. For example, as is acknowledged by the community, national, and social level of analysis, lower-level entities can be public safety organizations that are influenced by higher-levels factors that set boundaries, influence, and constrain them (Aguinis et al., 2013). Figure 3.3 provides a summary of human capital concerns as well as other organizational and group factors to be considered with regard to the current crisis.

When integrating micro and macro-levels influences, specifying whether the nature of a lower-level relationship is contingent upon a higher-level factor is essential. Such an effect would be labeled a cross-level interaction effect (Aguinis et al., 2013). Although the integration of multilevel theory and principles is scant in existing research, those who do adopt such an approach tend to investigate cross-level effects of the group or organization on individual relationships. In the context of COVID-19, for example, one might examine how the individual-level association between personality and compliance with COVID-19 restrictions is influenced by higher-level factors, such as organizational policies and practices. Namely, a particular focus could be on whether certain organizational policies attenuate or strengthen key individual-level relationships.

Although an extensive discussion of the implications of the current crisis on human capital management processes is beyond the scope of the present chapter, it is clear that COVID-19 will impact these processes for public safety organizations. Public safety organizations must consider the implications of the current situation at each stage of the human capital management lifecycle. Namely, organizational attraction, assessment, selection,

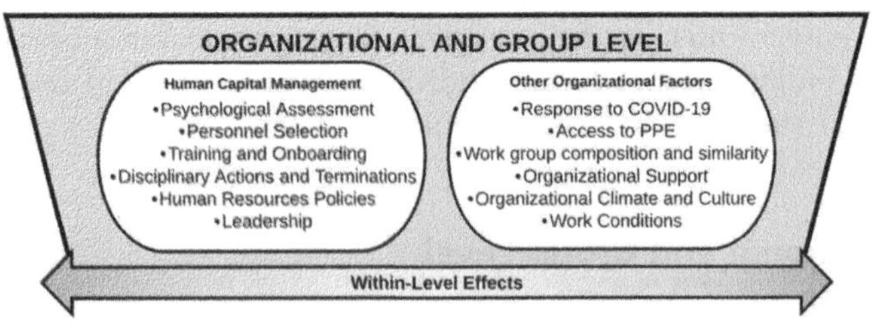

Figure 3.3 Organizational and group-level influences for public safety professions.

training and onboarding, leadership, and HR policies and procedures will be impacted by the present crisis in both the short- and long-term.

At the start of this lifecycle, the way in which public safety organizations attract talent may be affected by crises such as COVID-19. Given the medical nature of certain first responder roles, concerns regarding the risk of infection in this profession may impair organizational attraction, while some individuals may find meaning in serving as an essential worker in a public safety profession. Further, given the stability and essential nature of most public safety roles, organizations may leverage this benefit to attract applicants.

In terms of assessment and selection, crises such as COVID-19 may fundamentally challenge the essential knowledge, skills, abilities, and other characteristics (KSAOs) needed to be successful in these roles, thereby affecting how public safety personnel are evaluated and selected. Even during "normal" times, Garb et al. (2018) note that screening for public safety positions is one of the most important, but difficult tasks facing psychologists. Crises such as the COVID-19 pandemic may create a shift in the focus of public safety organizations and the KSAOs that are critical to success. More specifically, a greater focus may be placed on health, safety, compliance, and well-being of current and potential employees. Further, given the stressors and strains associated with crises such as COVID-19, an increased focus may be placed on reducing physical (i.e., tardiness, absenteeism, turnover) as well as psychological withdrawal behaviors (i.e., disengagement, burnout, reduced organizational commitment, and job satisfaction).

As a result of social distancing concerns, public safety organizations may elect to migrate certain training and onboarding practices that were previously conducted in person to online or virtual environments. The careful development of training content remains essential to creating effective training programs. Although meta-analytic results have suggested some potential benefits for web-based instruction compared to classroom instruction (Sitzmann et al., 2006), organizations should be mindful of the development and delivery of training to ensure its efficacy, particularly as it relates to the adjustment and socialization of organizational newcomers. Given the essential nature of their work, training may focus on the prevention of occupational exposure to COVID-19. For example, training public safety personnel on elements of infection prevention, the use of PPE, and the implementation of other safety measures. With that said, organizations often have little time or resources to implement training. The addition of such training programs may affect the training of traditional activities for public safety officials. Research should examine the effectiveness of such training programs, and for whom these programs are most effective.

The rapidly-changing nature of the COVID-19 situation has required human resources (HR) departments and managers to quickly adjust their policies and practices (Rudolph et al., 2020). In a typical public safety organization, many personnel functions are solely the superior's responsibility. The duty of implementing and ensuring the success of many of the aforementioned human capital management processes falls under the purview of these groups. Since public safety is a critical industry that cannot shut down its capacities, the current crisis has necessitated actions on the operational side of organizational practices. Although practices such as social distancing, the utilization of PPE, and sanitization practices can be implemented relatively easily, common practices such as reducing the social density of shifts or moving away from standard eight-hour shifts may be less feasible for public safety professions.

These essential professions often necessitate interactions with others. As a result, there is a need to foster positive hygiene cultures that ensure the health of the workforce. Public safety organizations can reference insights from public health research demonstrating the efficacy of interventions for hygiene procedures (Rudolph et al., 2020). As just one example, research in a hospital setting suggests that positive deviance change procedures can result in a 50% decrease in infection rates (Lindberg et al., 2009). Positive deviance practices include setting concrete, measurable goals for the initiative, identifying groups that already demonstrate these behaviors, and adjusting policies to provide communication, leadership, and support for these initiatives (Sternin, 2003). As part of setting COVID-19 policies and guidelines, public safety organizations must also navigate the difficult task of disciplining employees for failure to abide by safety precautions.

Although research on the occupational health consequences of COVID-19 are still emerging (see Lai et al., 2020; Zhu et al., 2020 for examples), past research on infectious diseases outbreaks indicate that healthcare workers, in particular, experience stressors and strains associated with the crisis (Brooks et al., 2018; Lee et al., 2018). Research on leadership emergence during the pandemic crisis will be key for understanding effective change management, communication, and the implementation of COVID-19 safety measures. Researchers have called attention to the critical role of immediate supervisors for effective implementation of proactive employer policies and practices to ensure workplace safety (Kristman et al., 2020; Shaw et al., 2020).

An organization's response to and communication regarding COVID-19 will be similarly critical for maintaining worker well-being. Existing research suggests that fears of infection are pervasive and positively associated with feelings of distress (Wong et al., 2005; Zhu et al., 2020). As the increased demand for PPE led to a national shortage of PPE, many public safety organizations struggled to replenish their rapidly diminishing PPE. Accordingly, many first responders were forced to make difficult ethical decisions about how to best protect themselves, their families, and the public (Maguire et al., 2020). A lack of access to proper PPE and low perceived organizational support have been found to be associated with strain symptoms and concerns over one's personal and family health (Maunder et al., 2006; Nickell et al., 2004). Further, as was evidenced by the PPE shortage, daily work becomes particularly taxing when the allocation of treatment resources is not enough to help those who may need them (Wright et al., 2020).

Thankfully, research suggests that actions taken by organizations can have a profound impact on workers. Individuals who perceived higher organizational, supervisor, social, and COVID-19 specific organizational support were more likely to report better outcomes (Charoensukmongkol & Phungsoonthorn, 2020; Labrague & De los Santos, 2020; Zhang et al., 2020). With that said, in highly intransigent (i.e., rigid or inflexible) workplace climates, a frequent characteristic of public safety organizations, supervisor support does not lower the perceived uncertainties of employees (Charoensukmongkol & Phungsoonthorn, 2020).

What emerges from the aforementioned research is the notion that group and organizational factors can have a profound effect on the individuals within them. Moreover, these effects cannot be divorced from research highlighting key individual-level variables. The response to COVID-19 has been ever changing as new information has emerged and organizations have tried different approaches to navigate the crisis. There is a need for research that both qualitatively and empirically investigates the organizational and group factors that have constituted successful responses to COVID-19. More specifically, research should call attention to the characteristics of organizations that handled the crisis well compared to those that did not.

Community, National, and Societal Level

As of October 2020, well over 6 months into the present crisis, the United States alone has witnessed over 8 million confirmed cases of COVID-19 with over 200,000 deaths (World Health Organization, n.d.). During this time, the United States also hit its first peak in new infections since July of 2020, prompting epidemiologists to label this spike in infections as the "third wave" of COVID-19. Conversely, in countries such as New Zealand, the swift implementation of risk-informed national COVID-19 suppression measures resulted in low relative burden of disease, low levels of population disease disparities, and the initial achievement of COVID-19 elimination (Jefferies et al., 2020). While some may point to observed differences between countries such as the United States and New Zealand, it is clear that community, national, and societal factors can have a profound impact on the handling of crises such as COVID-19.

At the highest level of the proposed conceptual model, the community, national, and societal levels of analysis acknowledge that public safety organizations are nested within broader communities, and thereby influenced by higher-level factors such as municipal, state, and national governments, collective social factors, and systemic factors that have effects on both organizations and individuals within a system. Although the consideration of these highest levels introduces complexity into our understanding of the factors influencing public safety organizations, crises such as COVID-19 necessitate a comprehensive approach. Past research on pandemics and epidemics suggests that the effectiveness of policies are conditional upon a host of factors, including the manner of development of the specific disease (Kilbourne, 2006; Taubenberger & Morens, 2006), the characteristics of the underlying population (Bootsma & Ferguson, 2007; Farmer, 1996; Hunter, 2007), and the available medical (Bandayrel et al., 2013) and communication technology (Chew & Eysenbach, 2010; Galaz, 2009) at the time. Figure 3.4 provides a summary of the community, national, and societal-level influences for public safety organizations.

Compared to most other organizations, public safety organizations are especially beholden to various governmental and regulatory agencies. Public safety personnel are generally nested within the organizations for which they work, which are further nested within their state's government and infrastructure. Municipal, county, state, and federal governments affect the provision of public safety services, and directly impact the response to crises such as COVID-19. The variation in governance, laws, and regulations creates a complex set of influencing factors for public safety organizations.

While the available research at the time of writing may be considered preliminary, a large hand-coded dataset of over 13,000 government policy announcements across more than 195 countries has provided insight into these influences (Cheng et al., 2020). Past research has indicated that the type of policies that governments have implemented in response to COVID-19, when they decided to implement them, who they were targeted towards, and a state's capacity to make and effectively implement policies have all significantly influenced how the virus has affected health outcomes

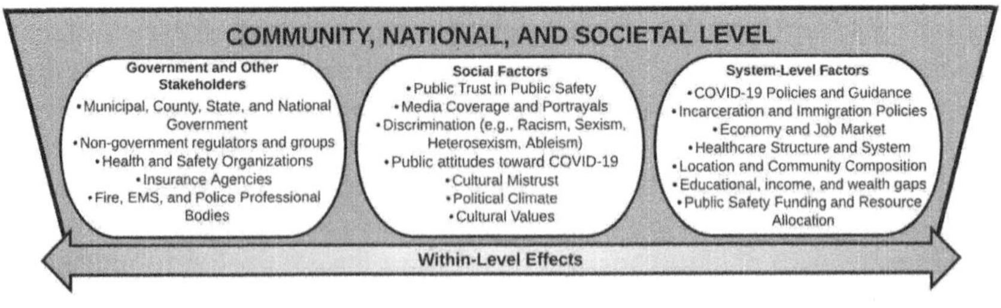

Figure 3.4 Community, national, and societal-level influences for public safety professions.

both within and across different countries (Cheng et al., 2020). Institutional and political factors, such as the authoritarian or democratic nature of a country, have also been found to play an essential role (Cheng et al., 2020). Existing research has already revealed how lockdown policies affect political attitudes (Bol et al., 2020), have led to increased authoritarianism in some countries (Lührmann et al., 2020), and had serious negative mental health consequences for many around the world (Torales et al., 2020).

Various collective social factors at this highest level of analysis exert meaningful influence on public safety organizations as well. Collective attitudes about COVID-19, trust in public safety, cultural values, and discriminatory ideology (e.g., racism, sexism, etc.) are shaped in a bottom–up way by the attitudes and beliefs of the individuals within a society, but also reciprocally exert top–down influences. Although each individual has their own distinct personality, attitudes, and predispositions, overlaid are a set of tendencies and assumptions that reflect the collective they belong to.

Recent research has shown that cultural values play a role in perceived risks and psychological maladjustment related to COVID-19 (Germani et al., 2020). In the context of COVID-19, there has been a particular focus on the cultural values of individualism and collectivism. Individualism corresponds with a preference to place the individual or personal self-interests over the social group, while collectivism corresponds to an emphasis on the group over the individual and considerations of how a person's behavior impacts the whole collective (Hofstede, 2001). To mitigate the effects of crises such as COVID-19 there is a need for collective cooperation and compliance from individual citizens that may come less naturally to those shaped by individualistic or culturally "loose" societies (Guan et al., 2020). Although it is acknowledged that collective cultural values shape the individuals within a certain society, it is not to suggest that all individuals within a society share the same values. In any society, there are members who have a low level of identification or may not be aligned with the collective norms and actions of a nation (Guan et al., 2020). A multilevel approach, such as the one proposed in our conceptual model, acknowledges collective influences and the uniqueness of individuals.

As it relates to trust in public safety, collective perceptions of police misconduct and discrimination are heavily influenced by media portrayal and consumption (Dowler & Zawilski, 2007). The majority of public knowledge about crime and law enforcement is largely derived from their portrayal in the media (Dowler & Zawilski, 2007). For police in particular, a recent study investigated the extent to which policing has become a "tainted" or stigmatized profession (Chatterjee & Ryan, 2020). Results indicate that the media coverage between 2011 and 2016 used a more negative tone over time when discussing police–citizen interactions, and that policing was categorized as a pervasively stigmatized job (Chatterjee & Ryan, 2020). The death of George

Floyd at the hands of the police in May 2020 reignited outrage surrounding the state of policing in the United States. This constituted a dual shock for law enforcement organizations as they began to face backlash while still grappling with the advent of the pandemic. Although the influence of trust in public safety may be less pronounced for EMS and fire professions, the notion that collective attitudes and trust in public safety influences their work and interactions with those they serve is essential.

The historic mistreatment of minority groups in places like the United States are often intertwined with attitudes toward law enforcement and the healthcare system more broadly. The historical mistreatment of Black people by law enforcement and in medical settings, in particular, has led to what many describe as "cultural mistrust" (Whaley, 2001). The effects of such beliefs may be evinced during crises like COVID-19 as well, either by public safety personnel themselves or those they serve.

In addition to collective prejudiced ideology and beliefs, prejudice may also become embedded as normal practice within a society or an organization (e.g., systemic or institutionalized racism). Well-documented disparities in education, work opportunities, and access to healthcare associated with race, gender, and social class present challenges and barriers for minority groups. Black people in the United States, for example, face many barriers to receiving health services, both historically and presently. This disparity can be ascribed to systemic barriers to accessing the healthcare system as well as the mistreatment of Black people in the healthcare system (Novacek et al., 2020).

Research suggests that racial and ethnic minority groups also bear a disproportionate burden of illness and death related to COVID-19 (CDC, 2020b). These groups face additional risks due to a variety of factors such as living conditions, underlying health conditions, labor market and workplace discrimination, and lower access to care (CDC, 2020b). Millet et al. (2020) found that counties that are disproportionately Black experience higher rates of COVID-19 diagnoses and death resulting from infection. This effect was observed even after controlling for characteristics such as age, poverty, comorbidities, and epidemic duration (Millet et al., 2020).

Since the first reported case of COVID-19 was recorded in Wuhan, China, many Asians have been scapegoated for the introduction of the virus (Kantamneni, 2020). For example, racialized references to COVID-19 as the "Chinese virus" perpetuate animosity towards Asians. In fact, nearly 30% of people from the United States blame China for the emergence of COVID-19 (IPSOS, 2020). In the United States, historians have indicated that the fear of Asians as it relates to infectious diseases is rooted in a long history of prejudicial policies (Natividad, 2020). Although viruses do not discern between hosts as a function of race, ethnicity, nationality or immigration status, misrepresentations of Asians as carriers of disease have been used historically to perpetuate discriminatory public health and immigration policies (Natividad, 2020). As highlighted by these findings, collective prejudice against minority groups can manifest in the treatment of these groups by law enforcement and the healthcare system more broadly. The consideration of these social factors sheds light on the different experiences of individuals within a society, as well as the potential for differential experiences with public safety organizations and the services they provide.

Finally, research must also consider the material and geographic properties of a community (e.g., population density, demographic composition), as well as system-level factors that determine the organization and provision of public safety services (e.g., healthcare system, funding, and resource allocation). The material characteristics of a community may impact behavior in general, and specifically as it relates to COVID-19. For example, densely populated communities may increase the spread and risk of infection, while sparsely populated areas may be harder to effectively and quickly provide services to.

Early research on community characteristics investigated the impact of a community's income level and "perceived danger" on police force decisions (Bayley & Mendelsohn, 1969; Slovak, 1986; Smith, 1986; Werthman & Piliavin, 1967). While early research was unequivocal in its findings, recent research has supported the notion that force is more likely to be used in poorer communities (McCluskey et al., 2005; Terrill & Reisig, 2003). Similarly, for firefighters, Scarborough (2017) found that firefighters often categorize neighborhoods as "good" and "bad" based on the cost of housing and oral history of recent calls. It was found that discussions between firefighters often conflated race and class, and race was used as a scapegoat for social problems associated with poverty (Scarborough, 2017).

Public safety organizations operate in government and healthcare systems that vary as a function of location. The funding and resource allocation to public safety organizations directly affects their capacity to handle crises such as COVID-19. Given that the budget of public safety organizations is, in part, determined by the local government, researchers have sought to assess citizens' attitudes about public services and their inclination to fund enhanced service levels and quality (Donahue & Miller, 2006). Research suggests that direct experience and media exposure affect attitudes, and these attitudes are associated with willingness to pay (Donahue & Miller, 2006). An acknowledgment of system-level factors such as funding and resource allocations highlights the difficulty of creating one-size-fits-all solutions and recommendations for public safety organizations. Taken together, it is clear that there is great value and insights that emerge from the consideration of community, national, and societal factors. Namely, the services provided by first responder organizations are influenced by various community, national, and societal-level influences that have implications for understanding the effects of the pandemic.

DISCUSSION

In light of insights from the proposed conceptual framework, it is clear that public safety organizations must be flexible and agile in the face of the current crisis. The COVID-19 pandemic has not only accelerated the pace at which the organizational landscape evolved but also made the work of public safety organizations more critical. Research suggests that while agility in public sector organizations right after a crisis increases significantly, it tends to reduce over time (Dowdy et al., 2017). It is theorized that this increase is because, in times of sudden crises, strict rules and hierarchy are relatively relaxed, encouraging personnel at different levels to look for solutions and act fast. However, once the initial shock of a crisis passes, old rules and hierarchies are reinforced leading to a reduction in agility and quick action. This is especially dangerous in the case of a pandemic because it usually lasts a relatively long time and is often unpredictable.

In the midst of the current crisis, public safety organizations have had to make a number of critical decisions on how much to change for the pandemic while keeping up with their traditional activities. The long-lasting effects of COVID-19 on the traditional activities of public safety organizations are still unknown. For instance, organizations may consider permanent changes to safety protocols or their emergency management plans. As previously noted, strong cultures tend to return to old practices unless the entire HR system is revamped or there is commitment or replacement of those at the top. As we emerge from the other side of the COVID-19 pandemic, public safety organizations will again face critical decisions surrounding the traditional activities and management of public safety personnel. In the following sections, we describe several recommendations for public safety organizations to consider in effectively managing the current crisis and similar crises in the future.

Recommendations for Managing Current and Future Crises

Over the last few decades, public safety organizations such as EMS and police have been increasingly characterized by "getting tough" (Goff et al., 2019) with firm rules and policies as well as a strict hierarchy or chain of command, and performance being primarily evaluated at the individual level with little change over time. All of this has resulted in a system that is not only rigid and bureaucratic but also one that lacks public trust and is too slow to adapt to changes in the external environment.

A recent report by McKinsey and Company (Dowdy et al., 2017) suggests that some classic problems seen within public sector organizations include slow information circulation, budgets that fail to keep up with the required operational changes, senior leaders' inability to quickly execute solutions, and limited or incomplete guidance for frontline workers. As mentioned, an underlying theme here seems to be slow and bureaucratic processes that are difficult to change. This is unfortunate because the external world is becoming increasingly volatile, uncertain, complex, and ambiguous (VUCA), requiring organizations to be flexible and agile to keep up. With these emerging challenges in mind, three classic challenges that plague in public sector organizations include: inherent risk aversion, functional silos, and organizational complexity.

Public sector organizations are generally more risk averse than private sector companies and often lack the infrastructure that promotes new or improved processes. Because of this, information travels slowly and organizations err on the side of gathering as much information as possible before implementing any changes. This is further intensified by the diverse range of stakeholders (e.g., state officials, citizens) they need to satisfy and the heightened risk of scrutiny from the media. Moreover, public sector organizations tend to operate in function silos that have little communication or collaboration between each other. Moreover, the rigid, bureaucratic structure usually only allows leaders high up in the organization to authorize cross-functional initiatives that span all levels of an organization. These structures generally inhibit rapid decision-making at lower levels, further slowing down the process of adaptation over time.

Finally, public sector organizations are some of the largest and most complex organizations. While this adds some value, it can also be dysfunctional and limiting. The myriad of rules and policies in the public sector not only take significant time and effort to navigate but also result in reduced transparency and slower decision making. While public sector companies usually succeed in working around these challenges in the face of crises, these effects do not last long.

In order to effectively react to crises and establish lasting change, public safety organizations need to readjust their priorities and focus on additional outcomes at every level. Specifically, a focus on leading with empathy and compassion is critical to enhancing public trust, working on developing long-term agility and collaboration at the organizational and group level can enable quick decision-making and action, and finally, promoting well-being at the individual level can help reduce burnout and turnover within their personnel.

Leading with empathy and compassion involves focusing on understanding the challenges faced by those we hope to help and meeting them where they are. In a society that is becoming increasingly more polarized, it is critical to keep citizens in mind and be thoughtful when making decisions or taking action that could affect them. Research suggests that approaching situations in an empathetic and compassionate manner can help build trust as well as lead to increased satisfaction, better compliance, and lower rates of malpractice litigation. In the medical field, empathy is also related to increased well-being and lower levels of burnout amongst medical professionals (Hojat, 2009).

To develop agility, public sector organizations can look at some of the most successful large private sector companies. According to research from McKinsey and Company (Dowdy et al., 2017), companies that are most successful tend to embody the two hallmarks of agility: stability and dynamism. In other words, these are companies that have stable operations but are open to change and have the capability to make fast and rapid decisions. While most public sector companies are not considered agile, there are four key opportunities that can help them become more agile, namely, strategy, structure, people, and processes. Agile companies tend to have a clear vision and mission that drives every decision they make. Clarity around the vision and purpose serve as the bedrock of an agile organization and define the direction in which they hope to move. Beyond that, it allows employees to react to changing circumstances and harness new opportunities in order to achieve this vision. In terms of structure, companies that have a simple structure with top level leadership allocating budgets and mid- and lower-level teams with clear missions, autonomy to make key decisions, and end-to-end ownership of their processes is key. In terms of processes, agile organizations tend to have a few standard rules of operation that are important and allow employees to make continuous improvement and be flexible in most other ways.

Finally, people or employees are key to the success of an agile organization. Once the foundation of a clear, shared vision and a common culture is set, allowing employees the opportunity to engage in self-improvement through stretch goals and creating an environment that allows for the exchange of feedback in a safe and effective manner can help organizations keep up with the external changes.

To increase focus on personnel well-being, there are several things that can be done. Research suggests that first responders often have high levels of depression, post-traumatic stress disorder, and suicidal thoughts (Newland et al., 2015) with many having little or no access to mental health or fitness related services (National Association of Emergency Medical Technicians, 2016). Since public safety professionals work under extremely stressful conditions, access to mental health resources are critical. Employee

Assistance Programs (EAP) and access to counseling or other kinds of training (e.g., stress management, resilience) can be a fruitful investment. Additionally, building a culture that emphasizes social connections and meaningful relationships can help and prioritize recovery can encourage employees to embrace these programs and prioritize their own mental health. This can not only reduce strain and burnout but in the long run, also lead to lower turnover and cost saving. Finally, providing avenues to promote physical health through fitness programs or nutritious snacks or meals can complement investment programs focused on mental or emotional health. Organizations should carefully examine the characteristics of physically and psychologically healthy workplaces and seek to create actionable steps to achieve a safe work environment for all employees.

CONCLUSION

It is clear that public safety organizations must be flexible and agile in the face of the COVID-19 pandemic. Furthermore, they must maintain this agility in the face of potential threats in the future. It is our hope that the insights emerging from our conceptual model will not only guide and improve applied practices for public safety organizations to the current crisis but also build a foundation of knowledge for responding to future outbreaks. In order to build a more replete organizational theory, future research and practice should address or acknowledge the various multilevel influences by examining the top–down, bottom–up, within-level, and cross-level effects of the factors identified in the proposed conceptual model. Communities around the world rely on the essential services of first responders during crises. Identifying the challenges faced by first responders and their respective organizations can improve outcomes for individual public safety personnel, their organizations, and those they serve.

REFERENCES

Aguayo, R., Vargas, C., Cañadas, G. R., & De la Fuente, E. I. (2017). Are sociodemographic factors associated to burnout syndrome in police officers? A correlational meta-analysis. *Annals of Psychology, 33*(2), 383–392.

Aguinis, H., Gottfredson, R. K., & Culpepper, S. A. (2013). Best-practice recommendations for estimating cross-level interaction effects using multilevel modeling. *Journal of Management, 39*(6), 1490–1528.

Allisey, A. F., Noblet, A. J., Lamontagne, A. D., & Houdmont, J. (2014). Testing a model of officer intentions to quit: the mediating effects of job stress and job satisfaction. *Criminal Justice and Behavior, 41*(6), 751–771.

Bacon, A. M., & Corr, P. J. (2020). Coronavirus (COVID-19) in the United Kingdom: A personality-based perspective on concerns and intention to self-isolate. *British Journal of Health Psychology.*

Bandayrel, K., Lapinsky, S., & Christian, M. (2013). Information technology systems for critical care triage and medical response during an influenza pandemic: A review of current systems. *Disaster Medicine and Public Health Preparedness, 7*(3), 287–291.

Baron, A., & Armstrong, M. (2007). *Human capital management: achieving added value through people.* Kogan Page Publishers.

Bayley, D., & Mendelsohn, H. (1969). *Minorities and the police.* Free Press.

Beaton, R., Murphy, S., & Pike, K. (1996). Work and nonwork stressors, negative affective states, and pain complaints among firefighters and paramedics. *International Journal of Stress Management, 3*(4), 223–237.

Bennett, P., Williams, Y., Page, N., Hood, K., Woollard, M., & Vetter, N. (2005). Associations between organizational and incident factors and emotional distress in emergency ambulance personnel. *British Journal of Clinical Psychology, 44*(2), 215–226.

Blau, G. (2011). Exploring the impact of sleep-related impairments on the perceived general health and retention intent of an Emergency Medical Services (EMS) sample. *Career Development International, 16*(3), 238–253.

Bol, D., Giani, M., Blais, A., & Loewen, P. J. (2020). The effect of COVID-19 lockdowns on political support: Some good news for democracy? *European Journal of Political Research.* https://doi.org/10.1111/1475-6765.12401

Bolger, P. C. (2015). Just following orders: A meta-analysis of the correlates of American police officer use of force decisions. *American Journal of Criminal Justice, 40*(3), 466–492.

Bootsma, M. C., & Ferguson, N. M. (2007). The effect of public health measures on the 1918 influenza pandemic in US cities. *Proceedings of the National Academy of Sciences, 104*(18), 7588–7593.

Brito, C. S., Luna, A. M., & Sanberg, E. L. (2009). *Benchmarks for developing a law enforcement pandemic flu plan.* Bureau of Justice Assistance: U.S. Department of Justice. https://www.publicsafety.gc.ca/lbrr/archives/cnmcs-plcng/cn34974-eng.pdf

Brooks, S. K., Dunn, R., Amlôt, R., Rubin, G. J., & Greenberg, N. (2018). A systematic, thematic review of social and occupational factors associated with psychological outcomes in healthcare employees during an infectious disease outbreak. *Journal of Occupational and Environmental Medicine, 60,* 248–257.

Careless, J. (2020a, July). The calls that never came: 9-1-1 volume plunges with pandemic. *EMS World.* https://www.emsworld.com/article/1224591/calls-never-came-9-1-1-volume-plunges-pandemic

Careless, J. (2020b, October). COVID-19's impact on EMS jobs. *EMS World.* https://www.emsworld.com/article/1225077/covid-19s-impact-ems-jobs

Carvalho, L. F., Pianowski, G., & Gonçalves, A. (2020). Personality differences and the COVID-19: Are extraversion and conscientiousness personality traits associated with engagement in containment measures? *Trends in Psychiatry and Psychotherapy, 1,* 1–6.

Centers for Disease Control and Prevention. (2020a, July 15). *Interim guidance for emergency medical services (EMS) systems and 911 public safety answering points (PSAPs) for COVID-19 in the United States.* https://www.cdc.gov/coronavirus/2019-ncov/hcp/guidance-for-ems.html

Centers for Disease Control and Prevention. (2020b, July 24). *COVID-19 in racial and ethnic minority groups.* https://www.cdc.gov/coronavirus/2019-ncov/need-extra-precautions/racial-ethnic-minorities.html

Charoensukmongkol, P., & Phungsoonthorn, T. (2020). The effectiveness of supervisor support in lessening perceived uncertainties and emotional exhaustion of university employees during the COVID-19 crisis: The constraining role of organizational intransigence. *The Journal of General Psychology*, 1–20.

Chatterjee, D., & Ryan, A. M. (2020). Is policing becoming a tainted profession? Media, public perceptions, and implications. *Journal of Organizational Behavior, 41*(7), 606–621.

Cheng, C., Barceló, J., Hartnett, A. S., Kubinec, R., & Messerschmidt, L. (2020). COVID-19 government response event dataset (CoronaNet v. 1.0). *Nature Human Behaviour, 4*(7), 756–768.

Chew, C., & Eysenbach, G. (2010). Pandemics in the age of Twitter: content analysis of tweets during the 2009 H1N1 outbreak. *PloS one, 5*(11), e14118.

Collins, P. A., & Gibbs, A. C., (2003) Stress in police officers: A study of the origins, prevalence and severity of stress-related symptoms within a county police force. *Occupational Medicine, 53*(2), 56–64.

Czeisler, M. É, Tynan, M. A., Howard, M. E., Honeycutt, S., Fulmer, E. B., Kidder, D. P., Czeisler, C. A. (2020). Public attitudes, behaviors, and beliefs related to COVID-19, stay-at-home orders, nonessential business closures, and public health guidance — United States, New York City, and Los Angeles, May 5–12, 2020. *Morbidity and Mortality Weekly Report, 69*(24), 751–758. https://doi.org/10.15585/mmwr.mm6924e1

Deery, S., Walsh, J., & Zatzick, C. D. (2014). A moderated mediation analysis of job demands, presenteeism, and absenteeism. *Journal of Occupational and Organizational Psychology, 87*(2), 352–369.

Department of Homeland Security Science and Technology Directorate. (2017, January). *The international forum to advance first responder innovation.* https://www.dhs.gov/sites/default/files/publications/First_Responder_Market_Overview_Synopsis_2017_508C.pdf

Donahue, A. K., & Miller, J. M. (2006). Experience, attitudes, and willingness to pay for public safety. *The American Review of Public Administration, 36*(4), 395–418.

Donnelly, E. (2012). Work-related stress and posttraumatic stress in emergency medical services. *Prehospital Emergency Care, 16*(1), 76–85.

Donnelly, E. A., & Bennett, M. (2014). Development of a critical incident stress inventory for the emergency medical services. *Traumatology: An International Journal, 20*(1), 1–8.

Donnelly, E. A., Siebert, D., & Siebert, C. (2015). Development of the emergency medical services role identity scale (EMS-RIS). *Social Work in Health Care, 54*(3), 212–233.

Dowdy, J., Rieckhoff, K., & Maxwell, J. R. (2017). *Organizational agility in the public sector: How to be agile beyond times of crisis.* McKinsey & Company. https://

www.mckinsey.com/industries/public-and-social-sector/our-insights/how-the-public-sector-can-remain-agile-beyond-times-of-crisis

Dowler, K., & Zawilski, V. (2007). Public perceptions of police misconduct and discrimination: Examining the impact of media consumption. *Journal of Criminal Justice, 35*(2), 193–203.

Engel, R. S., & Calnon, J. M. (2004). Examining the influence of drivers' characteristics during traffic stops with police: Results from a national survey. *Justice Quarterly, 21*(1), 49–90.

Fannin, N., & Dabbs Jr, J. M. (2003). Testosterone and the work of firefighters: Fighting fires and delivering medical care. *Journal of Research in Personality, 37*(2), 107–115.

Farmer, P. (1996). Social inequalities and emerging infectious diseases. *Emerging Infectious Diseases, 2*(4), 259.

Fowler, H. (2020, May 28). *Some cops, sheriffs won't enforce 'unconstitutional' COVID-19 orders. Can they do that?* https://www.newsobserver.com/news/coronavirus/article243054951.html

Galaz, V. (2009). Pandemic 2.0: Can information technology help save the planet? *Environment: Science and Policy for Sustainable Development, 51*(6), 20–28.

Garb, H. N., Wood, J. M., & Baker, M. (2018). The Lackland behavioral questionnaire: The use of biographical data and statistical prediction rules for public safety screening. *Psychological Assessment, 30*(8), 1039–1048.

Germani, A., Buratta, L., Delvecchio, E., & Mazzeschi, C. (2020). Emerging adults and COVID-19: The role of individualism-collectivism on perceived risks and psychological maladjustment. *International Journal of Environmental Research and Public Health, 17*(10), 3497.

Gershon, R. R., Barocas, B., Canton, A. N., Li, X., & Vlahov, D. (2009). Mental, physical, and behavioral outcomes associated with perceived work stress in police officers. *Criminal Justice and Behavior,* 36(3), 275–289.

Gevers, J., Van Erven, P., De Jonge, J., Maas, M., & De Jong, J. (2010). Effect of acute and chronic job demands on effective individual teamwork behaviour in medical emergencies. *Journal of Advanced Nursing, 66*(7), 1573–1583.

Green, A. R., Carney, D. R., Pallin, D. J., Ngo, L. H., Raymond, K. L., Iezzoni, L. I., & Banaji, M. R. (2007). Implicit bias among physicians and its prediction of thrombolysis decisions for Black and White patients. *Journal of General Internal Medicine, 22*(9), 1231–1238.

Goff, P. A., Hinton, E., Measures, T. L., Sarnoff, C. N., & Tyler, T. R. (2019, September 10). *Re-imagining Public Safety: Prevent Hard and Lead with the Truth.* https://law.yale.edu/sites/default/files/area/center/justice/document/re-imagining_public_safety_final_9.10.19.pdf

Gregov, L., Kovačević, A., & Slišković, A. (2011). Stress among Croatian physicians: Comparison between physicians working in emergency medical service and health centers: Pilot study. *Croatian Medical Journal, 52*(1), 8–15.

Guan, Y., Deng, H., & Zhou, X. (2020). Understanding the impact of the COVID-19 pandemic on career development: Insights from cultural psychology. *Journal of Vocational Behavior, 119,* 103438.

Hayeslip Jr, D. W. (1989). Higher education and police performance revisited: The evidence examined through meta-analysis. *American Journal of Police, 8*(2), 49–62.

Hoffman, K. M., Trawalter, S., Axt, J. R., & Oliver, M. N. (2016). Racial bias in pain assessment and treatment recommendations, and false beliefs about biological differences between Blacks and Whites. *Proceedings of the National Academy of Sciences, 113*(16), 4296–4301.

Hofstede, G. (2001). *Culture's consequences: Comparing values, behaviors, institutions, and organizations across nations.* SAGE Publications.

Hojat, M. (2009). Ten approaches for enhancing empathy in health and human services cultures. *Journal of Health and Human Services Administration, 31*(4), 412–450.

House, R., Rousseau, D. M., & Thomas-Hunt, M. (1995). The meso paradigm: A framework for the integration of micro and macro organizational behavior. *Research in Organizational Behavior, 17,* 71–114.

Hunter, M. (2007). The changing political economy of sex in South Africa: The significance of unemployment and inequalities to the scale of the AIDS pandemic. *Social Science and Medicine, 64*(3), 689–700.

IPSOS. (2020, April 28). *New center for public integrity/Ipsos poll finds most Americans say the Coronavirus pandemic is a natural disaster.* https://www.ipsos.com/en-us/news-polls/center-for-public-integrity-poll-2020

Jefferies, S., French, N., Gilkison C., Graham, G., Hope, V., Marshall, J., McElnay, C., McNeill, A., Muellner, P., Paine, S., Prasad, N., Scott, J., Sherwood, J., Yang, L., & Priest, P. (2020, November 1). COVID-19 in New Zealand and the impact of the national response: a descriptive epidemiological study. *Lancet Public Health 2020,* 5(11), E612–E623. https://doi.org/10.1016/S2468-2667(20)30225-5

Johnson, R. R. (2011). Suspect mental disorder and police use of force. *Criminal Justice and Behavior, 38*(2), 127–145.

Kaminski, R. J., Digiovanni, C., & Downs, R. (2004). The use of force between the police and persons with impaired judgment. *Police Quarterly,* 7(3), 311–338.

Kantamneni, N. (2020). The impact of the COVID-19 pandemic on marginalized populations in the United States: A research agenda. *Journal of Vocational Behavior, 119,* Article 103439. https://doi.org/10.1016/j.jvb.2020.103439

Kilbourne, E. D. (2006). Influenza pandemics of the 20th century. *Emerging Infectious Diseases, 12*(1), 9.

Kochel, T., Wilson, D., & Mastrofski, S. (2011). Effect of suspect race on officers' arrest decisions. *Criminology, 49*(2), 473–512.

Kop, N., & Euwema, M. C. (2001). Occupational stress and the use of force by Dutch police officers. *Criminal Justice and Behavior, 28*(5), 631–652.

Kristman, V. L., Shaw, W. S., Reguly, P., Williams-Whitt, K., Soklaridis, S., & Loisel, P. (2017). Supervisor and organizational factors associated with supervisor support of job accommodations for low back injured workers. *Journal of Occupational Rehabilitation, 27*(1), 115–127.

Labrague, L. J., & De los Santos, J. A. A. (2020). COVID-19 anxiety among frontline nurses: Predictive role of organisational support, personal resilience and social support. *Journal of Nursing Management, 28*(7), 1653–1661.

Lai, J., Ma, S., Wang, Y., Cai, Z., Hu, J., Wei, N., Wu, J., Du, H., Chen, T., Li, R., Tan, H., Kang, L., Yao, L., Huang, M., Wang, H., Wang, G., Liu, Z., & Hu, S. (2020). Factors associated with mental health outcomes among health care workers exposed to Coronavirus disease 2019. *JAMA Network Open, 3*(3), e203976–e203976.

Lawton, B. A. (2007). Levels of nonlethal force: An examination of individual, situational, and contextual factors. *Journal of Research in Crime and Delinquency, 44*(2), 163–184.

Lee, S. M., Kang, W. S., Cho, A.-R., Kim, T., & Park, J. K. (2018). Psychological impact of the 2015 MERS outbreak on hospital workers and quarantined hemodialysis patients. https://www.facebook.com/ *Comprehensive Psychiatry, 87*, 123–127.

Leinfelt, F. H. (2005). Predicting use of non-lethal force in a mid-size police department: A longitudinal analysis of the influence of subject and situational variables. *The Police Journal, 78*(4), 285–300.

Liao, H., Arvey, R. D., Butler, R. J., & Nutting, S. M. (2001). Correlates of work injury frequency and duration among firefighters. *Journal of Occupational Health Psychology, 6*(3), 229–242.

Lindberg, C., Norstrand, P., Munger, M., DeMarsico, C., & Buscell, P. (2009). Letting go, gaining control: Positive deviance and MRSA prevention. *Clinical Leader, 2*, 60–67.

Lührmann, A., Edgell, A. B., & Maerz, S. F. (2020). Pandemic backsliding: Does Covid-19 put democracy at risk. *V-Dem Policy Brief, 23*, 1–4.

Maguire, B. J., Shearer, K., McKeown, J., Phelps, S., Gerard, D. R., Handal, K. A., Maniscalo, P., & O'Neill, B. J., (2020, April 10). The ethics of PPE and EMS in the COVID-19 era. *Journal of Emergency Medical Services*. https://www.jems.com/2020/04/10/ethics-of-ppe-and-ems-in-the-covid-19-era/

Martin, C. E., Tran, J. K., & Buser, S. J. (2017). Correlates of suicidality in firefighter/EMS personnel. *Journal of Affective Disorders, 208*, 177–183.

Maunder, R. G., Lancee, W. J., Balderson, K. E., Bennett, J. P., Borgundvaag, B., Evans, S., Fernandes, C. M. B., Goldbloom, D. S., Gupta, M., Hunter, J. J., McGillis Hall, L., Nagle, L. M., Pain, C., Peczeniuk, S. S., Raymond G., Read, N., Rourke, S. B., Steinberg, R. J., Stewart, T. E., . . . Wasylenki, D. (2006). Long-term psychological and occupational effects of providing hospital healthcare during SARS outbreak. *Emerging Infectious Diseases, 12*(12), 1924–1932.

McCall, J. P. (2001). *A correlational study of firefighter personality traits and emotional exhaustion* [Unpublished doctoral dissertation]. George Fox University.

McCluskey, J. D., & Terrill, W. (2005). Departmental and citizen complaints as predictors of police coercion. *Policing: An International Journal of Police Strategies & Management, 28*(3), 513–529.

McCluskey, J. D., Terrill, W., & Paoline, III, E. A. (2005). Peer group aggressiveness and the use of coercion in police–suspect encounters. *Police Practice and Research, 6*(1), 19–37.

Millett, G. A., Jones, A. T., Benkeser, D., Baral, S., Mercer, L., Beyrer, C., Honermann, B., Lankiewicz, E., Mena, L., Crowley, J. S., Sherwood, J., & Sullivan, P. S. (2020). Assessing differential impacts of COVID-19 on Black communities. *Annals of Epidemiology, 47,* 37–44. https://doi.org/10.1016/j.annepidem.2020.05.003

Meronek, J. S., & Tan, J. A. (2004). Validity study personality predictors of firefighter job performance and job satisfaction. *Applied HRM Research, 9*(1), 39–40.

Montrose, L. (2020, April 15). *Wildfire smoke worsens coronavirus risk, putting firefighters in extra danger.* The Conservation. https://theconversation.com/wildfire-smoke-worsens-coronavirus-risk-putting-firefighters-in-extra-danger-136016#:~:text=5%20air%20pollution%2C%20which%20is,may%20make%20coronavirus%20particularly%20deadly.&text=Taken%20together%2C%20these%20findings%20suggest,develop%20severe%20COVID%2D19%20symptoms

Morabito, E. V., & Doerner, W. G. (1997). Police use of less-than-lethal force: Oleoresin Capsicum (OC) spray. *Policing: An International Journal of Police Strategies & Management, 20*(4), 680–697.

National Association of Emergency Medical Technicians. (2016, August 14). *2016 national survey on EMS mental health services.* http://www.naemt.org/docs/default-source/ems-health-and-safety-documents/mental-health-grid/2016-naemt-mental-health-report-8-14-16.pdf

Natividad, I. (2020, February 12). *Coronavirus: Fear of Asians rooted in long American history of prejudicial policies.* Berkeley News. https://news.berkeley.edu/2020/02/12/coronavirus-fear-of-asians-rooted-in-long-american-history-of-prejudicial-policies/

Newland, C., Barber, E., Rose, M., & Young, A. (2015). Survey reveals alarming rates of EMS provider stress and thoughts of suicide. *Journal of Emergency Medical Services, 40*(10). https://www.jems.com/special-topics/survey-reveals-alarming-rates-of-ems-provider-stress-and-thoughts-of-suicide/

Nickell, L. A., Crighton, E. J., Tracy, C. S., Al-Enazy, H., Bolaji, Y., Hanjrah, S., Hussain, A., Makhlouf, S., & Upshur, R. E. G. (2004). Psychosocial effects of SARS on hospital staff: Survey of a large tertiary care institution. *Cmaj, 170*(5), 793–798. https://doi.org/10.1503/cmaj.1031077

Niculită, Z. (2013). Personality traits that foster ambulance workers' professional performance. *Procedia-Social and Behavioral Sciences, 78,* 385–389.

Novacek, D. M., Hampton-Anderson, J. N., Ebor, M. T., Loeb, T. B., & Wyatt, G. E. (2020). Mental health ramifications of the COVID-19 pandemic for Black Americans: Clinical and research recommendations. *Psychological Trauma: Theory, Research, Practice, and Policy, 12*(5), 449–451. https://doi.org/10.1037/tra0000796

O'Brien, S. G. (1996). *The predictive validity of personality testing in police selection: A meta-analysis* [Unpublished master's thesis]. University of Guelph.

Paoline, E. A., & Terrill, W. (2004). Women police officers and the use of coercion. *Women & Criminal Justice, 15*(3/4), 97–119.

Paoline, E. A., III, & Terrill, W. (2007). Police education, experience, and the use of force. *Criminal Justice and Behavior, 34*(2), 179–196.

Pew Research. (2020). *Health concerns from COVID-19 much higher among Hispanics and Blacks than Whites.* https://www.pewresearch.org/politics/2020/04/14/health-concerns-from-covid-19-much-higher-among-hispanics-and-blacks-than-whites/

Pilárik, L. U., & Sarmany-Schuller, I. (2011). Personality predictors of decision-making of medical rescuers. *Studia Psychologica, 53*(2), 175–184.

Prentice, C., Zeidan, S., & Wang, X. (2020). Personality, trait EI and coping with COVID 19 measures. *International Journal of Disaster Risk Reduction, 51*(101789). https://www.ncbi.nlm.nih.gov/pmc/articles/PMC7418749/

Ranney, M. L., Griffeth, V., & Jha, A. K. (2020). Critical supply shortages—the need for ventilators and personal protective equipment during the Covid-19 pandemic. *New England Journal of Medicine, 382*(18), e41.

Rudolph, C.W., Allan, B., Clark, M., Hertel, G., Hirschi, A., Kunze, F., Shockley, K., Shoss, M., Sonnentag, S., & Zacher, H. (2020). Pandemics: Implications for research and practice in industrial and organizational psychology. *Industrial and Organizational Psychology: Perspectives on Science and Practice, 14*(1/2), 1–35.

Ruggs, E. N., Hebl, M. R., Rabelo, V. C., Weaver, K. B., Kovacs, J., & Kemp, A. S. (2016). Baltimore is burning: Can IO psychologists help extinguish the flames? *Industrial and Organizational Psychology, 9*(3), 525–547.

Rydberg, J., & Terrill, W. (2010). The effect of higher education on police behavior. *Police Quarterly, 13*(1), 92–120.

Scarborough, R.C. (2017), Risk a Lot to Save a Lot: How Firefighters Decide Whose Life Matters. *Sociological Forum, 32*(Suppl 1), 1073–1092.

Shaw, W. S., Main, C. J., Findley, P. A., Collie, A., Kristman, V. L., & Gross, D. P. (2020). Opening the workplace after COVID-19: What lessons can be learned from return-to-work research? *Journal of Occupational Rehabilitation, 30*(3), 299–302.

Sheikhbardsiri, H., Sarhadi, M., Abdollahyar, A., Dastres, M., Sheikh Rabari, A., & Aminizadeh, M. (2015). The relationship between personality traits and post-traumatic stress disorder among EMS personnel and hospital emergency staffs. *Journal of Critical Care Nursing, 8*(1), 35–42.

Sitzmann, T., Kraiger, K., Stewart, D., & Wisher, R. (2006). The comparative effectiveness of web-based and classroom instruction: A meta-analysis. *Personnel Psychology, 59*(3), 623–664.

Skibba, J. S. (2002). *Personality and job satisfaction: An investigation of central Wisconsin firefighters* [Unpublished research paper]. University of Wisconsin-Stout.

Slovak, J. (1986). *Styles of urban policing.* New York University Press.

Smith, D. (1986). The neighborhood context of police behavior. *Crime and Justice, 8,* 313–341.

Stepanikova, I. (2012). Racial-ethnic biases, time pressure, and medical decisions. *Journal of Health and Social Behavior, 53*(3), 329–343.

Sternin, J. (2003). Practice positive deviance for extraordinary social and organizational change. In D. Ulrich, L. Carter, M. Goldsmith, J. Bolt, & N. Smallwood (Eds.), *The change champion's fieldguide* (pp. 20–37). Best Practice Publications.

Stogner, J., Miller, B. L., & McLean, K. (2020). Police stress, mental health, and resiliency during the COVID-19 pandemic. *American Journal of Criminal Justice, 45*(4), 718–730.

Taubenberger, J. K., & Morens, D. M. (2006). 1918 influenza: The mother of all pandemics. *Revista Biomedica, 17*(1), 69–79.

Teachman, B. A., & Brownell, K. D. (2001). Implicit anti-fat bias among health professionals: is anyone immune? *International Journal of Obesity, 25*(10), 1525–1531.

Terman, L. (1917). A trial of mental and pedagogical tests in a civil service examination for policemen and firemen. *Journal of Applied Psychology, 1*(1), 17–29.

Terrill, W., & Mastrofski, S. D. (2002). Situational and officer-based determinants of police coercion. *Justice Quarterly, 19*(2), 215–248.

Terrill, W., Paoline, E., & Manning, P. (2003). Police culture and coercion. *Criminology, 41*(4), 1003–1034.

Terrill, W., & Reisig, M. (2003). Neighborhood context and police use of force. *Journal of Research in Crime and Delinquency, 43*(3), 291–321.

Torales, J., O'Higgins, M., Castaldelli-Maia, J. M., & Ventriglio, A. (2020). The outbreak of COVID-19 coronavirus and its impact on global mental health. *International Journal of Social Psychiatry, 66*(4), 317–320.

Vaulerin, J., Colson, S. S., Emile, M., Scoffier-Mériaux, S., & d'Arripe-Longueville, F. (2016). The big five personality traits and French firefighter burnout: the mediating role of achievement goals. *Journal of Occupational and Environmental Medicine, 58*(4), e128–e132.

Vettor, S. M., & Kosinski Jr, F. A. (2000). Work-stress burnout in emergency medical technicians and the use of early recollections. *Journal of Employment Counseling, 37*(4), 216–228.

Volk, A. A., Brazil, K. J., Franklin-Luther, P., Dane, A. V., & Vaillancourt, T. (2021). The influence of demographics and personality on COVID-19 coping in young adults. *Personality and Individual Differences, 168*(110398). https://www.ncbi.nlm.nih.gov/pmc/articles/PMC7492069/

Werthman, C., & Piliavin, I. (1967). Gang members and the police. In D. Bordua (Ed.), *The police: Six sociological essays* (pp. 58–59). Wiley.

WHO Coronavirus Disease (COVID-19) Dashboard. (n.d.). World Health Organization. https://covid19.who.int/

Wong, T. W., Yau, J. K. Y., Chan, C. L. W., Kwong, R. S. Y., Ho, S. M. Y., Lau, C. C., Lau F. L., & Lit, C. H. (2005). The psychological impact of severe acute respiratory syndrome outbreak on healthcare workers in emergency departments and how they cope. *European Journal of Emergency Medicine, 12*(1), 13–18.

Whaley, A. L. (2001). Cultural mistrust and mental health services for African Americans: A review and meta-analysis. *The Counseling Psychologist, 29*(4), 513–531.

Wright, A. L., Meyer, A. D., Reay, T., & Staggs, J. (2020). Maintaining places of social inclusion: Ebola and the emergency department. *Administrative Science Quarterly, 66*(1), 42–85. https://doi.org/10.1177/0001839220916401

Zajenkowski, M., Jonason, P. K., Leniarska, M., & Kozakiewicz, Z. (2020). Who complies with the restrictions to reduce the spread of COVID-19? Personality and perceptions of the COVID-19 situation. *Personality and Individual Differences, 166*(110199). https://www.ncbi.nlm.nih.gov/pmc/articles/PMC7296320/

Zhang, S. X., Sun, S., Jahanshahi, A. A., Alvarez-Risco, A., Ibarra, V. G., Li, J., & Patty-Tito, R. M. (2020). Developing and testing a measure of COVID-19 organizational support of healthcare workers–results from Peru, Ecuador, and Bolivia. *Psychiatry Research, 291*, 113–174.

Zhu, Z., Xu, S., Wang, H., Liu, Z., Wu, J., Li, G., Miao, J., Zhang, C., Yang, Y., Sun, W., Zhu, S., Fan, Y., Hu, J., Liu, J., & Wang, W. (2020). *COVID-19 in Wuhan: Immediate psychological impact on 5062 health workers.* medRxiv. https://doi.org/10.1101/2020.02.20.20025338

CHAPTER 4

FROM TELECOMMUTE TO TELECOMMUNITY

How Disabled Onto-Epistemologies Inform Post-Pandemic Professional Practices

Martina Svyantek
University of Virginia

Rua Mae Williams
Purdue University

Our abstract was submitted in the wake of COVID-19's immediate impacts on Spring 2020. Since March, the authors have both dealt with shifts in access to institutional resources, childcare, setting up home offices, and the complete upheaval of pre-existing work patterns and communication channels. Since March, the drain of constantly shifting frames of reference, time, space, and community have taken their toll on our own personal productivity, anxiety levels, and overall capacity to care about long-term plans. The fact that this chapter exists is a testament to the privilege of working in

Crisis, Chaos, and Organizations, pages 97–117

academic settings that made abrupt rearrangements to working hours and location expectations possible. We understand that not all our peers have been able to produce their own scholarship under pandemic conditions. Academic situations, in some ways, reflect an optimal workplace for teleworking. If, however, academic professionals have not been able to maintain productivity, what has been the impact of this change to teleworking on other types of organizations?

This chapter, "From Telecommute to Telecommunity," will contextualize the COVID-19 pandemic's effects on office-based and academic workspaces using a critical disability studies approach. Disabled scholars and activists have been frustrated by the simultaneous embracing of telework practices previously denied to disabled people coupled with efforts to categorize these practices, implemented inexpertly and under duress, as inferior in the drive to "return to normal"; by and large, the large-scale experiences of the move to "working from home" (WFH) has more in common with problematic disability simulations than an authentic telework situation.

This is a time of chaos, uncertainty, and new opportunities and challenges. What do we want to emerge out of this chaos? What considerations do we want to continue, and what can we, as a community, point to as a best practice versus something that should be discarded and moved away from out of societal level?

Crisis healthcare policies are poised to disproportionately devalue and endanger the lives of disabled people, while at the same time, the pandemic has and will continue to produce more vulnerable and disabled lives. Therefore, when imagining the "new normal," we must look to disability communities for guidance in forging just communal practices of work, sociality, and care.

2020's ABRUPT SHIFTS

Disability is entangled with and in the pandemic narrative. Uncertainty about the mechanics of SARS-CoV-2 viral spread, prognosis, and mortality risk factors drove response policies that sent many white-collar workers home. Suddenly, businesses were devoting logistical and financial resources to working accommodations such as home workstations, networked video conferencing, and VPN access. The same accommodations previously categorized as "unreasonable" adjustments for disabled employees became not only possible, but urgent (Anderson et al., 2020; Cirruzzo, 2020; Jagannathan, 2020).

Simultaneously, uncertainty surrounding the medical system's capacity for handling pandemic case-load led many hospitals to engage triage policies which compelled nurses and physicians to ration or deny crisis care to disabled people, including people with "underlying risk factors." Such risk factors included conditions like heart disease and diabetes, conditions which are known to disproportionately affect people of color, and which are attributed to the stress of labor exploitation and the trauma of racism. And yet, economic uncertainty demanded that jobs which could not be conducted "from home" were marked as "essential"—ostensibly because our capitalist system has made our basic needs dependent upon a constantly operating, single-day supply chain. Disproportionately performed by working-class people of color, such "essential work" is often minimum-wage, contingent labor, with no benefits, and no hazard pay. The very people who were placed at the highest risk of infection were also the most likely to receive inadequate medical care due to implicit bias and policies that devalue disabled lives.

Disability again becomes conspicuous as "pandemic fatigue" and national interests in "capital" compel corporate executives and institutional administration to demand a "return to normal." As the public grows tired of being #AloneTogether, disabled people become the sole shepherds of their own contagion risk, responsible for tightening their isolation to compensate for the apathetic recklessness of others. As workplaces demand their workers return on-site, those who have "underlying risk factors" or those caring for family members who do, are then forced into highly regulated games of disclosure in order to maintain safe working conditions. The same workplace accommodations previously denied to disabled people, given so freely in the wake of global crisis, are again becoming "precious" resources for which disabled people and their families must prove themselves worthy of. Those that "pass" as "vulnerable enough" or "vulnerable-adjacent" are rewarded with the unequal responsibility to isolate. We have forced disabled and sick people into a sort of COVID-19 closet, their isolation a requisite for our own sense of normalcy.

We argue that this desire for normalcy is based in part on an incomplete understanding of how equitable work-from-home structures might develop. While pandemic responses moved many people into provisional telework scenarios, these conditions are not comparable to the work-from-home structures previously advocated for by disabled workers. This is a time of crisis. Our workplaces are in chaos. Events of 2020 are not the "new normal" but a rupture in the facade that has obstructed our understanding of social norms in work and home life. The work-from-home experience is very different when there is a dedicated home office with appropriate seating, desk space, the equipment, and lighting; many of us have been dealing with an outdated laptop in a quiet closet trying to avoid pets, children, and partners. In reflecting on the many facets of "working from home," we contest assumptions that moving from an office computer to a home computer can truly be a seamless and orderly transition, and ask for a commitment to the constant communal negotiation and struggle required to enact equity in our day-to-day interactions.

First, we illustrate the experiences of disabled professionals navigating and, in most cases, fighting for workplace accommodations that are now considered essential for millions of able-bodied white-collar workers internationally. Then, we delimit how the pandemic WFH conditions are not representative of the conditions which disabled people have been advocating for, and what WFH looks like when imagined by disability advocates. We use examples from disability simulation critiques to contextualize this analysis. Finally, we contest the ableist practices that are already emerging as institutions of higher education negotiate a "return," and propose how such a return might be imagined otherwise.

TELEWORK IS NOTHING NEW

Driving people back into this COVID-19 closet is an attempt to draw harsh lines between what is acceptable in the modern workplace and what is not. However, "telework prophet" Jack Nilles began the discussion of remote work to mitigate the need for physical travel to a workspace as early as 1973 (Nilles et al., 1976). In the nearly 5 decades since it was coined, numerous terms—such as work from home, remote work, flexible work, flextime, flexiplace, alternative work schedule, compressed week, and work arrangement—have emerged alongside a significant body of research that investigates different permutations, advantages, and drawbacks to telework (Baltes et al., 1999; Baruch, 2001; Chiru, 2017; K. Daniels et al., 2000; Garrett & Danziger, 2007; Haddon & Brynin, 2005; Lamond et al., 1997; Ruth & Chaudhry, 2008; Schiff, 1993; R. J. Thompson et al., 2015). With so many competing definitions, we have chosen a basic way to understand what we mean by telecommute/remote work for this paper—working away from a central, in-person location associated with your employment and coworkers.

These remote work options are not available to everyone, even in a pandemic. "Essential workers," the individuals who have to be there, in some cases to literally keep the lights on, represent many fields of "service work" including social work, health care, the food supply chain, transportation, and utilities (Robertson & Gebeloff, 2020) do not have the option or the opportunity to work from home, because their work creates a demand for physical presence. As a society, we recognize this work as essential, but fail to remunerate those doing it, with the much-lauded "hero" pay quietly disappearing as the pandemic dragged on for unimagined months (Corkery, 2020).

Our own understanding of remote work is tied to accessible technology and disability accommodations, while at the same time being circumscribed by gendered disparities in professional and family labor and socioeconomic divides in digital access and in digital possibility. Society's shifting relationships with technology bring emergent and intensifying surveillance practices and hostile workplace relationships to the foreground.

Imani Barbarin (2020) issued a Twitter thread on March 12 contextualizing why so many disabled people are disgruntled about workplace pandemic response, stating, among other details:

> So, you've probably seen mine and other disabled people's pissed off tweets about the response to the #CoronaVirus... So, imagine my surprise (all disabled people's surprise) when because of the #coronavirus all of the accommodations we have been denied because we're disabled have suddenly become available... Quelle FUCKING surprise! A lot of the things disabled people have long demanded have instantly manifested now that nondisabled people need them too. Disabled people asked for telecommuting, and you called us "lazy."

The fact that nearly everyone and everything could pivot is proof that telework was an option all along. The previous unavailability of telework as a widespread, long-term option is a direct condition of "hostile accommodations" that involve an arduous burden on individuals who seek them while creating a sense of resentment in their peers and coworkers (Gernsbacher et al., 2016; Nario-Redmond et al., 2019; D. Thompson, 2013).

Now, people globally have been pushed out of workplaces and into their own homes, which are not necessarily any more accessible than more public spaces (Ho et al., 2007; Maisel et al., 2008; Mann et al., 1994; Stephens et al., 2017). To complete remote work, a set-up is required. This can be as rudimentary as a laptop and utilities (power and internet), or as elaborate as dedicated rooms, complete with furniture, storage spaces, and equipment such as noise-cancelling headphones to help concentration. Everyone newly teleworking is "suffering" because we are trying to jam work into the home sphere, when so much of how society is constructed is based around going to a physical workplace, separate from the rest of our lives.

Research, however, shows that people who telework are happier, more likely to remain in their jobs, and are more productive (Bloom, 2014; Dubrin, 1991) It is counterintuitive to make people come back, but working remotely becomes an issue of surveillance, control, and establishment of trust between employees and their supervisors (Baker et al., 2007). Moving work, and schooling, into the home has led to increased surveillance of personal spaces in ways not typically associated with employment. Our families, our pets, and our personal habits are on display via webcam. We stare into the online meeting void from closet spaces, backyard chairs, and vehicles parked on campuses trying to mimic inflexible routines and scripts for how to demonstrate we are participating as we move Zoom from a noun to a verb in our collective vocabulary.

ENVIRONMENTAL CONSIDERATIONS

The wide variety of environmental factors that affect workplaces should also be part of this discussion of remote work. Where and when we do work has always been affected by issues largely outside of our personal control. Construction in and around buildings have long affected the work environment and commutes; sometimes this is remediation work to address asbestos, "sick building syndrome," gas leaks, or infrastructure upgrades. This leads to temporary space reassignments, adding in the labor of packing and moving workplaces (potentially many times). Activities such as fire drills, severe weather systems testing, and active shooter scenarios eat into the workday to address workplace safety.

The larger environment also plays a role in how work is conducted. In 2020 alone, the United States has seen fires burn over 13 million acres, with suppression efforts costing nearly $3.5 billion, and over 14,000 structures destroyed from (National Interagency Fire Center, 2020), displacing thousands from their home and work locations. Other natural phenomena such as hurricanes, severe storms causing flooding, earthquakes, and tornados all have the potential to have similar effects.

With more moves to shift the workplace into the home, it is important to remember that, as many discovered this spring, internet connectivity is not a given. There is a lack of access both to the internet (Lake & Makori, 2020; Strover, 2001; Whitacre & Mills, 2010) and to technology tools (Baraniuk, 2020) that has yet to be addressed. Even when internet connections are possible, overall connectivity speed and reliability are still issues (Schulman & Spring, 2011); not far beyond the campus boundaries of an R1, it has been a common refrain for people entering a meeting to thank other attendees in advance for their patience if the connection gets dropped due to the rain.

No More "Accommodations" to Go Remote

COVID-19 and the global crisis of contagion has exposed societal inequities that are most intense at the intersection of disability, race, class, and gender. The "pre-existing conditions" that predispose someone to a poor pandemic prognosis are conditions that are closely associated with chronic stress (Danese & McEwen, 2012), and have been noted to embody consequences of generational, racialized trauma (Williams & Jackson, 2005). At the same time, the classification of essential workers (both the "skilled labor" of nursing staff and the so-called "unskilled labor" of retail and restaurant staff) is also most often represented by working-class women of color (Frye, 2020; Powell, 2020; Robertson & Gebeloff, 2020). And so, the very people our society collectively pressured into heightened exposure are also those most likely to fare the worst once infected, and on top of that, are also the same people least likely to receive compassionate, thorough medical care (Dehon et al., 2017; Devakumar et al., 2020; FitzGerald & Hurst, 2017). The general (dis)comforting refrain of "but only the old and sick are at risk" is macabre on its face but also serves to deflect attention from the raced, gendered, and classed particulars of who is counted within those categories. Black thought leader James Baldwin would remind us, "No, we are just the ones who are dying fastest" (1968). Regardless of the individual identities of the 200k+[1] souls lost in the United States to COVID-19, it was racism and ableism that killed each of them—our cultural devotion to White supremacy and able-normativity created the conditions that have allowed this pandemic to proliferate.

Community Wisdom and Mutual Aid

> *Disability Justice asserts that ableism helps make racism, Christian supremacy, sexism, and queer- and transphobia possible, and that all those systems of oppression are locked up tight.*
>
> —Piepzna-Samarasinha, 2018, p. 22

Disability justice is a framework for communal action that centers poor, disabled, queer people of color in our concept and formation of community and belonging. What the Sins Invalid and disability justice community are trying to teach us is that there is no community without disabled community. Disabled communities know what it takes to care for each other when normative society will not, even and *especially* when that care cannot be reciprocated in the manner capitalist formulations of transactional equivalency have groomed us to expect.

Crip[2] mutual aid projects, like Disability Justice Culture Club's Power to Live movement or their emergency distribution of home-made hand sanitizer and PPE at the onset of COVID-19, help us understand mutuality not as transactional but as coalitional, just, and loving. These community organized actions of rescue, care, and aid are not about "this for that," but about "when you hurt, I hurt, and when we help each other we all heal."

Black thought leader and activist Huey P. Newton formed the concept of "intercommunalism" to articulate mechanisms of cross-community interrelations that could foster revolutionary changes in material conditions of oppression (Newton, 2019, pp. 193–212). Foundational to this concept is a recognition that "everything is in a constant state of change" (p. 193). Articulations of justice between and within communities require an understanding of the world as materially entangled and in constant flux.

Rooted by dialectical materialism, it becomes impossible to form or even desire prescriptive, procedural, one-time check-list fixes to issues of solidarity and justice. Instead, just acts are guided by a spirit of "prefigurative politics"—"imagining and building the world we want to see now" (Piepzna-Samarasinha, 2018, p. 149). It is our hope for this chapter to instill in readers a sense of purpose, and a commitment enacting justice in the nuanced, hyper contextual, entangled moments within and between relations and community.

When we think about accessibility, we have been historically conditioned to think about the architected space. Ramps, hallway and door widths, table heights; or software integration with screen readers and keyboard-only navigation. Such focus on the built environment often lends itself to a sense of helplessness. If the space we are in is simply, unthinkingly, built to exclude then we feel powerless in the face of so much concrete and metal. We forget the power of community—of refusing to use inaccessible spaces and to pay for inaccessible services, of protesting their sustained manufacture, and of hacking access, be it digitally or through plywood, cinder blocks, and obstinance.

When we think about accommodations, we tend to think of external services. Special software, contracted interpreters, separate meal prep. The notion of accommodation as a discrete set of services compels organizations to imagine accommodations as a resource that must be regulated, rather than a communal duty. Such configurations of access and accommodations as limited resources lead to systems of control that police and discipline disabled people for deigning to ask for equitable inclusion. ChrisTiana Obey-Sumner (2020) describes these systems of control as *hostile accommodations*: "Any process or offer of accommodation that is either so complex or so strenuous that most people on the receiving end would consider it hostile or violent... [T]he person requesting an accommodation...is met with physical, social, and/or political barriers during the process" (para. 4).

Returning to the disabled activist-scholars at the heart of disability justice, we are shown alternatives to our present and future that are rooted in a communal conviction that spaces of connection are meant for everyone. Mia Mingus (2017) tells us that #AccessIsLove, and describes *access intimacy* as "that elusive, hard to describe feeling when someone else 'gets' your access needs" (para. 4). Leah Lakshmi Piepzna-Samarasinha (2018) has described *collective care webs* as explorations in "'crip-made access'... turning on its head the model that disabled people can only passively receive care, not give it or determine what kind of care we want" (p. 41). Crip community isn't just a contestation of how disabled people can care for themselves, Crip community is a devotional, lived conviction that disabled people have something that everyone needs—love and belonging.

LASTING CHANGE?

We now have a new normal... In light of this, we are changing the policy for remote work requests for the spring 2021 term. For the spring 2021 term, except as outlined below, we expect faculty to return to campus to teach their courses and conduct their research and service.

—Yan, 2020

While companies including Dropbox, Microsoft, Reddit, and Twitter have announced permanent remote work options (Berliner, 2020; Keane, 2020; Mayer, 2020; McLean, 2020), administrative statements strongly suggest academic arenas will not experience such transformations. Administrative mandates for a campus return deployed a multi-pronged, often self-contradictory set of strategies to reinforce assertions that return was not only necessary, but desired and safe. While students were presumed to demand an on-campus experience, students were also never given the opportunity to explore well-planned remote instruction. Simultaneously, as administrations declared their student (and by implication campus) community was not "at risk" of serious complications from COVID-19 infection, members of the campus community that were at risk were quickly disposed of through early retirement options (Feliciano, 2020; UF Human Resources, 2020) or tightly controlled remote work provisions. Such provisions demand both a rigorous documentation and "outing" of sensitive medical information while ensuring a new kind of workplace invisibility in the COVID-19 closet.

Though many campus statements rely heavily on the narrative that a return to in-person instruction is "consumer-driven" (i.e., by students), and thus an academic "duty" (M. Daniels, 2020), responses by campus counseling services bely the traumatic nature of the campus-in-COVID-19 experience. In "Adjusting to the New Normal," Campus Therapist Theresa Nutten (2020) intimates the devastatingly stressful toll the pandemic is having on students, sharing advice that is pragmatic and compassionate. But the harsh reality behind advice like, "It's also okay (and encouraged) to seek help and support!" is that there really isn't much support to be had; even before COVID-19, nation-wide campus counseling services were unable to keep up with the caseload of student psychological needs (Harrison, 2020).

Campus disability communities' concerns about pandemic responses were shared during the summer and early into fall, but to unknown, if any, impact on planning (Accessible Campus Action Alliance, 2020; Disability Alliance and Caucus, 2020; Disability Culture at the University of Michigan, 2020). Now, when looking at Spring of 2021, there are so many conflicting messages about what has occurred and developing plans, even from within the same institutions.

Instructors trying to plan course "modalities" (between in-person, synchronous, asynchronous, hybrid, flex, and any other permutation) might receive notices in September that for Spring 2021, "course modalities should be developed with the assumption that the environment will largely be the same as it is this fall" (Clarke, 2020a). A month passes that finds instructors faced with the complete dissolution of spring break, with an admonition that individual days, scattered across the spring semester schedule, should be treated as a real break, as "critically important to the overall mental health and personal wellness of our students that they have the opportunity to use these distributed spring break days to rest, recalibrate, and enjoy time" (Clarke, 2020b). This is trailed by yet more messaging that says that, while course modalities are the responsibility of the instructor, the "estimates of the proportions of in-person or hybrid instruction planned for the spring are slightly lower than those for this fall. Clearly, this does not align with our commitment to make progress in advancing in-person learning" (Clarke, 2020c).

The commitment to in-person learning is just as clearly not aligned with disability justice or community needs (Accessible Campus Action Alliance, 2020; Disability Alliance and Caucus, 2020; Disability Culture at the University of Michigan, 2020; Mingus, 2017; Piepzna-Samarasinha, 2018). It is not even necessarily aligned with the demands of other employees at the same institutions, whose work that went remote as immediately as teaching and learning did and yet "will continue to operate as we have in the fall semester, and telework will remain an option for Spring 2021 for employees in roles that can be performed remotely" (Garey, 2020).

The entire push to re-open campuses in the Fall of 2020 was a push to return to normal, an act of theater to mask (pun intended) the pre-existing condition of the pandemic on work, school, and life in general. The common refrain of students wanting to come back is based on what is really being asked: If they want there to be a pandemic, and unsurprisingly, they do not. They want to pretend it was all a dream, they want their universities to "go back to normal"—they want to party, they want to use the facilities, and they want to participate in the "normal" college experience, not the reality that 2020 has delivered.

When we perform "normal," without a commonly defined framework to understand what normal is in the first place, we simply put on an "act of appearing normal" (Force, 2010, p. 333), a show devoid of the substance of addressing and confronting any of the underlying concerns or conditions (Kuppers, 2015; Sheppard, 2020). This push to return to our "normal" is a push to consider all of the remote work done in the wake of COVID-19 as a disability simulation—badly enacted, and with an overall sense of dread for its potential for our workplaces.

SHIFTING POLICY TO REFLECT NEW REALITIES

The abrupt shifts away from campuses this spring have turned into trickles back this fall, rife with constantly updating dashboards to inform us of community health metrics. The long-haul of this pandemic is already breaking down under the weight of our societal expectations of normal. Instead of meekly returning to the status quo that refused to acknowledge the presence of disabled faculty, staff, and students beyond "reasonable accommodations," we should take this as an opportunity to re-imagine what the "new normal" should and could be.

While we are making these considerations and basing suggestions through a critical disability lens, it cannot be overstated the fact that this current chaos does not just affect people in a single identity category. Considerations of the economic impacts of family dynamics cannot be overstated. The availability of childcare in different areas has been intensified by those locations where this is already a scarce commodity due to available spaces and costs, meaning even more people are trying to cobble together care for their children. With K–12 schools across the country being open, virtual, or some sort of hybrid, daily schedules have changed drastically; school is no longer a setting that parents and caretakers can rely on regularly, impacting university faculty and staff.

If we don't learn from the disability community now, we will revert to what we have all pretended is "normal." The return to our previous workplaces will be akin to the aftermath of disability simulation writ large across our collective imagination; as Nario-Redmond et al. (2017) demonstrate, such "simulations can subvert their intended educational value and distort the realities of life with disabilities" (p. 324).

In the immediate wake of office shutdowns, Accessible Campus Action Alliance (2020) created a multi-page statement on how universities should move forward, framing "reopenings" and "return to normal" as a civil rights issue. With that foundation in mind, we make the following recommendations that should be incorporated into the policies dictating workplace practices at large:

1. *Remote accepted as default.* Telework and remote participation should exist as an accepted, default option—even as a "best practice" that needs more actual practice. When dealing with new pandemics, or even the "common" flu which causes an estimated 12,000 to 61,000 deaths a year in the United States (CDC, n.d.), we should not be requiring people to work in person.
2. *Remove paper barriers.* As a corollary, we should remove the layers of administrative paperwork and bureaucracy necessary to "qualify" for remote work. There are many barriers to official documenta-

tion, including cultural bias in obtaining diagnosis; bias from medical personnel; structural issues with lack of transportation, financial stability, and access to healthcare resources; and the increased risks of visiting medical offices during the pandemic. The entire world swerved on its axis in March 2020 to encourage physical distancing for teaching and learning—we've seen the lack of documentation be possible. As people such as Robert Kingett, someone who has wanted remote work for years, have pointed out, "This is a great middle finger to the excuse of, 'We just don't have the technology to do remote work... This recent shift... proves that they can actually do most work-from-home, given no other option" (Jagannathan, 2020).

3. *Build accessibility in practice.* We are 30 years past the passage of the Americans with Disabilities Act. This is the time when we are all moving and learning new ways of communicating and being; we need to build accessibility into our practices now, as people move into new ways of working and learning. Using meeting platforms with embedded captioning, ensuring that written communications (such as websites, emails, and digital flyers) have color contrast, practicing good data management—all of these things are vital for access considerations but they also make life better and easier for everyone. Some example of how to do this include:
    a. *Stop paying for inaccessible tools and materials.* Do not sign contracts with vendors or for tools without VPATs and ADA compliance metrics.
    b. *Provide captions.* Our organizations should recognize the need for captioning funds for internal and external audiences. Captioning also serves to transcribe meeting materials and free up energy to actually participate in real-time. The Graduate Student Assembly at Virginia Tech has seen this to great effect where they acquired captions prior to the start of COVID-19, modeling best practices for the entire institutions of what captions should be. Being literally ahead of the game, the GSA raised the practice of captioning to the level of the Board of Visitors and institutional town halls. The impact of COVID-19 on the institution has turned into securing a centralized captioning fund solely for the purpose of providing such services across Virginia Tech's campus (Accessible Technologies, 2020). This sort of fund should be commonplace; there should be some sort of funding mechanism, a policy, and people who serve as the contacts for such resources.
4. *Hazard pay.* If people must be on-site, they should receive hazard pay. This includes and starts with the housekeeping staff who are

working to ensure hygienic space is available for the community's use. This hazard pay would be for those who are literally putting their lives (and the lives of their families) on the line in order to meet with you in person; it is selfish of institutions to work harder to find ways around liability for what they're requiring of their employees then to figure out how to compensate them.

5. *Cost sharing.* LinkedIn (2020) recently conducted a poll regarding employer employee responsibilities for work from home office space; with more than 76,000 responses, over 60% were in favor of employers covering remote work expenses. The increased cost of utilities and better internet connections are now being born by the employee, where they would typically be part of what employers covered at a workplace. This is reminiscent of the gig economy (where companies attempt to designate workers as contractors, not employees) and this is a precedent that we hope to avoid. Non-essential employees and those whose work could be conducted from an alternative location have been doing so since March; for public universities it should be a matter of record to observe changes to operational costs such as utilities. Capital projects therefore might be places that could be reconsidered. Why do we need a space together if all this work can be done from alternative locations?
6. *Consider overlapping roles and responsibilities.* When thinking about workplace rules and norms, and higher education academic settings specifically, it is crucial not to ignore the graduate, professional, and postdoc populations. The overlapping roles and responsibilities mean that policies written for students might not take into consideration the instructional, research, and administrative components while employee rules might ignore the learning components. This results in conflicting policies as opposed to those that are universally focused, designed to be flexible and easy to understand.
7. *Shorter meetings.* There is no reason to try to mimic and recreate a 3-hour discussion seminar virtually. Even with the most interesting topic in the world, it is going to be easier to disengage and re-engage virtually. Instead of shaming those who need a break, think about what the virtual experience affords in terms of presentations and audience; different modes of expression, such as creating a class hashtag or an *unessay* (Nair, 2019) can be explored. Same goes for departmental meetings; informational meetings could and should be emails, or a shared document that everyone can contribute to instead of becoming "Zoombies" (Bryant et al., 2020; Petriglieri, 2020; Silard, 2020; Wellner, 2020).

8. *Address mental health needs.* We know mental health and wellness are so overused as buzzwords to be meaningless, but we need them to be meaningful. The alterations to Spring Break 2021 that have already been announced at universities impact everyone in academic settings, spiraling outwards, affecting not only students, but instructors and staff as well who have traditionally used that time as a way to metaphorically catch their breath before the last push of the semester. Conversations about mental health needs should no longer be treated as a joke, but as one of the ways to avoid collective burnout—even if that means going as far as faking a commute to telework (Harrington, 2020).
9. *Redesign conferences and professional gatherings.* We need to rethink professional travel; so far, 2020 has been a series of discoveries that conferences and large gatherings take more than just creating links to an online meeting. Professional gatherings have a variety of goals, such as presentations and networking, and we need to think about how to move them to virtual platforms in an intentional manner. As with other points, there are accessibility considerations (such as CART services) that need to be addressed, and additional security concerns to keep in mind; it is vastly different to deal with a meeting being zoombombed via a remote dialer and allowing entry to venues based on name tags.

We acknowledge that these recommendations only work for certain positions, specifically those where you don't "have to be there" to perform. In solidarity, people should start listening to the labor unions and including workers from outside their own office walls (i.e., the staff that make their pre-COVID-19 spaces function) in discussions about work, workplaces, and what the "new normal" could be.

SUMMARY

As much as this crisis has revealed the systemic inadequacies and outright violence of compulsory capitalism and austerity, this is only a "revelation" for those already privileged enough not to notice these issues prior to the pandemic. In this chapter, the authors explored how grassroots movements of mutual aid, disability justice, and carework must inform our "new normal," to make a choice other than shoehorning people back into a COVID-19 closet. Some in higher education are starting to recognize a need for change as a result of this chaos:

> While higher education leaders have been discouraged and dismayed by these issues, nothing has made us say, "Enough!" We haven't been willing to make different choices. But now, COVID-19 is wreaking havoc on the American economy and public health, not to mention the business-as-usual operations of colleges and universities. Candidly, I believe it may be the shove we need to accelerate change. (Sands & Shushock, 2020, para. 4)

We, too, want to witness this change occurring, starting with the acknowledgement that the previous lack of societal support for remote work options are inherently ableist and predicated on the desire of employers to surveil and supervise their employees. We want the intersections of our roles, responsibilities, and identities honored in developing policy. We want hazard pay, recognition of mental health priorities, and meaningful online opportunities for professional development. We want access, the way we have always dreamed it can be.

Ultimately, in times of a pandemic, those who can stay home, *should*. This rises to the level of a moral obligation to do so to help protect those who can't—those essential workers in service industry jobs where they have to be in a certain location to complete their work. There is no "good" plan—everything that office and academic spaces have attempted to cobble together since March is a band aid measure, with the stickiness frayed by constant exposure to concerns around personal and community health; access to childcare, internet connectivity, and other resources; and a fading sense of local and national economic security. The "Zoom fatigue" that people have complained about is a reminder that this has not been the ever present reality for most people before; the constant reminders of our own embodiment fraying has highlighted how non-disabled people completely ignore that "the COVID-19 related stress they have been experiencing . . . already [has] vocabulary for it all because everything already has a place within disabled experience" (Person, 2020).

It is time to learn from the disability community when we imagine the new normal. This chaotic miasma is an opportunity to redefine our assumptions of what work means and how it happens; it is an opportunity to reassess our expectations regarding the space and time for that work. Remote work might not be for you, and that's okay too. In the disability community, we call that a competing access need, and recognize that only together can we work to address all of our access needs, both in academia and in wider workplace culture.

NOTES

1. Due to COVID-19's impacts on the publication process, this number has increased to 780k+ within the United States by the time of publication.

1. *Crip,* as a term, is both a reclamation and recognition of disability identity. It is controversial, even within the community, serving as a rebellion against ableist attitudes and a way to take ownership of historically oppressive language, while also voicing critical differences (see Samuels, 2017). Crip can be used as a noun, verb (e.g., "cripping" a field to apply a critical disability-focused perspective), or as a way to denote movements focused on disability justice and pride such as #CripTheVote and Crip Camp.

REFERENCES

Accessible Campus Action Alliance. (2020). *Beyond "high-risk": Statement on disability and campus re-openings.* https://bit.ly/accesscampusalliance

Accessible Technologies. (2020). *Live captioning.* https://www.assist.vt.edu/services/captioning/live-cap.html

Anderson, A., Lyon, J., & Shew, A. (2020, October 2). *Disability studies and the pandemic* [Podcast]. https://www.brown.edu/academics/humanities/meeting-street-episode1

Baltes, B. B., Briggs, T. E., Huff, J. W., Wright, J. A., & Neuman, G. A. (1999). Flexible and compressed workweek schedules: A meta-analysis of their effects on work-related criteria. *Journal of Applied Psychology, 84*(4), 496–513. https://doi.org/10.1037/0021-9010.84.4.496

Baraniuk, C. (2020, July 25). *No end to COVID-19 webcam shortage.* BBC News. https://www.bbc.com/news/technology-53506401

Barbarin, I. [@Imani_Barbarin]. (2020, March 12). *So, you've probably seen mine and other disabled people's pissed off tweets about the response to the #CoronaVirus* [Tweet]. Twitter. https://twitter.com/Imani_Barbarin/status/1238213582787092483

Baruch, Y. (2001). The status of research on teleworking and an agenda for future research. *International Journal of Management Reviews, 3*(2), 113–129. https://doi.org/10.1111/1468-2370.00058

Berliner, U. (2020, June 22). *Permanent work from home is coming. Businesses, workers see benefits: NPR.* NPR. https://www.npr.org/2020/06/22/870029658/get-a-comfortable-chair-permanent-work-from-home-is-coming

Bryant, P., Rao, S., & Raouf, L. (2020, August 20). *How to ward off "Zoom zombies" and boost creativity.* ChiefExecutive.Net. https://chiefexecutive.net/how-to-ward-off-zoom-zombies-and-boost-creativity/

Centers for Disease Control and Prevention. (n.d.). *Burden of influenza.* https://www.cdc.gov/flu/about/burden/index.html

Chiru, C. (2017). Teleworking: Evolution and trends in USA, EU and Romania. *Economics, Management & Financial Markets, 12*(2), 222–229.

Cirruzzo, C. (2020, March 17). Disabled people have worked remotely for years, and they've got advice for you and your bosses. *Washington Post.* https://www.washingtonpost.com/lifestyle/wellness/disabled-people-have-worked-remotely-for-years-and-theyve-got-advice-for-you-and-your-bosses-/2020/03/17/f99dfd54-67d1-11ea-b313-df458622c2cc_story.html

Clarke, C. (2020a, September 25). *Message from Provost Cyril Clarke: Planning for spring 2021 course schedules and modality.* https://www.provost.vt.edu/provost-messages/provost-message-planning-spring-21.html

Clarke, C. (2020b, October 26). *Message from Provost Cyril Clarke: Spring break 2021.* https://www.provost.vt.edu/provost-messages/provost-message-spring-break-2021.html

Clarke, C. (2020c, October 28). *Message from Provost Cyril Clarke: In-person instruction for spring 2021.* https://www.provost.vt.edu/provost-messages/provost-message-in-person-instruction-spring21.html

Corkery, M. (2020, July 14). 'Hero' pay raises disappear for many essential workers. *The New York Times.* https://www.nytimes.com/2020/07/14/business/coronavirus-essential-workers-pay-raises.html

Danese, A., & McEwen, B. S. (2012). Adverse childhood experiences, allostasis, allostatic load, and age-related disease. *Physiology & Behavior, 106*(1), 29–39. https://doi.org/10.1016/j.physbeh.2011.08.019

Daniels, K., Lamond, D., & Standen, P. (2000). *Managing telework.* Cengage Learning EMEA.

Daniels, M. (2020, May 25). We have a responsibility to open Purdue University this fall—The Washington Post. *The Washington Post.* https://www.washingtonpost.com/opinions/why-we-have-a-responsibility-to-open-purdue-university-this-fall

Dehon, E., Weiss, N., Jones, J., Faulconer, W., Hinton, E., & Sterling, S. (2017). A systematic review of the impact of physician implicit racial bias on clinical decision making. *Academic Emergency Medicine, 24*(8), 895–904. https://doi.org/10.1111/acem.13214

Devakumar, D., Shannon, G., Bhopal, S. S., & Abubakar, I. (2020). Racism and discrimination in COVID-19 responses. *The Lancet, 395*(10231), 1194. https://doi.org/10.1016/S0140-6736(20)30792-3

Disability Alliance and Caucus. (2020, September). *DAC pandemic recommendations.* Disability Alliance at Virginia Tech. https://disabilityalliancevt.wordpress.com/dac-pandemic-recommendations/

Disability Culture at the University of Michigan. (2020, September). *DC @ UM letter in support of GEO & RA strikes.* Google Docs. https://docs.google.com/document/d/1WIP2nmYWwmBdotSYeD7McNtEjnV3KkGrhBI7o9FgW_s/edit?usp=sharing&fbclid=IwAR2K3ZVdl7skOM_DpD5P8txTvvw_TCKUOLZp3_CU-F2XBUW4sU45Y8cWfDU&usp=embed_facebook

Feliciano, A. (2020, May 1). Fall semester postponed until Aug. 31. *The Independent Florida Alligator.* https://www.alligator.org/article/2020/05/fall-semester-postponed-until-aug-31

FitzGerald, C., & Hurst, S. (2017). Implicit bias in healthcare professionals: A systematic review. *BMC Medical Ethics, 18*(1), 19. https://doi.org/10.1186/s12910-017-0179-8

Force, W. R. (2010). The code of Harry: Performing normativity in Dexter. *Crime, Media, Culture, 6*(3), 329–345. https://doi.org/10.1177/1741659010382333

Frye, J. (2020, April 23). *On the frontlines at work and at home: The disproportionate economic effects of the coronavirus pandemic on women of color.* Center for American Progress. https://www.americanprogress.org/issues/women/reports/2020/04/23/483846/frontlines-work-home/

Garey. (2020, October 29). *Vice President for Human Resources Bryan Garey gives an update on spring work plans, leave, and resources*. VT News. https://vtx.vt.edu/articles/2020/10/hr-bryan-garey102020.html

Garrett, R. K., & Danziger, J. N. (2007). Which telework? Defining and testing a taxonomy of technology-mediated work at a distance. *Social Science Computer Review, 25*(1), 27–47.

Gernsbacher, M. A., Raimond, A. R., Balinghasay, M. T., & Boston, J. S. (2016). "Special needs" is an ineffective euphemism. *Cognitive Research: Principles and Implications, 1*(1), 29. https://doi.org/10.1186/s41235-016-0025-4

Haddon, L., & Brynin, M. (2005). The character of telework and the characteristics of teleworkers. *New Technology, Work and Employment, 20*(1), 34–46. https://doi.org/10.1111/j.1468-005X.2005.00142.x

Harrington, K. (2020, October 19). "Fake commuting" to work—Why I do it for my mental health. *Stylist*. https://www.stylist.co.uk/health/mental-health/fake-commuting-to-work-from-home/438491

Harrison, R. (2020, August 13). As colleges reopen, they should recognize that COVID-19 will collide with the campus mental health crisis (opinion). *Inside Higher Ed*. https://www.insidehighered.com/views/2020/08/13/colleges-reopen-they-should-recognize-covid-19-will-collide-campus-mental-health

Ho, P.-S., Kroll, T., Kehn, M., Anderson, P., & Pearson, K. M. (2007). Health and housing among low-income adults with physical disabilities. *Journal of Health Care for the Poor and Underserved, 18*(4), 902–915. https://doi.org/10.1353/hpu.2007.0098

Jagannathan, M. (2020, May 5). *'I was told I could never work remotely': Before coronavirus, workers with disabilities say they implored employers to allow them to work from home.* MarketWatch. https://www.marketwatch.com/story/theres-no-excuse-for-not-offering-remote-work-the-coronavirus-induced-work-from-home-revolution-feels-like-vindication-for-some-workers-with-disabilities-2020-05-01

James Baldwin: How to cool it. (1968). *Esquire*. https://www.esquire.com/news-politics/a23960/james-baldwin-cool-it/

Keane, S. (2020, October 9). *Microsoft will let employees work from home permanently*. CNET. https://www.cnet.com/news/microsoft-reportedly-letting-employees-work-from-home-permanently/

Kuppers, P. (2015). Performance. In R. Adams, B. Reiss, & D. Serlin (Eds.), *Keywords in disability studies* (pp. 137–139). New York University Press.

Lake, R., & Makori, A. (2020, June 16). *The digital divide among students during COVID-19: Who has access? Who doesn't?* Center on Reinventing Public Education. https://www.crpe.org/thelens/digital-divide-among-students-during-covid-19-who-has-access-who-doesnt

Lamond, D., Daniels, K., & Standen, P. (1997). Defining telework: What is it exactly? In P. J. Jackson (Ed.), *Proceedings, Second International Workshop on Telework: "Building Actions on Ideas"* (pp. 117–187). Tilburg. https://www.academia.edu/20588552/Defining_telework_What_is_it_exactly

LinkedIn News. (2020, October). *Poll: Should companies pay for WFH expenses?* https://www.linkedin.com/feed/update/urn:li:activity:6719641116251168769/

Maisel, J. L., Smith, E., & Steinfeld, E. (2008). *Increasing home access: Designing for visitability* (p. 117). AARP Public Policy Institute. http://idea.ap.buffalo.edu/idea/wp-content/uploads/sites/110/2019/07/IncreasingHomeAccess.pdf

Mann, W. C., Hurren, D., Tomita, M., Bengali, M., & Steinfeld, E. (1994). Environmental problems in homes of elders with disabilities. *The Occupational Therapy Journal of Research, 14*(3), 191–211. https://doi.org/10.1177/153944929401400307

Mayer, K. (2020, May 12). *Twitter to work remote permanently.* Human Resource Executive. https://hrexecutive.com/twitter-tells-employees-they-can-work-from-home-forever/

McLean, T. (2020, October 27). *Reddit announces permanent work from home, eliminates cost-of-living pay compensation.* SF Gate. https://www.sfgate.com/bayarea/article/Reddit-permanent-work-from-home-15679060.php

Mingus, M. (2017, April 12). *Access intimacy, interdependence and disability justice.* Leaving Evidence. https://leavingevidence.wordpress.com/2017/04/12/access-intimacy-interdependence-and-disability-justice/

Nair, A. (@DisabilityStor1). (2019, December 9). *Thread #twitterstorians #histmed 1. Since some of you asked how I set up the #unessay assignment in my courses, here is how I do this* [Tweet]. Twitter. https://twitter.com/DisabilityStor1/status/1204204880421892096

Nario-Redmond, M. R., Gospodinov, D., & Cobb, A. (2017). Crip for a day: The unintended negative consequences of disability simulations. *Rehabilitation Psychology, 62*(3), 324–333. https://doi.org/10.1037/rep0000127

Nario-Redmond, M. R., Kemerling, A. A., & Silverman, A. (2019). Hostile, benevolent, and ambivalent ableism: Contemporary manifestations. *Journal of Social Issues, 75*(3), 726–756. https://doi.org/10.1111/josi.12337

National Interagency Fire Center. (2020). *National large incident year-to-date report.* https://gacc.nifc.gov/sacc/predictive/intelligence/NationalLargeIncidentYTDReport.pdf

Newton, H. P. (2019). *The Huey P. Newton reader* (2nd ed.). Seven Stories Press.

Nilles, J. M., Carlson, F. R., Gray, P., & Hanneman, G. J. (1976). *The telecommunications-transportation tradeoff.* Wiley.

Nutten, T. (2020). *Adjusting to the new normal.* Purdue Counseling & Psychological Services. https://www.purdue.edu/caps/covid-19/adjusting-to-new-normal.html

ObeySumner, C. (2020, February 11). Opinion: The violence of hostile accommodations. *South Seattle Emerald.* https://southseattleemerald.com/2020/02/11/opinion-the-violence-of-hostile-accommodations/

Person, R. (@lilririah). (2020, October 3). *More so irritation The entirety of covid, abled folk have been creating new terms to articulate the covid related stress* [Tweet]. Twitter. https://twitter.com/lilririah/status/1313745573279866880?s=20

Petriglieri, G. (2020, May 14). We are all Zoombies now, but it has to stop. *Financial Times.* https://www.ft.com/content/34fea7ea-83c5-11ea-b6e9-a94cffd1d9bf

Piepzna-Samarasinha, L. L. (2018). *Care Work.* Arsenal Pulp Press. https://arsenalpulp.com/Books/C/Care-Work

Powell, C. (2020, June 4). *The color and gender of COVID: Essential workers, not disposable people.* Council on Foreign Relations. https://www.thinkglobalhealth.org/article/color-and-gender-covid-essential-workers-not-disposable-people

Robertson, C., & Gebeloff, R. (2020, April 18). How millions of women became the most essential workers in America. *The New York Times.* https://www.nytimes.com/2020/04/18/us/coronavirus-women-essential-workers.html

Ruth, S., & Chaudhry, I. (2008). Telework: A productivity paradox? *IEEE Internet Computing, 12*(6), 87–90. https://doi.org/10.1109/MIC.2008.132

Sands, T., & Shushok, F. (2020, October 16). *The COVID-19 higher education shove.* Educause Review. https://er.educause.edu/blogs/2020/10/the-covid-19-higher-education-shove

Samuels, E. (2017). Six ways of looking at crip time. *Disability Studies Quarterly, 37*(3), Article 3. https://doi.org/10.18061/dsq.v37i3.5824

Schiff, F. (1993). *Comments on the origins of flexiplace.* Mid-Atlantic Telecommuting Advisory Council.

Schulman, A., & Spring, N. (2011). Pingin' in the rain. In P. Thiran & W. Willinger (Eds.), *IMC '11: Proceedings of the 2011 ACM SIGCOMM Conference on Internet Measurement Conference* (pp. 19–28). Association for Computing Machinery. https://doi.org/10.1145/2068816.2068819

Sheppard, E. (2020). Performing normal but becoming crip: Living with chronic pain. *Scandinavian Journal of Disability Research, 22*(1), 39–47. https://doi.org/10.16993/sjdr.619

Silard, A. (2020, May 1). Don't become a 'Zoombie' during quarantine: Commentary. *Orlando Sentinel.* https://www.orlandosentinel.com/opinion/guest-commentary/os-op-zoom-too-much-time-20200501-zdys5k2hbrg3lhnworysnzz6zq-story.html

Stephens, L., Spalding, K., Aslam, H., Scott, H., Ruddick, S., Young, N. L., & McKeever, P. (2017). Inaccessible childhoods: Evaluating accessibility in homes, schools and neighbourhoods with disabled children. *Children's Geographies, 15*(5), 583–599. https://doi.org/10.1080/14733285.2017.1295133

Strover, S. (2001). Rural internet connectivity. *Telecommunications Policy, 25*(5), 331–347. https://doi.org/10.1016/S0308-5961(01)00008-8

Thompson, D. (2013, May 14). Well, this is just awful: "Renting" disabled people to skip lines at Disney World. *The Atlantic.* https://www.theatlantic.com/business/archive/2013/05/well-this-is-just-awful-renting-disabled-people-to-skip-lines-at-disney-world/275840/

Thompson, R. J., Payne, S. C., & Taylor, A. B. (2015). Applicant attraction to flexible work arrangements: Separating the influence of flextime and flexplace. *Journal of Occupational and Organizational Psychology, 88*(4), 726–749. https://doi.org/10.1111/joop.12095

UF Human Resources. (2020). *COVID-19 retirement incentive for staff.* University of Florida. https://hr.ufl.edu/wp-content/uploads/2020/06/2020_June-16_HR-Forum.pptx

Wellner, G. (2020). *The Zoom-bie student and the lecturer; reflections on teaching and learning with Zoom.* The Society for Philosophy and Technology. http://www.spt.org/the-zoom-bie-student-and-the-lecturer-reflections-on-teaching-and-learning-with-zoom/

Whitacre, B. E., & Mills, B. F. (2010). A need for speed? Rural Internet connectivity and the no access/dial-up/high-speed decision. *Applied Economics, 42*(15), 1889–1905. https://doi.org/10.1080/00036840701749001

Williams, D. R., & Jackson, P. B. (2005). Social sources of racial disparities in health. *Health Affairs, 24*(2), 325–334. https://doi.org/10.1377/hlthaff.24.2.325

Yan, M. (2020, October 23). Faculty expected to return to campus for spring semester per updated remote work policy. *The Huntington News.* https://huntnewsnu.com/63797/campus/faculty-expected-to-return-to-campus-for-spring-semester-per-updated-remote-work-policy/

CHAPTER 5

ORGANIZING THEMSELVES

Jenifer Neale
Public School Educator

The purpose of this contribution is to explore the experience of elementary teachers as they moved from their brick-and-mortar classrooms into their digital classrooms resulting from the COVID-19 global pandemic. The context is a large, urban school district in the southeastern United States with over 20,000 teachers and 200,000 students. The district is situated within a state with a decades-long history of legislated mandates related to education that have become increasingly heavy-handed over the past several years.

The abrupt change in delivery model came about as a result of a global crisis that happened to teachers and schools all at once, and therefore was different from any reform tied to a school grade, a new curriculum, a top–down administrative decision, or a legislative action. Teachers were told that year-end state-mandated accountability measures would be cancelled, that school grade measures would not be implemented, and that their own year-end performance evaluations would be suspended.

This situation presented teachers with the unique circumstance of being able to adopt a new delivery model, along with their students, in an environment with no real penalty for failure. This is an exceptional

Crisis, Chaos, and Organizations, pages 119–146

context in the field. At the same time, many teachers knew very little about teaching in the digital environment, so the risk of failure was real. While the penalty was minimal teachers were conditioned over years to function in an environment of punitive, high-stakes accountability measures. How would teachers now respond?

I interviewed four elementary teachers, from two different schools, to explore this environment. The two schools were very different public elementary schools. One of the schools consisted of mostly Hispanic students and students receiving free and reduced priced lunch. The other school had no one single ethnic majority, with less than half of the students receiving free or reduced priced lunch. Both schools were of similar size, between 600–800 students. More specific information about school demographics is contained below. The small sample size does present some limits to generalizability. Very shortly after this research project was approved, a moratorium was placed on all research projects involving any school level participation in the school district being studied here. COVID-19 safety guidelines and protocols were explained to me as the reason for this. There were no opportunities for me to expand this research beyond my original scope.

The methodology was a critical discourse analysis focusing on the experience of elementary teachers during this episode in history. I examined how they talked about their abrupt move from brick-and-mortar to virtual classrooms resulting from the pandemic. My initial theory was that teachers formed ad-hoc groups to support their own growth, including social media groups, friend groups, family groups, and school groups.

When provided little more than an online shell for loading their course materials, how did teachers navigate this new world? How did teachers deal with the movement to virtual learning? What happened when teachers were an active part of the change effort (and it was not being done TO them)? What communities of support emerged? How did years of state-mandated student accountability measures impact teachers' efforts as they moved forward with their virtual teaching?

In a state where professional learning community meetings are mandated, the answers to these questions may help us understand how real communities of support form and advance learning for teachers. While change efforts are often driven by legislative mandate, findings may also inform our understanding of what drives real change. As we advance the art of teaching, this research may help us to understand the impact of the years of punitive, state-mandated accountability measures on teachers and teaching. This might also help us to gain an understanding of teacher resilience.

HISTORICAL BACKDROP

Accountability

Public school accountability has moved from a singular focus on inputs, such as school attendance, to a focus on outputs, such as testing and graduation rate (Rippner, 2016, p. 100). This state first issued school grades in 1999, based on standardized testing. Since then the stakes have been incrementally increased. This reflects a national trend. "Improvement and accountability have focused on standardized test scores, and policy debates have focused on levers to increase that performance" (Rippner, 2016, p. 107). Only teachers with more than 20 years of teaching experience have experienced teaching outside the confines of high-stakes accountability measures. "This has impacted the way teachers teach" (Rippner, 2016, p. 100).

In this state, the accountability has gone from testing all regular education students in Grades 3–12 in math and reading to including ALL students in Grades 3–12 regardless of exceptional student status or English language proficiency. Measures include science, growth, lower quartile growth, college readiness, graduation rate, accelerated coursework, biology, geometry, civics, science, and a requirement for testing at least 95% of all students. "Student academic achievement can be parsed by racial, ethnic, gender, socioeconomic, or other subgroups" (Rippner, 2016, p. 80). Also mandated are additional sanctions for schools failing to earn a school grade of C or higher. This involves an additional sanction for elementary schools with reading scores defined as being in the lowest 300 in the state. Initially this sanction was targeted at the lowest 100. "Data have become important, if not king" (Rippner, 2016, p. 80).

Accountability measures for schools graded as D or F have also been expanded in this state and have become increasingly demanding over time. Initially these schools were provided support from state education specialists in implementing best practices. Those efforts targeted teacher development at the school level while also supporting principal growth. Schools were given a specified number of years to turn around, with a penalty of being taken over by the state. Schools are now given 2 years to turn around and bring a school grade of D or F to a school grade of C or higher.

State take-over of schools is no longer an option in this state, however. The options provided by the state department of education for a failing school includes converting it to a charter school or private school, or school closure. If closed, the students are required to be rezoned to a school with a grade of C or higher. Sanctions are further intensified with a new definition of perpetually failing schools that looks at 5 years of school grades, even if a school has been a C or higher for the last 2 school years. State support of failing schools still includes support from education experts, but the effort has moved beyond simply the school and its principal to include district-level employees and systems.

Accountability measures also now incorporate teacher performance based on a value-added model (VAM) that includes only annual state-wide testing. "The view of what schools should be about are performance scores, and results to excess has lost sight of all the other things that characterize teaching" (Hargreaves & Fullan, 2012, p. 10). Teacher VAM scores, as required by state legislation, inform district decisions about which teachers can stay at a school identified as needing to turn around. "Given the focus on increasing student achievement, it is not surprising that there is a complementary focus on ensuring only quality teachers are in front of the classroom" (Rippner, 2016, p. 101). Schools are now even compelled by state legislation to move "ineffective" principals, defined as those leading D or F schools.

All of this leads to an overall culture of high-stakes accountability supported by state mandated punitive measures. "In the last decade or so, improvement and accountability have focused on standardized test scores, and policy debates have focused on levers to increase that performance" (Rippner, 2016, p. 107). This outlook is echoed by Ball (2008) when he writes that the "public discourse around... test results brought the notion of 'good schools' and 'bad schools,' as defined by performance, into common parlance, making them a vehicle for further policy" (p. 112). Ball describes a culture in which the focus on high-stakes test scores simply increases the policies focused on those test scores. This all results in what Ball refers to as "institutional performances" (p. 140). He goes on:

> One of the key elements in the new policy ensemble is the use of highly prescriptive systems of accountability—performance indicators, inspections... and achievement targets. Schools are rated and compared in terms of "achievement" measured by tests and examinations, for which students are carefully prepared. Institutional... increases or reductions in test scores are taken to be indicators of rising or failing standards of schooling. (p. 150)

This is the prevailing culture of our public schools, perpetuated by the accountability measures in place since 1999.

New Leadership

The school district that was studied was also experiencing a transfer of leadership, with a new superintendent coming onboard officially just weeks prior to the school closure. The superintendent, hired from another school district, brought several upper-level leaders into the district. Many of the district leaders under the prior administration were either transferred to lower-level positions or were let go altogether. New leaders were in place in nearly every department, with school closure related to the pandemic (including district offices) hampering any efforts at developing relationships and establishing a new vision for the district.

Understanding these dynamics provides a framework for this research. Teachers operate within a culture of accountability that has been normalized over the past 2 decades even as that culture of accountability has become more and more intrusive into their work. It is also important to understand the instability that comes with a new superintendent. This particular school district has a history of stability in that office, with, until now, only three superintendents since the onset of school grading in 1999. Those three superintendents were all internal candidates.

It was against this backdrop that students, parents, teachers, school board members, and the new superintendent experienced the global pandemic caused by COVID-19. A very sudden shift away from this existing culture of accountability occurred when nearly all schools across the nation were closed abruptly. In one moment, and for a quantifiable period of time, everything about schooling seemed to change. It is this moment in time that is the focus of this research, specifically a focus on teachers and how they managed their own swift transition into a new world of distance learning under a new superintendent, and with no accountability measures in place.

Professional Learning Communities

Professional learning communities (PLCs) are the principal way of work for teachers in this district. PLCs in this state are mandated by legislation as part of the accountability movement described above. Originally, PLCs were being brought into practice outside of the accountability movement nationally, but both movements were coming of age during roughly the same period. "At the same time that PLCs were percolating through education, there was also a call for greater accountability" (Neill, 2018, p. 79).

As the concept of the PLC developed, so too did the need for educators to prove they were meeting the needs of 21st century learners. "There was a push for 'data-driven' education . . . The PLC offered a way to use data as part of a reflective process and so make classroom practice accountable" (Neill, 2018, p. 79). The PLC became the vehicle for exerting internal control, by local school boards, state legislators, and even federal legislation. PLCs rely on a common vision, with shared values and norms. "In education, however, a developed vision had to align with an overall vision determined by government policy" (Neill, 2018, p. 79). The author goes on to write that PLCs have really become think tanks for assessment analysis (Neill, 2018, p. 80). Kanold (2011), in his book about PLCs, describes the discipline of accountability and celebration as "the leadership work of delivering specific improvement in student achievement results and monitoring stakeholder actions that lead to those results, with consequences" (p. 36). PLCs have become an evolving movement (Kanold, 2011). "What attracts us to pursue PLCs as a movement is their ability to build adult knowledge and skill capacity and empower every teacher and school leader to improve student learning" (Kanold, 2011, p. 186).

DuFour (2007) writes that the PLC allows the school to create a systematic process for examining issues related to student achievement. DuFour warns, however, that "the concept of a collaborative culture of a professional learning community is powerful, but like all powerful concepts, it can be applied badly" (p. 61). This element of poor application may be illustrated in the state's mandate for PLCs. Once mandated, the practice is established in every school regardless of desire, leadership competence, or presence of a shared vision. "Trying hard to make good leadership decisions without the training necessary to identify the values and beliefs behind those decisions or... will eventually render you ineffective" (Kanold, 2011, p. 4). Hargreaves and Fullan (2012) caution that PLCs should not be an end in themselves. They should, instead, be a means of developing the profession. "The promise of the PLC as applied to schooling was that it would open up dialogue about the purpose of education and the process of learning" (Neill, 2018, p. 10).

PLCs have attained some permanence. Those who thought that PLCs were a fleeting concept have come to learn that they are part of the education culture. To borrow an old adage, if PLCs can be established everywhere, then PLCs can be established anywhere. This belies the fact that effective PLCs require strong ownership. Ownership "refers to commitment to project goals and tasks, taking responsibility, and showing enthusiasm" and "that collective ownership refers to strong positive attitudes, intentions, and aligned behavior of members who reinforce each other in doing so" (DuFour, 2007, p. 130). Kanold (2011) echoes this sentiment when writing that a vision never "sticks" if the leader is the only person who owns it (p. 19). "Ownership signals real engagement and commitment to actions that reflect the vision" (p. 21). These qualities are hard to mandate. Still, PLCs are the way of work, even if implemented with greater or lesser success.

STUDY DESIGN

Purpose

The purpose of this research is to explore the experience of elementary teachers as they moved from their brick-and-mortar classrooms into their digital classrooms. The context is a large, urban school district in the southeastern United States with over 20,000 teachers and 200,000 students. The district is located in a state with a history of legislated mandates related to education that have become increasingly heavy-handed over the past several years.

An abrupt change in delivery model came about as a result of a global crisis that happened to all teachers and schools all at once, and therefore was different from any reform tied to a school grade, a new curriculum, a top–down administrative decision, or a legislative action. Year-end state-mandated accountability measures would be abandoned, school grade measures would not be implemented, and year-end teacher performance evaluations would be suspended. How would teachers now respond?

Methodology

The methodology is a critical discourse analysis (CDA) focusing on the experience of elementary teachers during this episode in history. I investigated how they talked about their abrupt move from brick-and-mortar to virtual classrooms resulting from the pandemic. The title derives from my initial theory that teachers formed ad-hoc groups to support their own growth, including social media groups, friend groups, family groups, and school groups. When provided little more than an online shell for loading their course materials, how did teachers navigate this new world? This research sought to answer the following questions:

1. How did teachers deal with the movement to virtual learning?
2. What happens when teachers are an active part of the change effort (and it is not being done TO them)?
   a. What communities of support emerged?
      i. Who did they lean on for support?
      ii. How did they develop relationships of support?
      iii. What resources did they utilize?
   b. How did years of state-mandated student accountability measures impact teachers' efforts as they moved forward with their virtual teaching?
      i. How creatively did teachers engage students?
      ii. How constrained did teachers feel in providing content?

The method this research will use to investigate the move from brick-and-mortar schools to exclusively virtual education is a CDA. The purpose of CDA is to analyze structural relationships of dominance, discrimination, power, and control as revealed in language. "CDA states that discourse is socially constitutive as well as socially conditioned. Furthermore, discourse is an opaque power object in modern societies and CDA aims to make it more visible and transparent" (Blommaert & Bulcean, 2000, p. 447).

GATHERING TEXT FOR ANALYSIS

Participants

This study was focused on four elementary teachers from two separate schools within one large school district located in the Southeastern United States. The district has over 200,000 students, over 20,000 employees, and over 125 elementary schools. The two elementary schools represented two very different sets of demographic data (see Table 5.1).

One participant at each school was purposefully selected based on my prior knowledge of their experience. Each of those two original participants then provided an additional participant. While I knew two of the participants in a professional manner, I had no prior knowledge or relationship with the other two participants. None of these participants were related to my work within the district. The schools selected resulted from the choice of the first two participants. Each participant agreed to an interview, which took from 30 to 45 minutes. Each was provided with a written transcript of the recorded interview as a way to check the accuracy of the text. These teachers will be referred to by number. Teachers 1 and 2 represent teachers from Palm View Elementary. Teachers 3 and 4 represent Southern Pine Elementary.

These interviews were semi-structured, providing some consistency in questioning, allowing common themes, domains, and factors to be isolated (Schensul et al., 1999, p. 151). This is important, because "the domains yield factors that are identified because they appear repeatedly in the text data" (Schensul et al., 1999, p. 153). However, while providing some consistency in questioning, the semi-structured format allows for further questioning as the opportunity presents itself.

Lens of the Researcher

An analysis of discourse is about understanding exactly how specific statements come to be formed, how specific statements come to be possible

TABLE 5.1 Elementary School Demographic Information

School	Number of Students	Students Receiving Free/Reduced Price Lunch	White	Black	Hispanic	Asian	Last Two School Grades
Palm View (Teachers 1 & 2)	800+	40%	25%	18%	20%	25%	A, A
Southern Pine (Teachers 3 & 4)	600+	95%	5%	5%	85%	0%	C, C

at all, and how these statements exclude the possibility of other statements. The discourse cannot be separated from its social context. It is the social context which provides the umbrella under which all discourse takes place. All of the data gathered from the texts described above will inform any understanding of discourse practices and social practices.

My own experiences within the district will inform my research and my understanding of the discourse and social practices. My experiences include 34 years of employment in this district (my entire adult working career), including 11 years as an elementary music specialist, 10 years as an elementary teacher of the emotionally handicapped, half a school year as an elementary reading specialist, 4 years as an elementary assistant principal, and 8 years as a district level administrator.

Protections

In order to provide protections for the participants, all individuals and schools will be referred to by pseudonyms. This particular school district is so large that this will provide ample protection for those involved. There are over 20,000 employees and over 145 elementary schools, ranging in demographics from urban to suburban to rural, and including every conceivable mix of financial status and race/ethnicity.

ANALYSIS OF TEXT

Gee (2005) writes that processing and organizing language is an initial step in critical discourse analysis. He is concerned about ways in which the research can begin to consider the grand task of analyzing the data, and "initial ways into a text" (p. 118). What Gee stresses is that the analyst looks "for patterns and links within and across utterances in order to form hypotheses about how meaning is being constructed and organized" (p. 118). This is a reciprocal and cyclical process in which the analyst considers a piece of language, situated meanings, and relationships in a specific context (p. 118). By dividing the text into lines and stanzas we are representing patterns as expressed by the speaker while simultaneously representing patterns which the analyst believes to be present.

The analysis began with arranging the typed transcript into lines and stanzas as defined by Gee. Lines, according to Gee, are small spurts of language and composed, usually, of one salient piece of new information "as the focus of the intonation contour" (Gee, 2005, p. 124). Each spurt of language is isolated by "a pause, slight hesitation, or slight break in tempo" (Gee, 2005, p. 124). Stanzas are collections of lines with a specific focus, such as time, event, idea, or character. The larger body of information is "composed of stanzas, each one of which takes a single perspective on an event, state of affairs, or character" (Gee, 2005, p. 128). Fairclough (1992) writes of a similar concept. Fairclough writes of "the clause" in a similar manner to Gee's lines and stanzas. "People make choices about the design and structure of their clauses, which amount to choices about how to signify social identities, social relationships, and knowledge and belief" (1992, pp. 75–76).

Coding began with a review of the theoretical framework and research questions. The method for coding, informed by Auerbach and Silverstein (2003), began with the recommendation that research concerns and the theoretical framework be present visually while editing text, in order to be continually attentive to those themes. "Your theoretical framework determines your biases. Stating it explicitly will force you to acknowledge your lack of 'objectivity' and will help you read the text in a more focused way" (Auerbach & Silverstein, 2003, p. 46). This process, as laid out by Auerbach and Silverstein (2003), allowed me to find a starting place into the texts, yet allowed those texts to find their own spaces.

As laid out by Auerbach and Silverstein (2003), my analysis then moved to reducing the transcript texts to relevant text, text related to "specific research concerns" (p. 37). Detailed knowledge of the transcript texts was critical in determining what pieces of the text were relevant. Cutting down the text into manageable, relevant pieces required having the research questions in mind, and editing for pieces of text that would be helpful in examining language text, discourse practice, or social practice.

Analysis progressed into editing for repeating ideas. "It is progressive in that you first develop, out of the data, major code clumps by which to sort the data. Then you code the contents of each major code clump, thereby breaking down the major code into numerous subcodes" (Glesne, 1999, p. 135). Auerbach and Silverstein refer to this as sorting into repeating ideas, and they do this by describing how to move each entry in the relevant text transcripts files into individual files that match each repeating idea. The master list of repeating ideas was used as a tool in the creation of major themes.

The next step involved developing theoretical constructs from the themes. "A theoretical construct is an abstract concept that organizes a group of themes by fitting them into a theoretical framework" (Auerbach & Silverstein, 2003, p. 67). This began with the creation of a master list of themes. This then allowed for themes to be grouped together into theoretical constructs, which brought the analysis back full circle to the original criteria for including relevant text. The process for developing theoretical frameworks from the texts utilized the same procedures as that of developing themes from repeating ideas. Richards (2009) writes that for a satisfactory research outcome the analysis should answer the research questions, offer an analysis and not simply a description, and should offer an explanation. Richards goes on to include arriving at something more than any of the participants could have reported, making an adequate report that makes sense to others (p. 138).

RESULTS OF ANALYSIS

How Did Teachers Deal With the Movement to Virtual Learning?

The move to virtual learning came just around the time of spring break in the school district. Teachers had planned trips and activities around what was expected to be a normal spring break. As the break approached, however, the idea that schools might be closing became conceivable. Teacher 3 describes an "inkling" about possible school closings. "When we left here I had a feeling we weren't coming back." Teacher 1 said that she believed that, "the news and everything started 'picking up' with regards to school closing being a possibility." Certainly, the teachers in this study were aware that the possibility for schools closing was real, and proximate, even while being told that, according to Teacher 2, "Our plan is to come back after spring break. We have spring break off, we'll come back after spring break."

Late in the week of spring break official notification from the superintendent was sent out to teachers in the form of an email. "I didn't know anything about it until I got back from my weekend away," said Teacher 1. Others, however, knew sooner. Teacher 2 mentioned learning of the school closures from social media, following the school district on Facebook and Twitter. That was how she was informed, having not seen the email due to it being lost in the "eight million emails" she had amassed over spring break. Teacher 3 said that the communication "had to have been from (the superintendent)." It is noteworthy that none remember specifics about receiving an official email from the school district.

Even after school closures were announced, it was widely accepted that it would be for a short amount of time, around a week or so. Teachers were allowed back into their schools to retrieve materials on a schedule assigned by their principals. The time was limited, and they were only given one opportunity to gather materials. At Palm View, teachers were given 1 day, and neither teacher felt as if they had collected adequate materials for an extended school closure. Teacher 2 stated:

> Like the one day they told us we could come get stuff, I didn't know what, how long we would be there, what I needed to take. I just, just grabbed whatever I could. But there was definitely times when I was like, oh sitting on this table or bookshelf at school I really could have used today, or really needed that paper, or that lesson, or whatever.

The teachers from Southern Pine were given 2 days, and while they spent their time gathering materials they also spent time putting together supplies and materials for their students. Teacher 3 put it this way:

> We got book bags from (a local grocery store) and we packed bags of materials, like the PrepareU book. We packed bags of pens, books from our classroom libraries, anything math books, anything that they might need that we thought would take us, we didn't really think it was going to last this long. So whatever we thought was gonna be easy for us to use with our population, that's what we packed as a fourth grade team.

These teachers prepared for distance learning, for both themselves and their students, they turned to a variety of sources for support. They sought support for technology, lesson planning, curriculum modifications, and emotional stability. This will be described below.

What Happens When Teachers Are an Active Part of the Change Effort?

Teachers did not feel like an active part of the change effort. They, instead, felt trapped within it. One theme that resonated across participants was a feeling of being overwhelmed by all that was happening. This feeling resulted from a lack of technology expertise, the number of trainings presented to them, and a lack of meaningful district support. For example, Teacher 3 spoke of the number of trainings being, "so overwhelming." Teacher 1 was "overwhelmed" by the professional development offered because of her limited skills with computers. Teacher 2 described the period of distance learning as being in "survival mode."

These teachers did not view this as an opportunity, but as a circumstance that they needed to get through. They managed distance learning by reaching out for support. They looked to each other, their teams, their school administrators, and their families. They did the work they had to do to make their work "work." These teachers were the face of the change effort, yet it didn't behave like any typical educational change. This was something that no one was leading. There was no one giving directions, no one with a teacher's manual, and no committee to give out assignments. Teachers worked this out as they went. One way they did that was through PLCs.

What Communities of Support Emerged?

As described earlier, PLCs are the way of work for teacher professional development at the school level. This structure gave teachers a mechanism for beginning to look for support. Both sets of teachers began searching for support from their immediate PLC team. The support then branched off and away from the main PLCs as more organic groups formed.

At Palm View, the teachers met in their first grade team almost daily. "We had almost daily Zooms to kind of vent and help each other and share information and things like that," describes Teacher 1. These regular Zooms took place through the entire school closure. Teacher 2 added, "We would meet almost daily as a whole team. There were seven of us. So all seven of us would bounce ideas off of each other and talk." This extended to lesson planning as well, where Teacher 2 describes how they "did the same plans, essentially. We would just change our names at the top and work together."

Quickly, though, alliances were formed based on teacher need. The team "kind of naturally, like, split," said Teacher 2. Teacher 1 was very distressed about her lack of technology skills. This was a primary concern for her. She originally thought that she just couldn't do it. "I can't do it. I had no idea. Literally, I had no idea about Google docs, I had no idea about the Zoom, I had no idea how to work with Brightly." She relayed that she only knew Zoom as a television show. Even as the whole team would continue to meet, she relied on Teacher 2 for technology support. Feeling the need for a more "personal touch" than what was offered through district trainings, she "cried to one of my teammates, who came to my house and sat down and said, 'This is what we're gonna do.'" She "held my hand" every step of the way.

A similar phenomenon occurred at Southern Pine as well. While talking about their teams, Teacher 3 also described two different sets of teachers in the grade level, and while she and her partner departmentalize (one teaches language arts, the other math and science), the other two teachers are co-teachers in the same classroom. "Well, we have two groups. So it was really two sides. Us and them."

Teacher 3 was unique however, in describing a source of support outside of the school itself. She describes participation in a writing PLC. This group was formed by the district elementary writing supervisor and included writing resource teachers from across the district. The writing supervisor "did a really good job of helping us like have a place where we could talk and figure things out. And so, that's who else we relied on. Other people that were trying things out." She went on to explain how she "got all of those ideas from that writing PLC when she would let us do our Zoom meetings together."

Teacher 4, also at Southern Pine, spoke mostly in terms of working alone, relying on himself. He did mention "stealing" an idea from his team. When he spoke of team meetings, it involved mainly the logistics of scheduling and keeping students generally in line with the curriculum content. When talking about ideas and his classroom practices, the conversation revolved around things he had done of his own accord. When asked who he relied on, he responded, "Honestly, during that time, it was basically me and myself."

The PLC structure, having been established as common practice, allowed a structure for these teachers as they searched for support. These PLCs, and the groups into which they split, were the strongest sources of support within the school. Others in the school building could be helpful on some level. While useful, these other sources of support never overtook the importance of the alliances formed through PLCs. For Hargreaves and Fullan (2012), this is just as it should be, "finding the time to develop collaboration, trust, and respect doesn't just happen accidentally or completely spontaneously—though it is possible to create platforms where spontaneous collaboration will occur (p. 114). School closure may have provided just that platform where PLCs could function with true collaboration and trust.

Principals and assistant principals, together forming the school administration, were less helpful when it came to assisting with classroom level concerns. According to Teacher 3, "They kinda sat back and watched because they didn't really know how to dive into the distance learning process, especially in elementary. I don't think they knew how to support us in a sense, because we were kind of on our own and we were remote." Teacher 1 added that the assistant principal "was very good about answering if she could" and that she was helpful in resolving a student password issue she had. I referred the parent to "the assistant principal and she helped her figure it out, it was some kind of a glitch."

Outside of school, family members served to support these teachers. Two teachers described their husbands, and one spoke out about her own children. One husband, after trying to fix a faulty school issued computer, went out and purchased a laptop for his wife. Another husband was a computer science major who was good about answering questions and pointing his wife in the right direction for advice. This teacher had access to quality technology at home as well. The middle and high school aged children of one teacher served to help inform their mother about the utility of Brightly, and how it might be utilized in its most simple form. Brightly was used regularly in middle and high schools in the district, as a means of communicating with families regarding grades. Students also used it as electronic access to assignments. In elementary schools it was commonly only used as a grade book for teachers. Full use of this electronic platform beyond use of the grade book had never previously been utilized for elementary schools.

Additionally, Teacher 2 mentioned following a Brightly Help Group online, through Facebook. This teacher, also through social media, found links to videos of other teachers nationally experiencing distance learning and how they were managing it. This same teacher also discussed finding out about school closures through social media. Teacher 4 mentioned following news outlets, "Just listening to the decisions being made, it was kind of firsthand from wherever it was coming from. So I kind of paid attention to that more and not word of mouth."

Teachers used these support mechanisms in various ways. Examples included supports for use of technology and some teaching strategies. PLCs were also instrumental in helping teachers determine content for their students.

How Constrained Did Teachers Feel in Providing Content?

All teachers felt at least basically responsible for providing the content as put in place by the school district. Being constrained by the content, all four teachers sought ways to adapt and supplement the provided curriculum to better meet the needs of the students, and almost more notably, to adapt to the needs of what the technology available to a student could manage.

The school district provided content through their digital platforms Brightly and Portrait. The generalized officials at the school district level were often referred to as "they." Teacher 4 stated, "They started putting lesson plans in there. They had lesson plans, pre-written and activities done." Teacher 2 stated, "Whatever the plans were, there was a little tiny icon on Brightly, that said distance learning plans or whatever it said, they kind of pushed out. That's where they would go to have general plans to get their kids to do. And, for I guess, for us teachers, have a general guide to do this." This description lacks clarity about what was actually required.

This lack of clarity was mirrored by Teacher 1. "We had what the online suggested, for lack of a better term, the pacing guides, the lessons. We had that, which we kind of used to frame our lessons." Again, it is obvious that the district supplied something for teachers, but any mandate to follow them was implied and indirect.

It also became apparent that many students did not have access to computers or the internet. While this was not a problem at Palm View, it was a focal issue at Southern Pine, where many students did not have computers or internet access. For situations like this, the district created printable packets to be sent home. For Southern Pine, this meant, according to Teacher 3, that "if the kids were getting packets then we wanted it consistent across" the team.

The idea of keeping all the curriculum consistent seemed to be a compelling factor for why these teachers chose to use the district created distance learning curriculum. However, the curriculum created several problems and teachers found creative ways of adapting and supplementing what was provided to better meet the needs of their students. As they continued to work within their selected work groups, teachers got better at managing the curriculum for their students. Teachers 1 and 2 worked together as they "pretty much created lessons using a rough outline of what (the district) provided."

The teachers were focused on how to adapt and supplement the provided curriculum to meet their students' needs. Teacher 1 believed that "they provided way too much for first graders to use, in a short time frame." Teachers 1 and 2 supplemented the curriculum through the use of a weekly student periodical. Teacher 4 seemed to incorporate several adaptations, describing how he "adapted some lesson plans because I would have to translate a lot for our population. So I translated all of the directions and stuff so parents would understand that and help the kids get through it. But I did make it familiar so that if a kid saw it they would kind of understand what to do, if the parent didn't know." He also supplemented his plans to include, for example, YouTube videos for word work. He utilized a video of his personal fish tank to engage the students in a more active science lesson. Teacher 2 described adapting a lesson as well. Here she discusses using ReadMe, an online virtual library.

> So we took whatever story they were supposed to read on ReadMe, and kind of adapted it, with tasks that we had already talked about in, together, in person and said okay, from this for character traits or whatever with this ReadMe story.

Her teammate, Teacher 1, reported, "We used books from ReadMe, using it and supplemented, using things like looking at the text features in this story today." They were supplementing the district supplied texts with content that their students were familiar with, thus adapting what was provided to more appropriately work for their students.

Still other adaptations came as a result of technology limitations. At Southern Pine, many of the students lacked computers or reliable internet. The teachers there had to contend with this as they sought to educate their students. The biggest problem of access seemed to be resolved through the use of cell phones. However, this caused several problems with the district online platform. Many of the functions of the platform either did not work at all on cell phones, or they worked poorly. So, according to Teacher 3, "That's why we definitely, we had to work out the kinks and the things that we did could possibly be done on either the phone or an iPad." Along with her team, they ended up simply uploading copies of the printable packets for their students. While unhappy with this solution, they "wanted to be consistent across the ELA fourth grade." Here is how it was explained:

> So we took whatever was in the packet and we just transformed it onto Brightly so that there would be just consistency and if someone didn't have a packet then it wasn't more work, it wasn't less work, it was everybody pretty much.

In other words, students would get the same work regardless of the device they used to access it. She talked repeatedly about "keeping it simple" so that students could access their work through Brightly on a cell phone. She added:

> We tried to use Brightly and as we got going we figured out how to make it very simple and then as, as it got later into the year and closer to the end of the year, we got better at it with being able to make quizzes on there, or questions and answers where they just had to input it.

Teacher 4 was also reliant on cell phones. "The easiest way for me and these families in this community was ParentComm (a text app for communicating between school and family). Because they all have cell phones, and some kind of service. Using the phone for video and things like that." This teacher talked about creating YouTube videos, something easily accessed through cell phones.

While none of the teachers mentioned that they had to comply with the use of the district curriculum, they all took pains to do so. They adapted and supplemented the curriculum as they desired, yet that was focused on the delivery of the curriculum. Even after they discovered that students would be graded very leniently, these teachers still maintained adherence to the district-supplied curriculum. They were all more concerned with how to deliver the content rather than tinkering with the actual content of the curriculum.

How Did Years of State-Mandated Student Accountability Measures Impact Teachers

All teachers in this study viewed the school closures as temporary and remained dedicated to upholding the desires of the district. They all felt a sense of responsibility to their students and their future success. Teacher 4 stated, "I was trying to get as much into them because I knew the district was moving them all on. And I wanted them to be successful next year whether they were with me or not." This teacher is referring to whether or not they were promoted to the next grade level for the next school year.

All teachers did remain acutely aware of the ever-present state mandates regarding student testing and teacher evaluations. One teacher talked about "levels" referring to the scores received on state standardized testing. Worried about a lack of student progress during distance learning, Teacher 3 said, "We'll never close any type of gap, we'll never do, like the levels." Students are expected to make learning gains and moving up a level is one way to illustrate that gain. Level 3 is often equated to proficiency. A student's "level" is important for both student grade promotion as well as the overall school grade.

Speaking to the need to try to maintain the teaching of required skills, Teacher 4 remarked:

> I didn't want to just tell my parents, because they're not being tested, I'm not going to give them everything they would have gotten. I kept the expectation high because I knew they're gonna need it regardless.

This comment relates to the fact that teachers were told that, barring a parent request, most students would simply be promoted to the next grade level if they made attempts at distance learning.

The emphasis on standardized testing even trickled down to the parents. Teacher 1 relayed a story about a parent upset about the lack of testing. "I had one parent who was upset," about the lack of testing. She wanted her son to be able to test at the end of the year, "just to see how he had grown since January."

When asked how she felt about the cancellation of the end-of-year state mandated standardized testing, Teacher 3 said she was relieved, not for herself or the impact to her evaluation, but:

> I don't think it was a relief that it wasn't going to count. And I think it wasn't fair that if we had to, especially for our population, that they were going to be tested on it. So the relief was that they're not going to be tested and they're not going to be held accountable of whether it's a pass (Level 3) or, passing on to the next grade, or their scores, because they don't have the resources. But it's because I couldn't physically teach them to the best of my ability and then that made me feel relief.

The teachers at Palm View were focused on the impact to their own teacher evaluation score. Teacher 2 described how she had completed all of the lengthy paperwork associated with her pre-observation interview. It was completed, and that, "it's there, in your (online) journal so they can look back at it if they wanted to." She was disappointed that it was not completed. Teacher 1 had a similar story when asked about the lack of formal teacher evaluation this year. It is important to know that numerical scores are assigned to teachers each year, with five being the highest.

> It angered me for one reason. Because I've always done very well on my evaluation, I'm a Level 5. I'm a great teacher, the State thinks I'm fabulous. My formal observation that I did this year was a science lesson. When I say that I did well, I was like reading my observation when it was over with. I'm like holy moly, holy moly. This is phenomenal. Oh my gosh, oh my gosh, this is amazing. That amazing observation now counts for nothing. Counts for nothing. And I would have scored like beaucoup, up there.

This teacher prides herself on her high evaluation scores annually and was disappointed that there would be none issued by the state this year. This rating is tied to financial incentives as well. Without test scores, the normalized method of measuring success, both intrinsically and extrinsically, had been removed.

The difference in attention to student level or teacher level may also involve the school grade for both of these schools. Palm View is a traditionally "A" rated school. There may be less anxiety about the immediate impacts of missing face-to-face teaching on student performance at Palm View. Southern Pine is, at least for the last few years, a "C" rated school with a large number of English for speakers of other languages. Attention to student achievement and growth is helpful in them maintaining their "C" grade. These teachers may be much more concerned about student performance and the "gap" that Teacher 3 mentioned, especially with students missing live interactions with teachers. As Teacher 4 said, they are "5 months behind."

A CLOSER LOOK

The text represented the views of four teachers, trying to teach while caught up in a world-wide pandemic and a state-wide shut down. The above analysis illustrates several themes that emerged from the text. These included a sense of being overwhelmed, a reliance on the PLC structure as a place to turn for support, adapting and supplementing the district supplied curriculum, and the cancelling of state-wide, high-stakes student testing and subsequent teacher evaluation.

This portion will take a closer look at the text through a discourse analysis. Fairclough (1992) examines "language as a form of social practice" (p. 63). It is only by examining language as it sits within context that we can seek understanding. Gee (2005) writes:

> Discourse analysis is always a movement from content to language and language to content. We gain information about a context in which a piece of language has been used and use this information to form hypotheses about what the piece of language means and is doing. (p. 14)

District Curriculum

As the teachers spoke, their responses were influenced by the greater discourse practice. It is in this dimension that effects of power become illuminated. Earlier it was noted that the school district did not overtly state that the provided curriculum was required. Yet all of the teachers interviewed made every attempt to utilize this curriculum. They adapted, and supplemented, but their use of the district curriculum remained. This curriculum is aligned with the state standards for students and has been developed to purposefully address those standards. The district curriculum is utilized in every school throughout the district, and is the only endorsed curriculum for teachers. However, during the school closure, teachers were allowed some flexibility to meet the needs of their students. Teacher 1 stated:

> We modified it some,
> like we used,
> we incorporated a weekly student periodical.

Another stated, that as they discussed in their team, the district curriculum was:

> It was very much,
> this is the plan,
> this is the general plan,
> it's gonna work for most of you, you know,
> I guess we can adapt from there.

Recall that Teacher 3 felt like

> So we took whatever was in the packet
> and we just transformed it onto Brightly

Even when working to simplify the online curriculum for their students they opted to simply use a different version of the district provided curriculum. Teacher 4 relied on the district curriculum:

> I kind of followed what the district gave us
> And I followed what we did in class
> So if we had reading in the morning I would do
> Reading in the morning

Teachers were willing to adapt and supplement, but around what was perceived to be the required curriculum. Teachers added additional resources, made videos for YouTube, and sent home materials for students. In every case, books sent home to students included PrepareU workbooks, adopted by the district. Some made herculean efforts at home visits, and even reported becoming tech support while the computer sat on the hood of the car. None, however, reported any novel teaching strategies or approach to teaching. The efforts were about assisting their students in accessing the district curriculum. Teachers felt, however, that their adaptations were an important addition. Referring to the use of a weekly student periodical, Teacher 1 stated that

> We could embed that into our plans,
> kids could bring that up and they could look at it and use it,

> so we used that as our science and social studies,
> and kind of embedded that and it's not even mentioned in the district's plans.

The teachers interviewed are used to a district mandated curriculum and operating within that curriculum. Their attitude toward use of the curriculum for teaching was no different during the time of school closure. None drifted away from the district curriculum, instead using it as a planning tool and tweaking it to make for a better fit for their students. These teachers all consented to this vision for content and curriculum. As a critical analyst might put it, it was common sense!

Pushing the Envelope

One teacher mentioned "pushing the envelope" on getting a computer signed out to a family.

> At first,
> because it was,
> what was followed by the rules,
> they have to come,
> they have to sign it out,
> right,
> until I pushed the envelope,

Eventually she was allowed to take the computer to the student's house to have the parent sign it out. When asked who she was pushing against, she responded that it was the principal or probably the district. She felt empowered to advocate for the family, but also felt she was pushing hard against the rules put in place by someone above her in the hierarchy that mandated the parent be present at the school to physically sign out the computer. This is an indication of her position in the hierarchy, but also of some measure of empowerment.

PLCs

These teachers relied on the structure of PLCs for support. This structure, while mandated by law, was not described by any teacher as having been mandated during the school closure. Each of these teachers found their way to their PLCs as an initial way in for support. Even from the very beginning, Teacher 1 describes learning about the impending school closure from her teammates (PLC):

there was a lot of
talking with
my teammates
back and forth,
getting information from my teammates and things like that

The PLC provided a means for communication that was easily accessible. Teacher 2 described the quick reliance on PLC team members:

We all kind of got together and
were brainstorming
and we figured out that there was a way,

Teacher 3 quickly mobilized the team to provide materials for their students:

The other thing we also did was, as a group,
there was four teachers, um,
we got book bags from a local grocery store
and we packed bags of materials.

All relied on their PLCs for support. PLCs, while mandated, have become the way of work for teachers. They are mandated by legislation and provide the mechanism for teachers to plan together and evaluate student data in order to make improvement. The presence of this structure proved to be instrumental in allowing teachers to quickly summon the support they needed.

Even a district-level PLC provided an easily accessible source of assistance. Teacher 3 talked in length about the Writing Resource Teacher PLC, and that it was a prime source of help for her. This PLC provided an open forum for any teacher willing to join.

These PLCs were an obvious choice for teachers when seeking support. The structure provided a quick source of support that could then be customized as needed. Teachers utilized this structure for their own benefit, even while maintaining the PLC structure and utilizing the support found to continue the district curriculum.

Comfort From Administrators

These teachers found comfort from their administrators. Each spoke in very gracious terms about their school administrators. The comfort these individuals offered is difficult to minimize. When asked to point to something important that helped them manage, this type of response, from Teacher 1, was typical:

> Somebody
> not being too critical
> of what I was doing.
> "It's okay,
> we're all learning,
> we're all doing the best we can.
> Just do the best you can."

These teachers were truly operating in an environment free from much penalty, except what they created for themselves. They were offered flexibility with the curriculum, a structure in PLCs to provide immediate support, and they were buoyed by their administrators. Taken together, the district provided curriculum, the PLC structure, and a compassionate administration represented some calm in a raging world. Teachers knew the district's way of work regarding curriculum, and they were intimately familiar with the standards underlying it. They were also familiar with the PLC structure, and 7 months into the school year they were familiar with their PLC team members. These teachers knew their administrators, and their role as instructional leaders yielded to simple human compassion. These structures, impacted by legislative mandate and ever-increasing high-stakes accountability, were familiar. This familiarity allowed for some sense of normalcy.

Earlier it was stated that, "Teachers did not feel like an active part of the change effort. They, instead, felt trapped within it." Principals and administrators supported teachers through their kind words and empathy. This did not go without notice.

THE LARGER DISTRICT CONTEXT

Outside the circumstances created by a global pandemic, education exists within a highly politicized world of high-stakes testing. Students are leveled, teachers are leveled, and schools are graded. Students, teachers, school administrators, and even district administrators are all held accountable based on the data produced as a result of statewide standardized testing. Students are penalized for not being "proficient." Teachers are penalized if their students fail to attain proficiency or show growth. Schools are penalized through letter grades. It is within this atmosphere that the teachers interviewed are now experiencing school closures due to a worldwide pandemic.

"They"

These teachers view the district, all of the people at that level making decisions, as a singular entity. These interviewees spoke of "the district" as "they" without attention to specific individuals. "They" were the ones making decisions. "The district" and "they" were terms employed by all of the teachers included in this study. The participants referred to the district as "they" over 50 times, always in the context of something that was being told to them or something they felt they needed to be doing. The following lines illustrate some examples of teachers referring to "they":

1. By the time they made that decision
2. Now that they have moved to Portrait
3. Over spring break is when they officially made the call
4. They kind of pushed it out
5. They offered it
6. They wanted us to click on this
7. If they're closing schools or not

The use of the term "they" in the context of decisions puts "them" in a position of power. "They" made the decision and it is our responsibility to follow. It is important to note that the teachers view themselves as subjects of the district. These teachers view themselves in relation to information and edicts coming from above them in the hierarchy, the "they" the teachers refer to. This seemed very matter-of-fact when inserted into our conversations.

Change in Tone

The tone of these teachers changed dramatically when discussing how this pandemic might be handled moving forward. In that context, "they" and "their" subsequent decisions caused a great amount of frustration and anger. The teachers were all asked if they were better prepared, this time around, if a school closure became necessary.

To understand their responses, it is important to know that distance learning during school closure was based on the Brightly digital platform. This made sense because it was already in use by middle and high school students. It was only a matter of bringing elementary students and teachers on board to have a platform for all students in the district. In the background, however, a new digital platform was in the final stages of approval. This platform was due to roll out at the start of the 2020–2021 school year. This coincided with the introduction of a new superintendent who brought to the district a new curriculum.

As I interviewed teachers, they had before them the prospect of continuing with distance learning, with a new curriculum and a new digital platform. These things were rolling out to teachers through digital communication only, even while new materials were being delivered to their school sites. The introduction of a new platform and new curriculum caused a great amount of anxiety amongst these teachers. Here are some of their comments:

> Now that they have moved to
> Portrait
> and modules and coursework,
> and had they have kept it
> at Brightly
> I could have picked up and said,
> okay, I can do this now.
> But because we went to Portrait
> and there's 45 steps to get to something,
>
> Go back to what they,
> they should never have implemented Portrait.
> Never, ever, ever
> should they have,
> if they bought Portrait,
> this was not the time or the year to roll this out.
> This is not the year to roll out a new curriculum,
> this is not the year to roll out this phonics program.
>
> I mean, I'm not even that comfortable
> doing it myself
> on Portrait,
> how am I supposed to
> do it and then
> push something out to the kids?
>
> To be honest
> It's too much at one time.
> New curriculum
> New way of meeting
> New online
> Platform
> It's too much.
> With the pandemic going on.
>
> It's worse because we had the platform Brightly and we just got the kids
> comfortable on Brightly
> and now we're starting a whole new program.

Clearly these teachers are distraught at the proposition of having to relearn everything. Instead of finding comfort in the systems before them, and their experiences within them, they are angry at having to learn everything all over again. These teachers are also worried about their students, who finally have gotten comfortable with one digital platform and may now have to move to another one. Here, the teachers continue to move forward, but the district does not have their consent. These teachers now feel coerced, and that has resulted in their anger.

CONCLUSIONS AND LIMITATIONS

It's Hard

This analysis began with the statement that teachers did not feel like an active part of the change effort. They, instead, felt trapped within it. In order to cope with a rapidly changing understanding of teaching, they sought support from those closest to them, their PLC team members, their administrative teams, and their family. These teachers did not view this as an opportunity for experimenting with new content and innovative ways of teaching, but as a circumstance that they needed to get through and to survive for both themselves and their students.

These teachers were frustrated over the circumstance of having to teach remotely. They felt as if they were going through the motions at times, struggling to provide something of meaning for their students. They described their frustration:

> It didn't hurt just the kids
> or hurt me
> It hurt me because
> I wasn't able to do the job the parents trusted in me to do
>
> It was all kids and parents teaching themselves.
> It was not me
> technically teaching.
>
> We have to keep it so simple.
> Even though it's just assigning
> and it killed me completely,

This situation presented to teachers was unique. Adopt a new delivery model, along with their students, in an environment with no tangible penalty for failure. Teachers responded as best they could, finding the help they needed from those at least metaphorically closest to them. These four teachers are not anxious to do it all over again. Against the prospect of having to repeat distance learning on a different platform with a new curriculum. Teacher 4 remarked,

Learning a new program and
fooling around
and making mistakes.
I don't have that time.
With the kids.
They're five months behind

As two participants stated, "It's hard."

Given the size of the study, with limits to generalizability, there are lessons here. These teachers work within a hierarchy, in a system typically driven by testing, test results, and data. This was normalcy for them. They all exhibited tremendous resilience by finding the support they needed within the system known to them. They all found a way forward in providing the prescribed curriculum in the very best they could for their students.

The hurdles these teachers faced during the pandemic were vastly different. Palm View students seemingly had all the technology necessary for successful eLearning. Southern Pine students, conversely, had none. While the hurdles were different, the teachers expressed the same reaction. Even with technology a non-issue, the teachers at Palm View struggled to provide meaningful content to their students. Teachers at Southern Pine struggled to provide meaningful content because their students had no access to the technology necessary. All had given it their best, yet none of the teachers were satisfied with their efforts to meet the students' needs.

Opportunities for Future Research

These teachers all showed tremendous resilience in dealing with the near instant switch from brick and mortar to online teaching. While it took a few weeks, they all seemed to find their "groove." None were pleased with their ability to deliver content but were at peace with the fact that they had done their best. Yet when these teachers discovered that they would be moving to a new digital platform, with a new curriculum, it seemed a bridge too far. These interviews all ended with teachers feeling angry and upset about what the future held for them. None were optimistic about their abilities to manage the platform and the curriculum moving forward. Looking forward, how has the organization adjusted to better meet the needs of the teachers? Should the pandemic end, will the teachers adjust to moving back to traditional delivery? What elements of distance learning might remain in place? How will the organization adjust? How will the lack of test scores impact teaching and evaluations? As we begin to receive our vaccines, and as the future begins to include schools filled to capacity with children, it will be interesting to see how teachers, school leaders, and school systems adjust.

REFERENCES

Auerbach, C. F., & Silverstein, L. B. (2003). *Qualitative data: An introduction to coding and analysis.* New York University Press.

Ball, S. J. (2008). *The education debate.* The Policy Press.

Blommaert, J., & Bulcaen, C. (2000). Critical discourse analysis. *Annual Review of Anthropology, 29,* 447–466.

DuFour, R. (2007). Professional learning communities: A bandwagon, and idea with considering, or our best hope for high levels of learning, *Middle School Journal, 39*(1), 4–8.

Fairclough, N. (1992). *Discourse and social change.* Polity Press.

Gee, J. P. (2005). *An introduction to discourse analysis: Theory and method* (2nd ed.). Routledge.

Glesne C. (1999). *Becoming qualitative researchers: An introduction* (2nd ed). Pearson Education.

Hargreaves, A., & Fullan, M. (2012). *Professional capital: Transforming teaching in every school.* Teachers College.

Kanold, T. D. (2011). *The five disciplines of PLC leaders.* Solution Tree.

Neill, S. O. (2018). Three innovations: Promises and perils. *Canadian Journal of Action Research, 19*(3), 73–90.

Richard, L. (2009). *Handling qualitative data* (2nd ed.). Sage Publications.

Rippner, J. A. (2016). *The American policy landscape.* Routledge.

Schensul S. L., Schedsul, J. J., & LeCompte, M. D. (1999). *Essential ethnographic methods: Observations, interviews, and questionnaires.* AltaMira Press.

CHAPTER 6

RADICAL ACCEPTANCE AND EXECUTIVE DECISION-MAKING IN THE AGE OF COVID-19

Susan Cannon
Fielding Graduate University

Ruth Middleton-House
Middleton-House & Company

This chapter integrates research and best practices on crisis decision-making and leadership needs during times of chaos and crisis with organizationally focused adult development theory. It includes data synthesized from interviews with executive leaders in the advertising industry responding to COVID-19. The results will include common themes that emerged in the immediate responses to the crisis, comparing those with leadership and organizational effectiveness in VUCA conditions (volatile, uncertain, complex, and ambiguous). It will highlight some desires for long-term changes to the way work is conceived, accomplished, and managed that are

Crisis, Chaos, and Organizations, pages 147–198

emerging as these executives guide their organizations through this crisis and beyond. The chapter will conclude with recommendations for leadership development drawn from the field of crisis decision-making.

Advertising agencies were chosen as a focus for this chapter due to (a) accessibility and (b) because they are cultural influencers and innovators who have had to draw upon their natural creative skills to innovate as their own industry navigated dramatic change in the previous decade. These particular leaders primarily represent flagship offices in agencies owned by four different publicly traded global holding companies, and one privately held agency. These flagship offices are located on the east coast, west coast, and midwest United States.

The agencies themselves also run offices in different countries, so the leaders manage a global context. They must navigate tensions between a predominantly financial-efficiency focused publicly traded holding company and a more talent-centric people oriented advertising agency culture.

Of the 15 interviewees, 10 are women. That predominance of gender was not by design, but part of an approximately 5-year trend in the advertising industry to promote gender equity and transform the "mad men" stereotype. This is evidenced by (a) the meteoric rise of the TIME'S UP Foundation, which is "committed to transforming the advertising industry and addressing the harassment and discrimination that harms our workspaces and stifles our creative potential" (TIME'S UP Advertising, n.d., para. 2) and (b) the industry's enthusiastic acceptance of The 3% Movement (n.d.) which seeks to increase the percentage of women industry creative directors (creative leaders) from 3% to 50%.

In an interesting twist, six of those senior women leaders had been recently promoted to their positions. Three of them had to take on the COVID-19 crisis within days or weeks of their promotions. This group includes two CEOs, a LatinX flagship office president, a LatinX chief operations officer (COO), a managing director (MD) of the flagship office of one of the most storied agencies in the world; and a chief creative officer (CCO) of one of the most venerable agencies charged with transforming its creative department. An auto company U.S. chief marketing officer (CMO) was promoted in the midst of the COVID-19 crisis.

Prior to COVID-19, in edited volume *Leadership 2050: Critical Challenges, Key Contexts and Emerging Trends*, Cannon et al. (2015) summarized current literature on future trends indicating that leaders across the planet were collectively facing a perfect storm of increasing complexity, accelerating change and near constant uncertainty and ambiguity (pp. 190–191). Among the prominent trends cited were transnational drivers such as sudden global economic disruption and runaway pandemics, which have become reality.

A summary of four recent (pre-COVID-19) global studies on leadership needs for the 21st century (Development Dimensions International & the Conference Board [DDI], 2015; Gitsham, 2009; IBM Corporation, 2010; Leslie, 2009) indicate that the conditions described above exceed the mental and emotional capacity of most leaders today. It points to an urgent need for post-conventional leadership assessment, training and development that disrupts current mental models and assumptions (Brown, 2013; Cannon et al., 2015; Kegan & Lahey, 2009; Rooke & Torbert, 2005).

The DDI's *Global Leadership Forecast* (2015) focused the study on leader readiness for the "VUCA" world, one that is volatile, uncertain, complex, and ambiguous. The term VUCA was first used by the U.S. military to discuss preparedness.

Even in normal times, executive leaders of organizations often face quick make or break and sometimes life or death decisions while they juggle multiple and conflicting priorities. In large, multinational organizations the complexity is staggering. No longer simply the topic of academic or military scenario planning studies, the COVID-19 crisis has provided organizations an immediate bootcamp experience of these transnational change drivers. It is the perfect storm in which they must learn to survive and thrive. Executive leaders are now forced to operate in conditions for which first responders and military personnel are trained (Endsley et al., 2003; Woo et al., 2018).

These leaders, however, may not feel prepared. Bob Johansen, renowned futurist and distinguished fellow with the Institute for the Future (n.d.) in Silicon Valley has focused for more than 30 years helping organizations prepare for and shape the future. In his 12 books on leadership for the future, he brought the acronym VUCA into popular use after learning it at the Army War College where he was a frequent presenter.

In *The New Leadership Literacies: Thriving in a Future of Extreme Disruption and Distributed Everything*, Johansen (2017), describes a massive acceleration of change that has already begun, one in which centralized and decentralized organizations will give way to truly distributed organizations that "have no center, grow from the edges, and cannot be controlled" (p. 1).

According to Johansen (2012), whose 40-year track record of forecast has been quite good (60–80% accuracy), "You cannot control the VUCA world but you can be prepared" (p. 22). He cites immersive learning as one of the best ways to prepare for VUCA environments, for example war gaming or simulations. In essence, the day-to-day world of an advertising executive is a natural VUCA immersive environment. This chapter will show that these executives were able to respond rapidly, performed at a high level and ended their mostly COVID-19 dominated year with results that exceeded their expectations.

METHODS

Data was collected via semi-structured hour-long interviews as well as internal documents and employee surveys, and published information about the leaders and their organizations. The interview question format was informed by Ken Wilber's integral framework, particularly the quadrants element (Duffy, 2020; Wilber, 2011). Quadrants are simply four irreducible perspectives or dimensions of reality that must be consulted to fully understand any issue. These represent the interior and exterior of the individual and the collective, or subjective/intentional; objective/behavioral & body; intersubjective/cultural; interobjective/systems & environment. Interview data was transcribed and coded to sort for themes.

SECTION 1: META-THEMES AND THE VUCA INDEX

COVID-19 thrust leaders across industries and across the globe into a VUCA environment. Abruptly, they were leading through volatility, uncertainty, complexity, and ambiguity. Circumstances previously routine only for first responders became the norm for all.

Throughout interviews with participants in this study were woven seven meta-themes that characterized their response to the VUCA explosion. Their examples demonstrated that they:

- radically accepted a new reality they neither chose nor liked;
- quickly shifted into crisis decision-making;
- balanced the needs of organizational stakeholders (holding company, agency, and clients);
- balanced the business needs of these organizations and the people's needs of their employees;
- aimed high to achieve goals and even surpassed expectations;
- exercised hope (they believed things tomorrow could be better than today, they forged alternate pathways to goals, they addressed obstacles);
- they remained resilient and empathetic in the face of sustained demand and unexpected obstacles; and
- they quickly created top team alignment and systematic communication protocols, while democratically engaging their employees.

These behaviors were consistent with the findings of DDI and The Conference Board (2015) in the VUCA index that codified effective leadership response (pp. 10–11):

1. Anticipate and react to the nature and speed of change.
2. Act decisively without always having clear direction and certainty.
3. Navigate through complexity, chaos, and confusion.
4. Maintain effectiveness despite constant surprises and a lack of predictability.

In the study, less than two-thirds of the more than 13,000 leaders representing over 2,000 organizations in 48 countries said they were either "highly confident" or "very confident" in their ability to meet the four VUCA challenges (DDI & The Conference Board, 2015, pp. 10–11).

Two agency priorities emerged that helped provide internal clarity in the crisis decision-making:

- *people first,* with a heavy emphasis on projecting jobs, caring for mental health, and acting with empathy; and
- *preserve culture,* keeping it creatively vibrant, socially connected, mutually supportive, collaborative, and fun.

These priorities are not surprising given that advertising is a talent-based rather than an asset-based business such as manufacturing or even technology. The product is ideas, not widgets. What was surprising is the degree to which the executives shifted their perspectives and appeared to grow in emotional intelligence (EQ).

These executive leaders were able to draw upon the "change muscle" they have developed responding to accelerating change in their industry. Digitization has been one of the key change drivers. According to Pfeiffer (2020), from the first digital ad that ran in *HotWired* in 1994 for $30,000, the digital ad industry in 2019 has grown to an estimated worth of $333.25 billion. An evolution of brands away from long-term Agency of Record contracts to shorter, fast turn-around project-based work, and the culture of intensive response to harried client demands layer on the need for speed and thinking out of the box. According to independent media consultant Brad Adgate (2020), we will see a long-lasting shift in the way people shop and engage with brands post-pandemic as a result created an opportunity for brands to modernize business models to focus more intently on digital experience and ecommerce strategy.

VUCA Index #1: Anticipate and React to the Nature and Speed of Change

Demonstrating radical acceptance and a quick shift to crisis decision-making, every executive had to shift their entire workforces and themselves from mostly urban high-density offices to working from home in less than a week, in some cases over a weekend. Given the technology and equipment requirements, it was a massive D-day like undertaking on very short notice to meet VUCA Index #1. In order to ensure continuity of their client's businesses—many of whom had expensive TV advertising campaigns that would have to be reworked immediately—executives had to manage frazzled clients and get the stressed and frightened workforce connected and up to speed while attending closely to those employees' safety, family needs, and mental health.

East coast Global Chief Talent Officer Amie Miller recognized a silver lining in the need for speed.

> If we had it to do over again, we would make the same decisions, and would have implemented them faster. The time pressure worked in our favor. Being cornered into making decisions quickly was a good thing. No easy way to do this but throw everyone in the pool at the same time.

The *Global Leadership Forecast* (DDI & The Conference Board, 2015) identified adaptability, flexibility, and decisiveness in the face of a constantly changing environment and under severe stress essential capabilities for agency executives now and in the future. In the case of COVID-19, leaders learned to embrace and be a driver of the change, running toward the danger like a first responder. As east coast flagship agency President Nancy Reyes recounted,

> As a leader, embracing change at this level was a big growth. There has always been change in our company but that was comparatively small. We now embrace change and we will be different, and layer our values over that once it settles. I would have been afraid to drive it this fast and this much before. (personal communication, October 23, 2020)

Sensing the writing on the walls given the global movement of the pandemic, three of the agencies anticipated and had the permission to experiment with trial "work from home" days just before the lockdowns came. Although the test window was relatively tiny, those three felt that it gave them an edge. According to Laura Maness, east coast flagship agency CEO, "We did a 24-hour test, and it was so smooth, we couldn't believe it. We sent out quite a bit of production equipment distributed to different homes to test our ability to create remotely should it ever get to that point. Then everything shut down, we were ahead of the curve" (personal communication, November 14, 2020).

People in the advertising industry often rely on "spidey sense," their colloquial term for the combined EQ skill and IQ skill to intuitively and analytically read clients and situations and pick up weak signals of danger.

Midwestern agency President Craig Conrad leaned into that and started planning early:

> Fortunately, we were sensing we would be impacted sooner than later. Mid to late February we started having serious discussions, if it hits us like other parts of the world, how do we ensure people and business are taken care of ? We put tests and separations in place to test out working from home. Had no idea that it would be 8 months. We didn't even think it would be 8 weeks. (personal communication, October 27, 2020)

For west coast CEO Evin Shutt, the early warning of the pandemic came up with their Singapore office:

> I was worried about our Singapore people, but felt it was in control. It came in waves and when it really hit it was global. We went into operational mode, extreme and tactical. Assess, keep our people safe, and protect them. Understand every business, where is the risk? Do we shut down or not? We work in advertising; it is not worth risking lives. Once we agreed we will all be remote, it was about the health of the business and our people. Couple that with—it was my first week as CEO. (personal communication, October 21, 2020)

Shutt's COO Patricia Rothenberg explained that the office was shut down on a trial basis Tuesday and Wednesday, then reopened on Thursday. The state lockdowns were enforced a day or two later, and the agency had already set up a system for scheduled IT equipment pickups from the office (personal communication, October 14, 2020).

VUCA Index #2: Acting Decisively Without Always Having Clear Direction and Certainty

All the executives reported that they were able, and had to, make decisions in quick succession with little clear direction or certainty. This was in part driven by their people first priority, a phrase that showed up in nearly every interview. In a talent-centered and relationship-focused industry, protecting the welfare of their people served as a powerful driver to make things happen and prioritize in the moment.

Some described having to become "battlefield generals" for their people and "turning fear into action." Others described having to learn to "fly by instruments" without previous practice. Johansen (2017) named one of the leadership literacies for the VUCA future as Voluntary Fear

Engagement. An important aspect of that is turning fear into something positive (p. 29). While Johansen was intending the use of gaming, simulations, and other safely constructed experiences, it makes sense that the less voluntary version would also provide a space for developing and demonstrating that leadership literacy.

The tension of balancing agency needs and holding company created a lack of clear direction and certainty, among other things. In early March, east coast flagship agency President Nancy Reyes sensed acutely that the threat level was high and that she had to get her employees working from home as soon as possible. However, she was constrained by the more conservative approach of her global holding company, which did not formally declare the office shut down until weeks later:

> I was told to calm down, don't be hysterical. While it might have been perceived as an emotional response, I was 100% confident it was the right action. I drove people to go home and not come to the office in the early days. That same emotional response drove me to action during the course of COVID. (personal communication, October 23, 2020)

She ultimately acted decisively but under the duress of resistance from those above her in the hierarchy, and with potential impact to her career. This is an example of acting with hope and heroism/morale courage, an antidote to paralysis in crisis decision-making (Lopez, 2013).

Reyes' CEO Rob Schwartz described another common strategy among the executives for decisive action, assuming the worst case:

> Once we understood how real this was, we had to assume the worst-case scenario, err on the side of extreme caution. Best case scenario, this was likely a stronger flu. Even if we were wrong, we were comfortable with the stigma of being helicopter parents to our people. (personal communication, October 12, 2020)

VUCA Index #3: Navigating Through Complexity, Chaos, and Confusion

The executives demonstrated their ability to navigate the complex, chaotic, and confusing environment. A common strategy was to develop, on the fly, their own versions of *dynamic steering*. This is an emerging agile management practice to constantly adapt and evolve the course in a situation of high uncertainty and rapid change (Robertson, 2015, pp. 129–130). Many common management practices are based on prediction and control-employing action plans, strategies, budgets all trying to evaluate risks and uncertainties to find a singular path. Robertson (2015) uses the metaphor of riding a bicycle, to keep it steady and moving requires continual dynamic input with a tight focus on finding the next concrete action that is workable now. Decisions can be revisited and changed at any time.

As Reyes described it,

> Another way of work has blossomed—just keep making decisions, then another and another. We are not reckless people. Just go ahead, and if we have to course correct make another one. The speed, it almost broke me. But at the end I found more strength in it. (personal communication, October 23, 2020)

Reyes' Executive Director of Talent Hanna Lentz was able to use the pressure of the crisis to upshift her leadership competencies from a rigid, rule-bound approach to a more fluid, flexible nuanced approach that could encompass dynamic steering.

> I tend to be more black and white. Had to let go of that. What is in front of me, how do I make the best decision today, maybe I change it tomorrow, and I have to be ok with that. Rapid, flexible, decision-making. (personal communication, October 12, 2020)

Balancing the business and people's needs, especially in the early days and weeks of the pandemic, required exceptional navigation capabilities. All the executives were acutely respectful of their employees' survival instincts to protect, cocoon, focus on family above all else, get kids online for school, take care of elderly parents, collect masks, toilet paper, food, and other provisions and systems needed for continuity and safety. Midwest President Craig Conrad described his dilemma of dealing with fearful employees before the final client presentation of a major pitch just days before lockdown:

> I had to balance the conflict, giving people room to take care of family and themselves in an unprecedented environment while being at the finish line of a significant piece of business. Winning this business would likely ensure we would not have to take aggressive action with employees, that is, headcount reduction. So those 72–96 hours were really tough. A lot of emotion, a slippery slope. I didn't want to mandate. I had to open people's eyes, not only how important it was for the agency, but for their livelihood and the livelihood of others. It would save jobs. That was really tough. I got yelled at, there were tears, lots of things. (personal communication, October 27, 2020)

In this example Conrad demonstrated *constructive depolarization,* one of Johansen's (2012) 10 leadership literacies for the VUCA World, the ability to calm tense situations where differences dominate and communication has broken down (pp. 109–113). Though typically used to describe situations with divergent cultures, in a complex organization the divergent worldviews of management and workers can and did become amplified under the survival threat to both life and business.

VUCA Index #4: Maintaining Effectiveness Despite Constant Surprises and a Lack of Predictability

After 9 months into the crisis, nearly all the executives surprised themselves with their better than expected creative work quality and business results, fulfilling VUCA index criterion #4. This was accomplished despite working from home, being unable to creatively collaborate in the accustomed fashion and with severe limitations in the ability, for example, to shoot TV spots on location. Despite that, most of the executives could point to what they assessed as an extraordinary body of creative work.

For example, east coast flagship agency CCO Chris Beresford-Hill engaged and collaborated with Director Aaron Stoller to produce a creatively improvised and industry-lauded TV commercial for a global laundry softener brand (McAteer, 2020). To adapt to the pandemic constraints, the work was shot in Stoller's own laundry room using his wife and four sons as cast and crew (Pfeiffer, 2020)

Given the dire business and economic environment in March 2020, all executives were expecting that their yearly financial forecasts would fall quite short in 2020. They prepared for the worst. Again, to their delight and surprise, nearly all were able to maintain most of their revenue, service their clients well, win new business, and project a reasonably healthy 2021 (though not without caveats of who knows what the future holds).

President Nancy Reyes summed up the office-to-home light speed transition that most experienced: "We did not miss a beat. Not a single client project, no delivery was missed because of our transition to remote working" (personal communication, October 23, 2020).

Her CEO Rob Schwartz spoke to an advertising industry key performance indicator, the craft quality and award-winning potential of the resulting creative work. "Super proud of our creative product. We have done some of the best work the agency has ever done" (personal communication, October 12, 2020). West coast flagship agency MD Jess Monsey noted, "Financially we are ending the year and entering Q1 in an astonishingly good place. And people are really happy with the [creative] work" (personal communication, November 2, 2020).

Justine Armour, a newly promoted CCO of a flagship east coast agency recounted,

> We've won pitches, had fun, made extraordinary work, and had a successful year financially—all things considered. Pride comes from a new resilience and having a sense of knowing that every time we get these things like a pandemic, a social justice movement, an election, a merger, people around me getting sick, some resigning—I can handle it. And I moved to a new house! (personal communication, October 23, 2020)

Armour names *resilience*, one of the most commonly cited capabilities that substantially contributed to maintaining effectiveness in an unpredictable situation. The unrelenting wave after wave of unexpected disruptions and chaos-generating situations during 2020 provided an extreme test of resilience. This was especially true for the six newly promoted executives (including two CEOs) who were also dealing with the complexity of climbing the learning curve of their new position with a greatly expanded remit, responsibility, and expectation of visibility, communication, and tone setting. According to Porter et al. (2004), promotion to CEO, even in normal times, typically comes with a host of surprises that test the leader's resiliency. Resilience as a critical leadership skill/capability in a VUCA environment will be further examined in Section 2.

Financially, the agencies finished the year out on a spectrum spanning being able to make everyone "whole," that is, protecting jobs, paying back pay cuts, and returning full pay, paying missed 401k contributions, and awarding year-end bonuses, to holding steady and keeping a financially and creatively healthy organization, though with leaner staff and a slimmed down financial picture. Despite where they landed on the spectrum, the executives expressed surprise and satisfaction at the unexpectedly positive outcome.

Scott Kavanaugh, MD of a major auto brand's U.S. advertising arm integrated within an east coast agency flagship office, recognized that in the VUCA environment his brand could make a major move that would not be possible in normal times. Johansen (2017) speaks of the near future in the VUCA world as a "scramble," where "lots of things that have been stuck will get unstuck" and many creative things will happen (p. 1).

> I was proud of how we stayed calm and led, didn't get flustered, and gathered ourselves. COVID leveled the playing fields with a lot of our competitor brands. It gave us an opportunity to expedite our growth and do things we wouldn't have had the license to do. Everyone was struggling. It gave us permission to reinvent ourselves. Proud we didn't blink, and doubled down on leading the resurgence and brand turn around. (S. Kavanaugh, personal communication, October 27, 2020)

Kavanaugh's auto brand counterpart, newly promoted U.S. CMO Allyson Witherspoon
recounted this:

> I just went. It was outside of my authority but it was needed. We had millions in the marketplace that were going to be wasted. I knew where it was going and I didn't need to wait for Finance. We pulled everything and rebuilt our messaging. We developed, concepted, produced, and launched in 2 days. When we got to an edit, FYI to my chairman. Not waiting for approval meetings. They were struggling with how we communicate with people if they don't come

> into the showroom. We worked with Facebook Live, talked about health and safety protocols, products, service, whatever they want to talk about. Rolled it out nationally. We were the first manufacturer to do that. (personal communication, November 17, 2020).

Kavenaugh and Witherspoon demonstrated the VUCA leadership literacy of *dilemma flipping* (Johansen, 2012, p. 56). This is the ability to take a dilemma, which unlike a problem is not solvable, and turn it into an opportunity. They were also an example of hierarchy flattening with indications of an organization developmental stage shift covered in Section 4.

Communication, both as a leadership capability and as organizational processes developed in the trenches was a critical and multi-faceted common theme for maintaining effectiveness in the face of constant surprises and unpredictability. "The ability to be clear, actionable, sympathetic, optimistic but realistic was an important piece. I focused on how to leave people feeling positive about a call when I really don't know what the future holds" (N. Reyes, personal communication, October 23, 2020). Related are the themes of leadership presence, top team alignment, making close one-on-one and frequent meaningful group connections cited as reasons and strategies for effectiveness covered in Section 2.

Balancing the holding company needs and agency needs was the next level up in the navigation of complexity, chaos, and confusion that the leaders had to navigate, as well as maintaining effectiveness in the VUCA environment. Publicly traded holding company executives are held by stakeholders, and ultimately Wall Street to strict financial targets and the share price that results. Only one of the seven organizations represented in this study is privately held.

The four holding companies did not significantly reduce their initial 2020 requirements for financial performance. However, they did allow a spectrum of flexibility in how the results were produced. The spectrum ranged from leaders receiving permission to do what they assessed as necessary to protect employees' jobs and get remote operations up and running, to restricting ability to hire critical staff, and having to adhere to strict labor metrics that required significant headcount reduction.

According to Amie Miller, in a split role between global chief talent officer of a worldwide collective and chief talent officer of an east coast flagship agency within that collective,

> Our offices around the globe were empowered to do what they needed to do to look out for the safety of employees. Employees were given permission to do what they needed as long as the work could get done. This made us very nimble while focused on the health and safety of employees. If we had tried to do this outside the pandemic it wouldn't have happened. (personal communication, October 19, 2020)

The flip side to these surprisingly positive business results was the human toll. It was generally acknowledged that this was partly due to mastering the learning curve of a pandemic, as well as running an extremely lean staff to accommodate holding company metrics. But whether or not publicly held, or how much autonomy the agency had to make decisions on behalf of their employees, every executive described in detail the pain and unsustainability of fatigue, burnout, loss of joy in work, and the difficulty maintaining a vibrant culture which is core to the success of a creative enterprise.

SECTION 2: LEADERSHIP IN COVID-19

The executives interviewed in this study demonstrated (and sometimes developed under pressure) a consistent set of skills/capabilities, and communication and team alignment strategies that were essential to meeting the VUCA index criteria described in Section 1. These skills/capabilities were both psychological (internal to the leader) and behavioral, or demonstrated outwardly in action. As described in Section 1, skills/capabilities of adaptability, flexibility, and decisiveness were evident and essential for meeting the four elements of the VUCA index, and won't be covered again here.

The key capability/skills identified in the data for individual leaders are:

- leadership presence
- resilience and acceptance of reality
- empathy/EQ

The key group capability/skills included:

- top leadership team alignment;
- communicating and interacting with others with consistency, transparency, and empathy;
- building trust, consensus, and commitment; and
- fostering employee creativity, learning, and innovation.

These key capabilities/skills map significantly to the critical skills identified by the *Global Leadership Forecast 2014|2015* that had the greatest impact on leader preparedness and confidence in addressing the challenges of VUCA (DDI & The Conference Board, 2015, p. 11) were:

- managing and introducing change,
- building consensus and commitment,
- inspiring others toward a challenging future vision, and

- leading across generations (this skill is key to forging a shared purpose despite diverse employee viewpoints and motivations).

Researchers contributing to the same report also developed an expanded *Leadership Agility Index* that included the four VUCA index capabilities used in Section 1 of this chapter, the VUCA critical skills 1 and 3 described above, plus the following leadership agility critical skills (DDI & The Conference Board, 2015, p. 22):

- communicating and interacting with others
- fostering employee creativity and innovation

"Agile organizations possess the ability to anticipate trends, respond to problems and adapt to change—important competitive advantages in a complex world" (DDI & The Conference Board, 2015, p. 23). The research showed that only 18% of the leaders in the study rated highly on the agility index, which is linked to the benefits of shorter time for a new leader to perform, faster company growth, and improved financial performance.

Individual/Self Capabilities

These are capabilities that reside within the leader and can be cultivated with practice and coaching. These were the top three that were described by the leaders that contributed to their ability to successfully navigate the COVID-19 crisis. They were also named by the leaders as desirable capabilities for future leaders they would choose, in addition to flexibility, adaptability, and decisiveness, all of which harmonize in the capability of dynamic steering as discussed in the previous section.

Leadership Presence

When asked about their own psychological, mental, and emotional response to the immediate crisis, the leaders responded with a similar set of capabilities that are combined here as *leadership presence.* In the *Harvard Business Review* article Deconstructing Executive Presence, John Beeson describes leadership presence as the "ability to project mature self-confidence, a sense that you can take control of difficult situations; make tough decisions in a timely way and hold your own with other talented and strong-willed members of the executive team" (Beeson, 2012, para 2). It is also described as "earned authority" that is key to inspiring others (Baldoni, 2010, p. 1) or the ability to command attention and connect authentically with others (Halpern & Lubar, 2003, p. 1).

Leaders found themselves working extremely long days, often 12 hours with few breaks, and due to videoconferencing, visibly in front of more employees at once than they were accustomed to. All eyes were on them, and that any indication of fear or inauthenticity would be amplified and impact trust. They consistently described the need to maintain a calm, cool, measured confidence, to show vulnerability and humility, to be transparent and authentic, empathetic, and have a sense of humor. They also emphasized the importance of being visible and truly present with their employees, which required some retooling on their part given the remote working environment. According to CEO Rob Schwartz,

> As a leader, I was very conscious about projecting calm, measured confidence. I'm a battlefield general, and the fight or flight mechanisms kicked in. It was about fight-mobilizing protocols, letting everyone in leadership know that we need to be very transparent, communicate early and often. We are in it now with a gung ho attitude. (personal communication, October 12, 2020)

The need to show up in a confident, decisive way was balanced with the recognition that people were afraid, that they needed comforting and empathy, moments of levity, and needed to see that their leaders were human. Nancy Reyes cited an important capacity she learned in the crisis was, rather than having to show up as superwoman, being able to "model taking care of yourself, and being vulnerable with people while you are also being strong and confident" (personal communication, October 23, 2020). Many described how important it was to admit publicly that they don't have all the answers yet and that the crisis was taking a toll on them too, bringing employees and leaders together creating a more level playing field. And after battling the triple waves of crises that besieged the west coast, MD Jess Monsey admitted, "It sounds flimsy, but I am proud that I maintained a sense of humor and hope" (personal communication, November 2, 2020).

Justine Armour, only 2 weeks into her job as CCO before the lockdown, emphasized being visible, confident, and authentic as a leader. "I know that when I'm showing up for others, I am authentic and helping them stay motivated and inspired" (personal communication, October 23, 2020) In a book on postmodern women's leadership development, Anderson and Cannon (2016) describe the capacity of "empowered radiant presence," an integration of masculine and feminine capabilities that are grounded, centered, and able to take a clear decisive stand, demonstrating congruence between inside experience and outside expression that makes space for others and encourages their best performance. Rather than performing or controlling, the leader inspires "trust, respect, and cooperation" simply by being their authentic self (p. 143).

In this vein leaders felt compelled to manage their reactivity, to calm themselves, and focus on being truly "present" in the sense of not compulsively multitasking during meetings, but trying to deeply listen. East coast office leader and head of production Lora Schulson noted that the job of a producer is about mitigating risk and managing things that go wrong, and the necessity to be calm on the outside when things get terrible:

> I was as calm and clear as I could possibly be, while still being honest and empathetic. But this was an area I had never navigated, and I was giving guidance on how we would figure this out. Inside I was dying a little bit. (personal communication, December 6, 2020)

Every executive grappled with projecting their presence through a screen and losing the subtle cues of body language and the comfort and intimacy of the physical presence of others. This required skill building of tele-presence. "On the computer, it feels a bit more hostile... eyes peering at you instead of a relaxed communal moment" (P. Rothenberg, personal communication, October 14, 2020). "Reading a room... that idea is not landing, that person has negative body language. I felt a bit that my superpower was taken away from me. I had to figure out how I could play that role and still use those talents but do it through a computer screen" (C. Conrad, personal communication, October 27, 2020).

Empathy

Although empathy was included by all of the leaders as an element of their crisis leadership presence they also elaborated on the need for more development of this critical emotional intelligence competency in themselves and others. Daniel Goleman coined the term "emotional intelligence" aka EQ or EI, with his groundbreaking research in the 1990s. Goleman (2006) describes emotional aptitude as a meta-ability that determines how well one can use other skills they have including raw intellect (p. 31). In particular, he describes empathy as "the fundamental people skill" (p. 37), the capacity to put oneself in another's shoes.

"I am pretty empathetic, but I needed to escalate that," explained CCO Eric Weisberg. "People who had soft skills really thrived. Those who are black and white, hard skill-driven, not so much. You needed to dial those [soft skills] up or learn them if you didn't!" (personal communication, November 9, 2020). Weisberg's office President Craig Conrad mused that he wished he had done a psychology minor. "I'm really trying to understand people, the wave of emotions, putting myself in their shoes" (C. Conrad, personal communication, October 27, 2020). CEO Rob Schwartz claimed his "biggest stretch" in the crisis was empathy. "I see it often on social media, just remember, people are trying to do their best in these trying times. I seem to remember that a lot. Empathy and gratitude" (personal communication, October 12, 2020). MD Scott Kavanaugh noted, "If your EQ is not strong and battle-tested, you would struggle now. Those who do not have faded into the background some, become more isolated. You have to really put yourself out there, be a connector more than otherwise" (personal communication, October 27, 2020.

Resilience

"At the beginning I was thinking how the heck will we do this?! I had to find resilience in myself. This is a team sport, I had to trust that it is our job to guide everybody to win, and we did!" (L. Schulson, personal communication, December 6, 2020). Resilience was one of the most commonly mentioned capabilities in the study, both to draw upon and develop. CCO Eric Weisberg noted, "The thing I learned most that I didn't need in previous jobs was resilience" (personal communication, November 9, 2020). According to the American Psychological Association (2012), psychologists define resilience as the process of adapting well in the face of adversity, trauma, tragedy, threats, or significant sources of stress—such as family and relationship problems, serious health problems, or workplace and financial stressors. The COVID-19 crisis, with the need for executives to support their employees with family issues arising from remote working, brought all of this into play.

Martin Seligman, founder of the field of Positive Psychology at the University of Pennsylvania, correlates resilience with life and professional success. At the request of General George Casey, he designed and delivered the U.S. Army Master Resilience Training course, one of the foundational pillars of the Comprehensive Soldier Fitness program (Reivich et al., 2011; Seligman, 2013). Executives in this study reached their personal limits, then discovered they could bounce back with newfound confidence and ability to handle whatever might come their way. CEO Evin Shutt described how the previous 6 months of dealing with the pandemic raised her pain threshold for disruption.

> I have increased tolerance for what comes next, it has to be pretty bad to get me paralyzed. Hard to imagine what could be worse . . . and then the fires on the west coast!! By the time that happened, it was not paralyzing. Last year it would have been. (personal communication, October 21, 2020)

"I'm glad how I've been stretched, the new pain threshold I have. Not too many things in the job I couldn't handle now. Not too many pressures I feel would be too much" (J. Armour, personal communication, October 23, 2020).

In positive psychology theory, resilience is the opposite of learned helplessness, an element of which is seeing a condition as permanent or constant rather than the more realistic narrative that the crisis is occurring at this time and has an end (Seligman, 2011, para. 5). In the darkest days the executives managed to avoid the learned helplessness trap and embrace the possibility of a changed world. "After we started to realize this wasn't going to be fast, it started to be exhausting. Then knowing it would last, we settled in, we proved we could do it, we can do this forever if we need to" (A. Miller, personal communication, October 19, 2020). MD Jess Monsey mused, "I definitely think I will continue to be resilient, although the wildfires almost broke me. It was the moment where I said to myself—really?" (personal communication, November 2, 2020).

Acceptance of reality. A key builder of resilience is acceptance of reality. In *The Myth of Stress,* Andrew Bernstein (2010) posits that the stress reaction is not caused by an event itself, but how one thinks about, or frames, the event. If one rails against the situation "it shouldn't be this way!" then physiological stress is generated and resilience is reduced. If one accepts the situation, that is, shifting from "I shouldn't have to have to deal with tedious remote collaboration" to "In reality, or at this time, I should because everyone is dealing with a global pandemic..." then the stress is relieved and constructive action can ensue. "I know a lot of people don't like to feel out of control, and the world feels uncertain. You can't change that, you can just change how you respond to it. Not getting swallowed up by the stress of others" (P. Rothenberg, personal communication, October 14, 2020).

One of the biggest challenges for this group of high performing executives, especially for creative leaders, was to confront the expectations, dreams, grand plans, and goals set for the year with the recognition that this crisis could drag on for a long time. The acceptance of the hard reality, letting go of those dreams and reframing expectations to a new definition of success allowed the leaders to psychologically move forward.

> I intuitively knew this pandemic would last a year. Within a week [of lockdown], I was really low. It was hard to drag myself out of bed...Then I was able to accept it...This year was supposed to be a year of amazing things. The greatest struggle was not having a real goal beyond just staying whole as we reoriented and changed plans. In September, we decided ok, focus on these pieces of work, these pitches. Execute them flawlessly, and we will end the year successful. Big unlock for me." (C. Beresford-Hill, personal communication, October 21, 2020)

Another CCO realigned her expectations and looked for the growth opportunity:

> I realized there is only so much you can really achieve. If I try to multitask, be on a call and email, it doesn't work. I have to be focused on the thing at hand. I can only do my best. The opportunity is to figure out how to scale my influence. I am giving myself some room, not expecting to achieve everything I planned for in 2020. (J. Armour, personal communication, October 23, 2020)

Interactive/Team Capabilities

Top Team Alignment

A more conservative midwestern agency dealt with a minority of powerful voices on their senior leadership team that initially challenged the push to work from home. The senior team finally reached consensus, although messaging issues about handling the pandemic persisted. Other agencies reported immediate and nearly full alignment on the need to leave the office and work from home, able to make swift crisis decisions together and to execute the messaging to their agencies. This top team alignment turned out to be an advantage for swiftly responding and adapting work processes to homes and maintaining morale and effectiveness.

CCO Chris Beresford-Hill observed that this smooth alignment was built on the trust and human connection already cultivated in the group:

> Our core leadership team genuinely cares about each other, likes and respects each other. That level of care and mutual respect is the only way you could survive this. We generally disagree very well, with no conscious undermining. Being a tight group, and having each other's backs, means we can right the ship, no weak links. (personal communication, October 21, 2020)

CEO Evin Shutt cited a collaborative leadership style as a driver for alignment. "When I made the call to close the office, they felt collectively part of it, not me handing down a directive" (personal communication, October 21, 2020).

At the tactical level, most senior executive teams met every day at the start of the crisis, creating something of a group command center. For many, these meetings were a source of comfort, a collective coping mechanism to the shock of suddenly leaving their work environment. As the crisis wore on and individuals adapted, the frequency reduced.

Over-Communicating and Interacting With Others With Empathy and Transparency

Communicating and interacting with others is one of the two of the critical skills cited in the *Global Leadership Forecast 2014|2015* for leadership agility. In the COVID-19 response, leaders cited the need to over-communicate, to build new communication skills, to be extremely transparent as well as empathetic in order to build trust, cohesion, and reduce fear. Senior leadership teams held larger and more frequent meetings and video conferencing events as a solution to company messaging and communication, team alignment, combating isolation, and fostering human connection. Weekly all company and departmental leadership meetings for the first few months of the pandemic were common solutions.

CEO Rob Schwartz, a self-described "people person" missed the spontaneity of walking the halls, talking to people, and sharing ideas. He created a weekly hour-long video conferencing practice for 5–7 new hires or existing talent that he dubbed "CEO coffee." This gave him a chance to deepen his relationship with employees at all strata of the organization in a way that was not possible before. "For the CEO coffee, I actually get to meet you, learn where you come from, what you are bringing to the agency. Before COVID-19 I would smile and say hi in the halls" (personal communication, October 12, 2020). Advertising agency leaders tend to be highly skilled communicators, and many expanded their repertoire once the pandemic put them on a war footing. According to Schwartz, "What emerged for me was more of the structures. I am creative by nature and anything with process is alien to me. I like to be in the ocean, see where the waves are and then get on my surfboard" (personal communication, October 12, 2020). Schwartz found himself like a battlefield general carefully structuring his all-agency communications to insure the COVID-19 information void was filled as well as possible, drawing from national, state, and local government sources, then holding company, down to what could be known about the office, ending with stories of people in the agency and gratitude.

According to CEO Barry Lowenthal, "The larger learning around COVID is that we all have to over communicate, especially leaders." He coached his agency to upskill their communications by going beyond face value and proactively probe for better understanding. "Don't assume people are stupid, bad, or misinformed. Assume good intent and ask, ask, ask" (personal communication, October 14, 2020).

One on ones. Leaders consistently found that working from home (WFH) paradoxically opened space for more rapport via one-on-one interaction with employees, particularly direct reports, and clients. MD Jess Monsey noted that ironically, her honest, empathetic and heartfelt nature has come out more in this WFH context and has been appreciated. "I may not be able to program 'fun' but at least I can be authentically very human" (personal communication, November 2, 2020).

President Craig Conrad found he could build better rapport with his direct reports while having his finger on the pulse of client business in a way he hadn't before. He structured his time to meet with all direct reports one-on-one 15 minutes every week, often 30, asking, "What are you focused on this week? How can I help? How are you doing (mental health-wise)? How is the team doing?" (personal communication, October 27, 2020). CCO Chris Beresford-Hill invited every single creative in his agency to a Friday lunch. Each week he would travel to a different borough or suburb and described it as just his desire to stay connected to his team, and from the feedback found, "It means more to people than I had known or planned" (personal communication, October 21, 2020).

Fostering Employee Creativity, Learning, and Innovation

The second of the two critical skills cited in the *Global Leadership Forecast 2014|2015* for leadership agility. This topic is mostly addressed in Section 3, "Resultant Organizational Shifts," as an acceleration of creativity and innovation catalyzed by the crisis. However, fostering employee creativity and innovation also shows up as a distinct and carefully considered leadership skill.

Leaders in a creative industry, selling a product that emerges nonlinearly from the imaginations of artistically talented people, had the challenge of helping their employees maintain a state of mind where they could, in the words of CCO Eric Weisberg, "Find the magic moment of creativity." Creatives in organizations tend to depend on comfortable open relaxed group spaces where teams can ideate together, kick back, be inspired. Being alone in one's basement or bedroom, dealing with concerns of job security, family safety, the election, the mixed messages from national leadership created "a lot of noise in people's minds." Further, early in the pandemic many of the clients pulled back from the more creative work and focused on tactical approaches to get people in the door (personal communication, November 9, 2020).

Leaders focused on keeping close contact with their creatives, giving them permission to take care of themselves, and also giving assignments that would be creatively satisfying so that the creative brain didn't atrophy. For a "maker" these kinds of projects were important in maintaining motivation and "juice" during the grind of fulfilling more tactical needs of clients who were busy pivoting their businesses and trying to survive.

SECTION 3: RESULTANT ORGANIZATIONAL SHIFTS

At this writing, the executives are in the midst of the pandemic, but have just enough information on the vaccines to begin to make some informed judgements about timelines for safely reopening their offices or moving into new ones.

All agree that life will not go back to the way it was in January 2020, and some degree of remote and flex working will persist. The question of degree varies widely, and none have finalized their plans. Questions abound about how to utilize the real estate, design the workspaces, and how much flex time will be allotted and for who, and how to categorize that flex time. Parents of small children? Long commutes? Special needs? Primarily tech and non-client facing? Employee surveys have been conducted about working from home, with one holding company requiring their agency HR departments to call and interview every employee in addition to surveys.

There is general agreement among the executives that creatives, employees making the creative product, are most likely to need to gather in person together to achieve the "creative alchemy" that their work requires. However, based on internal employee surveys, the degree of desire by the creatives themselves varied widely across agencies, from 95% wanting to continue to work from home, to 95% longing to be together in an office environment.

The Stigma of Working From Home "Obliterated" and Degrees of Permanent Flex Time and Remote Working Embraced.

The agencies in this study represent the mainstream in advertising, with management hewing to cultural remnants of organizational scholar Douglas McGregor's (2006) mid-century industrial era "Theory X" beliefs in motivation (Chapter 3, paras. 1–5). Theory X assumes that workers are not inherently self-motivated and trustable, requiring a level of authoritarian oversight and control to achieve objectives. The counter, participative Theory Y assumes that workers are motivated by higher level needs of esteem and self-actualization and given the appropriate conditions and environment will be self-directed and creative in achieving objectives. I use the term "cultural remnants" because advertising agencies are by their nature creative, loose, and depend on a high degree of self-direction compared to more predictable, highly controllable industrial processes that are more characteristic of Theory X management.

Holding companies, which exist to bring order and financial and operational rigor to agencies in order to maximize profit, apply pressure on management to be more controlling.

These Theory X remnants fell on a continuum of a mostly participative management culture that generally allowed working from home as needed, to a hard policy of 5 days a week "butts in seats" unless traveling for work, with rare exceptions. In the case of the more relaxed and allowing culture, or the rare policy exception, even executives who had been working part time from home pre-COVID-19 felt the subtle pressure and stigma that they were assumed to be taking it easy and that joining a meeting by videoconference or conference phone was substandard participation. They also experienced difficulty joining robustly in the conversation, felt unseen, excluded, and treated as an annoyance.

The COVID-19 experience of forced adaptation to remote working catalyzed a dramatic shift in management beliefs, though more at the agency level than the holding company. "If there was ever a fear and judgment around working from home, the stigma is gone. You're not allowed to say, 'Oh that person is working from home they are mailing it in.' Imagine how much more future-facing the organization can be if there is no stigma around that" (N. Reyes, personal communication, October 23, 2020). As a result, Reyes is actively planning to include not only flex time but "offshoring" in her 2021 objectives, to expand the full-time recruiting pool at her flagship east coast downtown agency to employees from across the country and around the world. A working parent with a long public transportation commute from the suburbs into the city, she also recognizes the productivity and work–life balance benefits of flex time, spending 3–4 days in the office focused on key meetings and 1–2 days at home with more opportunity to focus, think, and more effectively manage family issues.

Craig Conrad, president of a more traditionally managed midwestern agency expressed the classic Theory X-Y belief system contrast:

> I was more on the conservative side on the issue of flex time. I believed if you are not in the office you are not truly working. This COVID-19 experience opened my eyes—we are all big boys and girls. People, if left to their own devices, will not be screwing around. Small asterisk to that, we had no alternative. But I found that even as things slowly crept back to normalcy, people are responsible, getting their work done. I am a convert. So when we are back in the office, I am looking at flex time. (personal communication, October 27, 2020)

CEO Barry Lowenthal, who had been a stickler for the dress code in his company, noted that the COVID-19 response created a shift in his judgments of value from external perception to the actual results produced. "I used to say suit up to show up, show that you matter, that you have succeeded. Now it doesn't matter how you are dressed. It is the report you deliver" (personal communication, October 14, 2020). A Theory X leader is more inclined to judge and control-based on the visible perception of productivity and success—butts in seats, hours at the office, versus Theory Y focused on successful final results without needing to control how the employee got there.

Even without the overt stigma, Hanna Lentz, executive director of talent for an east coast flagship office voiced a common concern about the potential for a flex time policy to adversely impact careers, especially for working mothers who are likely to choose it. "What hallway conversations and spontaneous meetings will they be left out of? This keeps me up at night. How do we make it an equitable experience?" (personal communication, October 12, 2020)

Flattening of Hierarchy, Empowerment of Employees

Hand in hand with embracing a more democratic Theory Y-ish management perspective is a general shift, again on a continuum, toward a flattening of hierarchy and the empowerment of lower-level employees. For the most part this was precipitated by sheer necessity given the lean staffing and high volume of work that had to be handled. However, a common thorny issue in agency life is who gets to lead or direct the creative work, versus simply executing someone else's instructions. Creative departments, which are the heart of an advertising agency, are highly stratified by the perception of each creative's talent. Opportunities to lead the work often fall to a select few who show exceptional talent early. Later bloomers may not get much practice or get few assignments on accounts that have high potential for "creative opportunity," that is, resulting in work they can display in their portfolio/reel. Good creative opportunities beget more opportunities for the few, resulting in a catch-22 where many are relegated to a lower tier career and remain underdeveloped.

The pandemic appears to be a disruptive force in this quasi-feudal system, allowing a wider distribution of opportunity to engage in higher level thinking and making. CCO Justine Armour observed that "everyone is stepping up a level taking on more responsibility. It's impossible to stay deep on the breadth of things to manage—I had to trust people and be choiceful about my words and encouragement. Let the rest fall as it may" (personal communication, October 23, 2020).

MD Jess Monsey noted as did others, that most employees (not just creatives) were excited about the concept of more people getting an opportunity to lead things appropriate to their level (personal communication, November 2, 2020). This suggests a perspective shift beyond the necessity born of a shortage of hands, toward a more egalitarian mindset. A common theme was not just employees being empowered directly by their bosses, but employees taking initiative and assuming responsibility beyond their current job requirements on top of the higher degree of self-management the pandemic was driving. Agency executives for the most part embraced and facilitated this unprecedented sharing of power. "At the first couple agency meetings, leaders would get teary—it was incredible what people were doing and achieving, and how many people were going out of their way to make sure no ball was dropped" (A. Miller, personal communication, October 19, 2020).

Collective caring. A quality of care and caring for each other, not letting anyone down, emerged as the hierarchy relaxed. President Nancy Reyes described with wonder how employees spontaneously looked after each other, to the side (peers), below (less senior), above (their managers), and beyond (the clients; personal communication, October 23, 2020). President Craig Conrad observed, "People are rallying together to help fellow employees and clients. Now more than ever people are jumping in, chipping in, across a number of levels" (personal communication, October 27, 2020)

Building trust, consensus, and commitment. Employee initiative and collective caring were accelerated by the social justice crisis that exploded in late May 2020. Although it is not the focus of this chapter, agency leaders found it almost impossible to disentangle the unprecedented leadership and organizational challenge posed by COVID-19 from the racial justice movements that erupted within their organizations within 2 months of the lockdown. The cultural/political values within the agencies in this study tend to lean progressive, and most already had nascent or ongoing diversity, equity, and inclusion (DEI) initiatives. These became supercharged by a surge of employee activism, made more intense, raw, and emotional as working from home illuminated the socioeconomic divide inside the organization itself.

Agency leaders responded quickly, and with soul-searching. CEO Laura Maness explained,

> The health crisis was the catalyst to create the space, the rewiring, to prepare for the social justice movement. Interviewing our Black employees and understanding how isolating it is—and I had been beating my chest talking about "We are a family," and not realizing how offensive that was to many. (personal communication, November 14, 2020)

Using the remote working platforms that had been activated for the COVID-19 response, leaders were able to swiftly form democratic panels and groups to hear employees out and support employee initiatives. Employees self-organized to volunteer for, or formed, employee resources groups (ERGs) to develop DEI action plans for their agency's response. Emergent leaders (versus formally assigned leaders) were recognized and gained followership in various groups (Northouse, 2019, p. 50).

Accelerated Learning and Innovation

Related to the loosening and flattening of the hierarchy was an acceleration of learning and innovation across the board, embraced with gusto. "From an organizational standpoint, we've been scrappier and faster and craftier. People are really noticing it, saying things feel different in a good way. We are experimenting more, given permission to do things differently, there is less hierarchy" (J. Monsey, personal communication, November 2, 2020). President Nancy Reyes observed that her organization was able to harness the advertising industry's natural strengths of creativity, problem-solving, and collaboration in a way it had never done before (personal communication, October 23, 2020). Larry Clark (2020), MD, global learning solutions, at Harvard Business Publishing Corporate Learning, identified four key shifts that occur during a crisis that foster the conditions for new thinking and doing: uniting around a purpose, seeing the system differently, unfreezing the organization, and creating a bias toward action. During the COVID-19 response, all of these shifts were evident across the agencies, which tend to have an innate bias toward action even in normal times.

Reyes explained that the crisis had given the organization an opportunity to examine things they should be doing anyway such as flexible work and forced them to become less afraid of change. "We had no choice. That drives a spirit of let's embrace it, let's slay because the conditions are what they are. Instead of lamenting, it inspired more action and creativity-breakdown to breakthrough" (personal communication, October 23, 2020).

Evin Shutt, a newly minted CEO, found that the crisis accelerated her climb up the learning curve of this top role.

> I think, looking back, how close I was able to get to our business and so quickly on every single piece of business and every office. It would have taken me a year in the role under normal circumstances. Given the dynamics of a global agency I might not ever have gotten that deep. (personal communication, October 21, 2020)

Practically overnight, each agency was forced to reinvent the creative development and production of their product/service to accommodate working from home, social distancing, and limitations on travel. Beyond the technical challenges of managing, for example, an overseas shoot by Zoom video conferencing, or handling the disruption of a celebrity actor testing positive, the characteristically loose, spontaneous, and sometimes wasteful agency cultures became more focused, efficient and planful. As Head of Production Lora Schulson explained,

> A lot of our transactions and decisions used to be made in hallways, at watering holes. Now we have to be more focused and intentional with every exchange, set up a call to talk it through. Everyone in the company, especially producers and business affairs, had to do two things—push the limits of technology and up their project management skills by ten times. (personal communication, December 6, 2020)

Hyper-Collaboration

The *Global Leadership Forecast* (DDI & The Conference Board, 2018) focused on "digital-era" leadership and the performance advantage that digital-ready leaders bring. The pandemic basically forced executives in this study to leap ahead in this domain. Their responses catalyzed the potential for *hyper-collaboration*, or the capability to work relentlessly to break down silos and get people working together to solve customer's and organization's issues and cited as one of the strongest drivers of the performance advantage (pp. 14–15). With nearly everyone working by video conference and overseas travel limited, agencies connected within a holding company network or collective began to see the system differently. They discovered new synergies and efficiencies working directly with sister agencies to draw upon expertise, resources, and talent in other parts of the country and world.

Factors Impacting Shift Sustainability

Fatigue and burnout. The most universal complaint of the leaders is that they, and all their employees, have never been this exhausted and fatigued. The nature of their client-centric, often collaborative, service-based work translates into the energetic drain and physical and psychic strain of back-to-back meetings with clients, vendors, and colleagues without friendly banter and walks between meetings. Over the past 5 years, deadlines have become shorter and client budgets tighter. The working environment was already extremely fast paced and stressful, replete with unexpected changes and pivots.

> Fatigue, the one thing I have had to manage that I didn't before. I am relatively inexhaustible. But the Zoom fatigue, 8:00 a.m. to 8:00 p.m. My eyes, my brain, my ass are tired. I'm getting better at doing what I need to relieve it, like scheduling breaks to walk the dog. Still hard. (E. Weisberg, personal communication, November 9, 2020)

Pre-COVID-19, every organization's top team had to delicately balance the demand for profitability with the demand for keeping and maintaining top talent in a relationship-based, talent-centric industry. All except one executive in this study leads an organization owned by holding companies with stock price demands that in turn puts pressure on agency labor costs. The holding companies as of this writing appear to be unwilling to relent on this point due to worldwide economic uncertainty. The result has been attrition of the workforce, and with hiring freezes or limitations, leaving bare bones staff working extraordinary hours, including weekends, some for stretches of months on end. Employee burnout is universally cited as a top problematic result of the pandemic, with the leaders themselves speaking of "getting close to my breaking point," "nearly cracking," and seeking out therapists. The relentless waves of crises demanding leadership response—the Black Lives Matter, George Floyd protests and general civil unrest amplified the discomfort. West coast interviewees reported that the wildfires added an almost unbearable degree of physical, mental, and emotional pain. The orange ash filled air was inescapable, and the threat to the security of home and family with potential evacuation gave life an almost war-like feel.

An executive in one of the agencies (not interviewed directly for this chapter) recognized the physical and mental signs of his slide into a nervous breakdown. He was able to get psychiatric help and a reduced schedule before he had to be hospitalized. This was facilitated by his leadership team colleagues who volunteered to take over some of his workload and professed their care for him as a human being, encouraging him to take care of himself.

Loss of joy. Work at an advertising agency is demanding and intense but also highly social. Similar to the entertainment industry, one of the main attractors to it is the side benefit of fun, travel, glamour, and socializing with interesting, talented, and sometimes famous people.

With COVID-19 the counterbalances to the tough slog are gone.

> We used to film a giant campaign in an interesting place, eat a crazy dinner, bond on the road. Now to shoot in Europe, you're on Zoom from 1:00 a.m. to 9:00 p.m., getting comments, jumping back to the main camera feed. One team shot for 5 days in Kiev, normally the experience of your life. One guy told me that at the end he burst out crying; he felt so sad. Nobody has enjoyed it the way they used to. There used to be these pots of gold at the end of the rainbow. This is no longer magical. (C. Beresford-Hill, personal communication, October 21, 2020)

Maintaining a vibrant and "sticky" culture remotely. While this surfaced as a top priority across agencies and significant energy and time was invested to accomplish it, no one truly cracked the code to their satisfaction. The nature and appeal of the company culture is a powerful talent magnet, and a "sticky" culture means that top talent will stay and attract others, which has an immediate impact on the product and service that the agency provides. Attempts to facilitate an online replication of agency rituals with employees tired of staring at screens often fell flat. "Online happy hours are not fun! So awkward and weird, only one person can talk at a time" (H. Lentz, personal communication, October 12, 2020).

Coping mechanisms. The leaders for the most part had healthy coping mechanisms. Taking breaks, moving the body, walking in nature, gardening, meditation and yoga, Peloton, mountain biking, trying to eat healthy meals and snacks. They learned to set boundaries on their time, protecting weekends and family time as much as possible. Family time was a refuge for many. With their extreme workloads and exhaustion of screens no one seemed to have time for drinking too much, baking, or binge watching TV.

The coping mechanisms notwithstanding, fatigue, burnout, and loss of job are threats to the sustainability of the healthy and positive organizational shifts won to date in the battle with COVID-19.

SECTION 4: LONG TERM AND DEVELOPMENTAL ORGANIZATIONAL IMPLICATIONS

Leaders expressed general acceptance, whether they liked it or not, that where and how they work, the nature of their culture and the capabilities of employees they will seek to attract will be permanently changed. COVID-19 instigated a prolonged VUCA world experience and the changes wrought by that will likely persist in some form for years. Yet the final outcome in terms of organizational change is TBD—leaders say, "We are creating the road as we walk it." "When will the economy open up? No clear guide yet. A constant reminder, we are creating the new normal now. With the different generations in our company and the ability to think about what the culture of our company looks like in this new normal, it is exciting but daunting" (E. Schutt, personal communication, October 21, 2020).

They are enticed by the possibilities that open up when old silos collapse and the boundaries of time and space become malleable. Their surprising effectiveness in the face of chaos and uncertainty was the result of experimenting with remote working and pushing the limits of the tools and processes and their own psyches. As geographical limitations dissolve, workplace anyplace, outsourcing to global centers of excellence, offshoring, or sourcing talent anywhere—the leap in potential effectiveness is now tantalizing.

The primary constraints cited for these shifts becoming permanent were *ourselves*, reverting to old muscle memory, and the *holding companies* that would be resistant to reshaping the offices, real estate, and policies to support permanent remote and hybrid working.

Desirable competencies for future employees, ones that could thrive in a VUCA environment included flexibility, adaptability, resilience, tele-presence, empathy, and self-management. "Creatives are not inherently organized individuals. To be alone and in charge of your own schedule and deliverables is hard. It is a skill set of responsibility they've had to develop" (E. Weisberg, personal communication, November 9, 2020). Self-management refers not only to self but to the team context. "If you have to get on Zoom with your kid, do it but manage your workflow. You need to ensure that others on the team are not disproportionately affected. Just because you are a parent and have kids in school virtually doesn't mean that the 26-year-old on your team should be working 15 hours a day while you are working 4" (C. Conrad, personal communication, October 27, 2020). "Resilience, and the ability to persevere. It does feel like a grind, but we need someone who can roll with it, bounce back, be flexible and resilient—those are the people who will be successful out of this" (H. Lentz, personal communication, October 12, 2020).

CEO Rob Schwartz observed that the new normal will include the importance of maintaining culture through tele-presence, where one cannot rely on the conventional tropes of culture such as physical space:

> We seem to be transporting our culture in this tele-presence world. Interesting learning from Judaism. Throughout history, Jews were expelled from various and sundry cities and countries. They still manage to stay together. Someone referred to it as a "pop up religion." It survives because it is transportable through the rituals. When you get 10 people together they can hear and see it. That is enough to keep a culture together for over 5,000 years in extreme difficulty. (personal communication, October 12, 2020)

Developmental Stage Shift From Modern to Post-Modern. Will That Be Permanent?

A key conclusion of this study is that the agencies' response was also suggestive of a developmental stage shift of the organization and leadership, a mindset transformation in the direction of more complexity and nuance, allowing for the quick emergence of the capabilities/skills described in Sections 2 and 3.

The Developmental Perspective

Historically, whenever the pressures of "life conditions," or times of stress and constraint, consistently exceed the ability of humans to meet existential challenges, a new and more complex stage of culture and a corresponding advanced stage of adult maturity have emerged. The global COVID-19 crisis, which to this writing has extended nearly a year and has reshaped how humans work, live, transact, learn, worship, and embrace a digital life, has the earmarks of a life condition that is catalyzing a developmental shift in leaders, organizations, and potentially societies. One dispiriting trend for the mostly urban workforce in this study, is that many major cities such as New York, Los Angeles, Paris, Rome, and London have become hollowed out ghost versions of their former selves. In *Ten Lessons for a Post-Pandemic World,* acclaimed journalist, political commentator and author Fareed Zakaria (2020) noted that for centuries denizens of major cities have abandoned their homes in times of trouble, yet the cities come back transformed (p. 126). In particular, the Italian city-state of Florence which lost half its population during the Middle Ages to the bubonic plague, recovered and launched the Renaissance, setting the stage for the emergence of the modern industrial-scientific stage of cultural development.

The leadership and organizational development perspective taken in this section is grounded in constructive-developmental psychology (Brown, 2011, pp. 10–11) with a corollary organizational and cultural pattern. Individuals evolve through times of change or stability to stages of greater complexity and capacity. The interpretations, and the frameworks or "constructs" individuals use to make sense of what is happening, become more complex. Growth occurs in an identifiable sequence of stages from birth through adulthood, often likened to an ever-widening spiral (Cook-Greuter & Soulen, 2007, p. 183). Each later stage is "more differentiated, integrated, flexible and capable of optionally functioning in a rapidly changing and complexifying world" (Cook-Greuter & Soulen, 2007, p. 184), and most importantly, can be "encouraged and facilitated by appropriate support and challenge" (p. 184).

In other words, adult psychological capacity or "ego maturity" is developed in a stage progression—if the appropriate conditions are created.

Scholar-practitioners in the field of leadership development have defined ego maturity stages of combined cognitive-affective-behavioral growth using accurately measurable, statistically verified instruments (Cook-Greuter, 2000, 2004, 2014; Rooke, 2001; Rooke & Torbert, 1998, 1999, 2005).

Relationship Between Leadership, Cultural, and Organizational Stages of Development

The stages of a leader's growth have a direct correlation, and thereby a natural fit, with stages of organizational and cultural evolution. As shown in Table 6.1, a corresponding new techno-economic era encompassing a wider span of social organization and a new leadership paradigm has resulted (Anderson & Cannon, 2016, p. 23; Cannon et al., 2015, p. 193). Developmentalists generally agree that approximately five or six such cultural stages have emerged and are still in existence in various parts of the world (Beck & Cowan, 1996; Gebser, 1985; McIntosh, 2007; Wilber, 1996).

TABLE 6.1 Cultural and Leadership Stage Development Corollaries

Cultural Stage[a]	Techno-Economic Era	Social Organization	Adult Development Stage[b]	Leader Type Example[c]
Archaic	Hunting & Foraging	Clans	Symbiotic	Clan Wo/Man
Tribal	Horticultural	Tribes/Villages	Impulsive	Chieftain
Warrior	Early Agricultural	City-State Empires	Opportunist/ Egocentric	Emperor/ Dictator
Traditional	Late Agricultural	Kingdoms	Conformist/ Diplomat	Monarch
Modern	Industrial-Scientific	Nation-States	Expert and Achiever	Executive
Postmodern Networks	Informational	Virtual Transnational	Individualist/ Pluralist	Co-Leader/ Servant Leader
Integral (emerging)	(post-informational—emerging)	(global emerging)	Strategist/ Integral	Meta-System Transformer

[a] See McIntosh (2007)

[b] See Cook-Greuter (2014) and Rooke & Torbert (2005); the leading edge stage of adult maturity for that stage of culture; one of a variety of interchangeable terms used by developmentalists to designate that stage.

[c] These leader examples are representative of the leadership paradigm that emerged at the corresponding cultural stage, not the only kind of leader at that stage. No clear leader type existed at the Clan stage, though informal leadership would be taken by a particular Man or Woman given the existing conditions.

In a webinar on the transformative potentials of the pandemic, renowned Harvard developmental psychologist Robert Kegan (2020) observed that the amount of focused urgent collective attention on this crisis across the globe and for months, has generated enormous energy with the potential to lead to an "advance for the species." He compared this "shock to the system" to the experience of the bubonic plague in Europe that "broke the spell" of the divine right of a narrow class of nobles to rule over the many eking out a bare subsistence. Serfs observed that nobles died just as easily as they did, and according to Kegan, activating a consciousness shift that led to the emergence of a middle class and ultimately the end of the dark ages (minutes 7.00–10.15).

In *Reinventing Organizations*, Frederick Laloux's (2014) research at the nexus of organizational and adult development succinctly describes the unfolding of these stage changes and their corollary leadership. Emerging in the modern industrial scientific techno-economic era, the achiever stage is characterized by materialism, scientific rationality, individuality, fierce drive for success (material and status), and a hierarchy grounded in meritocracy and accountability, and an embrace of constant improvement and innovation. That prevailing worldview perceives the organization metaphorically as a machine and thus can value profit and task over people. The flowering of the achiever paradigm has manifested extraordinary levels of prosperity, well-being, and freedom in an historically short time period, and is currently the dominant worldview of global business.

Agencies, leaders, and holding companies in this study, prior to COVID-19, were mostly grounded in the achiever development stage (holding companies more so than agencies). However, the agencies and their leaders had already expanded their developmental leading edge, moving at least one foot into the postmodern information era's pluralist stage. As a result of the 2020 pandemic shock, all of the agencies made a significant move in the direction of postmodern pluralist.

All developmental stages have healthy characteristics as well as unhealthy or shadow downsides. The pluralistic worldview seeks to cure perceived insensitive, shallow, and greedy downsides of the achiever stage. This paradigm emerged in a significant way in industrialized western countries during the cultural revolutions of the 1960s and 1970s and has yet to become the dominant mindset or worldview on the planet. Pluralistic is more collectively oriented, egalitarian and flat, humanistic and emotionally sensitive. It values collaboration, consensus, diversity, and inclusion, but can value relationships above outcomes. Pluralistic "insists that leadership should be in service of those they lead . . . it is generous, empathetic, and attentive to others" (Laloux, 2014, Chapter 1.1, Pluralistic-Green paradigm, para. 8). The metaphor is organization as family. Whereas the Achiever paradigm is global, the Pluralist paradigm is planetary, caring for the environment and the beings on the planet. The agency priorities of people first and preserve culture; key leadership skills of empathy, collaboration, transparency, flattening of hierarchy and empowerment of employees; and the considerable focus on collaborative diversity, equity, and inclusion initiatives in the midst of the pandemic give evidence of this developmental move.

This outcome is surprising because the economic existential threat would more likely trigger a regression, a doubling down on achiever hyper-rational, hierarchical, and machine-like drive for success despite the human cost. Laloux notes that pluralist is a powerful paradigm for breaking down old structures but is idealistic and often less effective at formulating practical alternatives. However, the meta-themes of balancing business and people needs, as well as organizational stakeholder needs (holding company, agency, and clients) speak to the ability of the agencies to simultaneously hold achiever and pluralist values, or to "transcend and include" the best of both (Wilber, 2011, p. 25).

Pluralist is recognized as a transition stage into the emerging integral era and the meta-systemic strategist leader most capable of managing a VUCA environment (Brown, 2013; Cannon et al., 2015; Cook-Greuter, 2014; Rooke & Torbert, 2005). Cannon et al. (2015) notes that current leadership development practices are not effective at supporting or developing strategist level leaders able to navigate the future because they mostly focus on horizontal skill development at the same level rather than vertical development that creates an upshift in level (p. 196). One of the keys to vertical development is to engage in ongoing practices, trying out new and sometimes uncomfortable behavior and ways of thinking in order to catalyze a neural rewiring or upshift

(Brown, 2013, p. 16; Cannon et al., 2015, p. 59). This will be discussed in more detail in Section 6.

SECTION 5: GETTING VUCA-READY: PRACTICAL RECOMMENDATIONS FOR LEADERSHIP DEVELOPMENT

When the environment outside an organization shifts, people and systems within successful organizations shift to accommodate. The executive leaders who participated in our study shifted the way they thought, the way they behaved, the way they strategized, and the way they viewed the world. Teams and larger groups followed their lead. As a result, whole organizations shifted to succeed under circumstances that would have otherwise stymied them.

In this section we review the shifts by leaders and the shifts by teams that enabled success. We augment each one with a tip from the literature that can help you and your teams make the same shifts yourselves.

As an Individual Leader

In the Age of COVID-19, established ways of being and doing have been upended. The emotional and physical demands are dramatic. To help your organization succeed, you may need to change the way you think, the way you behave, the way they strategize, and the way you view the world. Best practices from our interviewees and from other research can help you...

- radically accept a new reality that you maybe did not choose and do not like;
- quickly shift into crisis decision-making;
- balance the needs of organizational stakeholders (your holding company's, your own agency's, and your client's);
- balance the business needs of these organizations and the people needs of your employees;
- aim high to achieve goals;
- exercise hope (believe things tomorrow could be better than today, forge alternate pathways to goals, address obstacles); and
- remain resilient in the face of sustained demand and unexpected obstacles.

Radically Accept a New Reality You Did Not Choose and Do Not Like

> I intuitively knew this pandemic would last a year. Within a week [of lockdown], I was really low. It was hard to drag myself out of bed...Then I was able to accept it...This year was supposed to be a year of amazing things. The greatest struggle was not having a real goal beyond just staying whole as we reoriented and changed plans. In September, we decided "OK," focus on these pieces of work, these pitches. Execute them flawlessly, and we will end the year successful. Big unlock for me. (C. Beresford-Hill, personal communication, October 21, 2020)

Amanda Ripley, an investigative journalist, interviewed survivors of disasters like 911 and Hurricane Katrina to determine what survivors did differently from those who were lost. She concluded there is a *survival arc*: disbelief, deliberation, and action. A person's choices at each of these phases along the arc enhanced or diminished her likelihood of survival (Ripley, 2008, p. xvi).

Denial was a more frequent reaction than panic. And it was persistent—even in the face of overwhelming evidence that pointed to risks. The resulting delay was often deadly. Ripley (2008) concluded that a person's risk was not dependent on the traditional calculation:

$$\text{Risk} = \text{Probability} \times \text{Consequence}$$

Instead, a person's risk could be better calculated if the dread factor were included:

$$\text{Risk} = \text{Probability} \times \text{Consequence} \times \text{Dread/Optimism}$$

(Ripley, 2008, p. 32)

Dread, in turn, can be calculated in this way:

$$\text{Dread} = \text{Uncontrollability} + \text{Unfamiliarity} + \text{Suffering} + \text{Scale of Destruction} + \text{Unfairness}$$

(Ripley, 2008, p. 33)

Dread increases the risk of denial and delay. Optimism reduces the risk of denial and delay. *Hope* now has a technical definition which includes a sense of agency. Not only does a person think the future will be better than today, she also believes she will have an active role in making it better.

Accelerate your survival arc. First, address the dread head on so you can move more quickly through deliberation to mindful action. Formulate your own dread calculation. Then take a closer look at it. Is the dread actually based on the current situation or on some past fear or failure? Is the dread that feeds your denial protecting you from reliving some earlier hurt? That was then and this is now. You are more knowledgeable, more skilled, more confident now. Picture the "protected self" the dread and denial are shielding. See your "today self" intervening and handling the situation differently. Free up your "today self" to deliberate and take action now (Van der Kolk, 2014, pp. 280–295).

Deal with your own resistance. If you resist giving up denial for acceptance, make a chart of the pros and cons. What are the pros of continuing to deny? What are the risks of continuing to deny? What are the pros of accepting the unwanted reality? What are the risks of accepting the unwanted reality? (Van Dijk, 2012, p. 109).

Frame the current reality to allow for a better future reality. Bessel Van der Kolk (2015) believes that the way we process and frame a situation facilitates or impedes our ability to accept an undesirable situation and move forward in spite of it. He tells the story of walking with a friend to Ground Zero the evening of September 12, 2001. His friend lived in downtown New York; and his 5-year old son, Noam, had witnessed the collapse of the Twin Towers from his classroom window. When Van der Kolk and his friend returned to the friend's apartment, they found that Noam had stayed up to show Van der Kolk the picture he had drawn of the tragic event.

Van der Kolk recognized the towers, the planes, the people jumping from the towers. But he was puzzled by a big, black dot between the two buildings. When he asked Noam about it, the boy explained, "That's a trampoline." Why a trampoline? "So that the next time when people have to jump they will be safe." Less than 24 hours later, the boy had extracted the learning he needed to make meaning from the tragedy and move forward (Van der Kolk, 2015, p. 51).

Deliberate with mindful reflection and assessment, not rumination. Sure, once may not be enough. You may need to describe the situation a number of times; you may need to express your feelings a number of times; you may need to rehearse possible actions a number of times. When is enough enough? Ask yourself, what am I learning from this? When the answer is "Nothing," it is time to move on to action (J. Kilkus, personal conversation, oncological psychologist, December 18, 2019).

Acknowledge and embrace the reality, then act. Something you did not choose and do not want is real and must be dealt with. One step at a time (Linehan, 2015, p. 344):

- Pay attention to what you are saying to yourself. Do you hear expressions of denial? "This can't be happening!" "There is some kind of mistake." "This isn't possible."
- Acknowledge the data. "This is the situation…."
- Recognize the history that led up to this moment. "This is how it happened."
- Acknowledge the distress.
- To tolerate the distress of the unwanted condition, begin by asking yourself: "If I accepted that this unwanted situation or circumstance is real, what would I do differently?"
- See a scene from the movie of your life in which you are living at peace with this change. What do you see yourself doing?
- Rehearse those things in your head.
- Do those things.

Quickly Shift Into Crisis Decision-Making

I just went. It was outside of my authority, but it was needed. We had millions in the marketplace that were going to be wasted. I knew where it was going, and I didn't need to wait for Finance. We pulled everything and rebuilt our messaging. We developed, concepted, produced, and launched in 2 days. When we got to an edit, FYI to my chairman. Not waiting for approval meetings. They were struggling with how we communicate with people if they don't come into the showroom. We worked with Facebook Live, talked about health and safety protocols, products, service, whatever they want to talk about. Rolled it out nationally. We were the first manufacturer to do that (A. Witherspoon, personal communication, November 17, 2020).

> Another way of work has blossomed—just keep making decisions, then another and another. We are not reckless people. Just go ahead, and if we have to course correct make another one. The speed, it almost broke me. But at the end I found more strength in it. (N. Reyes, personal communication, October 23, 2020)

> I tend to be more black and white. Had to let go of that. What is in front of me, how do I make the best decision today, maybe I change it tomorrow and I have to be ok with that. Rapid, flexible decision-making. (H. Lentz, personal communication, October 12, 2020)

Our "emotional brain" acts like a smoke alarm; but it only tells us there is smoke (danger). It doesn't tell us if the house is on fire and we need to run or if there is just a hamburger burning on the grill. When things work just right, our emotional brain sends the message to our "rational brain." The rational brain acts like a watchtower. Viewing the situation from the watchtower we can size up the danger, map out an appropriate response, and see how to adjust if conditions change (Van der Kolk, 2014, p. 60).

When things go wrong. The purpose of an alarm is direct action that results in safety or balance. If trauma disrupts or distorts the signal you laser-focus on survival. You fend off threats seen or unseen, real or imagined. No time or space then for relationships, reflection, play, planning, caring for others. You may reach out for help. If help isn't offered or if you don't recognize it, the rational brain will order "fight or flight" and send the alarm back to the emotional brain (Van der Kolk, 2014). At this point, you are likely to panic, deny reality, delay, seek comfort instead of safety, or simply not see what is right in front of you (Ripley, 2008).

When things go right. When things go right a strong clear signal gets from the smoke alarm to the watchtower; the watchtower is strong enough to function under the force of powerful emotion; and you are equipped to take the action needed to find safety and balance. You increase the odds of these things happening if you name the danger correctly to begin with. You can build a habit of doing that—even before a traumatic event—by routinely asking yourself guiding questions.

- Direct your decisions with guiding questions suggested by the Logos Institute.
- What do you have here? You look squarely at the naked facts. You do not make the worst out of a difficult situation by telling yourself or others a story with a heartbreaking outcome.
- What does it mean? You look at your options through a series of "if, then" statements. You eliminate those that would not get a good outcome or seem impossible to execute.

- What do you want? You clearly define the ideal outcome and the minimum acceptable outcome. Based on your definitions you narrow down the options you have not already eliminated.
- How do you make the less bad outcome happen? You empower yourself to make a difference for the better in this difficult situation. You remind yourself, "I influence life events; I find meaning in turmoil and look at adversity as a means for growth; I learn from both positive and negative events" (Garcia, 2017, p. 74).
- If the situation triggers a physical reaction that seems out of your control, first communicate directly with your autonomous nervous system.

Sometimes the emotion in a situation triggers a flashback that short-circuits the rational thought process and goes straight to the autonomous nervous system. In these instances, a cognitive protocol won't work. A physical intervention is the first step, then some grounding technique. At some point shift to separating the real from the perceived (J. Kilkus, personal conversation, oncological psychologist, April 22, 2020):

- Engage the physical senses through direct action: Touch something solid, touch something cold, put cold water on the face, dip the face in a bowl of cold water.
- Take other grounding physical action. As you gain control, shift to more finely tuned physical action. For example, when general deep breathing gives enough control to do so, shift to square breathing. (In for the count of four; hold for the count of four; out for the count of four; hold for the count of four).
- Audit the senses: Five things I can see, four things I can touch, three things I can hear, two things I can smell, one thing I can taste.
- Distinguish between the real and the perceived.
- Discern appropriate response: Do you need to escape a house on fire or take a smoking hamburger off the grill?
- Take the appropriate action (J. Kilkus, personal conversation, oncological psychologist, April 22, 2020).

Balance the Needs of Organizational Stakeholders (your client's, your own organizations', and the holding company/owners)

Our offices around the globe were empowered to do what they needed to do to look out for the safety of employees. Employees were given permission to do what they needed as long as the work could get done. This made us very nimble while focused on the health and safety of employees. If we had tried to do this outside the pandemic it wouldn't have happened (A. Miller, personal communication, October 19, 2020).

Prior to John Kotter and James Heskett's (1992) research for *Corporate Culture and Performance* it was generally believed that those companies most likely to succeed over the long haul were those who had the strongest culture. Kotter and Heskett found that strength alone wasn't the distinguishing quality. In an 11-year longitudinal study of 300 companies, they found that success over the long haul depended on a strong culture that equally valued three stakeholders: customers, employees, and owners.

In his seminal book *The Loyalty Effect* (1996), Frederick Reichheld quantifies the impact of your value for stakeholders on customer loyalty, employee loyalty, and shareholder loyalty. Then he goes on to establish the financial impact on the organization of loyalty from each of these groups.

The four holding companies in our study did not significantly reduce their initial 2020 requirements for financial performance. However, they did allow a spectrum of flexibility in how the results were produced. At one end of the spectrum leaders had permission to do what they deemed necessary to protect workers, jobs, and get remote operations up and running. At the other end leaders were unable to hire critical staff; to conform to strict labor metrics they were even required to lay people off.

Align your thinking, your language, your decisions, and your actions around a central value that impacts customers, employees, and owners. With unaltered financial targets and sharp resource restrictions, how do you focus on customers and employees as well as the owner's requirements? In *The Power of Alignment*, Labovitz and Rosansky (1997) conclude the key is keeping strategy, and people, customers, and processes centered on the same "main thing" (p. 55).

In *It's Time to Change the Way You Change*, House (2005) suggests you identify the "one word" you want your company to stand for.

How do you want to be known? What one word do you want customers, employees, and owners to think of when they hear the name of your organization? (It must be the same word for all three groups.)

- Why would people link your organization with the word you have chosen? What would it take for each stakeholder group to make that association?
- What, specifically, do you want to accomplish for each group?
- How will you do it? How can you make these things happen? (House, 2005, pp. 180–186)

Suppose, for example, your team chooses the one word, "success." Even that "boilerplate"-sounding word becomes nuanced when you see it through the eyes of different stakeholders.

Why would a client link "success" *for that client* to your company? For that client, success is likely to mean a quality product that appeals to that client's client, simplicity of use in a virtual work environment, on-time delivery, cost-effectiveness.

Why would an employee link "success" *for that employee* to your company? For that employee, success is likely to mean continued employment, a safe way to work, time to home school children, continued visibility to and connectivity with your chain of command.

Why would a holding company or shareholder link "success" *for that holding company or shareholder* to your company? For that holding company or shareholder success is likely to mean some indicator or predictor of ROI: revenue, margin, cost-effectiveness, share of market.

Adjust your internal operations to the changing external environment. Alignment among stakeholders isn't enough. It's critical to adjust internal operations to accommodate the changing circumstances outside your organization: political, economic, social, technological, environmental (geophysical), and legal. How can you take each of these variables into account at one time? House (2005) suggests you look at a common characteristic all these variables share: turbulence. How unpredictable and how rapid is change among these variables as a whole? Once you've answered that question, you can adjust management systems on the inside to match (House, 2005, pp. 81–95).

Strategy. When the external environment for your industry is stable and certain, you might be able to get away with a strategy by default; keep doing things the way you've always done them. In a turbulent, uncertain environment like this one, it is important to anticipate, be proactive.

Work. When the external environment for your industry is stable and certain, the requirements are stable too. If people just follow the rules, everything will be fine. In a turbulent, uncertain environment like this one, employees will need the tools to decide for themselves and shift quickly.

Motivation. Different people are motivated differently even when the external environment for your industry is stable and certain. In a turbulent, uncertain environment like this one, the same employee will need a larger range of motivators than usual. Safety and security have higher priority even for creatives; just the same, everyone will benefit from a sense of self-worth—that what they do matters. And they may be more dependent than usual on you to reassure them of that.

Structure. When the external environment for your industry is stable and certain, some functions will work just fine with a well-tuned hierarchy. In a turbulent, uncertain environment like this one, a flatter, more networked structure is likely to deliver better results.

Management. When the external environment for your industry is stable and certain, a more authoritarian approach may work in some functions. In a turbulent, uncertain environment like this one, a more interdependent approach will be essential.

Balance the Business Needs of These Organizations and the People Needs of Their Employees

I had to balance the conflict, giving people room to take care of family and themselves in an unprecedented environment while being at the finish line of a significant piece of business. Winning this business would likely ensure we would not have to take aggressive action with employees, that is, headcount reduction. So those 72–96 hours were really tough. A lot of emotion, a slippery slope. I didn't want to mandate. I had to open people's eyes, not only how important it was for the agency, but for their livelihood and the livelihood of others. It would save jobs. That was really tough. I got yelled at, there were tears, lots of things (C. Conrad, personal communication, October 27, 2020).

It is tough. On the one hand, it is important to communicate a sense of urgency to get the work of your organization done. Jobs depend on it. On the other hand, fear can immobilize; you need people in motion. Fear can have negative health consequences. You want a strong, healthy—even *vibrant* workforce.

What you need is a sense of urgency without immobilizing, damaging fear. How to achieve that? Bert Spector had some ideas about sparking urgency in a time of complacency that are equally relevant in a time of overwhelm.

Create a sense of urgency without triggering debilitating fear. Too often executives use fear to create a sense of urgency for change. Sometimes they even fabricate a crisis to justify doing so. Fear may get people moving alright—but not necessarily in the right direction! And it has profound negative side effects:

- It immobilizes some people.
- It stimulates action in some, but the action it stimulates may not be the action that was desired.
- People may "get back" at a person or situation that intimidates them.
- Fear takes a heavy toll on health. Lateness and absenteeism may go up.
- The sense of power in the person who used fear to motivate, encourages him or her to use it again and again. The side effects grow worse and worse. And the person using fear becomes more and more isolated.

Spector suggests four action categories that can help generate a sense of urgency without creating a damaging sense of fear:

Share competitive information. Traditionally information about gains and losses in market share have been confined to the executive suite. Get that type of information out into the organization. Have quarterly presentations by department heads to let employees know where the company and the department stand. Let employees know how to access ratings of the company and the competition in the *Wall Street Journal* and other publications.

Use models to create dissatisfaction with the status quo. Show people a better way. Use best practices from other companies in your industry. Publicize existing groups in your company that come the closest to meeting the ideal. Have employees use visionary analysis to develop their own models.

Point to behavioral dissatisfaction. Openly discuss your group's or your company's performance. What were your goals year to date? How close are you to achieving them? What can you do to close the gaps? *Note:* If individual performance is a problem, handle that privately and with respect.

Mandate dissatisfaction. It's better to avoid the "My way or the highway" approach. But you may need to let employees know that you are serious about the change. Let people know what will happen if the change fails. And on the positive side, look for ways to provide incentives to those who make progress on the change goals.

Throughout it all, be there: to encourage, to answer questions, and to listen (Spector, 1993, pp. 121–128). Neither you nor your staff can afford to spend time and energy on things that do not matter. That gets us to a second point:

Focus. "As long as you've got altitude and ideas, you're okay." —Captain Tammie Jo Shults

April 17, 2018. Southwest Flight 1380 took off from LaGuardia without incident; and for 20 minutes the flight was "business as usual." As the plane passed through 32,000 feet, "usual" came to an abrupt halt: a loud bang, rapid decompression in the cabin, and a chilling drop in temperature. In the cabin, passenger Jennifer Riordan tragically died as a result of the incident. Miraculously, hers was the only life lost (Haag, 2018, para. 4).

In the cockpit, Captain Tammie Jo Shults and First Officer Darren Ellisor focused on keeping everyone else alive. The plane vibrated violently. The noise was so loud that Shults and Ellisor used hand signals to communicate. The information they had was daunting: An engine had blown up, there was a hole in the side of the plane, a passenger had gone out. Yet 20 minutes later, they made a smooth landing in Philadelphia (McLaughlin, 2018).

Shults later said about her teamwork with Ellisor: "It was really just back to flying. Aviate. Communicate. Navigate. As long as you have altitude and ideas, you're okay. We had both" (Nemowitz, 2020, para. 10).

The pandemic has blown up normal work routines. You don't want it to blow up your projects or your life as well. But too much is happening too fast. You are in overload. How can you "land" this situation smoothly?

- Focus on what matters most.
- Aviate—keep your project (or your life) aloft.
- Navigate—move forward in the right direction.
- Communicate.

What is your "one next thing"? A common theme repeated over and over in *Griefshare* support group: overload. Too much happening too fast. The result? Over*whelm.* The suggested response? Do the *one next thing* you know you should do. You've brushed your teeth; next, put the top back on the toothpaste tube (otherwise, you'll have a bigger mess to deal with):

- Unload the overload and set the example for others.
- Declutter.
- Pay attention.
- Clearly define intent.
- Use all the training you've ever had.
- Audit yourself.

These things are hard to do when everything seems to be happening at once. Constable Ken Lam of the Toronto Police Service showed us how with the choices he made in a life-threatening situation.

April 23, 2018, Toronto.

1:25 p.m.: The first 911 call was received by Toronto law enforcement. A van had just run down pedestrians along a busy street. Ten people would die and many more were injured.

1:32 p.m.: Just 7 minutes later, the suspect was arrested without injury by Toronto Police Service (TPS) Constable Ken Lam. Constable Lam was the lone arresting officer. Videos of the arrest have gone viral: Observers around the world have praised Constable Lam's calmness and command of the situation.

Glenn Hanna, formerly RCMP (Royal Canadian Mounted Police), is one of those observers. He analyzed Constable Lam's behavior as the drama unfolded. Before you consider Hanna's observations, take a look at this video of the arrest (Hanna, 2018): https://www.youtube.com/watch?v=gUY9bytwCZs

Hanna (2018) refers to Constable Lam as "the Toronto cop who did everything right" (para. 4). Early in the encounter, Constable Lam *eliminated noisy clutter* by turning off the siren blaring from his car. He repeatedly called out for the suspect to "Get down!" as the suspect repeatedly shouted, "Shoot me! I've got a gun in my pocket! Shoot me!" (Nelson, 2018, para. 5).

Constable Lam *paid careful attention* to the action unfolding in context. He capitalized on safety provided by the *environment*. He positioned himself behind the engine block of his car, daylight provided a clear view of the suspect; and what he saw did not look like a gun. He focused his attention on *the work* at hand: He added nothing optional to his primary task of making a safe arrest. He observed the suspect's behavior in the *relationship*. The suspects behavior had all the hallmarks of an attempted "suicide by cop." The suspect did not assume a shooting stance. He remained upright with his shoulders back and appeared to be pointing a weapon at the officer, not aiming a weapon.

Constable Lam clearly defined intent, then he executed it flawlessly: De-escalate the situation; make an arrest without an injury or a fatality. Deadly force was authorized; but the Constable didn't deem it necessary. His intent to make a safe arrest was reinforced by his ability to minimize risk to himself and others. He did not allow his intent to be distorted by the heinousness of the crime.

Constable Lam's *training* paid off. His 24-weeks of training in defensive tactics, driving, firearms, neighborhood policing and investigation didn't provide "the answer" to the questions that arose during this encounter. His training did provide him with a framework to organize his observations, assess the situation, make a mindful decision, and provide a measured response.

Lam continuously *audited* himself in the situation. A one-time snap-shot of the situation would not have been enough. He continuously monitored the suspect's behavior, the suspect's ability to do harm, his own ability to take care of himself, his opportunity to make a safe arrest.

Aim High to Achieve Goals While Being Fluid in the Process of Getting There

> We did not miss a beat. Not a single client project, no delivery was missed because of our transition to remote working (N. Reyes, personal communication, October 23, 2020). Her CEO Rob Schwartz expressed the advertising industry complementary key performance indicator next to financials, the craft quality and award-winning potential of the creative work. "Super proud of our creative product. We have done some of the best work the agency has ever done" (personal communication, October 12, 2020). MD Jess Monsey noted, "Financially we are ending the year and entering Q1 in an astonishingly good place. And people are really happy with the [creative] work." (personal communication, November 2, 2020)

Practice dynamic steering, an emerging Agile management practice, to constantly adapt and evolve the course in a situation of high uncertainty and rapid change (Robertson, 2015, pp. 129–130). With the stakeholders' endpoint in sight, continuous collaboration and cycles of rapid feedback and iteration is key, both among team members and with project stakeholders, to make fully-informed decisions.

Exercise Hope

You may not always have a comfortable life and you will not always be able to solve all of the world's problems at once but don't ever underestimate the importance you can have because history has shown us that courage can be contagious, and hope can take on a life of its own.

—Michelle Obama

Hope is like the sun which, as we journey toward it, casts the shadow of our burdens behind us.

—Taniska Safir (2016)

It sounds flimsy but I am proud that I maintained a sense of humor and hope.

—J. Monsey (personal communication, November 2, 2020)

Act with hope and moral courage/heroism. Hopeful people believe the future will be better than today. They believe in their own agency, can envision many pathways to their goals, and find alternate pathways around any obstacles (Lopez, 2013). In controversial situations agency requires moral heroism, and leaders can deliberately build their capacity for it (Jones, p. 514; Ripley, 2018, p. 190).

Hopeful people get different outcomes. Shane Lopez (2013) tells us in *Making Hope Happen* that a hopeful person is more likely to . . .

- show up
- increase productivity
- have a sense of well-being
- enjoy good health
- live longer

Hopeful people get better outcomes (like the ones above); hopeful people hold different beliefs; hopeful people apply different skills. Lopez (2013) tells us that those different outcomes are driven by the different beliefs and enabled by the different skills.

So, if a person doesn't have these beliefs and skills right now, is he just out of luck? Lopez says no. He says people can learn them and enjoy those improved outcomes going forward.

Beliefs. Hopeful people believe . . .

- the future will be better than today

- they have the power to make it so
- there are many pathways to their goals
- none of these pathways is free of obstacles
- the future will be better than today

If you were watching a video of your hoped-for life, what would you see? What changes do you see that excite you? That have grown out of your strengths? That have a big impact on your life and the lives of others that you care about? Go ahead and actually experience that excitement now. Feel pride in your contribution to that better life. Enjoy the significant and positive impacts the changes have made in your life. See yourself experiencing these things—living that life. Let that image of yourself live in your mind and take hold.

Build Confidence That You Have the Power to Make It So

Continue to see yourself as the main character in your own story of that better future. Remind yourself with cues (perhaps an alarm every few hours on your wristwatch) to bring that image of yourself back into focus. Set up a periodic, regular check-in with an affirming friend. Remember how Odysseus instructed his crew to tie him to a mast to keep him from responding to the Sirens' call? You can make an "Odysseus contract" with friends to steer you clear of activities and patterns of thinking that obscure your image of that better future and bring you down.

Identify Alternative Pathways to Your Goals

Think of the route you take to work each day—even if it's just the 14 steps downstairs to your home office. Imagine yourself taking a different route each day for a week. What would those routes be? Now think of the straightest route to your goal. Imagine yourself taking five different routes. What old anxiety might you need to face down in order to identify alternate paths to your goals? What resource gaps might you need to fill? What strengths might you leverage? How can you incorporate play into your search for pathways? How can you "borrow" the hope of others and their confidence in you to find alternative pathways?

Accept That None of These Pathways Is Free of Obstacles. Then Plan Ways to Overcome Them

This is one of the differentiators between hope and wishful thinking. Hope takes the uncertainty we face into account. Look at that obstacle differently. What would you see if you were looking at it upside down? Inside out? Under a microscope? Through a telescope? Look for points of view that turn that obstacle into an opportunity. If that little voice in your head says, "That will never work," then ask, "What would it take to make it work?"

or pretend it could work and ask, "What would it look like?" The odds of gliding into that better future picture of yourself without encountering obstacles are slim. Expect them. Plan for them. Be ready for them.

SECTION 6: CONCLUSION

What can be learned from advertising agencies about crisis decision-making, and more broadly, the ability to effectively lead in an increasingly VUCA—volatile, uncertain, complex, and ambiguous—world? These agencies clearly met the Global Leadership Forecast 2014|2015 VUCA index for effectiveness while developing and deepening leadership and team skills critical to VUCA effectiveness and leadership agility. They cultivated a calm, attentive, empathetic, authentic, optimistic leadership presence that was consistently visible. They tapped and deepened reserves of resilience which enhanced their confidence. As a collective, they were able to muster swift top team alignment, from there communicated and interacted with consistency, transparency, and empathy. While embracing the spontaneous flattening of the organization and empowerment of employees (in part facilitated by the second tidal wave of racial justice crises). They built trust, consensus, and commitment throughout the organization, and fostered employee creativity, learning, and innovation.

A factor in this study was a preponderance of women executive leaders in this study, even though many of them had been recently promoted. In the article "Research: Women Are Better Leaders During a Crisis," Zenger and Folkman (2020) pulled 360-degree assessments for leadership effectiveness, 454 men and 366 women, between March and June 2020 from their existing database of 60,000. Consistent with their pre-pandemic analysis, they found that women were rated significantly more positively than men. Further, they found that the gap between women and men in the pandemic is "even larger than previously measured, possibly indicating that women tend to perform better in a crisis" (para. 5).

This is not meant to diminish the contribution of the male leaders in this study who were also VUCA effective. Rather, it is an indication that a full suite of well-integrated feminine and masculine skills and capacities (which both men and women can develop) is "especially suited to the constantly shifting ground that organizations and institutions are experiencing today" (Anderson & Cannon, 2016, p. 19).

These agencies also advanced in leadership and organizational developmental stage, able to learn and grow in the moment to meet the challenge. In his white paper *The Future of Leadership,* organizational and leadership transformation scholar and consultant Barrett Brown (2013) uses the business-friendly term *vertical learning* for this developmental stage-wise progression, or "the transformation of how a leader thinks, feels, and makes sense of the world" (p. 3). In other words, vertical learning is a mindset transformation whereas horizontal learning is competence/skill development within the same mindset. As Barrett shows, vertical learning is necessary for leaders and organizations to have the requisite up-to-date internal operating system with sufficient complexity and nuance to successfully respond in a VUCA world.

The agencies demonstrated both horizontal competence development as well as stage-wise vertical learning organizationally in leadership. They shifted toward a deepening embrace of the highly complex, adaptive, and recently emerging postmodern pluralist mindset, while still including healthy attributes of the historically earlier modern achiever mindset necessary for profitable business performance. An organizational mindset at the postmodern pluralist stage produces culture and leadership emphasizing collaboration, fluid networking versus strict hierarchies, diversity, sensitivity and care for human needs, and the development of emotional intelligence skills.

Are advertising agencies, by their nature and structure, more capable of dealing with crisis and change and more willing and able to uplevel their mindsets? In *Madison Avenue Manslaughter*, Michael Farmer (2017) charts the history of modern advertising agencies from the heydays of the 1960s and 1970s with the lucrative rise of television, to a peak in the 1990s when they were "at the top of their game" delivering big idea creativity and excellent client services. Since then, agencies have had to adapt to considerable changes in their operating environments: the rise of holding companies, the change from commission to fees, empowerment of procurement, the globalization of client relationships, the development of new digital and social media, and the fragmentation of their client relationships (pp. 175–176).

Even without the disruption of a pandemic, these changes have been leading to declining fees, rising workloads, and stretched resources (Farmer, 2017, pp. 28–30). From a modern/achiever perspective, these are factors arguing against a talented person committing to a career in the industry. Yet despite these changes, Farmer (2017) argues that advertising agencies "have been constant in their commitment to self-organizing management cultures that celebrate creative departments and allow other individuals to define their own rules and priorities" (p. 176). This may be a key insight.

Intrinsic to creativity-centric advertising agencies is the desire to fiercely protect a sacred space of seemingly unfettered chaos and self-determination that incubates and births creativity. Decentralization and self-organization are hallmarks of the postmodern pluralist stage and mindset, allowing organizations to be more fluid, nimble, and agile if the downsides of chaos can be managed. These agencies appear to be successful because they could deftly shift in the midst of crisis, and in a delicate dance operate semi-autonomously within the more hierarchical structures of the holding companies that helped secure them against the intense forces of economic breakdown. Agencies in turn nurtured and protected a seed of postmodern pluralism that sprouted and grew in the pandemic crisis conditions and enabled success.

Are the agencies' developmental gains sustainable? If holding companies remain entrenched in the more rigid, profit over people modern achiever mindset, agency vertical growth may experience downward pressure. Top teams worry that the long-term result will be an inexorable loss of competitiveness in the talent market that will translate into reduced quality of work and long-term degradation of the business and potentially the industry. Worse, it could lead to missed opportunities for advertising agencies/networks, or an evolved organizational form of such, to become innovative players and planetary influencers in the emerging post-COVID-19 future. From the developmental perspectives cited in this chapter that would most likely require leadership taking the next shift shown in Table 6.1, into the integral/strategist/meta-systemic stage of development (Brown, 2013; Cannon et al., 2015; Rooke, D., & Torbert, W., 2005).

How to fully realize that next development shift, which some agency leaders in this study are poised to make, is beyond the scope of this chapter. Nevertheless, the positive results that the leaders demonstrated under the pressure test of the COVID-19 pandemic suggest that the potential exists.

REFERENCES

Adgate, B. (2020, March 27). How the coronavirus will transform TV programming and advertising. *Forbes*. https://www.forbes.com/sites/bradadgate/2020/03/27/the-impact-of-the-covid-19-virus-on-programming-and-tv-advertising/?sh=74ed29881042

American Psychological Association. (2012). *Building your resilience*. https://www.apaservices.org/practice/good-practice/building-resilience.pdf

Anderson, S., & Cannon, S. (2016). *The way of the mysterial woman: Upgrading how you live, love, and lead*. She Writes Press.

Baldoni, J. (2010, May 5). Use your leadership presence to inspire. *Harvard Business Review*. https://hbr.org/2010/05/use-your-leadership-presence-t

Beck, D., & Cowan, C. (1996). *Spiral dynamics*. Blackwell Business.

Beeson, J. (2012, Aug 22). Deconstructing executive presence. *Harvard Business Review*. https://hbr.org/2012/08/de-constructing-executive-pres

Bernstein, A. (2010). *The myth of stress: Where stress really comes from and how to live a happier and healthier life*. Free Press.

Brown, B. (2011). *Conscious leadership for sustainability: How leaders with a late stage action logic design and engage in sustainability initiatives*. (Doctoral dissertation). Retrieved from Dissertations and Theses database. (UMI No. 3498378)

Brown, B. (2013). *The future of leadership for conscious capitalism.* MetaIntegral Associates. https://www.academia.edu/6605006/The_Future_of_Leadership_for_Conscious_Capitalism

Cannon, S., Morrow-Fox, M., & Metcalf, M. (2015). *The strategist competency model: The future of leadership development.* In M. Sowcik, A. C. Andenoro, M. McNutt, & S. E. Murphy (Eds.), *Leadership 2050: Critical challenges, key contexts, and emerging trends* (pp. 189–205). Emerald Group Publishing.

Clark, L. (2020, March 26). *Innovation in a time of crisis.* Harvard Business Publishing. https://www.harvardbusiness.org/innovation-in-a-time-of-crisis/

Cook-Greuter, S. (2000). Mature ego development: A gateway to ego transcendence? *Journal of Adult Development, 7*(4), 227–240.

Cook-Greuter, S. (2004). Making the case for a developmental perspective. *Industrial and Commercial Training, 36*(7), 275–281.

Cook-Greuter, S. (2014). *Ego development: A full-spectrum theory of vertical growth and meaning making.* Cook-Greuter and Associates. https://www.researchgate.net/publication/356357233_Ego_Development_A_Full-Spectrum_Theory_Of_Vertical_Growth_And_Meaning_Making

Cook-Greuter, S. & Soulen, J. (2007). The developmental perspective in integral counseling. *Counseling and Values, 51*(3), 180–192.

Development Dimensions International & The Conference Board. (2014). Working within the VUCA vortex. In *Ready-now leaders: Meeting tomorrow's business challenges. Global leadership forecast 2014|2015* (pp. 10–11). https://media.ddiworld.com/research/global-leadership-forecast-2014-2015_tr_ddi.pdf

Development Dimensions International & The Conference Board. (2015). *Global leadership forecast 2018.* https://media.ddiworld.com/research/global-leadership-forecast-2018_ddi_tr.pdf

Duffy, J. D. (2020, September 21). A primer on integral theory and its applications to mental health care. *Integral Psychiatry and the Science of Human Flourishing, 9*(1). Section 8. https://doi.org/10.1177/2164956120952733

Endsley, M., Bolte, B., & Jones, D. G. (2003). *Designing for situation awareness: An approach to user-centered design.* CRC Press.

Farmer, M. (2017). *Madison avenue manslaughter: An inside view of fee-cutting clients, profit-hungry owners and declining ad agencies* (3rd ed.). LID Publishing.

Garcia, H. F. (2017). *The agony of decision.* Logos Institute for Crisis Management and Executive Leadership Press.

Gebser, J. (1985). *The ever-present origin.* Ohio University Press. (Original work published as Part 1, 1949, and Part 2, 1953).

Gitsham, M. (2009). *Developing the global leader of tomorrow.* Ashridge and EABIS report. http://www.ashridge.com/Website/IC.nsf/wFARPUB/Developing+the+Global+Leader+of+Tomorrow+Report+-+2009?opendocument

Goleman, D. (2006). *Emotional intelligence: Why it can matter more than IQ.* [Kindle ed.]. Bantam Books.

Haag, M. (2018, May 10). Southwest pilot who landed fatal flight wasn't supposed to be on it. *New York Times.* https://www.nytimes.com/2018/05/10/business/southwest-pilot-interview-flight-1380.html#:~:text=the%20main%20story-,%E2%80%9CAs%20long%20as%20you%20have%20altitude%20and%20ideas%2C%20you',ago%2C%20said%20in%20the%20interview

Halpern, B. L., & Lubar, K. (2003). *Leadership presence: Dramatic techniques to reach out, motivate and inspire.* Penguin Group.

Hanna, G. (April 24, 2018). *Why didn't he shoot? The Toronto cop who did everything right.* The conversation. https://theconversation.com/why-didnt-he-shoot-the-toronto-cop-who-did-everything-right-95570

House, R. M. (2005). *It's time to change the way you change.* Middleton-House & Company.

IBM Corporation. (2010). *Working beyond borders: Insights from the global chief human resource officer study.* http://www-935.ibm.com /services/csuite/chro/study/

Institute for the Future. (n.d.). *Bob Johansen: Distinguished follow.* https://www.iftf.org/bobjohansen/

Johansen, B. (2012). *Leaders make the future. Ten new leadership skills for an uncertain future.* Berrett-Koehler Publishers.

Johansen, B. (2017). *The new leadership literacies: Thriving in a future of extreme disruption and distributed everything.* Berrett-Koehler Publishers.

Kegan, R. (2020, April 9). *The transformative potentials in our current crisis* [webinar Part 2]. https://www.youtube.com/watch?v=YG27QGm59GE&feature=youtu.be

Kegan, R., & Lahey, L. L. (2009). *Immunity to change.* Harvard Business Review Press.

Kotter, J. P., & Heskett, J. L. (1992). *Corporate culture and performance.* The Free Press.

Labovitz, G., & Rosansky, V. (1997). *Power of alignment.* John Wiley & Sons.

Laloux, F. (2014). *Reinventing organizations: A guide to creating organizations inspired by the next stage of human consciousness.* Nelson Parker.

Leslie, B. (2009). *The leadership gap: What you need and don't have when it comes to leadership talent.* Center For Creative Leadership. http://www.ccl.org/leadership/pdf/research/leadershipGap.pdf

Linehan, M. M. (2015). *DBT skills training and worksheets.* Guilford.

Lopez, S. (2013). *Making hope happen.* Simon and Schuster.

McAteer, O. (2020, April 21). *Inside chaotic Snuggle spot made in director's laundry room with family as actors and crew.* https://www.campaignlive.com/article/inside-chaotic-snuggle-spot-made-directors-laundr y-room-family-actors-crew/1680984

McIntosh, S. (2007). *Integral consciousness and the future of evolution.* Paragon.

McGregor, D. (2006). *The human side of enterprise* (J. Cutcher-Gershenfeld, Ed.; Annotated). [kindle version]. McGraw-Hill.

McLaughlin, E. C. (2018, April 23). *22 minutes of terror.* CNN. https://www.cnn.com/2018/04/22/us/southwest-1380-emergency-landing-moments/index.html

Namowitz, D. (2020, Sept. 24). *"Barn door in a hurricane" Capt. Tammie Jo Shults gives master class in emergency management.* Tammie Jo Shults. https://www.captainshults.com/barn-door-in-a-hurricane-capt-tammie-jo-shults-gives-master-class-in-emergency-management/

Nelson, S. (2018, April 24). Toronto van attack: Praise for officer's restraint as suspect Alek Minassian screamed "kill me." *Huffpost.* https://www.huffingtonpost.co.uk/entry/praise-for-officers-restraint-as-toronto-van-suspect-screamed-kill-me_uk_5adee41ee4b0b2e81132c3af

Northouse, P. G. (2019). *Leadership theory & practice* (8th ed.). Sage.

Pfeiffer, B. (2020, August 18). *The ads affair: How the industry has changed and is changing.* Business.com. https://www.business.com/articles/how-the-ad-industry-is-changing/

Porter, M. E., Lorsch, J. W., & Nohria, N. (2004, October 1). *Seven surprises for new CEOs.* https://hbr.org/archive-toc/BR0410

Reichheld, F. F. (1996). *The loyalty effect.* The Harvard Business School Press.

Reivich, K. J., Seligman, M. E. P., & McBride, S. (2011). Master resilience training in the U.S. Army. *American Psychologist, 66*(1), 25–34. https://doi.org/10.1037/a0021897

Ripley, A. (2008). *The unthinkable: Who survives when disaster strikes and why.* Crown Publishing.

Robertson, B. (2015). *Holacracy: The new management system for a rapidly changing world.* Henry Holt and Company.

Rooke, D. (2001). Organizational transformation requires the presence of leaders who are strategists and magicians. *Organizations and People, 4*(3), 16–23.

Rooke, D., & Torbert, W. (1998). Organizational transformation as a function of CEO's developmental stage. *Organization Development Journal, 16*(1), 11–28.

Rooke, D., & Torbert, W. (1999). The CEO's role in organizational transformation. *Systems Thinker, 10*(7), 1–5.

Rooke, D., & Torbert, W. (2005, April). Seven transformations of leadership. *Harvard Business Review, 83*(4), 66–76. https://hbr.org/2005/04/seven-transformations-of-leadership

Safir, T. (2016). Hope: A psychological perspective. *Indian Journal of Positive Psychology. 7*(1), 138–140.

Seligman, M. E. P. (2011, April). Building resilience. *Harvard Business Review.* https://hbr.org/2011/04/building-resilience

Seligman, M. E. (2013). *Flourish: A visionary new understanding of happiness and well-being.* Atria.

Spector, B. (1993). From bogged down to fired up. In T. Jick & M. A. Peiperi (Eds.), *Managing change: Cases and concepts* (pp. 121–128). Irwin.

The 3% Movement. (n.d.). *The mission.* https://www.3percentmovement.com/movement

TIME'S UP Advertising. (n.d.). *We're making gender equality the new normal.* https://timesupfoundation.org/work/times-up-advertising.

Van der Kolk, B. A. (2014). *The body keeps the score: Brain, mind and body in the healing of trauma.* Penguin.

Van Dijk. S. (2012). *DBT made simple.* New Harbinger Publications.

Wilber, K. (1996). *A brief history of everything.* Shambhala Publications.

Wilber, K. (2011). *A theory of everything: An integral vision for business, politics, science, and spirituality.* Shambhala.

Woo, G., Fotheringham, J., & Middleton-House, R. (2018, July 19). *Dangerous intersections: In-between, in crisis, in overload* [Alumni Track Session]. Fielding Graduate University Summer Session, Chicago.

Zakaria, Fareed. (2020). *Ten lessons for a post-pandemic world* [kindle version]. W.W. Norton & Company.

Zenger, J., & Folkman, J. (2020, December 30). Research: Women are better leaders during a crisis. *Harvard Business Review.* https://hbr.org/2020/12/research-women-are-better-leaders-during-a-crisis

CHAPTER 7

EMERGENCE AND SENSEMAKING IN A COMPLEX GLOBAL KNOWLEDGE SYSTEM

Implications for Leaders Post-COVID-19

Lisa Cuevas Shaw
Pepperdine University

Laura Hyatt
Pepperdine University

At the time of this writing, there is worldwide evidence of disastrous consequences associated with climate change, social unrest, and a global pandemic. The immediate threat of the global pandemic presents an opportunity to study leaders' response to systemic complexity, crisis, and chaos in real time and on an order of magnitude most of us have not witnessed in our lifetimes. The range of subsystems (Angst, 2020; Lynton, 1969) that leaders had to navigate to develop effective responses to the pandemic

Crisis, Chaos, and Organizations, pages 199–225

included intergovernmental ministries, international health organizations, national and local governments, global economics, political systems, social systems, and much more. The actions within these subsystems vacillated between collaboration and conflict, and coordination and chaos during the first several months following the pronouncement of a pandemic. One of the primary sources of tension for organizational leaders was the dizzying flow of information, misinformation, and disinformation (Kouzy et al., 2020). In fact, the proliferation of misinformation emerged as a central narrative, so much so that the World Health Organization (WHO) referred to the phenomenon as an *infodemic* (UN Department of Global Communications [UN DGC], 2020) to describe the "excessive amount of information about a problem, which makes it difficult to identify a solution" (UN DGC, 2020, para. 3).

The term infodemic is not new. It was coined in 2003 by a *Washington Post* reporter to describe a similar phenomenon in relation to a SARS virus outbreak (Rothkopf, 2003). Yet, it is especially apt in highlighting a key organizational and leadership challenge of the information age when a crisis or large-scale disruption strikes. Crisis, in this instance, is defined from the stakeholder perspective as "an event that is an unpredictable major threat that can have a negative impact on the organization, industry, or stakeholders if handled improperly" (Coombs, 1999, p. 2). During these events, as was witnessed in the early days of the current pandemic associated with the COVID-19 virus, there can be an abundance of information available and incoming from diverse sources, comprising everything from formal research reports to a range of news media to a largely unregulated yet highly influential social-media infrastructure. In this chapter, the totality of facts, information, and content from wide-ranging sources across various locally and globally situated contexts and networks are presented as the global knowledge system. This global knowledge system includes the accompanying cognitive, social, and cultural processes of interpretation and application of this information.

The efficient and productive sourcing, processing, and use of reliable information is critical when operating within a complex global system that is experiencing extreme uncertainty. So, how do organizational leaders identify and enact effective solutions in the midst of information (or misinformation) overload? Furthermore, how do they continue to process a dynamic situation and apply effective measures in response to new knowledge as it emerges or develops at such a rapid pace? Formal models of organizational knowledge management often present the process of acquiring, interpreting, and sharing knowledge in a linear or cyclical manner (Sensuse et al., 2014). However, in crisis or chaos, linear models or more protracted cycles for this institutionalized process may not be pragmatic or possible.

Within the theoretical construct of systems thinking, these critical questions are examined in relation to the course of *emergence*, which refers to "the arising of novel and coherent structures, patterns, and properties during the process of self-organization in complex systems" (Goldstein, 1999, p. 49), within and across the global knowledge system. Organizational *sensemaking* is explored, including the process describing how individuals, leaders, organizations, or communities make meaning of surprising or uncertain situations (Weick, et al., 2005; Weick & Sutcliffe, 2007) that take place across the global knowledge system. The distinct interplay between these two processes of emergence and sensemaking presents a conceptual construct that organizational leaders can learn to navigate and leverage in responding to a crisis situation. These concepts address some of the central challenges as well as opportunities of a crisis as complex and interconnected as a pandemic, but they can also be applied to less existential crises and forms of disequilibrium that organizational leaders are likely to encounter with increasing regularity in an era of extreme disruption and distributed everything, as futurist Bob Johansen (2017) expressed.

EMERGENCE AND SENSEMAKING IN ACTION

During the earliest days of the pandemic, no one was in the hot seat more than organizational leaders within the global science community, most especially public health officials. The systematic coordination of international, national, and local agencies to process and share new knowledge developments efficiently among themselves incurred challenges on multiple occasions during critical early stages of the outbreak (Forman, 2020; Jordana & Triviño-Salazar, 2020; Osterholm & Olshaker, 2020). Despite the myriad challenges with coordinating an effective global response, one phenomenon clearly emerged from the broader science community that highlights several aspects of emergence, organizational sensemaking, and their effective interplay. Responding to the systemic need to abate this global public health crisis, organizational members of the science communications community quickly unlocked paywalls to content; encouraged rapid, responsible data-sharing; aggregated content for ease in discovery; translated science communication into practical insights for the wider public; and formed new partnerships to mobilize and strengthen their efforts. These same members continued to adapt their activities as new information, new needs, and course corrections became apparent. The discrete study of this coherent response emerging within a significant aspect of the global knowledge system presents unique insights for leaders enacting change through the sensemaking process. This example is incorporated into the chapter to illuminate key concepts, lessons learned, and future implications for organizational leaders.

Systems thinking and, specifically, the process of emergence of new structures and properties within complex systems and organizational sensemaking are well developed yet still diversely interpreted constructs in organizational theory (Blitz, 1992; Bunge, 2003; Corning, 2002; Goldstein, 1999; Holland, 1998; Kim, 2016; Maitlis & Christianson, 2014; Weick, 1988, 1995, 2005). The unique interplay of these constructs applied to the global knowledge system distinguishes a new level of organization with respect to how leaders process and use information and facilitate organizational understanding and learning during and following disruptive events. The COVID-19 pandemic laid bare some significant complications and challenges of our global knowledge system that serve as a call to action for organizational leaders to deepen their understanding of various kinds of systems emergence, including those properties that are productive and those that present new challenges or are deleterious. This chapter offers leaders, researchers, educators, and information professionals

- a contemporary synthesis of complex adaptive systems (CAS), specifically identifying the organizational attributes and actions across the global knowledge system evidenced during the early stages of the pandemic;
- key insights into the processes and potential outputs of emergence and sensemaking during crisis and chaos;
- learnings from the science communications community's response to the pandemic; and
- implications for organizational leaders' own sensemaking processes, including a conceptual framework for this interplay between emergence and sensemaking within the global knowledge system.

These concepts encourage the continued investment in systems thinking and sensemaking theory development while offering practical value to leaders who are committed to future-oriented sensemaking, organizational learning, and sustainability.

CONTEMPORARY SYSTEMS THINKING

Much of contemporary systems thinking applied to organizations follows Checkland's (1993) goal of solving for real-world problems by taking into account the holistic attributes and needs of the system. Organizational systems theorists also acknowledge the high degree of complexity in which organizations operate and therefore, attempt to prepare for disruption that may lead to chaos (Anderson, 1999). Complex systems theory focuses on the connectivity and interdependence of many agents within a system as well as the emergence of new structures, processes, and behaviors of the system as a whole (Bar-Yam, 1997; Holland, 1998; Yolles, 2006). Viewing organizations from this lens provides a valuable framework from which to draw lessons for organizational leaders facing a crisis or periods of significant uncertainty. In this section, complex systems theory is used to frame and identify organizational attributes and actions evidenced across the global knowledge system during the initial stages of the pandemic that relate specifically to CAS. This is followed by a review of the emergence of new levels of organization across the global knowledge system during the crisis and the possibility of anticipating future patterns should a similar crisis arise.

Global Knowledge as a CAS

A CAS is an interdisciplinary, theoretical construct that can be used for studying and explaining systems of interdependent agents forming emergent, global-level properties that bring relative order to a given system (Holland, 1995). CAS was first popularized in the field of evolutionary biology, but its principles have been widely applied across organization science (Anderson, 1999; Brown & Eisenhardt, 1998; Dooley, 1997). The unifying notion of CAS is that at all levels of system analysis, "order is an emergent property of individual interactions at a lower level of aggregation" (Anderson, 1999, p. 219). In other words, behavior of complex systems can be modeled by examining the emergent order of individual interactions occurring between agents or within subsystems. One of the primary goals of applying a CAS construct is to simplify the complex by extracting what might be considered unnecessary information or minor phenomena relative to the more significant, ordered patterns that emerge (Simon, 1996). Organizational leaders regularly attempt to simplify the complex in order to pare back the volume of data and information available to them to make effective decisions that affect present and future states.

Anderson (1999) identified four common elements of CAS models that can enhance an understanding of the complex global knowledge system today. These include:

- *Heterogeneity of agents with various schemata.* Organizational agents of a CAS could include individuals, groups, collaboratives, institutions, communication channels, and forms of technology. Schemata are loosely defined to represent perspectives, rules, ideas, or any construct that might determine what action the agent will take in any given moment.

- *Self-organizing networks.* Agents are at least partially connected to one another by feedback loops, which might reinforce an agent's behavior through positive (or reinforcing) feedback or cause it to take a different path, usually owing to negative (or balancing) feedback. Unlike other organizational theories, in a CAS model, no one component determines the collective behavior of the system. The system self-organizes as a result of the dynamic feedback loops, actions, and interactions, occurring largely in a nonlinear fashion.
- *Coevolution to the edge of chaos.* Agents within the system coevolve to improve their states. This process is dynamic, with small adaptations producing small-, medium-, or large-scale change. CAS models are not intended to focus on purely chaotic states, wherein the slightest disruption causes large-scale change.
- *Recombination and systems evolution.* These systems evolve over time as agents transform themselves or enter and exit the system. The interconnectedness of the agents can change over time as well, with some relationships becoming stronger and others weakening or adjusting in some form (Anderson, 1999, p. 220).

Applying this basic CAS model to the global knowledge system includes a vast range of agents organizational leaders can engage with, each carrying distinct schemata relative to their roles, socially and culturally constructed identities, and core objectives within the system. As well, the global knowledge system is increasingly interconnected in large part because of technological advances, namely, widespread access to mobile and internet technologies that facilitate information exchange. The various interactive feedback mechanisms and resultant self-organizing through levels of adaptation can be accelerated and amplified via relatively efficient and accessible digital communication channels and networks. The overall interconnectedness of agents within the system is highly dynamic and complex, given the sheer number of agents, the potential pace of adaptation, and the power and influence of relationships across knowledge networks within the system.

Table 7.1 provides a summary of the key CAS characteristics and processes as applied to elements and examples within the global knowledge system that were especially pertinent to leaders and to the general public as the response to the pandemic unfolded. This summary consolidates a highly complex, increasingly technology-led or influenced system with a wide range of agents and social or cultural subsystems interacting at multiple levels. Distilling the view of the system in this manner facilitates a focus on the patterns and high-level order that emerged during the early days of the pandemic.

TABLE 7.1 CAS Attributes and Processes Applied to the Global Knowledge System During the Early Stages of the Pandemic

CAS Attribute or Process	Global Knowledge System Elements and Examples
Other CAS Influencing the System	Local and global political system, economic system, education system, environmental system, social system
Heterogeneity of Agents	
Institutions	Government agencies, universities, public health agencies, news media, NGOs and IGOs
Individuals	Subject matter experts (scientists, researchers, public officials), government leaders, public figure influencers
Social Networks	Social media, professional networks, personal networks
Content Types	Research reports, case studies, news, policies, opinion
Communication Channels	Internet, email, text, social media, broadcasting, word of mouth
Technologies	Data discovery and aggregation, automated alerts, automated filtering, artificial intelligence
Feedback Loops	Public behavioral responses; rate of infection/health indicators; proliferation of information and misinformation; public discourse; local, national, international ordinances; economic indicators
Self-Organizing Networks	Coordinated public health campaigns, collective enforcement of ordinances and recommended practices, public compliance and resharing of information, research collaboration
Coevolution to the Edge of Chaos	All resources on COVID-19, rapid dissemination, new collaboration, novel aggregation of information
Recombination and Systems Evolution	New networks (e.g., governors move from centralized interpretation to local interpretation and action), new task forces

COMPLEX KNOWLEDGE SYSTEM IN CRISIS AND CHAOS

The pandemic further evinced the complex interconnectedness of our global knowledge system as much as the volume and frenzied pace at which knowledge can be shared and constructed during a crisis. Within the global response to this public health crisis, there was ample evidence of systemic coherence that led to positive outcomes: Scientists sequenced the genome of the virus and developed several promising vaccine candidates in a matter of days (Gates, 2020); early prevention strategies in several countries, including those that are economically disadvantaged such as Mongolia, contained the spread (Erkhembayar et al., 2020); and Singapore, as with many other countries, effectively used various media outlets—news, television, radio, and social media—to improve public knowledge and awareness and thus minimize virus-related stigmas that could have otherwise negatively affected public intervention responses (Kuguyo et al., 2020). Each of these are examples that demonstrate an adaptive, self-organizing, largely coherent, and effective knowledge system at work through the various actors and dynamic interactions within the system.

Unfortunately, the global response also demonstrated several systemic issues within the global knowledge system, which resulted in devastating effects on economic and public health. It was documented that the Chinese government did not sound an early warning bell and supply the WHO with data and statistics to inform levels of intervention needed (Colglazier, 2020). The Reuters Institute released a study of the types, sources, and claims of COVID-19 misinformation (Brennen et al., 2020). The report documented the pervasiveness of formal campaigns that led to confusion and chaos, and further delayed action. In another study exploring the extent of the infodemic, an analysis of 700 Twitter feeds verified that the public was exposed to a substantial amount of misinformation among different members of the media and government as the global community tried to understand how to combat disease spread effectively (Kouzy et al., 2020).

Critical Feedback Loops During the Pandemic

Within the examples of positive systemic coherence and systemic errors, one can observe intricate external and internal feedback loops that reinforced and amplified certain responses among agents within the global knowledge system and feedback loops that regulated responses. In the early days of the pandemic, positive feedback, also referred to in systems literature as *reinforcing* feedback (Sterman, 2000), from various agents and subsystems resulted in both positive and negative outputs. For example, the globally shared goal and demand to quash the virus resulted in an unprecedented, accelerated discovery process among researchers for viable vaccine candidates. At the same time, an equally pervasive, globally shared desire for answers to questions surrounding virus spread and its related threats created a positive feedback loop in which online social networks fueled an intense demand for any information. The accelerated network effect of this demand contributed to the rapid propagation of misinformation, as people tried to fill the void of reliable information and answers (Törnberg, 2018). In this instance, the reinforcing feedback from the system for any data led to potentially confusing information. Unfortunately, leading public health institutions were not able to adapt quickly enough to respond to this network-type feedback to develop novel information-sharing techniques that might stave off the rapid spread of misinformation (DiResta, 2020). This resulted in added chaos rather than coherence within the system.

Similarly, there were instances in which negative feedback across the knowledge system helped to regulate structures, processes, and behaviors across the broader response. The most obvious example of this kind of feedback was the increasing infection rates, hospitalizations, and deaths, all of which caused local and national governments and public officials to construct public ordinances that would alter the public's behavioral responses. In another example of balancing feedback, the spread of misinformation was so highly visible to some information providers across the system that new campaigns and strategies for disseminating accurate information were priority adaptations for them.

Whereas the global knowledge system is largely decentralized, these and other examples of feedback loops, adaptation, and self-organizing demonstrate the system's propensity to form emergent properties and new capacities as a whole, especially in response to a crisis. Leaders look to establish or retool their strategies for managing knowledge acquisition, interpretation, and sharing during a crisis or state of uncertainty. A more intentional focus on emergent properties and any causal relationships therein may have alleviated the overwhelming effects inherent in simply trying to keep up with the voluminous and discordant information across the entire system and among its various actors and networks.

The Significance of Emergence for Organizational Leaders

Contemporary organization literature related to CAS often focuses on how and when emergence of a new order takes hold, specifically exploring the processes of adaptation, positive and negative feedback loops, and organizational learning (Bunge, 2003; Dooley, 1997; Holland, 1998; Kim, 2016). The common properties of emergent phenomena in complex systems are not only "novel" and "coherent" but also "dynamical, ostensive, and occur at a global or macro level" (Goldstein, 1999, p. 49). The retrospective and real-time study of patterns yielding emergent, higher-level order can yield insights into the adaptability of the global knowledge system and the new rules and structures being created and accepted across the system. For example, what if leaders had been even more intentional about monitoring the social network effects with information and misinformation, and had more profoundly transformed their social network and related communication strategies to anticipate better system dynamics (DiResta, 2020)? A greater focus on the relevant emergent properties of core communication may have helped to prevent or lessen the more reactionary responses and activities that ensued, which added to their constituents' sense of being overwhelmed and or confused.

There is another consideration for leaders regarding the significance of emergence. As Fulmer and Ostroff (2015) observed, leaders often serve as interpretive filters of the social aspects of organizations and are thus key to motivating required behaviors. As such, they may become agents for social influence and play active and influential roles in shaping and reinforcing the feedback loops, behaviors, and resultant emergent processes and outputs. Therefore, leaders' own awareness of the concepts, processes, and outputs of emergence during a crisis could be especially significant not only for navigating the system but for actively shaping their roles as potential agents of change within the system (Hyatt, 2020). Furthermore, active awareness of the process of emergence may be beneficial for leaders looking to develop the increasingly significant leadership literacy of foresight (Johansen, 2017). By paying attention to emergent properties, leaders might increase their ability to anticipate the unpredictable and burgeoning needs of the system more effectively.

Emergent Property Cues: What Organizational Leaders May Observe

Interest in complex systems remains high among contemporary organizational theorists, and yet there is no consensus or single typology used to define or ascribe meaning to emergent order occurring in organizations (Corning, 2002; Lichtenstein & McKelvey, 2011). A proliferation of meanings is understandable when one considers the range of systems and subsystems that organization sciences cover as well as the vast number of situations or problems being explored. Emergent order in the global economy may look different than the order that emerges within a single entity. The global knowledge system as a CAS refers to two dimensions of a CAS-related typology for emergence developed by Lichtenstein and McKelvey (2011). These dimensions frame observations leaders make to build awareness of the process and causality of emergence within this system, especially during a state of significant disequilibrium. This then provides cues specifically related to the global knowledge system under pressure.

The first of the dimensions within Lichtenstein and McKelvey's (2011) emergence typology relates to measuring the extent of agent heterogeneity. The second of the dimensions relates to measuring the degree of causal intricacy. A global knowledge system represents a highly diverse and complex system of intricately interconnected agents. The high degree of causal intricacy and complexity of relationships among agents and inputs creates nonlinear interactions across multiple levels, all of which lead to emergent contexts. Through the process of observing emergent patterns retrospectively and in real-time, leaders can develop a set of strategies that may be beneficial when responding to a crisis. According to Lichtenstein and McKelvey (2011), the global knowledge system as a CAS, even operating largely as a decentralized system, operates with a degree of "purposefulness" (p. 348), or an ability to change goals (Ackoff et al., 2005). Leaders, as agents of social influence within the system, may positively affect the purpose of the global knowledge system through effective use of retrospective and real-time system insights.

To apply these dimensions and characteristics of emergence in a CAS to a real situation, leaders may consider making the following intentional queries as they observe system contexts:

1. What specific behaviors are emerging across the range of agents and among constituents in particular?
2. What new structures and processes are emerging and for what purpose?
3. What are the top-down and bottom-up forces contributing to adaptation and self-organizing?
4. Who or what represent the most influential agents across the system at this time?
5. What kinds of positive (reinforcing) or negative (balancing) feedback loops are in motion, and how are they amplifying or dampening certain behaviors?
6. How are relationships among agents across the system changing, and what effect might those changes have on the organization?
7. What actions might support necessary disequilibrium, amplify positive behaviors or emergent properties, or dampen deleterious behaviors?

Two of the more commonly cited factors in systemic failure are weak system-wide understanding along with inadequate feedback (Buldyrev et al., 2010). Leaders who proactively seek to make meaning of the system, its emergent properties, and the feedback loops shaping them may contribute positively to an effective system response to a crisis. Given the expanse of active and intentional querying and observation required to monitor and make sense of a complex and dynamic system during a crisis, leaders also have an opportunity to foster rich organizational relationships and capacity-building that can support these efforts.

ORGANIZATIONAL SENSEMAKING AND EMERGENCE

Sensemaking has been studied among organizational theorists to provide insights into factors that surface as members of an organization address uncertain, ambiguous, confusing, and unexpected situations (Cornelissen, 2012; Maitlis & Christianson, 2014). Weick (1988, 1995, 2005), who is recognized as the founding theorist on sensemaking (Maitlis & Christianson, 2014), positioned this process specifically within the context of crises, which is fitting for the exploration of leader response to the pandemic. There are several characteristics and varieties of sensemaking that have been explored and developed during the past several decades. In their contemporary survey of the topic, Maitlis and Christianson (2014) called attention to a few especially prominent, recurrent themes among organizational theorists that are pertinent to sensemaking within the global knowledge system under pressure. The first of these themes is that the process of sensemaking is dynamic and ongoing. The sensemaking that took place during the early phases of the pandemic demonstrated this dynamism as well as a level of transience, as new information was shared, and new meaning constructed and reconstructed many times over by agents across the system. The second theme involves the specific activity of extracting cues, particularly from trigger events that represent the unexpected, and relates well to the pandemic context.

The third theme that Maitlis and Christianson (2014) called attention to is that sensemaking is social. Within the sensemaking literature, there are authors who explored the individual and cognitive aspects of the process (Klein et al., 2006; Starbuck & Milliken, 1988), yet most theorists agree that meaning-making involves social construction (Berger & Luckmann, 1966; Cunliffe, 2008; Gergen, 1999; Hosking & McNamee, 2006; Hyatt & Allen, 2018; Maitlis & Christianson, 2014; Taylor & Van Every, 2000; Weick et al., 2005). This view is resonant with sensemaking that occurs specifically within the construct of the global knowledge system, as this system promotes the social construction of knowledge through responsive discourse and communication, especially through influential social and related media. The fourth major theme is that sensemaking is more than the interpretation of stimuli or data; rather, it involves the active authoring of events and frameworks for understanding (Maitlis & Christianson, 2014). In other words, the process often involves an enactment of the interpretation, so that a more ordered reality might be realized amidst confusion or ambiguity. During the pandemic, this aspect of sensemaking was especially challenging, given the range of conflicting enactments that occurred across the various multiple agents. Some of the confusion stemmed from leaders who attempted to convey a message that the pandemic was not a serious threat, thereby dampening alarm and vigilance toward the public health threat (BBC, 2020a). These highly visible, public statements were counter to other global and local government leaders' move to shut down public activities almost immediately following the global pandemic proclamation (BBC, 2020b).

Sensemaking and Sensegiving

As the study of sensemaking has evolved, related concepts such as *sensebreaking, sensegiving, sensedemanding,* and *sensehiding* have been developed to build out a more robust and accurate account of the process of meaning making in organizations (Maitlis & Christianson, 2014). Sensebreaking refers to the destruction or breaking down of a previously accepted meaning or presumed reality (Pratt, 2000). Sensegiving refers to the process of meaning-making so that a deeper understanding is achieved or a desired reality is embraced or enacted (Gioia & Chittipeddi, 1991; Maitlis & Lawrence, 2007). Sensedemanding involves the more assertive effort to realize a certain coherence to a situation (Vlaar et al., 2008). Sensehiding involves the reinterpretation of a situation to create a desired view of reality or, at least, obfuscate an existing one (Vaara & Monin, 2010). Much of the research about these activities centers around organizational leaders and managers, as leaders play a significant role in enacting these aspects of sensemaking during a crisis (Maitlis & Christianson, 2014).

Bringing Emergence and Sensemaking Together: The Data-Frame Model

Further to these recurrent themes and concepts across the sensemaking literature, there is utility in Attfield's et al. (2018) perspective that sensemaking is ultimately a "quest for coherence" (p. 652). That is to say, it is often the lack of coherence, or consistency, of ideas or data regarding a specific issue that prompts the sensemaking process. Again, this view aligns with our depicting the global knowledge system as a CAS and studying the (coherent) emergent properties as much as the chaos that ensued in response to the pandemic. The lack of coherence across the system resulting from the volume, accelerated distribution, and processing of information and misinformation as well as the conflicting enactments of reality make a strong case for understanding how leaders apply or enact aspects of the sensemaking process within the global knowledge system to respond effectively to a crisis such as the pandemic.

One conceptual model that may be useful for sensemaking within the global knowledge system under pressure is the data-frame model (DFM) presented by Klein et al. (2007). The DFM has been popularized within the naturalistic decision-making community. The model essentially proposes that information from the world, or "data," can be made sense of through the application of an appropriate knowledge structure, or "frame" (Klein et al., 2007, p. 113). Sensemaking, from this perspective, then, is the ongoing interplay between data and frame. In the case at hand, data would include inputs, feedback loops, relationships, and adaptations observed across the complex global knowledge system during the pandemic. The frame or frames that leaders and agents may have used to represent and interpret the data could have related to a particular responsibility or role they play within the broader system; the depth of understanding regarding disease spread or the potential impact of a pandemic; and beliefs about personal freedoms relative to compliance measures and ordinances enacted. This type of frame extends beyond the inputs and feedback loops present within the CAS; rather, it uses background knowledge and expectations based on the relevant frame in order to create coherence (Attfield & Baber, 2017). A frame can also make the intake process of large amounts of information more efficient, though it also may bring certain expectations or biases.

The challenges demonstrated within the global knowledge system during the pandemic included the volume of information, accelerated pace of change, growing misinformation, and need to enact sensemaking efficiently in the wake of a crisis. Therefore, it is useful to view systems thinking as the broad frame through which leaders consider the incoming data from the global knowledge system. This would include a focus on emergent properties of the system as a flexible and appropriately dynamic means of sourcing, situating, and processing the volume of information. This approach can also act as an organizing frame for sharing or using this data. Specifically, framing the global knowledge system as a CAS and seeking emergent properties during the pandemic presents organizational leaders with the following potential benefits:

- provides a strategy for processing the volume of information by focusing on patterns;
- structures a method for more intentionally assessing the process of emergence across the system, so as to situate the organization within this process;
- mitigates the potential risk of overreacting to volumes of data and inputs;
- focuses the actual enactment of sensemaking on higher-level, and potentially more influential, ordering within the system, as needed; and
- presents a flexible data frame that can be adapted to suit specific organizational values, goals, and desired responses.

Table 7.2 offers a basic DFM focused on emergent properties to supplement leader queries presented as emergence cues earlier in the chapter. These queries specifically account for the CAS properties of the global knowledge system and the general response to the pandemic.

TABLE 7.2 Leader Sensemaking Related to Emergent Properties in the Global Knowledge System

CAS Attribute or Process	Global Knowledge System Elements and Examples	Properties
Other CASs Influencing the System	Local and global political system, economic system, education system, environmental system, social system	What top–down forces are shaping adaptations within the knowledge system?
Heterogeneity of Agents		
Institutions	Government agencies; universities; public health agencies; news media; NGOs and IGOs	How cohesive or fragmented are these institutions in providing current insights?
Individuals	Subject matter experts (scientists, researchers, public officials); government leaders; public figure influencers	Which of these agents is most influential in driving behavior? What is their underlying motivation?
Social Networks	Social media; professional networks; personal networks	Have I or my organization unwittingly created an echo chamber of biased, narrowly focused perspectives, sources of information?
Content Types	Research reports, case studies, news, public statements, policies, interviews, editorials/opinion	How dynamic or conclusive is the evidence presented in these information sources?
Communication Channels	Internet; email; text; social media; broadcasting; word of mouth	What are the strengths and weaknesses inherent to each communication channel? Are we relying too heavily on any one channel?
Technologies	Data discovery and aggregation; automated tools to measure diffusion of information; internet surveillance	Are we using technology effectively to build organizational capacity to monitor and interpret systemic patterns?
Feedback Loops	Public behavioral responses' rate of infection/health indicators; proliferation of information and misinformation; public discourse; local, national, international ordinances; economic and related macro system indicators	What are the root causes of positive and negative feedback loops? Are there viable solutions for stemming deleterious feedback loops? Are we supporting and investing enough in positive behavioral outcomes?

(continued)

TABLE 7.2 Leader Sensemaking Related to Emergent Properties in the Global Knowledge System (continued)

CAS Attribute or Process	Global Knowledge System Elements and Examples	Properties
Self-Organizing Networks	Coordinated public health campaigns; collective enforcement of ordinances and recommended practices; public compliance and resharing of information; research collaboration	Which networks are producing positive (or negative) results? What is my organization's role within or across these networks?
Coevolution to the Edge of Chaos	All resources on COVID-19; rapid dissemination; new collaboration; novel aggregation of information	Are the adaptations sustainable? How close are we to chaos and why?
Recombination and Systems Evolution	New networks (e.g., from centralized action to decentralized action and new regional/local networks); new task forces; new communication protocols	How is the structure and set of relationships changing? What implications does this have on the system itself and on my organization?

The DFM does not assume dependence on a single frame or knowledge structure. Therefore, values, other beliefs, and responsibilities can still be taken into account using this proposed frame of systems thinking and a focus on emergence. In fact, when values and beliefs are generally shared, the entire sensemaking process through this model may result in a more cohesive enactment and ordering of reality among the various agents across a system. To observe this more cohesive ordering in action, the pandemic response can be viewed as enacted by a subsystem within the global knowledge system—the research and or science communications community.

EMERGENCE AND SENSEMAKING IN ACTION: THE SCIENCE COMMUNICATIONS COMMUNITY'S RESPONSE TO THE PANDEMIC

The pressure to perform the critical function of providing data, evidence, and solutions to the myriad problems presented by COVID-19 was certainly felt by members of the science community. In fact, from a systems perspective, one could argue that the quality of the agent relationships and interactions within the science community and among other key influencers across the global knowledge system (government agencies, public health institutions, the media, etc.) was paramount to formulating and executing an effective local and global set of responses to the crisis. For that reason, the nature and substance of this system's sensemaking process and forms of emergence are considered to illuminate a few key learnings and future implications for organizational leaders operating within and making use of the global knowledge system.

The system of research-based knowledge production contains a vast number of interconnected agents (researchers, government ministries, funding agencies, publishers, universities, libraries, technology companies, intergovernmental agencies; the Organization for Economic Cooperation and Development [OECD], 2015) and components (e.g., journal articles, research reports, data, disciplinary fields) with multiple and evolving interactions (e.g., funding, citations, scholarly collaborations, and networked communications; Zeng et al., 2017). Based on these characteristics as well as the ones distilled earlier in the chapter, the science communications community can be considered as its own purposeful CAS, nested within the broader global knowledge network.

This community frequently acts on a commonly held, utilitarian view that research is a means to improving and doing what is best for society. Among members of this community, access to knowledge is often cited as a human rights issue, one that is affirmed in Article 27 of the United Nations' Universal Declaration of Human Rights (Tennant et al., 2016; UN General Assembly, 1948). Owing to this relative self-similarity in philosophy and shared goals, it is likely that the science communications community would experience an accelerated self-organization in response to the pandemic (Dooley, 1997). A review of public communications and activities across a variety of channels in this community evidenced as much.

Opening Up Information Channels: Emergent Behaviors, Policies, and Partnerships

A research study (Cuevas Shaw, 2021) employing discourse analysis was conducted of more than 75 press releases, blogs, and website updates across nonprofits, commercial publishers, government agencies, technology companies, and universities to identify emergent properties across the scholarly communications community, including (a) the range of support activities immediately undertaken following the proclamation of the pandemic; (b) the language and style of public discourse used, demonstrating how different organizations viewed their identities and roles during the crisis; and (c) specific patterns that emerged related to the process of organizational sensemaking. The findings suggested that the scholarly communications community responded to the crisis with a high degree of adaptability and self-organization that was observable at an aggregate level. The most prominent set of emergent properties resulting from this self-organization and coevolution related to the speed, openness, and enhanced global collaboration in producing and disseminating COVID-19-related research. The variety of adaptations made by this community included the following:

- greater accessibility to research and research tools related to COVID-19;
- the aggregation and curation of COVID-19-focused research;
- enhanced discoverability of research using AI and other technologies;
- free access to relevant content and tools;
- new content, products, and services to support a wide range of pandemic responses;
- new rules applied to the reward system for researchers, the production process for research, and other relevant processes; and
- new collaborations to support these activities.

The extent of these adaptations suggests that members of this system were willing and committed to self-organizing in order to take control of the highly dynamic and uncertain circumstances. Furthermore, there was repeated evidence of the prosocial nature of this collective action, which demonstrated a unified set of values.

With regard to how enacted sensemaking took shape in language use and style of public discourse among agents within this community, there was considerable alignment across overall messaging related to authentically expressed concerns about the pandemic; types of solutions offered; degree of service orientation, commitment, and resourcefulness demonstrated; the consistent focus on accelerating activity and working toward greater efficiency across all aspects of research and dissemination where possible; and the expressed desire to cooperate and partner internationally. There were only a few instances in which an organization did not reference collaboration, partnership, or some degree of connectedness to the global efforts being undertaken.

The process of sensemaking involves the ability to enact the environment as much as be constrained by it. The science communication community responded quickly to the call to action by key influencers to make content freely accessible and demonstrated the desire to make sense of the situation through action and mobilization.

Perhaps more interesting in the context of organizational sensemaking during this crisis was the degree to which multiple sensegiving strategies were employed across a majority of the communications. Whereas the purpose of these press releases largely centered around offering immediate and direct support for the research community, the frequency of ostensive expressions regarding how this crisis work should be carried out and what the current and future state of scholarly communications should comprise was high. The most frequently observed push for change centered around support for open science principles and practices, the need for cooperative and collaborative action on a global scale, the need for authoritative and quality content, the need for greater process efficiency, and the call to focus on serving the needs of individual researchers.

Learnings From the Science Community's Response

Although there were gaps in coordination and effectiveness across this system, the overall response demonstrated that this subsystem could sustain a level of focus and capacity to adapt, even as the broader global knowledge system faced more chaotic episodes. Organizational leaders may not have employed a specific emergence-focused DFM in ordering their reality during this time. There are several learnings relating to systems thinking, emergence, and sensemaking enactment that support the benefits of leveraging this frame when operating within the global knowledge system including the following promising benefits:

1. *A quick and focused assessment of what the system needed.* Within the same week of March that most of the world was shutting down due to the pandemic, this community had already quickly assessed the need to accelerate research efforts and make needed content discoverable.
2. *Understanding and focusing on one's role and capacity within the system.* Evidence points to members of this community focusing intently on matching their capacities to the needs identified.
3. *Paying attention and adjusting to ongoing feedback loops.* The community effectively identified and ramped up activities that were being positively received and of use to the system.
4. *Adapting potentially deleterious behavior.* At the same time, as the accelerated production of research yielded concerns about the quality of the research, the community adjusted processes and protocols to mitigate this increased risk.
5. *Actively reorienting relationships to accelerate goals.* New partnerships and new relationships with constituents were developed as needed to ramp up research efforts.
6. *Actively leveraging technology and new processes to accelerate goals.* Similarly, new technology to aid in aggregation and discovery of content or to address remote research and learning needs was actively employed.
7. *Leaning-in to a dynamic open system.* The overwhelming emergent property among this system was the relatively cohesive push to lean in to the dynamic open system, supporting transparency of process,

free access to previously locked content, and using this occasion to point out the long-term benefits of an open research infrastructure and process (Dooley, 1997, pp. 90–93).

These examples demonstrate how leaders can respond practically and effectively when interpreting a crisis and focusing their efforts.

IMPLICATIONS FOR LEADERS: FROM SENSEMAKING TO LEARNING TO SUSTAINABILITY

There are numerous potential challenges, real demands, and novel actions required of leaders who are navigating our complex and highly dynamic global knowledge system, especially in the time of crisis. In fact, as a result of the pandemic, the WHO launched its own efforts to advance our understanding of infodemiology, or "the science of managing infodemics" (WHO, 2020, para. 3), hosting its first infodemiology conference only a few months following the early days of the proclamation. This is not the first, nor will it be the last, infodemic that occurs. Planning and situating a more intentional strategy for acknowledging the dynamism of the knowledge system and all of its challenging realities presents a unique opportunity for current and future organizational leaders.

Given the level of dynamism and complexity inherent to global knowledge production, dissemination, construction, and use, such a framework requires flexibility if it is to serve as an effective tool for taking in the richness, unpredictability, and evolution of the system. There are limitations to what any leader or organization can achieve within a truly chaotic circumstance. However, during even the initial phases of the pandemic, the global knowledge system exhibited a sense of coherence as in the case of the science communication community's response.

Systems thinking provides one viable and practical broad frame through which to design such a flexible and still-organic approach to organizational sensemaking and, relatedly, enactment of an effective response and new reality. The specific focus on emergence as a primary data frame for the sensemaking process carries numerous potential advantages for crises and other moments of significant disequilibrium. This focus allows leaders to pare back more intentionally and strategically, process, and act on retrospective, real-time, or anticipated emergent properties that have a likelihood of influencing the system in some way. Attention to emergence, if applied soundly, also does not preclude the leader's ability to evaluate and scan the wide range of agents and interconnections across this complex system. Rather, it focuses such an effort and suggests a certain level of diverse sourcing of content and perspectives to synthesize appropriately the whole system. Furthermore, if this systems-oriented DFM is co-constructed with members of the organization, the opportunity for shared learning may increase, as the social and discursive aspects of the sensemaking process becomes more intentional and cohesive. This learning and capacity building may, in turn, assist organizational leaders in preparing for future uncertainty and needed evolution.

Visualizing the New Framework for Leaders

Figure 7.1 offers a visual of this new conceptual DFM framework for leaders that describes the sensemaking process within a systems frame. Specifically, this visual depicts the dynamic processes of (a) identifying and characterizing the emergent patterns across the global knowledge system; (b) enacting a response based on the processing of organizational sensemaking with teams and other constituents; and (c) the overlapping and continuous process of sensemaking that results from the ongoing identification, interpretation, and enacted response to system emergence.

SUMMARY

Leaders are called to make sense of increasingly complex global systems, not the least of which is the global knowledge system, which exhibits the core attributes of a CAS: heterogeneity of agents, self-organizing networks, coevolution to the edge of chaos, and recombination. As witnessed during the early days of the pandemic, this CAS under pressure carries characteristics of resilience as well as chaos, as a result of the increasing interconnectedness of a wide range of agents that are operating in an otherwise decentralized manner.

Coupled with advances in technology that make various digital networks and relationship causalities even more dynamic and complex, it is imperative to develop new mechanisms for navigating and influencing the disequilibrium characterized by ambiguity, uncertainty, and disruption. The mechanisms are not likely to be linear or predictably cyclical in nature, yet that does not preclude leaders from designing and constructing a strategic frame to address such dynamism. In fact, it is through a strategic frame that leaders can hone the habits and skills of learning about the whole system, including structures, interconnected relationships, processes, and characteristics.

The specific feature of emergence within a CAS offers a uniquely flexible yet sophisticated data frame through which leaders and their constituents can process events and properties related to the system. Emergence

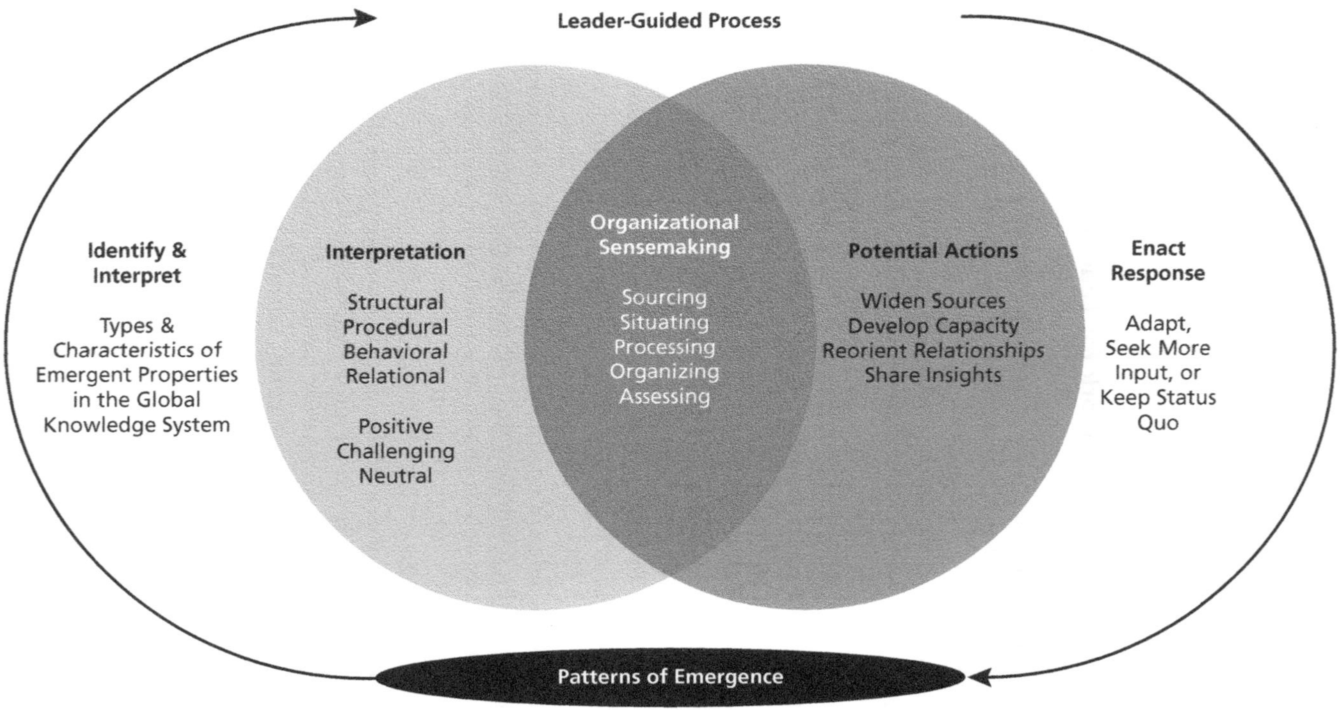

Figure 7.1 Emergence and sensemaking: A conceptual framework for leaders.

can relate to structures, processes, patterns of behaviors, and outputs of a system, all owing to the dynamic interplay of positive and reinforcing, or negative and reducing feedback loops. Leaders, their teams, and their networks can benefit from more consistently pulling back from the voluminous detail offered by the global knowledge system to observe the whole both retrospectively and in real time. Emergent properties can shape the sensemaking process without removing a leader's opportunity to enact sense or a specific order to some circumstances. Although certain moments of chaos may not afford the opportunity to control certain situations, leaders can benefit from situating themselves and their organizations within the higher-order patterns that emerge.

A novel DFM comprising a unique interplay of the constructs of emergence and organizational sensemaking can provide leaders with numerous benefits, especially during a crisis situation. First, it addresses the need to process a high volume and range of data, and in a more focused and intentional manner. Second, it may hone the skill set of observing critically influential and activating feedback loops. Third, it balances the sensemaking process between the needed focus on emergent phenomena that may be changing the system and the active authoring of the emergent or changing reality. Fourth, if co-constructed and shared with teams and constituents, it allows for a more intentionally designed, social learning process, which can be especially effective and critical during moments of crisis, as individuals personally situate themselves and their value systems within an otherwise unexpected and uncertain set of circumstances.

The science communications community, a subsystem within the global knowledge system, offers an example of a relatively cohesive and resilient response to the pandemic. In addition to illuminating the connections across systems thinking and sensemaking, this example also calls attention to the likelihood of a more open research infrastructure and set of resources that leaders may seek out for future sensemaking. Research and evidence may be less available to leaders during times of rapid change. However, through technology, the global knowledge system is adapting to make these resources more discoverable, transparent, and usable in an effort to coordinate and collaborate on wicked global problems such as pandemics.

REFERENCES

Ackoff, R. L., Emery, F., & Ruben B. (2005). *On purposeful systems: An interdisciplinary analysis of individual and social behavior as a system of purposeful events.* Aldine Transaction.

Anderson, P. (1999). Complexity theory and organization science. *Organization Science, 10*(3), 216–232.

Angst, M. (2020.). Bottom-up identification of subsystems in complex governance systems. *Policy Studies Journal, 48*(3), 782–805. https://doi.org/10.1111/psj.12301

Attfield, S., & Baber, C. (2017). Elaborating the frames of data-frame theory. In J. Gore & P. Ward (Eds.), *Naturalistic decision making and uncertainty: Proceedings of the 13th International Conference on Naturalistic Decision Making* (pp. 25–32). The University of Bath.

Attfield, S., Fields, B., & Baber, C. (2018). A resources model for distributed sensemaking. *Cognition, Technology & Work, 20,* 651–654. https://doi.org/10.1007/s10111-018-0529-4

Bar-Yam, Y. (1997). *Dynamics of complex systems.* Perseus Press.

BBC. (2020a, September 10). *Trump deliberately played down virus, Woodward book says.* https://www.bbc.com/news/world-us-canada-54094559

BBC. (2020b, May 10). *How world leaders adapted to the pandemic.* https://www.bbc.com/news/world-52744485

Berger, P. L., & Luckmann, T. (1966). *The social construction of reality: A treatise in the sociology of knowledge.* Anchor Books, Doubleday.

Blitz, D. (1992). *Emergent evolution: Qualitative novelty and the levels of reality.* Kluwer Academic Publishers.

Brennen, J. S., Simon, F., Howard, P. N., & Nielsen, R. K. (2020, April). *Types, sources, and claims of COVID-19 misinformation.* Reuters Institute. https://reutersinstitute.politics.ox.ac.uk/types-sources-and-claims-covid-19-misinformation

Brown, S. L., & Eisenhardt, K. M. (1998). *Competing on the edge: Strategy as structured chaos.* Harvard Business School Press.

Buldyrev, S., Parshani, R., & Paul, G. (2010). Catastrophic cascade of failures in interdependent networks. *Nature, 464,* 1025–1028. https://doi.org/10.1038/nature08932

Bunge, M. A. (2003). *Emergence and convergence: Qualitative novelty and the unity of knowledge.* University of Toronto Press.

Checkland, P. B. (1993). *Systems thinking, systems practice.* Wiley.

Colglazier, E. W. (2020, April 9). Response to the COVID-19 pandemic: Catastrophic failures of the science-policy interface. *Science & Diplomacy.* https://www.sciencediplomacy.org/editorial/2020/response-covid-19-pandemic-catastrophic-failures-science-policy-interface

Coombs, W. T. (1999). *Ongoing crisis communication.* SAGE Publications.

Cornelissen, J. (2012). Sensemaking under pressure: The influence of professional roles and social accountability on the creation of sense. *Organization Science, 23*(1), 118–137.

Corning, P. A. (2002). The re-emergence of "emergence": A venerable concept in search of a theory. *Complexity, 7*(2), 18–30.

Cuevas Shaw, L. (2021). From sensemaking to sensegiving: A discourse analysis of the scholarly communications community's public response to the global pandemic. *Learned Publishing, 34*(1), 6–16. https://doi.org/10.1002/leap.1350

Cunliffe, A. L. (2008). Orientations to social constructionism: Relationally responsive social constructionism and its implications for knowledge and learning. *Management Learning 39*(2), 123–139.

DiResta, R. (2020, May 6). Virus experts aren't getting the message out. *The Atlantic.* https://www.theatlantic.com/ideas/archive/2020/05/health-experts-dont-understand-how-information-moves/611218/

Dooley, K. (1997). A complex adaptive systems model of organization change. *Nonlinear Dynamics, Psychology, and the Life Sciences, 1*(1), 69–97.

Erkhembayar, R., Dickinson, E., Badarch, D., Narula, I., Thomas, G. N., Ochir, C., & Manaseki-Holland, S. (2020). Early policy actions and emergency response to the COVID-19 pandemic in Mongolia: Experiences and challenges. *The Lancet Global Health, 8*(9), E1234–E1241. https://doi.org/10.1016/s2214-109x(20)30295-3

Forman, R. (2020). 12 lessons learned from the management of the coronavirus pandemic. *Health Policy, 124*(6), 577–580.

Fulmer, C. A., & Ostroff, C. (2015), Convergence and emergence in organizations: An integrative framework and review. *Journal of Organizational Behavior, 37*(S1), S122–S145. https://doi.org/10.1002/job.1987

Gates, B. (2020, April 30). Responding to Covid-19—A once-in-a-century pandemic? *New England Journal of Medicine.* https://doi.org/10.1056/NEJMp2003762

Gergen, K. J. (1999) *An invitation to social construction.* SAGE Publishing.

Gioia, D. A., & Chittipeddi, K. (1991). Sensemaking and sensegiving in strategic change initiation. *Strategic Management Journal, 12*(6), 433–448.

Goldstein, J. (1999). Emergence as a construct: History and issues. *Emergence, 1*(1), 49–72. https://doi.org/10.1207/s15327000em0101_4

Holland, J. H. (1995). *Hidden order: How adaptation builds complexity.* Addison-Wesley.

Holland, J. H. (1998). *Emergence: From chaos to order.* Addison-Wesley.

Hosking, D. M., & McNamee, S. (2006) *The social construction of organization.* Business School Press.

Hyatt, L. (2020, March 2–4). *Effect of narratives on organization change* [Paper presentation]. International Technology, Education, and Development Conference, Valencia, Spain.

Hyatt, L., & Allen, S. (2018). *Advancing doctoral leadership education* (With Foreword by Ron Riggio, PhD). Edward Elgar Publishing.

Johansen, B. (2017). *The new leadership literacies: Thriving in a future of extreme disruption and distributed everything.* Berrett Koehler Publishers.

Jordana, J., & Triviño-Salazar, J. C. (2020, May 23). Where are the ECDC and the EU-wide responses in the COVID-19 pandemic? *The Lancet, 395*(10237), 1611–1612. https://doi.org/10.1016/S0140-6736(20)31132-6

Kim, J. (2016). Emergence: Core ideas and issues. *Synthese, 151*(3), 547–559. https://doi.org/10.1007/s11229-006-9025-0

Klein, G., Moon, B., & Hoffman, R. R. (2006). Making sense of sensemaking 1: Alternative perspectives. *IEEE Intelligent Systems, 21*(4), 70–73.

Klein, G., Phillips, J. K., Rall, E. L., & Peluso, D. A. (2007). A data-frame theory of sensemaking. In R. R. Hoffman (Ed.), *Expertise out of context: Proceedings of the Sixth International Conference on Naturalistic Decision Making* (pp. 113–155). Lawrence Erlbaum Associates Publishers.

Kouzy, R., Abi Jaoude, J., Kraitem, A., El Alam, M. B., Karam, B., Adib, E., Zarka, J., Traboulsi, C., Akl, E. W., & Baddour, K. (2020). Coronavirus goes viral:

Quantifying the COVID-19 misinformation epidemic on Twitter. *Cureus, 12*(3), e7255. https://doi.org/10.7759/cureus.7255

Kuguyo, O., Kengne, A. P., & Dandara, C. (2020). Singapore COVID-19 pandemic response as a successful model framework for low-resource health care settings in Africa? *OMICS: A Journal of Integrative Biology, 24*(8), 470–478. http://doi.org/10.1089/omi.2020.0077

Lichtenstein, B., & McKelvey, B. (2011). Four types of emergence: A typology of complexity and its implications for a science of management. *International Journal of Complexity in Leadership and Management, 1*(4), 339–378. https://doi.org/10.1504/IJCLM.2011.046439

Lynton, R. P. (1969). Linking an innovative subsystem into the system. *Administrative Science Quarterly, 14*(3), 398–416.

Maitlis, S., & Christianson, M. (2014). Sensemaking in organizations: Taking stock and moving forward. *The Academy of Management Annals, 8*(1), 57–125.

Maitlis, S., & Lawrence, T. B. (2007). Triggers and enablers of sensegiving in organizations. *Academy of Management Journal, 50*(1), 57–84.

Organization for Economic Cooperation and Development. (2015). Making open science a reality. *OECD Science, Technology and Industry Policy Papers* (No. 25). http://dx.doi.org/10.1787/5jrs2f963zs1-en

Osterholm, M. T., & Olshaker, M. (2020). Chronicle of a pandemic foretold. *Foreign Affairs, 99*(4), 9–24.

Pratt, M. G. (2000). The good, the bad, and the ambivalent: Managing identification among Amway distributors. *Administrative Science Quarterly, 45*(3), 456–493.

Rothkopf, D. (2003, May 11). When the buzz bites back [Opinion]. *Washington Post.* https://www.washingtonpost.com/archive/opinions/2003/05/11/when-the-buzz-bites-back/bc8cd84f-cab6-4648-bf58-0277261af6cd/

Sensuse, D. I., Sucahyo, Y. G., Rohajawati, R., & Anggia, P. (2014). Models and frameworks of knowledge management: A literature review. In N. Sapporo (Ed.), *2014 International Conference on Information Science, Electronics and Electrical Engineering* (pp. 1166–1170). IEEE. https://doi.org/10.1109/InfoSEEE.2014.6947854

Simon, H. A. (1996). *The sciences of the artificial* (3rd ed.). MIT Press.

Starbuck, W. H., & Milliken, F. J. (1988). Executives' perceptual filters: What they notice and how they make sense. In D. C. Hambrick (Ed.), *The executive effect: Concepts and methods for studying top managers* (pp. 35–65). JAI Press.

Sterman, J. D. (2000). *Business dynamics: Systems thinking and modeling for a complex world,* McGraw Hill/Irwin.

Taylor, J. R., & Van Every, E. J. (2000). *The emergent organization: Communication as its site and surface.* Erlbaum.

Tennant, J. P., Waldner, F., Jacques, D. C., Masuzzo, P., Collister, L. B., & Hartgerink, C. H. (2016). The academic, economic and societal impacts of open access: An evidence-based review. *F1000Research, 5,* 632. https://doi.org/10.12688/f1000research.8460.3

Törnberg, P. (2018). Echo chambers and viral misinformation: Modeling fake news as complex contagion. *PLOS ONE, 13*(9), e0203958. https://doi.org/10.1371/journal.pone.0203958

United Nations Department of Global Communications. (2020, March 28). *UN tackles "infodemic" of misinformation and cybercrime in COVID-19 crisis.* United Nations.

United Nations General Assembly. (1948). *Universal declaration of human rights* (217 [III] A). Paris.

Vaara, E., & Monin, P. 2010. A recursive perspective on discursive legitimation and organizational action in mergers and acquisitions. *Organization Science, 21*(1), 3–22.

Vlaar, P. W. L., van Fenema, P. C., & Tiwari, V. (2008). Cocreating understanding and value in distributed work: How members of onsite and offshore vendor teams give, make, demand, and break sense. *Management Information Systems Quarterly, 32*(2), 227–255.

Weick, K. E. (1988). Enacted sensemaking in crisis situations. *Journal of Management Studies, 25*(4), 305–317.

Weick, K. E. (1995). *Sensemaking in organizations.* SAGE Publications.

Weick, K. E. (2005). Managing the unexpected: Complexity as distributed sensemaking. In R. R. McDaniel Jr., & D. J. Driebe (Eds.), *Uncertainty and surprise in complex systems: Questions on working with the unexpected* (pp. 51–65). Springer-Verlag.

Weick, K. E., & Sutcliffe, K. M. (2007). *Managing the unexpected: Resilient performance in an age of uncertainty* (2nd ed.). Jossey-Bass.

Weick, K. E., Sutcliffe, K. M., & Obstfeld, D. (2005). Organizing and the process of sensemaking. *Organization Science, 16*(4), 409–421.

World Health Organization. (2020). *1st WHO infodemiology conference.* https://www.who.int/news-room/events/detail/2020/06/30/default-calendar/1st-who-infodemiology-conference

Yolles, M. (2006). *Organizations as complex systems: An introduction to knowledge cybernetics.* Information Age Publishing.

Zeng, A., Shen Z., Zhou, J., Wu, J., Fan, Y., Wang, Y., & Stanley, E. (2017). The science of science: From the perspective of complex systems. *Physics Reports, 714–715,* 1–73. https://doi.org/10.1016/j.physrep.2017.10.001

CHAPTER 8

A DIFFERING VIEW OF COMMAND IN A CONNECTED WORLD

Captain Brett Crozier and COVID-19 Command Decisions

Paul Nelson
Mission Next, LLC

Robert A. Norton
Auburn University

Greg S. Weaver
Auburn University

This chapter uses the case of Captain Crozier of the U.S. Navy to illustrate how the absence of a cohesive narrative or strategy among elected officials, government agencies, and the military itself typified not only the early COVID-19 response but also the complex issues related to messaging within

Crisis, Chaos, and Organizations, pages 227–239

TABLE 8.1 Timeline Compiled From the U.S. Naval Institute

Date	Event
11/01/2019	Captain Crozier assumes command of the USS *Theodore Roosevelt*.
12/31/2019	First reports from China RE cluster of illnesses later identified as COVID-19.
01/17/2020	USS *Theodore Roosevelt* deploys from San Diego, CA to the Indio-Pacific AOR.
03/05–29/2020	USS *Theodore Roosevelt* arrives in port in Da Nang, Vietnam. 39 sailors are quarantined following possible contact with COVID-19 positive individuals. All test negative but members of crew begin testing positive on 03/24. By 03/29 the number reaches 53.
03/30–31/2020	Captain Crozier sends unclassified email to superiors requesting quarantine of crew. Appears in *San Francisco Chronicle*.
04/02/2020	Captain Crozier relieved of command.
6/19/2020	Navy upholds decision to relieve Captain Crozier.

the military and federal government. The attempt to balance the health of the crew of the USS *Theodore Roosevelt* (and others) while not negatively affecting the U.S. position in the Pacific reflects a strategy-to-policy inversion and disjointed interpretation of strategy that resulted in courses of action that were both valid and contradictory to one another.

In communicating to his superiors, he expressed concerns related to the health of personnel under his command. Rapidly spreading COVID-19 infections among the crew risked not only the health of personnel, but also the loss of a strategic U.S. capability in the Pacific. CAPT Crozier's letter leaked to the press, and he was quickly relieved on command—which appeared to indicate the Department of the Navy and larger Department of Defense were attempting to suppress the medical concerns of the U.S.S. Theodore Roosevelt for the sake of keeping the aircraft carrier at sea. Some members of the press interpreted the events as evidence of a "cover up." The situation became more confused when, after openly criticizing CAPT Crozier (who incidentally was infected with COVID-19), the Acting Secretary of the Navy Thomas Modly resigned. The timeline shown in Table 8.1, compiled from the U.S. Naval Institute (2020), provides partial context of the events.

POWER PROJECTION AND COMMAND

Command duty at sea is one of the most difficult challenges that Navy officers will face during their careers. The mission of U.S. aircraft carriers is highly complex, given that they are warships which act not just as mobile airbases for Navy based aircraft, but also as a means of highly effective means of achieving "power projection," sometimes called "force projection." Power projection can be thought of as a function of statecraft. Aircraft carriers are highly mobile, contain massive lethal firepower in the form of aircraft capable of carrying bombs and missiles, which because of the aircraft carrier, can be rapidly deployed as needs arise. In this way, aircraft carriers serve the function of acting as powerful deterrents to malign actors and hostile states that may choose to politically or militarily challenge the United States, our allies and global trading partners, or the sovereignty of nations. Regardless of project massive military might and achieve both strategic and tactical dominance, should warfighting capabilities be needed. Furthering this mission, aircraft carriers serve to achieve, what are envisioned as the four operational concepts of future "joint" (meaning multi-service) warfare; those being (a) dominant maneuver, (b) precision engagement, (c) focused logistics, and (d) full-dimensional protection (Lee, 1999). The totality of these capabilities is often framed in the term "hard power," which is calculated in terms of the number of aircraft, personnel, armaments (tanks, artillery, etc.) and ordinance (bombs, missiles, etc.), which the nation can bring to a conflict.

Carrier battle groups (CVBG) are also important tools for the non-lethal projection of state power, since they can also participate in global rescue or humanitarian efforts, through the deployment of their carry reconnaissance aircraft and aircraft for search and rescue efforts, as well as the delivery of humanitarian aid. One interesting aspect of nuclear-powered aircraft carriers is that they are equipped to produce massive amounts of potable water, which likewise can and have been used in humanitarian efforts.

Power projection by the United States is now frequently framed in terms describing the "soft power" capabilities that can be brought to bear, humanitarian efforts being only one example. Soft power is a term that was first described by the political scientist Joseph S. Nye (1990). In that essay, the author posited great power shifts were occurring in the world in part as a result of the failure of the Soviet Union. He claimed these global power shifts in turn necessitated de-emphasis of hard power, while necessitating the need for increased emphasis by the United States on soft power elements:

> Proof of power lies not in resources but in the ability to change the behavior of states. Thus, the critical question for the United States is not whether it will start the next century as the superpower with the largest supply of resources, but to what extent it will be able to control the political environment and get other countries to do what it wants. (p. 155)

The United States is very good at projecting hard power, but often less than successful in persuasion. As always, other countries serve their own needs first and cooperate only to the extent when U.S. needs and desires mesh well with their own goals, or can at least be used by those nations to neutralize the power offered by other nation state competitors. "For Nye, the basis of U.S. soft power was liberal democratic politics, free market economics, and fundamental values such as human rights—in essence, liberalism" (Li, 2018, para. 3).

Global trade is considered an essential element in soft power projection, the thought being that trading partners are less likely to go to war. Although that theory has been proven wrong on several occasions throughout history, global trading partners (e.g., China) can be reminded with a not-so-subtle message that the United States can project power wherever and whenever it chooses, through the presence of an aircraft carrier group arriving in international waters. As global tensions continue to rise with potential hostile nations, like North Korea, China, and Iran, U.S. aircraft carriers increasingly cruise in or near contested waters like the Persian Gulf or the South China Sea.

Because of both the lethality inherent to an aircraft carrier, the Navy requires its officers to be the best and most experienced, since there is no room for error and zero tolerance of failure. Blunders on the part of these officers can cause shooting wars and diplomatic disasters. Major errors in command judgement, willful dereliction of duty or disobeying orders, whether in reality or in spirit, would therefore be considered as the highest level of failure and a betrayal of both the Navy and its commanders. Captain Crozier was considered worthy of such trust by the Navy, or else he would not have been assigned such an important mission. He had arrived at the pinnacle point of trust by the Navy in his career and appeared destined to achieve further rank advancement to Flag Officer status (starting with Rear Admiral Lower Half; O-7). Then COVID-19 arrived.

OFFICERS AND THE PROFESSION OF ARMS

Military officers are regularly required to make rapid decisions that at their least can be impactful to those who serve under their command, or at their most serious can cost lives, either of the enemy or the various personnel that serve under those officers' commands. The American military ethos is framed in the descriptor, "A Profession of Arms," which is typified by a shared code of values, ethics, and standards to be adhered to by all of its members. The Department of the Navy describes core values as including, honor, courage, and commitment (Military Leadership Diversity Commission, 2009).

The U.S. Department of the Navy Code of Ethics (2005) contains a list of "dos and don'ts," which outlines a number of principles such as loyalty to U.S. law and the U.S. Constitution (including the appearance of avoiding illegal or unethical behavior), honesty, and being a good citizen.[1] Ethical conduct is further codified by Navy leadership in the "Leadership Commitment to Ethical Conduct" which states: "It is essential that all Department of the Navy personnel adhere to the highest standards of integrity and ethical conduct. The American people put their trust in us and none of us can betray that trust" (U.S. Department of the Navy, 2013). Additionally, in elaborating "Bedrock Standards" in the Core Values Charter—which elaborates the values of honor, courage, and commitment—the following is stated, "I will conduct myself in the highest ethical manner in relationships with seniors, peers, and subordinates" (U.S. Department of the Navy, n.d.).[2]

One of the responsibilities an officer has is to maintain operational security (OPSEC), which generally refers to various measures related to protecting critical information and reducing the likelihood that an adversary can access information and gain an advantage from it. OPSEC is designed to protect both military personnel and missions. In a July 20, 2020 memo to all Department of Defense (DOD) personnel, Defense Secretary Mark Esper released a memo about its importance. In the memo he stated,

> Proper Operations Security (OPSEC) is critical to protecting our forces, ensuring our mission success, and implementing the National Defense Strategy. History is full of examples of poor OPSEC leading to the unnecessary loss of life and mission failure, and it can mean the difference between our winning and losing as we face great power competitors that will not hesitate to exploit and weaponize information. (Esper, 2020, para. 1)

This sentiment was further echoed in a Department of Defense (2020) memorandum released on the following day.[3]

OPSEC is not a new concept to the military, but its practices and principles need to be scrupulously adhered to, for the desired outcomes to be assured.

> Operations Security (OPSEC) as a concept is probably as old as war itself. Nevertheless, the fact that poor OPSEC practices have been costly in loss of human life and lost objectives in every American war demonstrates that, despite its venerated age, Operations Security/as a doctrine needs to be learned afresh by each generation. (National Security Agency, 1993)

The processes and standards, which have evolved since "Purple Dragon," a military program (team) that stood up during the Vietnam War, determined that publicly released information by the Pentagon was being used by the North Vietnamese to anticipate U.S. military missions and flights. The information was not classified information. The Vietnamese had not deciphered classified and encrypted communications, but the end result was almost as serious in that its release had caused the loss of both military aircraft and more importantly, as substantial loss of life.

The first OPSEC definition developed by Purple Dragon is compelling in the current context. OPSEC is "the ability to keep knowledge of our strengths and weaknesses away from hostile forces" (National Security Agency, 1993, p. 4). All military officers and enlisted personnel receive OPSEC training and are held to the standards of the training. In the modern context of complex Navy missions, the Second World War slogan, "Loose Lips Sink Ships," seems apropos. The release of information related to the health of a crew is an example of information that although not classified is sensitive, since it can give a picture to potential adversaries of the readiness of a ship to respond to military challenges.

The Secretary of the Navy designated the responsibilities of OPSEC in a guidance (SECNAV/OPSEC) dated December 16, 2016. Current guidance documents rules and procedures were most recently released on May 29th by the Office of the Secretary of Defense (2020):

> This final rule sets forth the Department of Defense's (DOD) policies and processes governing the issuance and use of guidance documents. By issuing this final rule, DOD also responds to the Executive Order titled: "Promoting the Rule of Law Through Improved Agency Guidance Documents," which requires federal agencies to finalize regulations, or amend existing regulations as necessary, to set forth processes and procedures for issuing guidance documents. (para. 7)

Citing the authority of 5 USC 552a, under Subsection 339.1, the rule document reads,

> (c) For purposes of this part, the term guidance document includes any statement of agency policy or interpretation concerning a statute, regulation, or technical matter within the jurisdiction of the Department that is intended to have general applicability and future effect on the behavior of regulated parties, but which is not intended to have the force or effect of law in its own right and is not otherwise required by statute to satisfy the rulemaking procedures specified in 5 U.S.C. 553 or 5 U.S.C. 556.

In other words, a guidance document interprets statutes and regulations, which are already in place and does not supplant them.

Several elements of the guidance are very relevant to the review of Captain Crozier's performance during the COVID outbreak on his ship. The directive frames the importance of this security posture since

> current threats require that we redouble our efforts to protect critical information... Exploitation of internet based capabilities, publicly released information, and other UNCLASSIFIED but potentially sensitive data gives adversaries the ability to undermine our technological edge, threaten our personnel, and potentially compromise our operations. (Secretary of the Navy, 2016, para. 2)

The Secretary of the Navy (2016) guidance of December 16th lists several "key elements of the policy..." including:

> a. OPSEC is explicitly the responsibility of each Commanding Officer or equivalent.
>
> b. OPSEC must be considered and incorporated into all operational planning and execution. c. A requirement for commands to develop, resource, and maintain effective OPSEC programs.
>
> d. OPSEC is clearly defined as an Operations rather than a Security function...
>
> i. Each Command shall develop and implement enforcement mechanisms to reduce disclosures of critical information per SECNAVINST 3070.2...

Using this framework as the standards for commanders, it becomes clearer that Captain Crozier may have violated Navy requirements for commanders to enforce OPSEC, which included development of a program for the ship, as part of the larger OPSEC program for the CVGB and Navy. Rather than a security violation, it appears the email[4] discussing the onboard medical condition of the crew was interpreted by Navy command as an operational violation, since OPSEC is an operations responsibility. It is not clear who leaked the email to the press. However, staff from the *San Francisco Chronicle* was in communication with an officer onboard of the Roosevelt, as indicated in the original article, about the crew COVID case numbers (Gafni & Garofoli, 2020). In the strictest sense, it does not matter because using an email as a means of communicating unclassified, but sensitive information is not considered proper under OPSEC standards.

Nonetheless, it is also clear that there is another element in play. Navy command was surprised and predictably acted swiftly, possibly in anger. Captain (ret) Kevin S. Eyer (2020) explained in a U.S. Naval Institute blog post,

> It is fundamentally understood by the Navy's commanders that the Navy will be not grateful to those who unilaterally decide to make "family business" a matter of raging, politically fraught debate. The danger is that to quell the noise, the Navy may be forced to take actions, which may be contrary to either the "good order and discipline" so vital to an effective fighting force or decisions which lead to unintended, unwanted other consequences. (para. 4)

Eyer (2020) then explains the crux of the problem from the Navy perspective:

> More important, Captain Crozier precipitated the removal of one of the Navy's few, most powerful strategic assets from the playing board. This hole cannot be filled without machinations that leave other holes and drag thousands

> of sailors back to long deployments early. The Navy was not allowed to work to a strategic "soft-fall," and our potential enemies were given a wrong signal. That, if nothing else, cannot be forgiven. (para. 5)

The USS *Roosevelt* had been operating in waters that are increasingly problematic, because of the increasingly belligerent military postures of China. The email leak occurred also in a time of great domestic uncertainty associated with the escalation of domestic COVID numbers. The public health responses by the Trump administration had become a political football, with each side of the aisle vying for attention (read votes) by the public, given 2020 is an election year. It is clear the Navy had the full authority and precedent to discipline Captain Crozier, like any Naval officer who had stepped outside of the bounds of acceptable behavior, but Secretary of the Navy, Thomas B. Modly, decided to make his chastisements of Captain Crozier more personal, and in doing so, made the situation even worse:

> Secretaries of the Navy do not involve themselves in individual ships. That is not their place. While on deployment, that aircraft carrier was and is the operational responsibility of U.S. Indo-Pacific Command, Admiral Philip S. Davidson. Even within Navy's administrative chain, Modly sat some five echelons removed from Crozier. Further, Modly's actions reportedly were contrary to the advice of that chain of command including the Chief of Naval Operations Admiral Michael M. Gilday. (Eyer, 2020, para. 8)

In short, Modly was inexplicably outside of his lane and jumping complex and well-tested lines of authority.

CIVIL-MILITARY RELATIONS

The previous section highlights ethics and related decision-making of Navy officers, a point that connects to civil-military relations which are briefly discussed here. There is an extensive literature focusing on civil-military relations, and a comprehensive review is beyond the scope of the current essay. Fundamentally, the concept of civil-military relations emphasizes the dynamic between military officers and the state. As the officer ranks are increasingly viewed as a profession, their position in relation to civilian, state organizations and individuals becomes complex (Huntington, 1957). As such, there is concern about using the military to accomplish political goals and at the individual level, how decisions by officers can be influenced by political issues. Some scholars suggest that ideally, the military as an institution and the individuals within it should be apolitical. President Eisenhower's warning of a growing "military-industrial complex" is but one example. Similarly, Goltz (2003) makes the point of the long-held notion that to be political is to be self-serving, which is arguably related to ethical behavior. Brooks (2020) notes that an increasing number of military personnel disagree with this sentiment. Further and more importantly as it relates to the current examination, the author notes that apolitical decisions can have political consequences, which is arguably the crux of the Crozier controversy, particularly if she is correct in the assertion that President Trump views the military as a political ally.

THE VERDICT

One may make a reasonable argument that Captain Crozier is a modern-day Navy hero. Recognizing the potentially dire and rapidly medical conditions evolving situation aboard the ship under his command, he acted decisively with the best information available. OPSEC violations, whether by Captain Crozier directly or made under his command, were a small price to pay when the lives of his sailors and the overall long-term fighting capacity of his commanded ship, were in question. He acted knowing the professional price he would pay to defy an insular and politically entrenched Navy bureaucracy. Reports of the outbreak aboard his ship had already appeared in press, meaning they could not be ignored. He made the difficult decision to put the lives of his sailors first by elevating the emerging disease outbreak into the news, while ensuring that his ship would survive to be available to fight another day. Using this perspective, he upheld in the finest way the traditions of Naval command, and the Naval bureaucracy was wrong in their actions.

On the other hand, one may make an equally compelling argument that Captain Crozier was, at best, negligent in his duty to protect the strategic national asset entrusted to him as he clumsily navigated the political firestorm of press he created. At worst, his hubris undermined the chain of command and damaged America's strategic interests and resolve in the Pacific, undercutting our national military strategy in ways that are still emerging. Senior Naval leadership was fully justified by their swift actions as they removed a rogue sailor from command. Public insubordination required a public punishment to send a strong message that the Navy remains a disciplined fighting force and under civilian control.

While each of these arguments on face value is reasonable in reality, neither one fully captures the essence of the primary actions taken by Captain Crozer or the subsequent reactions by the Naval leadership. While we do not, and may never know, all of the events that occurred leading up to the removal of Captain Crozier, each protagonist, the Naval commander and the Navy chain of command, acted predictably based upon a bureaucratic politics model of decision making as well as the individual leadership beliefs of the protagonists.

A different model would be to look at the political and strategic environments that underpin the decision makers. In this model, an overall national strategy would inform operational and tactical decisions. Commanders at all levels would be held accountable for their decisions. However, in the Spring of 2020 (and into 2021), the nation was ill-prepared to coalesce around a coherent national security strategy in dealing with the impact on COVID-19. This political process, between the executive and legislative branches, between the military leaders and domestic "generals" (including the public health professionals and economists), failed to articulate or coalesce around a national strategy.

President Trump declared himself a wartime president, and the nation rapidly assumed a wartime footing, with lockdowns and restriction of commerce. However, the nation never effectively coalesced around a politically negotiated national strategy to fight COVID-19 as part of a broader national strategy. While one may choose to rest sole blame on the commander in chief ("the buck stops here"), this approach would underestimate the role of other political actors and oversimplify the negotiated and horizontal process of strategy development that a democratic republic undergoes (Huntington, 1960).

Further complicating the situation was the national partisan polarization that was occurring after an impeachment process (the justification for or against is beyond the scope of this paper) running up to a contentious national election. Finally, because the enemy was a poorly defined virus, the national security apparatus was unable to fully conceptualize the nature of the conflict and articulate in cohesive ways through the interagency process. Principal actors such as the Department of Defense were unable to re-conceptualize their role and fell back to preparing for the "familiar battle," that is a conflict with China. This is not to say that the PRC is not a threat to United States influence around the world, or that they may have covered up COVID-19 initially and up to present. Rather, COVID-19 exists as a new challenge to the great power competition between a rising China and an established great Pacific power, the United States.

Other principles including the Health and Human Services and Centers for Disease Control, jockeyed for power with the Treasury Department and other agencies as we lurched from fighting at least four conflicts at once. First was the "war on COVID-19," framed initially as an existential threat to the multiple sectors of our strategic infrastructures. Second was the normal conflict in the interagency process as the nation engaged in the political process between competing interests in the bureaucracy of the federal government. Third was the "war against China" and the "China Virus" as a rising great power. Finally, was the hyper-partisan political "war" and lack of effective leadership to bring the nation together around a single articulated strategy.

Into this complex and poorly-defined environment sailed Captain Crozier and the crew of the USS *Teddy Roosevelt.* Captain Crozier was trusted with command of a strategic national asset, and Naval captains were given great leeway in the command of their ship while underway. With this great trust comes great responsibility, especially in times of war. However, Captain Crozier found himself at the very beginning of a poorly defined strategic political landscape, one that has, in fact, not been better defined in the intervening 6 months since he was removed from command.

While the rank of Naval captain (06) is considered a "senior rank" by virtue of command, in reality it is the entry level position for senior officers exposed to the political environment that is our national decision-making process. Most senior officers who have this level of political exposure have a flag rank. Further, the most exposed positions (the 09-010 positions are politically confirmed positions and considered terminal rank (unlike Captain Crozier). The expectation for these most senior officers is that they are in the political arena, and that they can be sacrificed politically at any time, and they can resign without prejudice.

This was not the case with Captain Crozier. He was a relatively junior officer in a poorly defined series of wars, and had no easy answer. Only with the lens of history and further information, much of it likely classified for years to come, will we be able to fully analyze Captain Crozier's actions and the response of the Naval leadership. The authors' belief, however, is that all protagonists will likely emerge as honorable men and women, and that each was sacrificed by his lack of political consensus about the nature of the conflict, and a failure to develop and execute a coherent strategic national strategy in 2020.

NOTES

1. The U.S. Department of the Navy (2005) Code of Ethics can be accessed at https://www.secnav.navy.mil/Ethics/Pages/codeofethics.aspx.
2. See U.S. Department of the Navy (n.d.) Core Values Charter for a complete description.
3. The information in the memorandum mirrored Secretary Esper's (2020) guidance which included the following:

    1. Be deliberate and careful with all classified, controlled unclassified, and predecisional policy information and proposals. Just because someone has a clearance, or previously worked for DOD, does not mean they have a need to know. You must protect non-public information appropriately when communicating with any party, including ensuring that the person receiving the information is authorized access and has a need-to know or lawful government purpose for such information prior to any disclosure.

2. Comply with DOD policies regarding public disclosures. Ensure that an appropriate DOD Public Affairs office authorizes the release of official DOD information to the news OSD00627 5-20/C M D007704-20 media, or that information is released according to appropriate procedures (e.g., Freedom of Information Act).
3. Comply with all prepublication review policies, with which you are required to comply even after you retire, resign, or are dismissed from your government service or contract.
4. Comply with security clearance-related obligations to report certain contacts to your security offices.
5. Review current DOD-wide and organization-specific OPSEC and traditional security practices, and ensure compliance with those procedures.

4. Crozier's email was sent to at least three persons in his immediate chain of command, and cc'd to at least seven other relevant authorities on and off the USS *Roosevelt*. See Snodgrass (2020).

REFERENCES

Brooks, R. (2020). Paradoxes of professionalism: Rethinking civil-military relations in the United States. *International Security, 44*(4), 7–44.

Esper, M. (2020, July 20). *Memorandum for all DOD personnel. Subject: Reinforcing operations security and the importance of preventing unauthorized disclosures.* https://media.defense.gov/2020/Jul/21/2002460476/-1/1/1/REINFORCING_OPERATIONS_SECURITY_AND_THE_IMPORTANCE_OF_PREVENTING_UNAUTHORIZED_DISCLOSURES.PDF

Eyer, K. S. (2020, April 17). *Don't reinstate Captain Crozier.* U.S. Naval Institute Blog. https://blog.usni.org/posts/2020/04/17/dont-reinstate-captain-crozier

Gafni, M., & Garofoli, J. (2020, March 31). Exclusive: Captain of aircraft carrier with growing coronavirus outbreak pleads for help from Navy. *San Francisco Chronicle.* (Updated 8 June) https://www.sfchronicle.com/bayarea/article/Exclusive-Captain-of-aircraft-carrier-with-15167883.php

Goltz, S. M. (2003). Considering political behavior in organizations. *The Behavior Analyst Today, 4*(3), 354–366.

Huntington, S. P. (1957). *The soldier and the state.* Harvard University Press.

Huntington, S. P. (1960). Strategic planning and the political process. *Foreign Affairs, 38*(2), 285–299.

Lee, P. A. (1999, April). *Power projection: A comparison of the aerospace expeditionary force and the battle group* [Research report submitted to the faculty]. Air Command and Staff College, Air University. https://apps.dtic.mil/dtic/tr/fulltext/u2/a425333.pdf

Li, E. (2018, August 20). *The rise and fall of soft power.* FPNews. https://foreignpolicy.com/2018/08/20/the-rise-and-fall-of-soft-power/

Military Leadership Diversity Commission. (2009). *Department of defense core values.* https://diversity.defense.gov/Portals/51/Documents/Resources/Commission/docs/Issue%20Papers/Paper%2006%20-%20DOD%20Core%20Values.pdf

National Security Agency Center for Cryptologic History. (1993). *Purple dragon: The origin and development of the United States OPSEC program.* https://www.governmentattic.org/docs/Purple-Dragon_Origin-US-OPSEC_NSA-Ctr-Cryptologic-History_1993.pdf

Nye, J. S., Jr. (1990). Soft power. *Foreign Policy, 80*, 153–171.

Office of the Secretary of Defense. (2020, May 29). *Federal Register, 85*, 32996–32300. https://www.federalregister.gov/documents/2020/05/29/2020-11551/dod-guidance-documents#sectno-reference-339.1%20

Secretary of the Navy. (2016). *New SECNA guidance on operations security (OPSEC) and the protection of critical information* (R 131700Z DEC 16). https://www.navy.mil/Resources/ALNAVs/Message/Article/2235823/new-secnav-guidance-on-operations-security-opsec-and-the-protection-of-critical/

Snodgrass, G. (2020, April 17). *Return crozier to the roosevelt, restore faith in the navy.* U.S. Naval Institute Blog. https://blog.usni.org/posts/2020/04/17/return-crozier-to-the-roosevelt-restore-faith-in-the-navy

U.S. Department of Defense. (2020, July 21). *Memorandum on reinforcing operations security.* https://www.defense.gov/Newsroom/Releases/Release/Article/2281405/memorandum-on-reinforcing-operations-security/

U.S. Department of the Navy. (2005, November 10). *Navy code of ethics.* https://www.secnav.navy.mil/Ethics/Pages/codeofethics.aspx

U.S. Department of the Navy. (2013). *Secretary of the Navy statement on ethics.* https://www.secnav.navy.mil/Ethics/Pages/default.aspx

U.S. Department of the Navy. (n.d.). *Department of the Navy core values charter.* https://www.secnav.navy.mil/Ethics/Pages/corevaluescharter.aspx

U.S. Naval Institute. (2020, June 23). *Timeline: Theodore Roosevelt COVID-19 outbreak investigation.* https://news.usni.org/2020/06/23/timeline-theodore-roosevelt-covid-19-outbreak-investigation

CHAPTER 9

THE URGENCY OF ORGANIZATIONAL CHANGE WITHIN COLLEGES IN CRISIS

Jennifer McLean
Appalachian State University

Carrol Warren
North Carolina State University

This chapter will outline the responses of postsecondary institutions, specifically community colleges to the COVID-19 pandemic. Framed by two theoretical approaches, stakeholder theory (Freeman, 1999) and the organizational life cycle theory (Hatch, 2018) this chapter will explore the impact of COVID-19 through a theoretical lens. Guided by research and theory, the chapter will give insight into the impact of research and theory on the practice of navigating higher education during COVID-19. This chapter presents case studies specific to institutions of higher education that will provide an opportunity for practical application both within higher education and within organizations which may be outside of the scope of education.

This chapter will prompt thought and promote insight into how educational institutions view the urgency of organizational change, specific to

Crisis, Chaos, and Organizations, pages 241–256

colleges in crisis. Framing the chapter is an introduction to the Warren and McLean model of solution focused outcomes. As this chapter presents many ideas relative to change within higher education, it aligns trends which center on the change resulting in a post-pandemic era. An informative historical overview guides the way to the exploration of the roles of stakeholder theory and the organizational life cycle in times of crisis. Equilibria in organizations as previously described by research remains out of sync, and the effects on power in times of crisis will have far-reaching outcomes, which will be revealed by emerging trends and symbols.

Sprinkled within this chapter are two case studies highlighting two hypothetical scenarios faced by educators working in higher education settings. These case studies are designed to promote critical thinking through the lens of the theories discussed in this chapter and to shift from the challenges presented within each case to solutions based on emerging trends.

Organizations, specifically in higher education, have the potential to become self-destructive when presented with challenges by allowing power to interrupt the solution process (Gergen, 2012). The Warren and McLean Model of solution focused outcomes posits that organizations must acknowledge limitations when resolving the challenges presented by crisis and accept input to solutions from stakeholders both internal and external to the organization, leaders within the organization, and the organization must embrace a culture of change that will contribute to positive solutions. The model suggests that there is a shift that occurs with the normal or standard organizational practices and policies that take place when a crisis occurs. When organizations seek the input of stakeholders, when the leadership is receptive to the input of the stakeholders, and the value of suggested change is supported by both the leadership and stakeholders, the outcomes are solution focused. Driven by the need to adapt to change quickly and develop a plan with collective input from both internal and external stakeholders, this model promotes the absorption of chaos and crisis with outputs of solutions in mind. Figure 9.1 demonstrates the Warren and McLean model of solution focused outcomes.

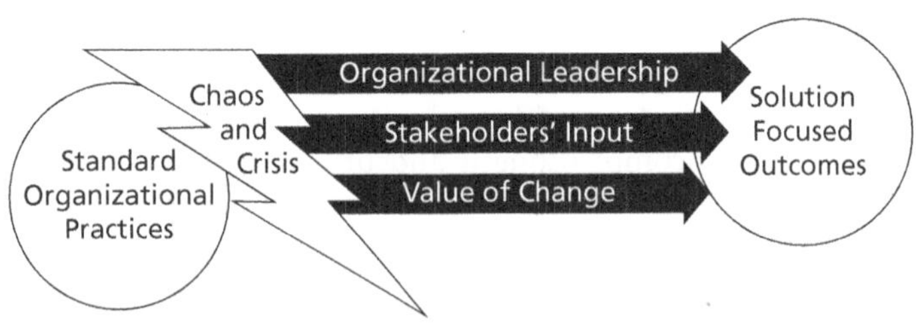

Figure 9.1 Warren and McLean model of solution focused outcomes.

HISTORICAL OVERVIEW

The history of the community college in America stretches back to the 1940s when the Truman Commission Report was issued calling for the rebirth of the junior college into a new institution, the community college (Beach, 2011). When created, the community college became what Beach (2011) noted as an institution that would "promote democracy, social mobility, and economic development" (p. 17). These institutions are crucial gateways into higher education that serve two functions in the United States; to feed the workforce pipeline and to prepare citizens for the 4-year college. The focus of these organizations are the communities in which they are located. In North Carolina for example, no citizen lives more than 30 minutes from a community college. This is a privilege as North Carolina is the third largest community college system in the nation. For other states, the community college service area may be larger, and collaborations are crucial to assist citizens. Community colleges are able to collaborate and integrate into their communities and serve their needs, especially in rural areas. These two purposes allow the college system to be flexible to their areas' unique needs which was on display during the COVID-19 pandemic.

While the pandemic was a brutal awakening for many in education, community colleges were able to adapt and quickly pivoted to meet their communities' needs. News articles were filled with reports of colleges distributing desperately needed items during the shutdown of states across America. When healthcare organizations began to experience shortages of personal protection equipment (PPE), local colleges gathered the PPE utilized by their health science programs and distributed them to local hospitals and community organizations (Fauver, 2020).

Colleges also emptied their food stores, sharing the bounty with area households (Mahoney, 2020). When classes were abruptly switched to online learning, colleges extended their Wi-Fi into the parking lots so students could study and complete coursework while social distancing (Leckrone, 2020). While the colleges shined and truly demonstrated the community in their names, they were also faced with dramatic organizational change as the institutions faced economic uncertainty and disruption within their traditional organizational system.

Colleges braced for a fiscal downturn amidst the pandemic, with their dependency on state dollars tested with the collection of state tax deadlines extended and legislative focus centered on recovering from the devastation wreaked by COVID-19. Leaders discussed the possibilities of a precipitous drop in enrollment combined with a squeeze on state monies. Among faculty and staff, whispers began of the possibilities of a reduction in force and how the survivors of this strategy would handle the workload. This will be the biggest challenge facing community colleges since their inception and organizational change will be necessary to survive. It will be essential for community colleges as well as all postsecondary institutions of education to adapt in coordination with the community surrounding the campus, with students, and with organizations who can contribute as stakeholders to a new vision for higher education.

STAKEHOLDER THEORY

Business organizations have long touted stakeholder theory as the foundation upon which change manifests best (Freeman, 1999; Freeman et al., 2010). Stakeholder theory is what drives the value of creating new ideas and concepts in business. When applied to the lens of higher education, stakeholder theory can be envisioned in a similar fashion, removing the traditional business focus of capitalism, but with the focus remaining upon the way value is created and trading among one another (students, educators, administrators, and community members).

Research suggests that stakeholder theory can guide an understanding of how an organization can be more socially responsible (Freeman et al., 2010). At the core of stakeholder theory, the impact that strategic management can have upon the success of an organization is of great emphasis. Iterations of stakeholder theory have invited many versions over the past 2 decades including the idea to rethink traditional practices with the theory at the helm (Freeman et al., 2010).

STAKEHOLDER THEORY APPLIED IN EDUCATIONAL SETTINGS

When applied in educational settings, stakeholder theory can take on a different implication, one that promotes the growth of the engagement of external organizations who are closely tied with the business of educational operations. Considering the economic impact higher education has on its surrounding communities, stakeholders from external organizations take on the roles of serving on committees to establish the viability of new programs, informing educators of content application outside of the classroom, serving as hosts for internships, work-based learning opportunities, apprenticeship programs, and the list goes on. Stakeholders who serve in the capacity of board members, committee members, or donors can have tremendous influence on the operations, leadership decisions, and the organizational change that takes place in institutions of higher education.

As you integrate what you read with what you already know, let's pause for a moment and consider an application to practice. Case Study 1.1

represents a common challenge postsecondary administrators faced and continue to face during the pandemic. Once you review the case as presented, take a moment to reflect on the questions.

CASE STUDY 1.1

President of West Community College, Dr. Smith is receiving criticism for his leadership of the institution throughout COVID-19. Dr. Smith delayed the closing of the institution, placing faculty, staff, and students at risk—he reasoned the decision to close after March 30th was due to the concern for those who did not have reliable access to internet connection to complete work. Complaints were made to local media outlets and rumors are circulating that he is relying on his chief of staff to provide a response. To make matters worse, when the state decided to re-open in the fall, Dr. Smith encouraged faculty to teach in person courses and resources were limited for employees who had to work remotely, as well as students who were now learning remotely. The leadership of the institution has been poor with communicating decisions to the campus and the news is reporting that students are withdrawing from West Community College at a high rate. After a consultation with the vice president of finance the institution is also facing a significant budget deficit if enrollment continues to decline.

Reflecting on Case Study 1.1

Consider the following questions:

1. What next steps should Dr. Smith take to create a plan to move forward?
2. How should the chief of staff work to respond to the complaints being taken to the media?
3. What type of organizational shift could create a better fiscal outcome?
4. How could the institution shift services to best serve the needs of faculty, staff, and students?

ORGANIZATIONAL LIFE CYCLE

Larry Greiner, an organization theorist posited that organizations proceed through stages, similar to psychological stages of development (Hatch, 2018). In an analysis of Hatch's (2018) organizational life cycle theory, the concept of navigating through a crisis can result in remarkable change is highlighted. A crisis breaks the organizations monotony and leads to major change, as well as the next stage of development. Each crisis has the potential to lead to organizational death or growth (Hatch, 2018). The introduction of COVID-19 in early 2020 caused many organizations to involuntarily embark on the road to change. The community college system, as many higher education institutions, were stuck in predictable bureaucratic strongholds of complacency. The pressure was on and the pull of performative leadership that is prevalent in bureaucracy was powerful. The urgency of this pandemic was combined with the glare of the students, parents, and community watching to observe how the community colleges would handle this emerging threat.

PUNCTUATED EQUILIBRIUM MODEL

While Griener believed that organizations process through stages, Tushman and Romanelli (1985) postulate that organizations vacillate between periods of equilibrium and revolution. The periods of equilibrium are long with small progression of change dispersed with what Romanelli and Tushman (1994) describe as "brief periods of intense and pervasive change" which "break the grip of strong inertia" (pp. 1142–1143). In the punctuated equilibrium model organizations do not show significant change unless they are in a period of revolution (Romanelli & Tushman, 1994). This revolutionary time typically does not last longer than 2 years while in Griener's model, stages of change have no distinguished period of time (Romanelli & Tushman, 1994).

The COVID-19 pandemic qualifies as a dramatic period of change for higher education. Institutions that were comfortable with their class offering delivery were suddenly forced to switch to online platforms at a rapid rate. For most of higher education, these transformative decisions were made over weeks in the Spring of 2020. The revolution continued in the fall as colleges debated the merits of opening campus for in-person classes, adjusted academic calendars to remove fall break, and balanced staff and faculty presence on campus. Among college personnel there were discussions on the prudence of providing COVID-19 testing to all students, staff, and faculty. Suddenly higher education was debating the merits of performing duties typically assigned to their community public health departments. In the end, for community colleges, most collaborated with health departments and provided the space and resources for testing while not conducting the test with college personnel.

What does this mean for higher education in the future? If we agree with Romanelli and Tushman (1994) that "revolutionary transformation is the most common mode of fundamental transformation" (p. 1162), the pandemic will permanently alter the education landscape in America. Or will we see what Griener suggests in that the pandemic will be another stage in the organizational development of higher education? Regardless of the applied approach, higher education has experienced a metamorphosis in the past year and will continue to change as the pandemic extends into 2021.

PANDEMIC DECISION-MAKING

As a result of the impact of COVID-19, remarkable changes occurring within organizations are the result of the recognition that higher education administrators were working under bounded rationality, in that they had limited information to make their decision, uncertainty was rampant and time was of the essence (Hatch, 2018). Administrators serving in higher education organizations had to make decisions during the COVID-19 pandemic that will result in long-term organizational shifts towards online teaching and learning. These quick decisions broke through the traditional bureaucratic red tape of rigid rules and policies, producing change that many had been advocating for years. Unprecedented is the term many institutions have used to describe the transition of services to students, many of whom are without resources to maintain a connection to their education.

COVID-19 has also spotlighted existing inequities of community college students. Many students were without reliable broadband access before the pandemic and the issue worsened due to the strain on the current infrastructure. Even a decade before students have admitted to me that they worked on their homework at McDonalds and after the pandemic a colleague shared that a student completed her English paper on her cellphone due to lack of access to a computer. These inequities have led to another organizational stage that Hatch (2018) refers to as a period of unification. The overwhelming aspects of dealing with a pandemic led institutions to allow for redistributed workloads and more autonomy for their personnel (Hatch, 2018). Community colleges have worked as a team to extend their Wi-Fi access to their parking lots so students may access services with social distancing and collaborate with community organizations to host graduation drive-through events for local high schools. When facing a crisis, Zdziarski et al. (2007) suggested that it is the duty of professionals, specifically educators, to provide more attention to approaching service to our communities with a more humanistic touch. While these efforts will not resolve inequities, community colleges will continue to build social capital while meeting the needs of their area. Does this remain a truth even in the current era?

Resources for postsecondary education institutions have been limited. On-campus housing refunds, tuition refunds, and reduced enrollment, colleges have struggled to keep their doors open.

During the collaboration phase leaders must switch from an emphasis of control to one of motivation (Hatch, 2018). While adapting to the new environment brought about by COVID-19, community colleges must continue to lead with their community in mind. During this time of transition trust becomes paramount in leadership styles (Hatch, 2018). Thoughtful, dedicated leadership will allow for these institutions to be responsive to new challenges. Leaders that were flexible with their staff work schedules and responsive to mental health needs provided a compassionate example of pandemic leadership. One potential hopeful outcome of this crisis could be a change in the organizational approach to employees. Higher education institutions have quickly adapted to allow many employees to work from home due to the contagious nature of COVID-19. Employees that are trusted with this opportunity are experiencing the oft-touted work–life balance that has eluded 21st century workers. Caring for staff, students, and the community are the core values of higher education institutions (Zdziarski et al., 2007). By demonstrating compassionate leadership, administrators can align the institution's goals with their identity and past as recommended by Hatch (2018) in order to inspire and encourage employees for the future.

Community colleges will play a pivotal role in rebuilding the national economy. Higher education institutions provide resources such as "customized job-training programs, hands-on counseling, technical help, and management assistance" (Shaffer, 2015, p. 54). States have become wise to the services provided by community colleges and harnessed the power to drive an economic movement. Gradually states have shifted from what Shaffer (2015) notes as fiscal motivation to attract employers to a knowledge first approach. Higher education institutions will be successful in stimulating the economy if they continue to engage their local stakeholders and maintain a collaborative mentality.

As we adjust to COVID-19 as a part of our lives, institutions must guard against burnout and the potential to slide into another phase, the crisis of renewal (Hatch, 2018). This phase is marked by exhaustion from the stress of additional responsibilities and Hatch (2018) indicates this phase will either transform the organization or lead to decline and death. Characteristics of this decline and death include a focus on personal objectives regardless of institutional goals, institutional power whittles down to a select few, and the organization is no longer able to meet previous standards and demands (Lester et al., 2003). The toll of managing COVID-19 may lead personnel to experience psychological symptoms such as interruptions in normal sleep patterns, digestive challenges, a feeling of fatigue, or challenges with sleep disturbances, indigestion, fatigue, or even difficulties with maintaining civility in interpersonal relationships (Zdziarski et al., 2007). According to the U.S. Bureau of Labor Statistics higher education institutions are going through a threat that has led to thousands losing their jobs (Tomac, 2020). The fiscal ramifications of COVID-19 have strained relationships among administrative and faculty divisions at odds over tough decisions to soften the financial impact related to student attrition (Tomac, 2020). It is too early to determine if this will be the death knell of higher education as we know it as has been reported for decades.

We can hope that our colleges will emerge a slimmer, more streamlined institution that has emerged from a crisis with a new perspective on their identity. Leaders must be willing to evolve and allow the institution to progress into a new form (Hatch, 2018). Small missteps of maladaptive strategies will lead the institution on a path to organizational death (Hatch, 2018). In order to serve their community, colleges must continually adjust their strategies and allow their employees flexibility to try new approaches to remain socially relevant. As the life cycle continues, the organization will face another crisis in the future. Our educational system must continue to grow, be flexible, and evolve to survive the crises that await us. While some institutions may not survive COVID-19, those that utilize adaptive strategies will continue to serve students and the communities in which they reside.

Considering the challenges faced by educational institutions across the nation, Case Study 1.2 centers around enrollment. As you review the case study, think about the change that occurs when enrollment numbers decline in colleges and universities.

CASE STUDY 1.2

Enrollment Challenges at North Community College

The following case study provides an example of the decisions that are currently made every day during the COVID-19 pandemic. While reading, consider how you would assist "Ray" and answer the reflection questions.

Ray: "I can't go back... I need to work extra hours because my father lost his job."

Versa nodded her head, knowing the student could not return to classes, even virtually. She had heard this from multiple students over the past few months. As director of the Advising Center at North Community College she was worried about the effects of COVID-19 on her staff, students, and college.

Versa: "Do you think you will be able to enroll next fall?"
Ray: "I'm not sure... when is the deadline?"

Ray has no idea what next month will be like and cannot imagine the next year. His father lost his job at the restaurant and has struggled to find a job. His unemployment only has one more month and his mother is disabled. Between working additional hours and taking care of his sister he has not had any time to see his friends.

> **Versa:** "How about I check in with you over the summer?"
> **Ray:** "That will be great, thanks."

Versa made a note in his file and finished her meeting with Ray. So many students had withdrawn this semester, and this was on top of the low enrollment numbers. The state legislators were focused on rebounding the economy in response to COVID-19 so she knew that budgets will be tight next year. Her college spent so much money in March to switch all classes online, so she knew they were operating at a deficit. North Community College was in a rural area where many students did not have reliable access to the internet. This caused headaches in the spring that were still not fully resolved this fall. She had heard that one of the businesses in the area was going to donate laptops, but she was not sure if this was just a rumor.

Versa sighed. Her staff were suffering too. She had one advisor that was exposed to COVID-19 last week so she would be out of the office in quarantine for 1 more week. They were already so short-staffed Versa worried about budget cuts. If North decided to implement a reduction in force how would their office manage?

As Ray walks to his car he shuffles his feet. He was so excited to attend North Community College. He was the first in his family to attend college and his mom cried when he enrolled for classes. He missed his friends but knew it would be a long time before his dad found work again. The state had lifted some of the mandates, but restaurants were hard hit. What if he could not go back to college? What would he do?

Reflecting on Case Study 1.2

Consider the following questions:

1. How should Vera approach finding resolutions to the challenges Ray is facing?
2. What approach could North Community College administrators take as they consider serving students who are similar to Ray?
3. If you were supervising Vera how would you provide support for her and her team?

EQUILIBRIA IN ORGANIZATIONS

As the pandemic prompted organizations to shift from traditional work routines to a more flexible model, Tushman and Romanelli's (1985) and Romanelli & Tushman's (1994) work on maintaining the equilibrium of organizational transformation remains relevant. The impacts of punctuated equilibrium theory allows space for the evolution of organizational change over time while brief disruptions of transition create change that adapts to the shift (Gersick, 1991; Miller & Friesen, 1984; Romanelli & Tushman, 1994; Tushman & Romanelli, 1985). In March of 2020, organizations, specifically higher education, shifted abruptly to remote education, for what was expected to be a brief timeframe to shelter in place during the pandemic brought about by COVID-19. Earlier conclusions of the work surrounding the punctuated equilibrium model confirmed that it was through the brief and intermittent implementation of transformation that change occurred; however, since the world has experienced a health crisis, it can be concluded that an exploration of forced transformation for an extended period is worth further research.

The pandemic created opportunities for organizations to reconsider their policies, extend outreach to those in need, and increase empathy beyond what is expected. The inequities that existed in higher education before COVID-19, were highlighted when students or educators were without internet connectivity due to their rural location, or when access to technology was limited. Work–life balance became a challenge as people began working from home while monitoring their children who were forced to learn from home. Equilibria within organizations is being reconsidered as balance remains out of control.

EFFECTS ON POWER IN TIMES OF CRISIS

Organizations originate in the social structure to share power and serve the community (Hatch, 2018). The structure of educational organizations like community colleges allows for stability to a system as a whole under normal circumstances to serve the community. It also contains inflexible characteristics which did not lend well to the COVID-19 crisis that began in March 2020. Higher education leaders across the nation raced to push information technology staff and faculty members to transition all courses online, thrust new cleaning expectations on facility staff, and worried with their business office staff about financial ramifications to adjust to what was speculated as the new normal. These fast-paced changes led to altered power dynamics in colleges across the nation.

The bureaucratic organizational structure of community colleges naturally leads to a rigid hierarchy and top-down decision-making. For select institutions, their educational leaders regularly demonstrated silent power that can be categorized under what Steven Lukes termed the three faces of power (Hatch, 2018). While the first face of power resembles an open democracy of shared power, the second and third faces seek to limit or dominate decision-making, regardless of the consequences (Hatch, 2018). Educational leaders that utilized the silent s*econd face of power* that limits decision-making within their institutions were faced with difficult decisions when the COVID-19 crisis caused all classes to be transitioned to the virtual environment (Hatch, 2018). These colleges, after years of refusing to update their virtual offerings, were sent scrambling in early 2020 when nationwide governors began to enact shutdowns that restricted movement of citizens. The leaders that suppressed and controlled the conversation were then forced to call on those that were unable to participate in the decision-making process to then provide the solution to their crisis. Time will tell how this quick shift of business as usual to immediate needs from staff will translate into higher education institutions in the future.

COVID-19 also spotlighted workers in our system that do not typically gain notice in our day to day life. Leaders and influencers began to tout healthcare workers and frontline workers as those that keep the country running during the pandemic. Commercials and banners across communities hailed these individuals as heroes. These examples demonstrate strategic contingencies theory where Hatch (2018) states individuals within organizations gain power through their skillset to fulfill an institutional need or solve problems quickly. In higher education institutions these individuals were typically the facilities personnel that maintained the campus buildings and the information technology personnel that quickly implemented and trained staff and faculty on new educational platforms. The capacity to deal with uncertainty along with their skill set make these personnel invaluable to their organization (Hatch, 2018). The workers were suddenly a pivotal member of their college and influenced the ability of their institution to adapt to new expectations. As the COVID-19 pandemic continues; however, how will our educational system face it when the workers are unable to continue to carry the heavy burden of frontline work? If various strains of COVID-19 continue to appear, institutions must recommence evolving, supporting their employees and encouraging their stakeholders for the educational system to survive.

Why were some higher education institutions able to respond rapidly to the COVID-19 complications? Organizations that have developed crisis management teams understand that placing collaborations and organizational structure into their plan enables them to respond nimbly to a variety of crises. These teams are tasked with creating a deliberate crisis plan as well as developing relationships with individuals in the community that will be imperative during a crisis. These teams form bonds with media in the community, first responders, insurance agents, and nonprofits to prepare for various calamities their institution may face. As referenced in Zdziarski et al. (2007), organizations should develop a psychological first aid plan within their broad institutional crisis plan. The first aid plan outlines how the institution will support their personnel and the community in the aftermath of a crisis (Zdziarski et al., 2007). The ultimate goal of this plan is to support the individual or group towards their pre-crisis balance (Zdziarski et al., 2007). While the first step of the first aid plan is aimed toward addressing immediate needs, the second step begins the work of maintaining control in the institution to maximize your resources (Zdziarski et al., 2007). While managing a crisis, chaos will be prevalent and this step sets the stage for a structured response. Colleges will have a crisis management team that will determine which staff member will control communication, who will provide resources to students, and the individuals that will be responsible for making decisions (Zdziarski et al., 2007). This arrangement allows for power to be distributed so that individuals can flexibly respond to the crisis. It also allows for collaboration as shown during the COVID-19 crisis when community colleges offered their campus for drive-in graduations for local high schools, extended their Wi-Fi access to campus parking lots, and provided food and technology distribution to their students. In times of crisis, leveraging the power of individuals and the institution will assist the community and not only serve the local area, but build capital for the future.

EMERGING TRENDS AND SYMBOLS

COVID-19 brought a sense of panic to institutions of higher education, specifically to the institutions who lacked awareness of protocols in the event of a crisis. For organizations that were prepared with contingency plans, the shift experienced with remote work transitions and online learning was less damaging. Institutions of higher education that found themselves in a panic during the transition, sought guidance from external sources often, modeling what other colleges were implementing. The beginning of the pandemic was not a time to recreate the wheel, so organizational leaders of colleges found solace in adapting plans they had with new ideas sourced from other institutions. The diffusion of innovation theory, (Rogers, 2002, 2003; Rogers & Agarwala-Rogers, 1976; Rogers & Shoemaker, 1971), is a way for organizations to consider how communication can be used to implement innovative change. Rice and Rogers (1980) reinvention is a way to connect the new ideas with the old ideas in an innovative way (Rice & Rogers, 1980). Taking an idea that has been around for a while and recreating it, in a sense, can result in gaining the attention of a new population of users (Rice & Rogers,

1980). The diffusion of innovation theory can play a critical role to support the communication of ideas, including those related to social justice (Ratts & Wood, 2011). When leadership has an awareness of an organizational need and is willing to be accepting of the time and ideas of others, the ideas have the opportunity to thrive early (Ratts & Wood, 2011).

When innovation occurs, there is potential for risk of failure. Perhaps, innovation sparks a renewal, but due to fatigue or barriers, there is no action for the new ideas to thrive and continue. Consistent with findings of Svytanek and DeShon (1993) organizational change efforts which consider chaos theory are better understood and lend practitioners additional insight into the failures and success of change. We must realize that failure can result in change and can be the prompt for new ideas. Design thinking emerged in the 1980s as a result of the examination of multiple theoretical explanations for problem solving (Rowe, 1987). Brown and Katz (2019) brought about a reemergence of design thinking, introducing it as a way to connect the development of products to a collective and collaborative change process within organizations, with a customer-centered approach. The approach is beaconed as a transformative experience for those who create and implement change within product effectiveness because of the results from former failures.

With reduced budgets, less time spent on work-related commuting or travel, and increased use of technology, emerging trends brought about by the shift to a remote work environment included the increased recognition of technology reliance, the efficacy of solution-driven leadership practices, and the value of stakeholder input in problem solving.

As organizations shifted their focus from normal day-to-day practices to an abrupt period of chaos, they went from standard organizational practices to solution focused outcomes based upon the input of their stakeholders, organizational leadership practices, and the value that the organization saw in changing.

CONCLUDING THOUGHTS

This chapter has provided an introduction of the Warren and McLean model of solution focused outcomes specific to postsecondary educational institutions navigating through change. A historical context of change within higher education was presented and followed by an exploration of theory, pandemic responses to change, and other models and ideas supporting equilibria within organizations. The case studies presented an opportunity to apply the context to practical application. As change continues to be a constant in higher education, it will continue to be the source for research, innovation, and solution focused outcomes.

REFERENCES

Beach, J. M. (2011). *Gateway to opportunity? A history of the community college in the United States.* Stylus Publishing.

Brown, T., & Katz, B. (2019). *Change by design: How design thinking transforms organizations and inspires innovation* (Vol. 20091). HarperBusiness.

Fauver, M. (2020, April 3). *College donates personal protective equipment to local hospitals.* https://www.waketech.edu/post/wt-news-story/4822

Freeman, R. E. (1999). Divergent stakeholder theory. *Academy of Management Review, 24*(2), 233236.

Freeman, R. E., Harrison, J. S., Wicks, A. C., Parmar, B. L., & De Colle, S. (2010). *Stakeholder theory: The state of the art.* Cambridge University Press.

Gergen, K. J. (2012). Brown, M. C., Eds. Organization Theory in the Postmodern Era. *Organization and Governance in Higher Education, Fifth Edition, 36,* 524–536.

Gersick, C. J. G. (1991). Revolutionary change theories: A multilevel exploration of the punctuated equilibrium paradigm. *Academy of Management Review, 16*(1), 10–36.

Hatch, M. J. (2018). *Organization theory: Modern, symbolic, and postmodern perspectives.* Oxford University Press.

Leckrone, B. (2020, May 15). *Expand access to Wi-Fi.* https://www.chronicle.com/article/expand-access-to-wi-fi/

Lester, D. L., Parnell, J. A., & Carraher, S. (2003). Organizational life cycle: A five-stage empirical scale. *International Journal of Organizational Analysis, 11*(4), 339–354.

Mahoney, M. (2020, April 21). Distribute food and supplies to the local community. *The Chronicle of Higher Education.* https://www.chronicle.com/article/distribute-food-and-supplies-to-the-local-community/

Miller, D., & Friesen, P. H. (1984). *Organizations: A quantum view.* Prentice Hall.

Ratts, M., & Wood, C. (2011). Counselor preparation, the fierce urgency of now: Diffusion of innovation as a mechanism to integrate social justice in counselor education. *Counselor Education and Supervision, 50*(3), 207–223.

Rice, R., & Rogers, E. (1980). Reinvention in the innovation process. *Knowledge Creation, Diffusion, Utilization, 1*(4), 499–514. https://doi.org/10.1177/107554708000100402

Rogers, E. (2002). Diffusion of preventive innovation. *Addictive Behaviors, 27*(6), 989–993.

Rogers, E. (2003). *Diffusion of innovations* (5th ed). Free Press.

Rogers, E., & Agarwala-Rogers, R. (1976). *Communication in organizations.* The Free Press.

Rogers, E., &n Shoemaker, F. (1971). *Communication in organizations.* New York.

Romanelli, E., & Tushman, M. L. (1994): Organizational transformation as punctuated equilibrium: An empirical test. *Academy of Management Journal, 37*(5), 1141–1166. https://doi.org/10.5465/256669

Rowe, P. G. (1987). *Design thinking.* MIT Press.

Shaffer, D. F. (2015). Higher education systems are assuming a larger role in the economic development efforts in their states. *Economics, Management, and Financial Markets, 10*(1), 54–79.

Svyantek, D., & DeShon, R. (1993). Organizational attractors: A chaos theory explanation of why cultural change efforts often fail. *Public Administration Quarterly, 17*(3), 339–355. http://www.jstor.org/stable/40861593

Tomac, J. W. (2020, August 27). The future of the academic work force. *The Chronicle of Higher Education*. https://www.chronicle.com/article/the-future-of-the-academic-work-force

Tushman, M. L., & Romanelli, E. (1985), Organizational evolution: A metamorphosis model of convergence and reorientation. In L. L. Cummings & B. M. Staw (Eds.), *Research in organizational behavior* (pp. 171–222). JAI Press.

Zdziarski, E. L., Dunkel, N. W., & Rollo, J. M. (2007). *Campus crisis management: A comprehensive guide to planning, prevention, response, and recovery*. Wiley & Sons.

CHAPTER 10

A THEORETICAL ANALYSIS OF ORGANIZATIONAL CHANGE DURING COVID-19

Steps, Stages, and Themes for Implementation

Theodore J. Wiard
Southwestern College

Mary J. Selke
Grand Canyon University

Genevieve Oswald
Golden Willow Retreat Inc.

The year 2020 brought with it one of the greatest global health crises the world has ever seen. What was first thought to be pneumonia cases of an unknown origin in Wuhan China, in December of 2019, was subsequently identified as a previously unknown coronavirus. The rapid spread of the

Crisis, Chaos, and Organizations, pages 257–280

virus resulted in global lockdowns, supply chain disruptions, and an overall international crisis (Ali et al., 2020), requiring continued rapid and focused response.

Crisis situations require strong leadership to reestablish a sense of normalcy during and after the crisis experience (Boin et al., 2013). Leaders are forced into making difficult choices on a daily basis, choices that will have a long-term impact on the working relationships between employers, their employees, and stakeholders for decades to come. COVID-19 has impacted all aspects of life and no matter the specific impact it has had on the myriad organizations around the world, it is certain that the status-quo of pre-pandemic life will be forever altered.

Leadership behaviors during the management of resulting changes are a factor in effecting successful organizational transitions through the disruptions of the COVID-19 crisis and into a "new normal." Leaders who are capable of sharing the vision of a new normal, which key stakeholders of an organization can buy into with confidence, make the difference between successful change and attempted change that could have been successful but devolved during transition processes.

A basic understanding of how to best manage change is a warranted contribution to professional literature at this point in time. Implementing Kurt Lewin's three-stage change management model—unfreezing, transitioning, and refreezing—and focusing specifically on the nature of employer-employee relationships during organizational change initiatives will be crucial. Operationalizing these three stages can be accomplished by viewing them through a lens of three themes for enacting change (Wiard, 2018): (a) know your audience and walk your talk; (b) implement vision, communication, trust, and buy-in; and (c) inspire residual passion and perseverance. A thorough knowledge of leadership behaviors which enable an employee to trust a leader's vision, embrace change, and facilitate the passionate implementation of necessary change will help secure success in rebuilding many aspects of a new post-COVID-19 world. Related information will be applicable during the COVID-19 crisis or any other current or future challenging organizational transition.

At the center of this chapter's discussion is the element of managing crisis and change through the human components of trust and residual passion as antecedents for change outcomes. Lawrence et al. (2014) noted emotional resistance to change results in responses such as anxiety, depression, confusion, self-doubt, grief, and uncertainty. It appears the COVID-19 global health crisis, followed by global economic collapse, has generated at least one of these emotions for every human on the planet since the beginning of 2020. This means emotional resistance to a current world crisis is inevitable. Understanding and implementing the leadership behaviors which facilitate trust and passion during an organizational change, to mediate emotional resistance and resistance in general, provides a potential advantage for enacting successful, effective, change processes in a context of challenge or crisis.

GENESIS OF COVID-19

The mystery virus first began to appear in December of 2019. By the first week of January 2020, Chinese authorities identified the virus as a mutation of the coronavirus, which causes the coronavirus disease-2019 (COVID-19), primarily a severe acute respiratory syndrome (Dong et al., 2020; Ölcer et la., 2020). Despite efforts by Chinese authorities to contain it, the virus and the disease it causes spread rapidly through Hubei province, and then to other neighboring countries. By March 11, 2020, the rapid, vast spread of the virus across the globe resulted in the World Health Organization (WHO) declaring it a global pandemic. By May 23, 2020, there were over 5.1 million reported cases affecting 210 countries and territories across the globe. By October 1, 2020, the death toll of the global crisis had crossed the million persons threshold and continued to increase.

At the beginning of 2020, few people outside the world of infectious diseases would have been aware of, much less able to decisively prepare for the crisis that would disrupt the entirety of life worldwide. According to the literature, crises arise from sudden and unexpected events that disrupt routine and proceedings (Meisler et al., 2013; Meisler & Vigoda-Gadot, 2014). While change is nothing new to organizational management, the drastic, rapid, and dramatic change that swept the world with the onset of COVID-19 in the Spring of 2020 became a crisis that left many people in all sectors of life scrambling, trying to prepare for and live through mass quarantines and worldwide shutdowns.

To slow the spread of the virus without a vaccine, governments and organizations employed non pharmaceutical interventions such as social distancing and mass quarantine to minimize the death tolls (Desvars-Larrive et al., 2020). Many countries throughout the world instated a deliberate complete or partial shutdown across all sectors of the economy with global travel restrictions and local quarantines in early spring (Desvars-Larrive et al., 2020). As a result of the global shutdown, an unprecedented economic crisis arose on top of a worldwide health crisis (Pennington & Stanford, 2020).

Transitions were hectic, sudden, and rapidly mitigated. Organizational systems throughout the world scrambled to adjust in an attempt to slow the spread of the disease and salvage the rapidly collapsing world economy. COVID-19 has affected every industry and organization across the private and public sector. The crisis continued into the Fall of 2020 as fear of a second wave of global shutdowns loomed in the near future.

ORGANIZATIONAL IMPACT

The most significant change, impacting all sectors during the COVID-19 pandemic, was social distancing and isolating at home to prevent exposure to the virus (Di Domenico et al., 2020; Termini & Traver, 2020). Social distancing and travel restrictions affected organizations across all sectors whether in a country or region where lockdowns were firmly in place or not enforced. Organizations that could take their operations online had employees stay home while operational adjustments were made. Schools rapidly transitioned to online learning platforms. Health care organizations have had to make difficult decisions, choosing between fully protecting the health of their employees and saving the lives of community members (Kuhlmann et al., 2020). Some governments enforced a broad spectrum of aggressive interventions, ordering mass quarantines and shutdowns of non-essential businesses, while others approached the pandemic with more laissez-faire strategies, hopeful that herd immunity would result with limited intervention (Desvars-Larrive et al., 2020). Risk assessment of the spread of the virus identified the vulnerabilities of personnel in a broad spectrum of business as well as in service industries such as hospitality, retail, tourism, and security (Koh, 2020). Attempted mitigation of human vulnerability to the virus across all sectors did not eradicated the virus, rather it has created more need to adjust to social and economic fallout from the pandemic.

Health Care

In the health care industry, fear of contagion from those working in the industry broke down the chains of effort or support systems that usually enable organizations to run smoothly. COVID-19 can be described as the new occupational disease of the 21st century (Koh, 2020). For example, even after the availability of vaccines, there is fear of medical personnel using public transit, a ride for a nurse may cancel, and front-line medical personnel working with COVID-19 patients may be ostracized in their communities or forced to distance themselves from their immediate families. David Koh (2020) noted an incident in which an ambulance driver was turned away from a food stall for fear he was infected.

Not all reactions toward health care workers are negative. There are also stories of support and gratitude, such as the nightly cheers for healthcare workers in cities around the world, during the early days of the pandemic. The social stigmas health care workers encounter in their day to day lives are minor in contrast to the safety concerns they encounter in the workplace. Vaccines are highly effective but breakthrough cases are common.

The nature of the virus places extra burdens on health care workers (Middaugh, 2020; Verhagen et al., 2020). Effects of COVID-19 on the respiratory system are so extreme that a disproportionate number of patients need to be placed on life support, using interventional resources that tend to be limited outside of major medical centers. In many cases worldwide, the number of patients requiring interventions has far outweighed the capacity of health care systems to administer interventions to all in need. Unfortunately, this places an unfair burden on health care workers, forcing them in some cases to choose between patients, to fundamentally decide who lives and who dies (Emanuel et al., 2020).

To mitigate these complexities, many nations and states ramped up emergency health care operations. Field hospitals were constructed beyond the walls of traditional institutions. Beds, supplies, and personnel from other areas were reallocated to COVID-19 units. Navigating these tremendous changes and transitions in rapid response required dedicated leadership, focused on solving a rapidly shifting array of problems.

Government

The burden on governments and government officials has been no less challenging. As the directors of social movement and the conductors of social constructs, the pressure of immediate need to slow the spread of the disease with little or conflicting information often proved overwhelming. Governmental personnel struggled to make choices for their populaces that would keep people alive and maintain an economic system that did not decompose into complete worldwide recession or worse, economic depression. The U.S. federal government, under the Trump administration, passed the responsibility to make such difficult choices onto the state governments. With no worldwide consensus on what was most effective to contain the virus, the many varying interventions or lack of interventions has created more strife as contrast in governmental policy or perceptions of COVID-19 severity propelled conflict among the populace.

Businesses

Social distancing and global shutdown affected businesses in every industry and every sector. The globe is more economically connected than ever before. A shut down of a factory in China can easily mean a disruption in the supply chain for a U.S. business (Pennington & Stanford, 2020). An infected government official in the EU could result in a halt to policymaking that would impact international relations and interfere with the institution of support stimulus to people left with no work or forced to stay at home under quarantine orders. One ill employee in a factory of thousands, as exemplified at the Tyson chicken processing plants across the

United States during the initial months of the COVID-19 pandemic, can infect many other employees and shut down key components or the entire operation, resulting in a rapidly burgeoning crisis. Again, despite readily available vaccines by summer of 2021, misinformation and unfounded rumors pertaining to the vaccines resulted in large numbers of people refusing to be vaccinated, even faced with workplace or federal mandates to do so, further exacerbating worker shortages.

CHANGE THEORY AND GROUP DYNAMICS

Crisis situations require strong leadership to reestablish normalcy to the organization or group, during and after the crisis experience (Boin et al., 2013). The seminal research of Kurt Lewin's change theory (1943) is based on the concept that a leader sets the tone for their followers. Lewin based his change theory in field theory and group dynamics, both of which share the component of understanding the environment in which a change will take place and the elements comprising the status quo of that environment (Lewin, 1951). Leaders who understand the underlying field and group dynamics of the environment are better able to prepare for various disruptions, knowing resistance to change will be part of the change process (Burnes & Bargal, 2017; Wiard, 2018).

In group dynamics, the identity of a group is not defined by perspectives of the individual members that make up the whole. Rather, it is the *collective response* of those group members that forms the identity of a group (Burnes & Bargal, 2017). While individual identities do not hold great gravitas in collective group identity, Lewin (1943) considered resistance to change to arise from personal relational experiences of belonging; any force placing that experience of belonging in jeopardy would be met with resistance. Expanding upon his own research and the knowledge that change implementations were short lived, if successful at all, Lewin developed the three-stage model of change management (Burnes, 2015).

FOUR BASIC STYLES OF LEADERSHIP

Lewin's three stages of change were recently enhanced through the work of Dunphy and Stace (1993) in which strategies to address change depend on environmental changes, that is, changes in the field. Dunphy and Stace (1993) identified four basic styles of leadership: collaborative, consultive, directive, and coercive. Collaborative style relies upon mass participation, involving group members who actively contribute to determining and enacting changes for the future. Consultive style involves garnering focused expertise from specific areas on a more myopic level regarding goals and decision-making. Directive leadership style is not dependent on follower participation; authority is used to formulate and implement decisions and actions. Coercive style involves the use of force, be it psychological, physical, financial, or political, in order to implement leadership-determined change.

Organizational leaders have implemented multiple approaches to decrease the negative social and economic impacts on health, government, and business sectors resulting from the COVID-19 pandemic. Strategies such as, but not limited to, social distancing, lockdowns, quarantines, herd immunity, and isolation were put into place utilizing all four of the Dunphy and Stace (1993) leadership styles (Luisetto & Latyshev, 2020). As the pandemic continued to wreak havoc across the world, many strategies were being enforced which depended, at least in part, on the leadership style used to implement them. As more information is forthcoming and additional strategies are able to be implemented, a scaffolding effect will impact how change initiatives are put into place and how they are passed on to followers for buy-in. Dunphy and Stace's (1993) four styles of leadership provide a basic operational schema for selecting and analyzing leadership behaviors in the midst of crisis and organizational change.

CONTEXTS OF CRISIS AND CHAOS

Crisis and chaos are two fundamentally different change initiators. Both propel organizational change but have different outcomes. Crisis is not synonymous with organizational change and crisis is also not synonymous with chaos. Classical definitions of chaos cover circumstances and theories to explain the collapse of perceived order and systems for a sustained period of time, after and out of which, a new order arises from the disarray, creating a new form or container for the previously existing systems (McBride, 2005). A crisis is defined as a sudden and unexpected event that disrupts routine proceedings and threatens the organization's position in the market (Meisler et al., 2013; Meisler & Vigoda-Gadot, 2014; Wiard, 2018).

For example, the sudden death of a CEO exemplifies an organizational crisis in terms of an opportunity for punctuated change that, when over, may be followed by reversion to old ways. Chaotic change on the other hand, in general leads to more drastic upheavals with unpredictable future events. The punctuated equilibrium model of Tushman and Romanelli (1985) proposes an organization evolves through relatively long periods of stability (equilibrium) punctuated by short bursts of fundamental change (revolutionary periods; Romanelli & Tushman, 1994).

Will life return to a more normal state, resembling life before the pandemic, after a vaccination has been made more globally available and utilized by choice or mandate? In regard to the COVID-19 pandemic, these authors think it is safe to assume yes is the realistic answer. While some systems will change permanently, the majority of social systems, global industrial systems, and political systems will return to conditions approximating normal operations. With this in mind, the focus of this theoretical chapter is on a crisis response rather than chaos theory.

While much of the literature on organizational change leadership is focused outside the context of crisis, research supports the fact that organizational change initiatives are minimally effective on the whole. Such change initiatives often do not address critical failure factors and the levels of inherent resistance to change at all levels, whether change is enacted in response to a crisis or through a slow and deliberate action plan (Baesu & Bejinaru, 2013; Decker et al., 2012; Parry, 2015; Wiard, 2018).

UNDERSTANDING THE FIVE STEPS FOR CRISIS LEADERSHIP

Effective leadership is fundamental in navigating a crisis such as those imposed on organizations during the COVID-19 pandemic (Grady & Grady, 2013). There are five steps essential for successful crisis leadership: (a) making sense of the crisis, (b) making solid decisions for undertaking and resolving the crisis, (c) framing the context of the crisis for stakeholders, (d) troubleshooting the crisis to reestablish normalcy, and (e) learning from the crisis experience (Meisler et al., 2013; Meisler & Vigoda-Gadot, 2014). Lewin's three-stage model for change management, in combination with Wiard's three themes for enacting change, provide a viable means for putting the five steps for crisis leadership into practice.

Effective leadership can be determined by followers' willingness to transition into and accept a new status quo (Atkinson & Mackenzie, 2015), a critical component of response to change in a crisis situation. Disruption to any state of status quo leads to resistance to change among the people impacted (Burnes & Bargal, 2017; Wiard, 2018). There are interventions a leader can set into motion to effect a change process and enable stakeholders to move into and accept a new status quo (Kotter, 1996; Lewin, 1951). Literature supports that maintaining follower trust, sharing a positive vision, and leading the way through example are strong behaviors that a leader can implement to navigate difficult transitions and reduce resistance to change (Wiard, 2018).

Mitigating resistance to change is key to successful organizational change (Ming-Chu & Ming-Hsiu, 2015; Vanderwood, 2013; Wiard, 2018). Followers support leaders during a change who are deemed legitimate and rational (Self et al., 2007; Wiard, 2018). Through trust, defined as a social construct that enables sensemaking about a decision or relationship (Lewis & Weigert, 1985), group cooperation is established and enabled, and uncertainty is alleviated (Balliet & Lange, 2013; Molm et al., 2000; Kenworthy et al.,

2015; Smollan, 2013). Lack of trust contributes to resistance to change (Ming-Chu & Meng-Hsiu, 2015; Wiard, 2018).

Leadership behaviors contribute greatly to a follower's experience of trust or distrust; for this reason, it is the leader's responsibility to behave in ways which enhance trust and decrease distrust at all levels in order to reestablish normalcy and create a new status quo (Meisler et al., 2013; Meisler & Vigoda-Gadot, 2014; Penava & Sehic, 2014: Wiard, 2018; Zhang & Zhou, 2014). It is critical that this be accomplished in the midst of the COVID-19 crisis if stakeholders are to buy in and help to facilitate responsive rather than reactive change. The success or lack thereof of those organizational change processes will depend on leaders' abilities to successfully implement the three stages in Lewin's (1943) change model, by enacting Wiard's (2018) three themes for change.

LEWIN'S CHANGE MODEL: UNFREEZING, TRANSITIONING, AND REFREEZING

The Lewin (1943) model of change management includes three stages of the organizational change process: unfreezing, moving, and refreezing. The premise of Lewin's (1943) change theory upon which the three-stage model is based, is that the status quo needs to be shaken up for a change to take place: unfreezing. After the habits of systemic thinking have been altered there is a time period of movement and organizational learning during which new systems are put into place: transitioning. As new learning becomes habitual effective behavior, a new normal is put in place for the status quo: refreezing.

Criticisms to Lewin's (1943) theory suggest that it is based on an assumption that organizations work in a stable state, and that the theory itself was only suited to small scale change implementations, and hierarchical management structures (Burnes, 2015). Lewin's (1943) work was founded in the belief that the resolution for any change was found in learning, assumes learning can and will take place, and could be facilitated through those who acquired fresh, expanded perspectives (Burnes, 2004). Critics of the work have themselves been criticized for misunderstanding the foundational nature of participatory group dynamics necessary to facilitate change. Criticism aside, in recent decades the literature pertaining to change theory and practice has changed course to focus more on application of the theory in the context of organizational learning, culture, and transformation (Burnes, 2015).

Stage 1 in Context of COVID-19: Unfreezing the Status Quo

In the context of the COVID-19 pandemic, the unfreezing process began in Wuhan City in Hubei province, central China, with the first outbreak of the virus (Koh, 2020). The first interventions to slow the spread of the virus took place in central China, with the shutting down of the seafood and wet animal market where the virus is suspected to have originated. After the virus continued to spread despite the market shutdown, more severe interventions were set in place, involving the shutdown of the entire province and the forced quarantine of all residents within that province (Koh, 2020; Ölcer et al., 2020).

Related information of what was being referred to at the time as an epidemic began to unsettle the rest of the world. Awareness of the supply chain connections which link China to the rest of the world began to unsettle many industries that rely on materials China supplies. While travel restrictions were quickly put into place to bar those from the province from leaving and those outside from getting in, awareness that the virus could have left the country before the restrictions were put into place unsettled those living in cities with robust international travel linking them to those cities and industries. The idea that leaving home was safe quickly became false as outbreaks began to spread across borders into neighboring countries such as Singapore and Thailand, across oceans on cruise ships, and through major airports to other continents. The status quo of daily life on earth changed remarkably fast in the knowledge that a deadly virus was not under control.

Stage 2 in Context of COVID-19: Transitioning Through Uncertainty

As outbreaks spread through Italy and Spain and into the United States in the early Spring of 2020, the call to address the virus with new interventions led to more significant lockdowns, more stay-at-home orders, and more closures of schools, businesses, and borders (Olcer et al., 2020). What many hoped would be a short-lived experience of discomfort evolved into months of uncertainty and unknowns. With mass closures of businesses, schools, borders, and service industries such as tourism, retail, hotels, and restaurants the resulting economic crisis presented challenges on a secondary level (Pennington & Stanford, 2020). Many workers were relegated to abrupt transitions to working virtually, in some cases with the challenge of teaching their children while keeping up with their own workload. Businesses deemed "essential" saw different struggles as employees became ill with the virus, expressed fear of becoming ill, and removed themselves from the workforce willingly or unwillingly. In some cases, initial closures brought the additional burden of an increase of demand in the midst of a simultaneous decrease in supply, as happened with basic products in grocery stores. Coupled with fear and uncertainty, employees and leaders in the "essential" business environments were also burdened with the psychological toll of their own fears, magnified by customer reactions to shortages or pandemic-related policies (Quinn & Laws, 2020). Prolonged closures perpetuated an unstable global economy as the unknown duration of the pandemic loomed.

Focusing on one specific country, The United States provides a snapshot of how the health care industry, government, and businesses across all sectors were disrupted and set into a perpetual state of uncertainty and discomfort. Early attempts by the federal government in 2020 to mitigate the complicated dynamics of the global pandemic had little positive effect. Thousands of people across the country contracted the disease daily, followed by medical institutions becoming overwhelmed by the lack of capacity to meet the needs of an influx of critically ill patients. By the end of March 2020, New York City had become a hotspot of infection.

Since the terrorist attacks on New York City in 2001, Americans, especially New Yorkers, have been guarded and grieving. The war on terror that followed began the American collapse of confidence in government which has been exacerbated over the past 2 decades. In addition, prolonged or unsuccessful military campaigns increased mistrust and lack of confidence in the government (Kilcullen, 2020). The concern over Russian operatives interfering with the 2016 presidential election, combined with an investigation and impeachment trial of sitting President Donald Trump spanning the course of 2019, did nothing to stave off the reluctance of many Americans to trust the government (Kilcullen, 2020). New York City being the epicenter of the first major outbreak in the United States did not help improve confidence of New Yorkers or citizens across the country.

In the literature on trust and crisis management there are four major drivers for trust in institutions through a crisis: culture, institutional setting, economy, and social outcomes (Kye & Hwang, 2020). The role of trust is increasingly identified as an element of better crisis management and simultaneously acknowledged as often lacking in a crisis management situation. The reasons for this continue to be discovered. For instance, it is known that the level of trust in institutions affects not only the success of a recovery from a crisis, it also affects the survival of the institution. It is also known that it is crucial to increase or at least maintain the level of trust in the institution through crisis management for favorable outcomes (James & Wooten, 2010; Kye & Hwang, 2020; Wiard, 2018). Without trust in government or institutional leadership, support for policy implementation becomes limited, principally where short-term sacrifices are demanded but long-term gains are less feasible (Kye & Hwang, 2020).

As an example of an outcome stemming from diminished trust in governmental leadership during the COVID-19 crisis, the preventable death of George Floyd on May 25, 2020, while in police custody, in Minneapolis, Minnesota, exacerbated an already growing uncertainty toward government

(Garfinkle, 2020). Within the stay-at-home culture of the COVID-19 pandemic, increasing numbers of people were interacting primarily through social media outlets. The death of Mr. Floyd was video recorded by an onlooker and shared live on social media platforms (Nwonka, 2020). The video soon went viral and ignited social unrest in a country that was already shaken by lack of trust that its diverse body of citizens would be adequately and equitably cared for during the pandemic.

The complexities of the circumstances surrounding the death of Mr. Floyd and the protests and riots that followed are entrenched in the fundamental identities of the nation itself (Garfinkle, 2020; Gibson et al., 2020; Nwonka, 2020). Despite the end of slavery in the 19th century, covert racism continued to pervade social systems (Gibson et al., 2020) and words written in the Declaration of Independence have paradoxically never been able to justify economic practices and social systems rooted in White supremacy. The resulting Black Lives Matter (BLM) movement was an expression of a longstanding distrust and lack of confidence in police, and by proxy government, to competently and safely care for United States citizens, primarily Black Americans, but not limited to Black Americans. The resulting social unrest and polarization of communities across the country, exacerbated by a lack of consistent leadership messages on the federal level, contributed to the downward spiral of social systems and the fundamental ability to trust governmental leaders during the COVID-19 crisis.

The U.S. government's initial lack of competence in dealing with the virus has dissolved social trust, exacerbated fear and uncertainty regarding the future, and dissolved the government's perceived capacity to provide responsible leadership (Kye & Hwang, 2020). With a presidential election set to take place in the first week of November 2020 the discomfort of the unknowns presented by COVID-19 could be summarized by economic collapse, social unrest, renewed spikes in cases of the virus with no vaccine in sight, and government distrust. Great challenges existed for American leadership to effectively navigate the transition stage and garner follower trust, decrease follower resistance, and share a strong and compelling vision for change.

Viewing the resulting societal context from the perspective of the five steps essential for successful crisis leadership, follower trust enables the first step of making sense of a crisis. If trust is compromised or absent, ability to successfully transition a group, an organization, or a nation through a crisis will also be compromised if not absent. Understanding the components that may exacerbate a crisis enables leadership to make solid decisions for undertaking and resolving the crisis. Framing the context of a crisis for stakeholders must be done in ways that remediate fear and cultivate social buy-in. Troubleshooting the crisis to reestablish normalcy would mean interventions that do not exacerbate the crisis and fear inherent in the crisis.

Learning from the crisis experience invites looking back not only at the current crisis but previous similar crises' and addressing the immediate situation with a broad base of knowledge (Meisler et al., 2013; Meisler & Vigoda-Gadot, 2014).

As noted previously, the key to successful organizational change begins with mitigating follower resistance (Lawrence et al., 2014; Meisler & Vigoda-Gadot, 2014). Leaders must express themselves in a way that followers deem legitimate and rational in order to generate support. Trust and follower support are key ingredients needed to generate group cooperation and alleviate uncertainty, because lack of trust contributes directly to resistance to change (Grady & Grady, 2013).

How a leader behaves impacts their followers' experiences of trusting or distrusting them (Meisler et al., 2013; Wiard, 2018). How leaders behave during times of transition will enhance or decrease follower trust and distrust on all levels of an organization or group (Meisler et al., 2013; Meisler & Vigoda-Gadot, 2014; Penava & Sehic, 2014: Wiard, 2018; Zhang & Zhou, 2014). In order to reestablish normalcy and create a new status quo in the midst of the COVID-19 crisis that all stakeholders can buy into, leaders in all sectors have a large ongoing task in front of them; building trust and enabling cooperation for the sake of the greater mission of the organization.

Stage 3 in Context of COVID-19: Looking Ahead to Refreezing

The third stage in the change process, refreezing, takes place when the systems learned in the second stage organically solidify (Lewin, 1951). During a time of upheaval and uncertainty, it is impossible to predict the duration of the transitioning stage and when or how the refreezing stage of a new status quo will take place. At the time this chapter went to press, we were simply not there yet in regard to COVID-19 related change processes internationally or in the United States.

Successful change implementations depend on a scaffold effect. The success of one change becomes the foundation upon which another is built. Leaders can implement behaviors from different strategies in order to unfreeze, transition, and refreeze any change process. The three stages of the process remain the same if the process is to be categorized as successful. Because change implementations are rarely successful, having a benchmark for success is necessary (Decker et al., 2012; Wetzel & Dievernich, 2014). Establishing a measurable benchmark for the third stage process of refreezing therefore is important to determine success. A set of three themes essential for putting the three stages of the Lewin (1943) model into practice can be used to facilitate the best possible outcomes.

WIARD'S THREE THEMES FOR ENACTING CHANGE

Lewin's three-stage model of change management was used as the seminal theoretical research base for *Leadership Behaviors in the Midst of an Organizational Change Initiative: A Case Study* (Wiard, 2018). The study was concentrated on a middle-sized organization during a large-scale change initiative, focusing primarily on the behavioral attributes of middle management leaders that enabled successful refreezing of a new status quo into the organizational culture. Wiard's (2018) research revealed new findings on passion and its effects on organizational change in the cross section of leadership behaviors and their effect on organizational culture. It was also noted in findings of the 2018 study that transformational and transactional leadership behaviors were not mutually exclusive to successfully refreezing the status quo by garnering follower trust and buy-in, affirming findings presented in previous crisis leadership literature (Boin et al., 2013; Meisler et al., 2013).

The predominant finding of the study (Wiard, 2018) applied directly to the three stages of change in Lewin's (1943) model. Three themes were found to coincide with moving from one stage of the change process to another, essentially providing a leadership behavioral context for operationalizing a change process. These three themes for change created a clearer picture of the leadership behaviors which enable or disable a change process: (a) know your audience and walk your talk; (b) implement communication, vision, trust, and buy-in; and (c) facilitate residual passion and perseverance (Wiard, 2018).

Wiard's Change Theme 1: Know Your Audience and Walk Your Talk

All organizations have unique, singular cultures. The culture of an organization affects followers' willingness to trust a leader and follow a leader through change with minimal resistance. Creating an organizational climate that fosters positive job attitudes is an antecedent to commitment to change (Green et al., 2016). Positive job attitudes can be fostered through a leader's behavior. Knowing your audience and walking your talk are two examples of leadership behaviors that can positively impact an organization's culture during an organizational change. Knowing your audience involves understanding the culture of an organization's status quo to attain stakeholder buy-in for an effective change implementation. Knowing your audience involves understanding the interplay between historical organizational dynamics, and current circumstances and climate.

Walking your talk is the leadership behavior of leading by example. At times easier to define than to enact, leading by example is a skill that reflects emotional intelligence (Ngirande & Timothy, 2014; Segon & Booth, 2015). Walking your talk encourages followership rather than submission or depletion of loyalty, similar to gleaning residual passion to promote motivation through trust. Leaders who lead by example through walking their talk, neutralize the negative effect of the followers' residual passion of wishing an organization was like it used to be, engaging follower trust and buy-in toward change (Wiard, 2018). This finding echoed previous research which emphasized leaders who work alongside their followers and have personal relationships with them are better able to facilitate their employees' willingness to buy into a change initiative and embrace the unfreezing of the status quo (Lawrence et al., 2014; Meisler et al., 2013; Meisler & Vigoda-Gadot, 2014).

Wiard's Change Theme 2: Implement Communication, Vision, Trust, and Buy-In

For an organizational change implementation to be effective, leadership must lead with behaviors that share a clear vision for the proposed change, enhance trust, and increase stakeholder buy-in. A clear and shared vision reduces follower stress and creates an organizational environment conducive to trust and follow-through (Williams et al., 2013). Knowing your audience and their residual passion enables communicating a clear vision through shared language (Wiard, 2018). Poor communication is among the major antecedents which lead to negative outcomes in change implementations (Saruhan, 2014). An effective implementation of a change process is 100% dependent on the person or persons effecting the change.

Clear communication of the vision for the change is a responsibility not to be carried lightly by leadership (Mangundjaya, 2015). Additionally, followers' residual passion for their roles in the organization, and the old ways of performing their roles, may generate resistance to the vision communicated by leadership. Leaders can mitigate such resistance and generate trust and buy-in from followers by using consistent, positive, collaborative communication and listening to follower feedback (Sharif & Scandura, 2014; Wiard, 2018). Leaders who communicate their vision with behaviors that build trust and do not discredit the foundation on which a change is being built can more readily engage follower buy-in for a change. Maintaining these behaviors throughout a change process results in successful and effective implementation of change.

Wiard's Change Theme 3: Facilitate Residual Passion and Perseverance

Residual passion and its relationship to leadership, when addressed in organizational change literature, is defined as a strong emotion that captures an intensity of feeling toward a company or an organization (Siren et al., 2016; Vallerand, 2012). In leadership research passion has historically been considered two parts; harmonious passion and obsessive passion, which can be identified in the way a person experiences passion. As is implied by their names the two types of passion are dualistic in nature. Harmonious passion is an antecedent of positive attitudes and behaviors, while obsessive passion leads to negative attitudes and behaviors (Siren et al., 2016; Vallerand, 2012).

A new phenomenon relating to obsessive and harmonious passion was identified in the 2018 Wiard study and labeled residual passion. This refers to passion in terms of motivation, buy-in, work ethic, and commitment to follow-through. Residual passion also relates to followers' attitudes toward prior leaders or a prior vision, encompassing a long-standing traditional culture of an existing organization. Understanding the role of residual passion in follower engagement, particularly regarding trust and resistance to change, can enable leadership to communicate a vision for change that reduces resistance to change during a change implementation.

Wiard's (2018) research demonstrated that the internal experience of residual passion could paradoxically imply the tone of negative and/or positive antecedent to effective organizational change implementation outcomes. In some cases, residual passion can be a negative antecedent to trusting new leadership. In other cases, with healthy leadership, there can be a positive tone, an assuring and wise tone, using lessons learned in the old status quo while creating the new norm. Tapping into old passions and wisdom (the residual passion), decreased knowledge silos and supported perseverance through resistance to change with an undaunting work ethic rooted in the love of the work itself.

Positive emotional attitudes related to one's work contribute directly to overall life satisfaction and fulfillment (Palaiou et al., 2016). Regardless of leadership behaviors, organizational behaviors, change processes, or perceived lack of vision, the internal stakeholders in the Wiard (2018) study indicated that residual passion for the work itself empowered followers to maintain their engagement during the challenging and uncomfortable processes inherent in organizational change. Happiness is elusive and difficult to define but the motivations and determinations of happiness are more easily qualified. Facilitating an environment in which residual passion can be fostered and nourished can provide motivation for perseverance during change processes and substantively reduce resistance to change.

Implementing Change: Lewin's Three-Stage Model and Wiard's Three Themes

This chapter is rooted in the seminal change theory research of Kurt Lewin (1943) and his resulting three-stage model of change management. To summarize, these three stages involve the unfreezing of the status quo, the transitioning stage, and the refreezing stage of a new status quo. Because resistance to change is expected, the focus during the unfreezing stage is to ally stakeholders to the purpose and value of the change initiative. Leaders need to have a clear conceptualization of how followers define and view the status quo and be able to clearly identify why and how it needs to change. Once the organization has been unfrozen then the change process can begin.

Planning and preparing for a change give leaders a clear advantage when it comes to communicating a vision for change that followers can buy into. Writing a plan is often the start of a change process. However, the start of the change process or the transition stage, is not always recognized before it begins. Crises are catalysts for change that begin a change process with little or no planning and preparation.

In all change processes, the transition stage is difficult, and people will struggle with change. People are most afraid during this time because the uncertainty of the future is most magnified. It is during this time that education and support of all stakeholders in an organization matters most. Engagement on a personal level during the transitioning stage has a positive effect on the outcomes which are solidified in the third stage, refreezing. Considered by Lewin (1943) to be the most important stage of the process, this third stage is the point at which new systems, cultures, behaviors, and goals are affirmed and put into place. It is also a time when organizational infrastructure is vulnerable to reverting to old ways; acknowledgment of the success of the change reinforces its value and purpose for continuity (Lewin, 1951).

Applying Wiard's three themes for enacting change in your organization during the COVID-19 pandemic, or during any other change implementation, may enhance your leadership's capacity to successfully implement change with minimal resistance. Start with a change plan and develop a vision for change while asking yourself who you are leading through the change and what is most important to them. If there is any doubt about the latter, go to the source and ask rather than assuming and basing a change on values that don't exist. Are you able to walk your talk through the process? Would you be willing to do what you are asking your followers to do?

Change is hard, people are inherently resistant, and there may be aspects of what you ask of your followers to which they may not want to adhere. Prepare your followers for implementation like a parent prepares a 4-year old for bed; give clear guidelines for where you are going, when, for how long, and why it's important. Communicating a clear vision and walking your talk before, during, and after the change develops trust in your followers; doing it consistently develops buy-in. Keep your followers committed by remembering what fuels them and add to their fire. For example, if you are in the outdoor recreation business, consider giving your employees some free outdoor recreation time in the midst of longer hours or reduced pay. Seek to implement behaviors that exemplify the themes of knowing your audience and walking your talk; implementing communication, vision, trust, and buy-in; and facilitating residual passion.

Operationalizing these themes into a change plan can involve actions as simple as including front-line in daily meetings, incorporating stakeholder input when determining organizational values, and transparently sharing the data when analyzing company metrics. Depending on the needs of the organization a more complicated approach could be used with more aggressive interventions, such as team retreats focused on the residual passion at the heart of the organization; restructuring of management to place leaders with the capacity to serve at the level the organization demands; logical consequences for poor and failing follow through. Leading through the scope of the three themes—know your audience and walk your talk, implement communication, vision, trust, and buy-in, and facilitate residual passion—means leading with a combination of emotional intelligence, transformational and transactional leadership behaviors and skills, and avoiding any vestige of a coercive leadership style.

CONCLUSIONS

The value of managing a change implementation during a crisis situation, through Lewin's three stages of change (1943) within the context of Wiard's (2018) three themes for change, can act as a positive antecedent for change outcomes. Crisis situations require strong leadership to reestablish a sense of normalcy to the organization or group during and after the crisis experience (Boin et al., 2013).

Sudden and complete global disruption of the world's status quo, as happened with the 2020 COVID-19 pandemic, impacts daily operations at every organization along with everyone's daily lives and change is inevitable. While the crisis is ongoing, it is impossible to predict what the final outcomes will be. However, it is clear that during a time of rampant, ongoing unknowns, choices can be made by leaders which will mitigate follower lack of trust, resistance to transition, and fear of the unknown.

It is also clear that strong leadership is greatly needed during this time, leadership that enhances trust and follower buy-in. Viewing the theoretical model of Lewin's (1943) three-stage model of change management through the lens of Wiard's (2018) three themes for change, it is clear that knowing your audience and walking your talk; implementing communication, vision, trust, and buy-in; and facilitating residual passion strongly enhance a leader's potential for success in creating and sustaining a new status-quo. The behaviors that demonstrate the leadership themes result in a hybrid leadership approach, empowered with the emotional intelligence of residual passion.

While the approach suggested in this theoretical chapter focuses on a top–down approach, the themes for change can also be utilized in a bottom–up grassroots manner. Follower buy-in is not relegated to following classical leaders in formidable roles. Follower buy-in and residual passion are emotional propellants that can compel communities to bring new local leaders to the forefront. Two contemporary examples would be Barack Obama (Kovaleski, 2008) and Alexandria Ocasio-Cortez (Alter, 2019), both of whom have early experience as grassroots community organizers that influenced their ability to unite and motivate constituents in subsequent political careers.

The COVID-19 pandemic presents the organizational leadership research community with an unprecedented opportunity to study leadership models and stakeholder commitment under long-term duress with unknown outcomes. Research on the subject of leadership behaviors which mitigate follower resistance and enhance follower buy-in through residual passion needs to be done during this time to add to the body of organizational change literature. This chapter demonstrates that moving a change implementation through Lewin's three stages of change (1943), within the context of Wiard's (2018) three themes for change, can have a mitigating effect on follower resistance while enhancing leadership effectiveness during the inevitable organizational changes stemming from the COVID-19 pandemic.

REFERENCES

Ali, S. H., Foreman, J., Capasso, A., Jones, A. M., Tozan, Y., & DiClemente, R. J. (2020). Social media as a recruitment platform for a nationwide online survey of COVID-19 knowledge, beliefs, and practices in the United States: methodology and feasibility analysis. *BMC medical research methodology, 20*(116), 1–11.

Alter, C. (2019, March 21). 'Change is closer than we think.' Inside Alexandria Ocasio-Cortez's unlikely rise. *Time.* https://time.com/longform/alexandria-ocasio-cortez-profile/

Atkinson, P., & Mackenzie, R. (2015). Without leadership there is no change. *Management Services, 59(2),* 42–47. http://www.philipatkinson.com/uploads/7/1/5/0/7150143/without_leadership_ther e_is_no_change_article.pdf

Baesu, C., & Bejinaru, R. (2013). Leadership approaches regarding the organizational change. *USV Annals of Economics & Public Administration, 13(2)*, 146–152.

Balliet, D., & Lange, P. A. (2013). Trust, conflict, and cooperation: A meta-analysis. *Psychological Bulletin, 139*(5), 1090–1112. http://dx.doi.org/10.1037/a0030939

Boin, A., Kuipers, S., & Overdijk, W. (2013). Leadership in times of crisis: A framework for assessment. *International Review of Public Administration, 18*(1), 79–91. http://dx.doi.org/10.1080/12294659.2013.10805241

Burnes, B. (2004). Kurt Lewin and the planned approach to change: A re-appraisal. *Journal of Management Studies, 41(6)*, 977–1002. http://dx.doi.org/10.1111/j.1467-6486.2004.00463.x

Burnes, B. (2015). Understanding resistance to change–building on Coch and French. *Journal of Change Management, 15*(2), 92–116. http://dx.doi.org/10.1080/14697017.2014.969755

Burnes, B., & Bargal, D. (2017). Kurt Lewin: 70 years on. *Journal of Change Management, 17*(2), 91–100. https://doi.org/10.1080/14697017.2017.1299371

Decker, P., Durand, R., Mayfield, C. O., McCormack, C., Skinner, D., & Perdue, G. (2012). Predicting implementation failure in organization change. *Journal of Organizational Culture, Communications & Conflict, 16*(2), 39–59. http://alliedacademies.org/Public/Default.aspx

Desvars-Larrive, A., Dervic, E., Haug, N., Niederkrotenthaler, T., Chen, J., Di Natale, A., Lasser, J., Gliga, D. S., Roux, A., Sorger, J., Chakraborty, A., Ten, A., Dervic, A., Pacheco, A., Jurczak, A., Cserjan, D., Lederhilger, D., Bulska, D., Berishaj, D., . . . Ten, A. (2020). *A structured open dataset of government interventions in response to COVID-19.* MedRxiv. https://www.medrxiv.org/content/10.1101/2020.05.04.20090498v1

Di Domenico, L., Pullano, G., Sabbatini, C. E., Boëlle, P. Y., & Colizza, V. (2020). *Expected impact of lockdown in Île-de-France and possible exit strategies.* MedRxiv. https://www.medrxiv.org/content/10.1101/2020.04.13.20063933v2

Dong, Y., Mo, X., Hu, Y., Qi, X., Jiang, F., Jiang, Z., & Tong, S. (2020). Epidemiological characteristics of 2143 pediatric patients with 2019 coronavirus disease in China. *Paediatrics*. https://doi.org/10.1542/peds.2020-0702

Dunphy, D., & Stace, D. (1993). The strategic management of corporate change. *Human Relations, 46*(8), 905–920.

Emanuel, E. J., Persad, G., Upshur, R., Thome, B., Parker, M., Glickman, A., & Phillips, J. P. (2020). Fair allocation of scarce medical resources in the time of Covid-19. *New England Journal of Medicine, 382*, 2049–2055. https://www.nejm.org/doi/full/10.1056/NEJMsb2005114

Garfinkle, A. (2020). The 'George Floyd' unrest: its strategic implications. *RSIS Commentaries.* https://www.rsis.edu.sg/rsis-publication/rsis/the-george-floyd-unrest-its-strategic-implications/#.YXYVjtlKhH0

Gibson, A. N., Chancellor, R. L., Cooke, N. A., Dahlen, S. P., Patin, B., & Shorish, Y. L. (2020). Struggling to breathe: COVID-19, protest and the LIS response. *Equality, Diversity and Inclusion: An International Journal.* https://scholarcommons.sc.edu/libsci_facpub/291/

Grady, V. M., & Grady, J. D. (2013). The relationship of Bowlby's attachment theory to the persistent failure of organizational change initiatives. *Journal of Change*

Management, 13(2), 206–222. http://dx.doi.org/10.1080/14697017.2012.728534

Green, A. E., Dishop, C. R., & Aarons, G. A. (2016). Organizational stress as moderator of relationship between mental health provider adaptability and organizational commitment. *Psychiatric Services, 67*(10), 1103–1108. https://doi.org/10.1176/appi.ps.201500191

James, E. H., & Wooten, L. P. (2010). *Leading under pressure: From surviving to thriving before, during, and after a crisis.* Routledge.

Kenworthy, J. B., Voci, A., Al Ramiah, A., Tausch, N., Hughes, J., & Hewstone, M. (2015). Building trust in a post conflict society an integrative model of cross-group friendship and intergroup emotions. *The Journal of Conflict Resolution, 60(6),* 1041–1070. http://dx.doi.org/10.1177/0022002714564427

Kilcullen, D. (2020). *The dragons and the snakes: How the rest learned to fight the West.* Oxford University Press.

Koh, D. (2020). Occupational risks for COVID-19 infection. *Occupational medicine (Oxford, England), 70*(1), 3. https://doi.org/10.1186/s13054-020-2818-6

Kotter, J. P. (1996). *Leading change* (1st ed.). Harvard Business School Press.

Kovaleski, S. (2008, July 7). Obama's organizing years, guiding others and finding himself. *The New York Times.* https://www.nytimes.com/2008/07/07/us/politics/07community.html

Kuhlmann, E., Dussault, G., & Wismar, M. (2020). Health labour markets and the 'human face'of the health workforce: Resilience beyond the COVID-19 pandemic. *The European Journal of Public Health, 30*(Suppl 4), iv1–iv2. https://dx.doi.org/10.1093%2Feurpub%2Fckaa122

Kye, B., & Hwang, S. J. (2020). Social trust in the midst of pandemic crisis: Implications from COVID-19 of South Korea. *Research in social stratification and mobility, 68,* 100523. https://dx.doi.org/10.1016%2Fj.rssm.2020.100523

Lawrence, E., Ruppel, C. P., & Tworoger, L. C. (2014). The emotions and cognitions during organizational change: The importance of the emotional work for leaders. *Journal of Organizational Culture, Communications and Conflict, 18*(1), 257–273.

Lewin, K. (1951). *Field theory in social science: Selected theoretical papers* (Dorwin Cartwright, ed.).

Lewis, J. D., & Weigert, A. (1985). Trust as a social reality. *Social Forces, 63*(4), 967–985. http://dx.doi.org/10.1093/sf/63.4.967

Luisetto, M., & Latyshev, Y. (2020). COVID-19 Pandemic and the Management Strategy for Business and Economy. *Journal of Economic and Business Studies, 3*(2), 1–3.

Mangundjaya, W. L. (2015). People or trust in building commitment to change? *Journal of Developing Areas, 49(5)*, 67–78. https://dx.doi.org/10.1353/jda.2015.0050

McBride, N. (2005). Chaos theory as a model for interpreting information systems in organizations. *Information Systems Journal, 15*(3), 233–254. http://citeseerx.ist.psu.edu/viewdoc/download?doi=10.1.1.485.7957&rep=rep1&type=pdf

Meisler, G., & Vigoda-Gadot, E. (2014). Perceived organizational politics, emotional intelligence and work outcomes: Empirical exploration of direct and indirect effects. *Personnel Review, 43*(1), 116–135. http://dx.doi.org/10.1108/PR-02-2012-0040

Meisler, G., Vigoda-Gadot, E., & Drory, A. (2013). Leadership beyond rationality: Emotional leadership in times of organizational crisis. In A. J. DuBrin (Ed.), *The handbook of research of crisis leadership in organizations* (pp. 110–126). Edward Elgar Publishers. https://www.researchgate.net/publication/270574588

Middaugh, D. J. (2020). Maintaining management during disaster: The COVID. *Medsurg Nursing, 29*(3), 211–212.

Ming-Chu, Y., & Meng-Hsiu, L. (2015). Unlocking the black box: Exploring the link between perceive organizational support and resistance to change. *Asia Pacific Management Review, 20*(3), 177–183. http://dx.doi.org/10.1016/j.apmrv.2014.10.003

Molm, L. D., Takahashi, N., & Peterson, G. (2000). Risk and trust in social exchange: An experimental test of a classical proposition. *American Journal of Sociology, 105*(5), 1396–1472. http://doi.org/10.1086/210434

Ngirande, H., & Timothy, H. T. (2014). The relationship between leader emotional intelligence and employee job satisfaction. *Mediterranean Journal of Social Sciences, 5*(6), 35–40. http://dx.doi.org/10.5901/mjss.2014.v5n6p35

Nwonka, C. J. (2020, June 8). *The protests over George Floyd's death show how film and culture can be tools of anti-racism, but we must continue to value them beyond this moment.* USApp—American Politics and Policy Blog. https://blogs.lse.ac.uk/usappblog/2020/06/08/the-protests-over-george-floyds-death-show-how-film-and-culture-can-be-tools-of-anti-racism-but-we-must-continue-to-value-them-beyond-this-moment/

Ölcer, S., Yilmaz-Aslan, Y., & Brzoska, P. (2020). Lay perspectives on social distancing and other official recommendations and regulations in the time of COVID-19: A qualitative study of social media posts. *BMC Public Health, 20,* 963.

Palaiou, K., Zarola, A., & Furnham, A. (2016). The dark side of personality predicts positive and negative work attitudes. *Personality and Individual Differences, 88,* 12–16. http://dx.doi.org/10.1016/j.paid.2015.08.029

Parry, W. (2015). *Big change best path: Successfully managing organizational change with wisdom, analytics, and insight.* Kogan Page.

Penava, S., & Sehic, D. (2014). The relevance of transformational leadership in shaping employee attitudes towards organizational change. *Economic Annals, 59*(200), 131–162. http://dx.doi.org/10.2298/EKA1400131P

Pennington, A., & Stanford, J. (2020). Rebuilding After Covid-19 Will Need a Sustained National Reconstruction Plan. *Journal of Australian Political Economy, 85,* 164–174.

Quinn, A., & Laws, M. (2020). Addressing community needs and preparing for the secondary impacts of Covid-19. *NEJM Catalyst Innovations in Care Delivery.* https://catalyst.nejm.org/doi/full/10.1056/CAT.20.0186

Romanelli, E., & Tushman, M. L. (1994). Organizational transformation as punctuated equilibrium: An empirical test. *Academy of Management journal, 37*(5), 1141–1166. http://assochange.it/wp-content/uploads/2016/07/romanelli-tushman-1994.pdf

Saruhan, N. (2014). The role of corporate communication and perception of justice during organizational change process. *Business & Economics Research Journal, 5*(4), 143–166.

Segon, M., & Booth, C. (2015). Virtue: The missing ethics element in emotional intelligence. *Journal of Business Ethics, 128*(4), 789–802. https://doi.org/10.1007/s10551-013-2029-z

Self, D. R., Armenakis, A. A., & Schraeder, M. (2007). Organizational change content, process, and context: A simultaneous analysis of employee reactions. *Journal of Change Management, 7*(2), 211–229. http://dx.doi.org/10.1080/14697010701461129

Sharif, M. M., & Scandura, T. A. (2014). Do perceptions of ethical conduct matter during organizational change? Ethical leadership and employee involvement. *Journal of Business Ethics, 124(2),* 185–196. http://doi.org/10.1007/s10551-013-1869-x

Sirén, C., Patel, P. C., & Wincent, J. (2016). How do harmonious passion and obsessive passion moderate the influence of a CEO's change-oriented leadership on company performance? *Leadership Quarterly, 27*(4), 653–670. http://dx.doi.org/10.1016/j.leaqua.2016.03.002

Smollan, R. K. (2013). Trust in change managers: The role of affect. *Journal of Organizational Change Management, 26(4),* 725–747. http://dx.doi.org/10.1108/JOCM-May-2012-0070

Termini, C. M., & Traver, D. (2020). Impact of COVID-19 on early career scientists: An optimistic guide for the future. *BMC Biology, 18*(1), 1–4. https://doi.org/10.1186/s12915-020-00821-4

Tushman, M. L., & Romanelli, E. (1985). Organizational evolution: A metamorphosis model of convergence and reorientation. *Research in Organizational Behavior, 7,* 171–222.

Vallerand, R. J. (2012). From motivation to passion: In search of the motivational processes involved in a meaningful life. *Canadian Psychology, 53*(1), 42–52. http://dx.doi.org/10.1037/a0026377

Vanderwood, R. S. (2013). *Leader behaviors and organizational change effectiveness* [Unpublished doctoral dissertation]. Capella University. http://gateway.proquest.com/openurl?url_ver=Z39.88-2004&res_dat=xri:pqdiss&rft_val_fmt=info:ofi/fmt:kev:mtx:dissertation&rft_dat=xri:pqdiss:3608822

Verhagen, M. D., Brazel, D. M., Dowd, J. B., Kashnitsky, I., & Mills, M. C. (2020). Forecasting spatial, socioeconomic and demographic variation in COVID-19 health care demand in England and Wales. *BMC Medicine, 18*(1), 1–11. https://doi.org/10.1186/s12916-020-01646-2

Wetzel, R., & Dievernich, F. E. (2014). Mind the gap. The relevance of postchange periods for organizational sensemaking. *Systems Research & Behavioral Science, 31*(2), 280–300. http://dx.doi.org/10.1002/sres.2198

Wiard, T. J. (2018). *Leadership behaviors in the midst of an organizational change initiative: A case study* [Unpublished doctoral dissertation]. Grand Canyon University.

Williams, V., Oades, L. G., Deane, F. P., Crowe, T. P., Ciarrochi, J., & Andresen, R. (2013). Improving implementation of evidence-based practice in mental health service delivery: Protocol for a cluster randomized quasi-experimental investigation of staff-focused values interventions. *Implementation Science, 8*(1), 1–10. http://doi.org/10.1186/1748-5908-8-75

Zhang, X., & Zhou, J. (2014). Empowering leadership, uncertainty avoidance, trust, and employee creativity: Interaction effects and a mediating mechanism. *Organizational Behavior and Human Decision Processes, 124*(2), 150–164. https://doi.org/10.1016/j.obhdp.2014.02.002

CHAPTER 11

DIGITAL COMMUNICATION STRATEGIES DURING PANDEMIC CRISIS

Lessons From Amazon Company

Ludovica Moi
University of Cagliari

Simone Serpi
Senior Management Consultant, Milan

Francesca Cabiddu
University of Cagliari

The unexpected outbreak of the coronavirus (COVID-19) pandemic has impacted people and organizations worldwide, triggering in-depth economic, political, and social changes of an unprecedented scale (Baum & Hai, 2020). Notably, it has raised the need for companies to design social media communication strategies more effectively than in the past to respond to the crisis underway and to create real connections with their customers that

Crisis, Chaos, and Organizations, pages 281–307

will outlive the pandemic's social and economic impacts (Mirbabaie et al., 2020; Walwema, 2021). People are increasingly employing digital tools to share and receive real-time experiences and information, about the multiple events related to COVID-19 (Islam et al., 2020; Zheng et al., 2020).

A growing body of literature has recognized that social media covers a key role in crisis communication (Cheng, 2018; Fraustino et al., 2017; Veil et al., 2011; Zhao et al., 2018). Despite this recognition, there is no systematic research about how companies could define effective digital communication strategies to react to a global emergency's various stages as the coronavirus spread.

In this chapter, we attempt to answer a compelling question posed by managers across firms: "What kind of digital communication strategies are required to successfully navigate crises like the COVID pandemic?" Accordingly, this study investigates and understands the types of communication strategies adopted by organizations during the pandemic underway, focusing on the Amazom.com Facebook page. We adopt an explanatory sequential mixed design (Creswell et al., 2003). Firstly, using a model based on data science and text mining techniques with R (Frau et al., 2019), we collected quantitative data to assess the overall sentiments expressed by customers towards the company over time. Secondly, with NVivo 10 software's support, we conducted an in-depth qualitative analysis (Moi et al., 2018b) to explore the recurring themes or topics in users' negative comments and then identify the type of communication strategy adopted by the firm to deal with customers' complaints.

Our findings offer a view of how social media communication strategies take place during a pandemic crisis. By extending current knowledge on crisis communication strategies in a social media context, we explain how, during a global pandemic crisis, organizations can learn about users, and what digital communication strategies may be adopted to increase corporate reputation, or to limit the effects of negative comments.

This chapter has crucial implications for practice as well. The chapter guides managers regarding effective and suitable communication strategies. The latest events made organizations rethink the way of doing business and redefine digital communication endeavors. As uncertain as the current times may be, a crisis is also a way to discover new paths. Considering the pivotal role of social media in people's lives, we believe in providing significant guidance to managers facing current business scenarios and implementing corrective actions in how they deal with customers' reactions, thereby adopting more informed communication strategies.

A crisis is generally defined as "the perception of an unpredictable event that threatens important expectancies of stakeholders related to health, safety, environmental, and economic issues and can seriously impact an organization's performance and generate negative outcomes" (Coombs,

2014, pp. 2–3). Thus, a particular circumstance during which "the normal order in a system is destabilized, which creates considerable uncertainty and requires rapid intervention" (Falkheimer & Heide, 2010, p. 514).

The condition of heightened volatility and uncertainty that characterizes marketplaces following a crisis pushes organizations to strongly use social media to accomplish important tasks to adapt to new market conditions and look for greater ways to focus straight on customer needs (Coombs, 2018). Social media increases the production and dissemination of information during a crisis (Jurgens & Helsloot, 2018; Liu et al., 2012). They work as "alternative discursive space" where people exchange information, express their opinions, share emotions and experiences, or stay informed about the events underway (Marken, 2007; Sweetser & Metzgar, 2007; Zhao et al., 2017). Organizations can then extract crucial people's opinions and thoughts in real-time (Dellarocas, 2003) and keep relationships with them (Argenti & Barnes, 2009; Hennig-Thurau et al., 2010; Kietzmann et al., 2011). On the other side, social media often makes crisis management more unpredictable and complex (Floreddu et al., 2014; Vanbruggen et al., 2010). The skepticism of customers towards organizations in a digital context is growing as "consumers are becoming more and more aware of organizations' hidden messages, and are likely to immunize themselves against persuasive online messages and social media content" (Valentini, 2015, p. 175). Hence, in today's online environments, customer voices may undermine organizational reputation (Aula, 2010). This is also known as the negative or "dark" side of social media (Baccarella et al., 2018; Floreddu et al., 2014). Among the recognized negative facets of social media, scholars highlight the sharing of fake news (Allcott & Gentzkow, 2017), the increased levels of anxiety and depression (Levenson et al., 2016), but also defamation (Baccarella et al., 2018). Other studies offer an overview of social media practices in managing risk and crisis communication (e.g., share timely information about risks; Veil et al., 2011).

In summary, in times of crisis, "comments and actions of online stakeholders have a significant effect on organizations [...] negative online comments can threaten organizations' reputation" (Coombs, 2011, p. 21). Greater attention in trying to engage with customers humanly and conversationally is then required to protect and enhance corporate reputation (Floreddu & Cabiddu, 2016; Jones et al., 2009; Kelleher, 2009; Moi et al., 2018a; Van Noort & Willemsen, 2012; Ye & Ki, 2018).

The field of crisis communication encompasses several strategies. Instructing information and adjusting information strategies aim, respectively, to protect public safety and to notify people about how the organization is performing to face the crisis (Sturges, 1994). Reputation repair strategy strives to reduce the adverse effects on corporate reputation brought by the crisis (e.g., by excluding organization's responsibility, by reminding past good work, or ensuring that a negative event will not occur anymore; Coombs, 2015). Within reputation repair strategies, a central role is played by "apology." By apologizing, organizations protect their image and reputation, inspiring positive feelings to the counterpart (Coombs, 1995, 2014; Coombs et al., 2010). Instructing and adjusting information strategies commonly represent organizations' first response strategies to safeguard reputation, purchase intention, and potential negative word-of-mouth (Coombs, 2015).

METHODOLOGY

We adopted an explanatory sequential mixed method research design (Creswell et al., 2003). Using a quantitative method, we identified the peaks of negative interactions across users' comments. Thus, we employed a qualitative method to support the in-depth explanation of the quantitative part of the research, that is, details about customers' main topics during the different peaks and the firm's kind of communication response strategy.

We focused our attention on the Amazon.com Facebook page. Amazon.com, Inc. is a U.S. global company, recognized worldwide as one of the most popular brands in the e-commerce industry. To conduct our analysis, we chose to select the U.S. Amazon Facebook page for the outstanding number of likes, comments, and followers compared to the other English-speaking pages of the company.

Data Collection and Data Cleaning

For the quantitative analysis of our research, we used a dataset of 441,707 records (posts and comments) extracted by the Amazon U.S. Facebook page from January 2020 to June 2020. The dataset was created by employing Facepager 3.6 and Ncapture (the browser application of NVivo 10 software), and then converted to an excel file. A first data cleaning process concerned the removal of a set of words related to the "hi-tech" world, numbers and a list of the most frequent 250 English adverbs. We then removed the English and Spanish "stop words" (i.e., articles, conjunctions, prepositions) by using the existing vocabularies stored in the "tm" R package (Meyer et al., 2008).

The quantitative analysis enabled us to recognize the main peaks of negative comments of users. We then realized a qualitative dataset selecting negative comments which were published during the timeframe analyzed. The dataset was uploaded into NVivo 10 software for the thematic qualitative data analysis.

Data Analysis

To perform the sentiment analysis, we used the text2vec R package (Selivanov & Wang, 2018). First, we created a document-term matrix (DTM). Second, we adapted a logistic regression model to the DTM, using "sentiment140" database (Go et al., 2009), which classifies a huge number of records as positive or negative. We then applied the logistic regression model to the data collected. The probability for each comment to be positive or negative ranges from 0 (*totally negative comment*) to 1 (*totally positive comment*). We fixed a probability threshold of 0.50 to divide the comments into positives or negatives. Once negative comments have been identified and selected, the probability of their positivity is lower than 0.50.

Our quantitative analysis was accompanied by a thematic qualitative analysis that enabled us to better explain the identified peaks of negative comments among users. Notably, we run four rounds of coding. During the first coding step, we analyzed the type of post shared by Amazon on its Facebook page to explore whether the company adjusted its post-related messages during the pandemic. Therefore, in the second coding step, we looked for descriptive and interpretative codes concerning customers' negative comments about the service provided by Amazon. The result of this step was a list of issues as stressed by users (e.g., refund, long delivery time, mistakes in the order received; Miles & Huberman, 1994). In the third coding step, we grouped the descriptive codes in thematic codes (Miles & Huberman, 1994), recurring themes, topics, and meanings discussed by users during the different peaks of negative comments. The result of this step was a list of topics. Finally, we identified the type of communication strategy adopted by the company to respond to users' negative comments, discussing the main factors shaping such strategy to engage with customers.

RESULTS

Figure 11.1 represents the distribution of users' negative comments. Throughout the entire time span analyzed (January 2020–June 2020), we discovered some periods in which the negative comments' distribution reached significant peaks. Notably, the highest peaks mainly concentrate between March and June 2020, which represent the "salient" months of the coronavirus spread worldwide and the period during which governments started implementing strict safety measures and protocols to reduce at most the risk of infection.

During the time that we analyzed (January 2020–June 2020), it is interesting to notice that the type of post and related message changed a lot from January and February to the following months. Until February 2020,

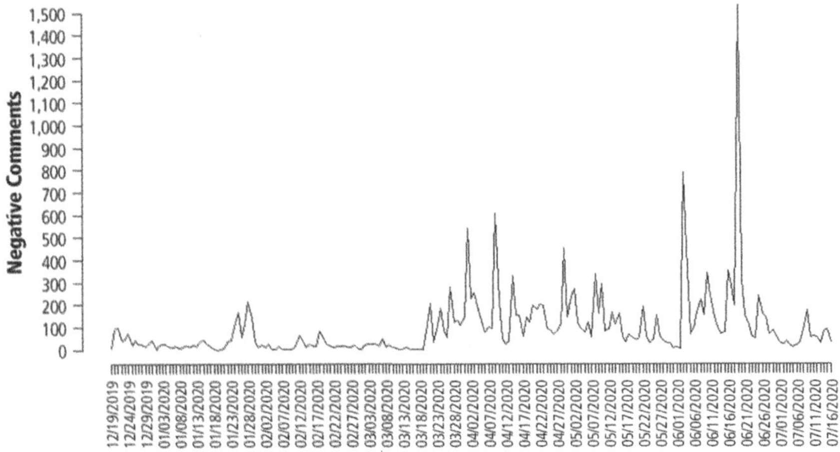

Figure 11.1 Projection curve of comments with peaks of negativity (January 2020–June 2020)

Amazon mainly communicated promotional messages, for example, general news about their products and services ("Wait, who's Alessa? Watch the big game on 02.02.20 to find out what we did #BeforeAlexa" [Amazon.com, 2020a] or "Scout, our delivery robot, made a special guest appearance on The Ellen DeGeneres Show yesterday!" [Amazon.com, 2020b]).

However, when the pandemic coronavirus hit our lives definitely, we noticed that Amazon changed the "tone" from a promotional communication to a more engaging interaction. An ample number of pandemic-related posts started being published on its Facebook page, suggesting in several ways how the company was at the forefront of tackling the event.

In some cases, Amazon looked for human contact with its customers by communicating its emotional closeness to them in addressing the difficult times they were experiencing:

> There's hope in togetherness, even when we're apart. Thanks to #believeinrainbows for the powerful reminder to thank all the helpers out there, near and far" (Amazon, 2020e) or "We're blown away by all the ways you're saying 'thank you' to helpers everywhere. A simple act of kindness can make all the difference. #thanksfordelivering #apartbuttogether" (Amazon, 2020f)

In other cases, the company adopted messages that try to safeguard its reputation communicating how all people working at Amazon were actively engaged in ensuring safety as a top priority: "We're doing everything we can to keep you protected. From increased cleaning to safer working distances to hand sanitizer stations, your safety is priority one" (Amazon.com, 2020c).

Finally, other recurring posts related to Amazon's intention to safeguard its reputation concern the promotion of Amazon's products and services emphasizing their ability to take care of the specific customer needs during the difficult moment of lockdown and social distance: "During these difficult times, we are committed to making Alexa and Amazon Devices more helpful and informative. We are building experiences so you can stay up-to-date with the latest on COVID-19, learn about social distancing, connect with family and friends, stream free content, and much more, all while staying home. Learn more [link]" (Amazon.com, 2020d).

In summary, in trying to address the pandemic coronavirus's challenges, the company has thoroughly maintained and protected its online reputation, thus improving brand awareness and people's attachment towards Amazon. The company communicated straightforwardly how it was close to them and how it was committed to facing the pandemic tangibly, such as through several initiatives of safety to protect its employees and the improvements made in their offerings to align with new customer needs and requests promptly. The aforementioned different kinds of posts and messages are summarized in Table 11.1.

The in-depth thematic analysis of the users' main negative comments, together with the type of response strategy adopted by Amazon to address users' complaints, led to identifying the following social media communication strategies: supportive, collaborative, and empathic. By conducting a cross-thematic analysis to seize whether the topic and the related communication strategy were limited to a single peak or consistently replicated by several peaks (Eisenhardt & Graebner, 2007), we observed that the identified strategies occurred throughout the period analyzed.

Our analysis reveals that users' negative comments are usually associated with specific topics: order delivery, the carelessness of Amazon's drivers, the bad customer service, and scam/hacking.

The negative comments related to order delivery "embrace" the greatest number of complaints expressed by users, such as the mistakes in the order received (i.e., wrong items), the problems with product integrity, and the wrong place of delivery or the long delivery time. These issues trigger disappointment, especially of "loyal" customers, that is, customers who use subscription services (such as Amazon Prime) and expect to receive a service that works perfectly.

Another recurrent topic in users' complaints regards the carelessness of drivers. People frequently express their disapproval about how the products are delivered, without taking care of the items bought. Users express their disappointment with the very bad customer service provided by Amazon during the pandemic. People report the difficulties of getting in touch with customer care services, thus remarking Amazon's employees' incapacity to address their needs and requests. Finally, an ample number of posts show

TABLE 11.1 Summary of Amazon's Type of Post and Message

Month	Type of Post	Message Description	Quote Example
January	Promotional-oriented	The company communicates general news/promotion about its products or services.	"Fully electric and zero carbon. Say 👋 to a few of our new electric delivery vehicles coming to India (Although we can't guarantee Jeff will deliver your order!). #ClimatePledge"
February			"We are excited to welcome explorer and elite endurance athlete Colin O'Brady to Amazon HQ today to share his adventures and discuss his book *The Impossible First: From Fire to Ice—Crossing Antarctica Alone.* [link]"
March	Emotional closeness-oriented	The company looks for a human contact with its customers by communicating its emotional closeness to them in addressing the difficult times they were experiencing.	"We're all in this together. Here's how we're supporting customers, employees, and communities affected by COVID-19. Head to our blog for more info."
April	Reputation safety-oriented	The company safeguards its reputation communicating how all workers are actively engaged in ensuring safety as a top priority.	"Millions of masks, gloves, and cleaning supplies add up to one thing: Safety. Our people's health comes first, and we've been working around the clock to get them what they need to stay safe. For more safety info, visit our blog. [link]"
April	Care-oriented	The company promotes its products and services by particularly emphasizing their ability to answer to the specific customer needs during the difficult moment of lockdown and social distance.	"Families, children, and readers now have access to a selection of free digital books to enjoy at home. Discover family fun reads, beloved Classics to fantasy, thrillers, historical fiction and more on the Kindle Reading App. A big thank you to the authors and educators supporting this new offer. To start reading, visit: [link]."
May			"During the COVID-19 pandemic, people around the country are taking comfort in titles and tunes they enjoyed decades ago—nostalgic favorites from classics to throwbacks. Here's a look at some of the music, movies, and books people are rediscovering at home."
June			"*Good Morning America* takes a look at Distance Assistant, a new innovative tool we're using to keep our people safe and promote social distancing. [link]"

Source: Authors' elaboration.

that customers manifest many issues related to scam/hacking, such as suspicious emails or movements in their accounts.

When dealing with users' complaints concerning these topics, Amazon exhibits to adopt mainly supportive and collaborative communication strategies alternatively. We observed that supportive is the most frequent communication strategy adopted by Amazon on its Facebook page. According to such an approach, the firm actively interacts with and answers customers who exhibit bad reactions within the brand's page for several issues, trying to provide the information required, and then finding a solution to a specific problem they faced. In other words, when addressing users' complaints about, for instance, malfunctioning delivery services, Amazon engages in always offering prompt support. The company tried to deepen the type of issue that customers encountered and then tried to understand the proper department with which the customer should immediately solve the problem. Notably, Amazon offers a direct link/a direct suggestion of the company's department through which the customer could request straight for help. Still, it also asks to have further information or update if the problem is solved to offer prompt assistance (see Figure 11.2).

Alternatively, a different communication strategy frequently adopted by Amazon in addressing customers' complaints about order delivery (e.g., long delivery time), the carelessness of Amazon's drivers, and bad customer service is collaborative. According to such an approach, the company is strongly committed to helping the customer throughout the different phases during which the problem occurred until it manages to solve it completely. This is evident in several cases in which a highly interactive

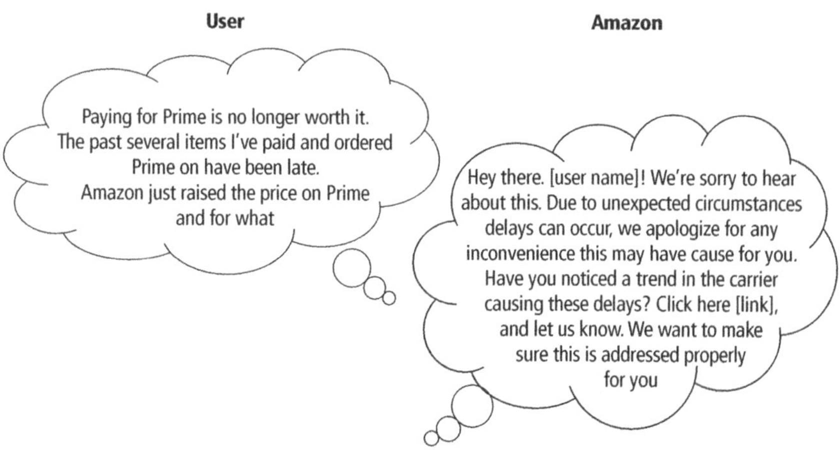

Figure 11.2 Supportive communication strategy. *Source:* Authors' elaboration.

Figure 11.3 Supportive communication strategy. *Source:* Authors' elaboration.

conversation among Amazon and its customers takes place, until concluding by saying "thank" to solve the problem (see Figure 11.3).

Table 11.2 reports some interesting examples of interactions concerning the supportive and collaborative communication strategies adopted alternatively by Amazon when dealing with the different topics.

Our findings reveal that a systematic communication strategy employed by Amazon is also what we call empathic. By adopting such an approach, the company answers to customers that manifest an issue by sharing a positive personal experience or opinion felt by the individual Amazon employee. In

TABLE 11.2 Summary of Supportive and Collaborative Response Communication Strategies by Topic

Topic	Quote Examples			Strategy
Bad customer service	"What in the hell is going on with you? Your customer service has been so bad for the last 3 months. I'm about to cancel my prime membership and just start going elsewhere [...] It's out of control, I'm so sick of arguing with your rude customer service reps" **[User]**	➡	"Thank you for reaching out to us today, [user name]. We're terribly sorry to hear of these poor experiences. This isn't the level of service we strive for here at Amazon [...] can you please provide us with a little more information, including if there's a current order that we could assist with? We're here to help however we can!" **[Amazon]**	Supportive
	"In a time that safety comes first, having amazon prime to help keep us from going to the store, especially when I am at high risk, would be amazing . . . except that amazon has locked us out of our account for over a month, with no one willing to help, no phone numbers to contact . . . it would be nice if someone from you Company could actually help us, so we can stop going to the store.. very unhappy" **[User]**	➡	"Hey there, [user name]. I'm really sorry to hear that. Just to confirm, do you have any emails from our Account Specialists on this? Be sure to check your spam/ junk folders" **[Amazon]**	
	"I tried to contact Amazon for weeks about a cancel order but still no refund, is no phone customer service, not live chat either, I try to call the prime credit card no phone customer service finally email Amazon support and literally nobody replied UNBELIEVABLY!!" **[User]**	➡	"Thank you for that information. We'd like to work with you in real time on this issue. When you have a moment, can you please contact us via chat here: [link]? We'll help in any way we can" **[Amazon]**	

(continued)

TABLE 11.2 Summary of Supportive and Collaborative Response Communication Strategies by Topic (cont.)

Topic	Quote Examples							Strategy
Bad customer service	"Is a computer considered a house hold staple ? I had to order one due to schools closing and going online and it hasn't shipped but still says arrival is Thursday . . ." **[User]**	➡	"Hi there, [user name]! Thanks for the question. We always intend to delivery your package on the promised delivery date given at check-out. If your order hasn't arrived by 9 PM on the promised date, please let us know, and we'll do everything we can to further assist" **[Amazon]**	➡	"Amazon.com thanks for the quick reply" **[User]**	➡	"Our pleasure!" **[Amazon]**	**Collaborative**
	"Need help someone changed the email associated with our account. No way to reset the password or recover the account that we've had for years. There is no customer service to contact right now either" **[User]**	➡	"Hi, there. Thank you for reaching out to us today. Since, you are unable to access your account, please use this link: [link] to reach our Account Specialists directly. They will be in the best position to assist you" **[Amazon]**	➡	"Thank you so much! They were very helpful!" **[User]**	➡	"You're welcome!" **[Amazon]**	

(continued)

TABLE 11.2 Summary of Supportive and Collaborative Response Communication Strategies by Topic (cont.)

<table>
<tr><th>Topic</th><th colspan="9">Quote Examples</th><th>Strategy</th></tr>
<tr><td rowspan="4">Carelessness by drivers</td><td colspan="4">“Your driver broke my sprinkler heads last month, with his fast curb parking tell them to not curb to close or run over grass” [User]</td><td>➡</td><td colspan="4">“We’re sorry this happened. Just to clarify, which carrier was assigned to deliver this package? You can find this information here [link]. Please keep up posted” [Amazon]</td><td rowspan="3">Supportive</td></tr>
<tr><td colspan="4">“Agreed with the knocking at my door . . . I watched one driver just practically toss my package and take off. What’s up Amazon Prime?!?!” [User]</td><td>➡</td><td colspan="4">We’re sorry to hear about this happening, [user name]. Was this on a recent order? Can you please confirm the carrier that this happened with? Please let us know, we’re here to help!” [Amazon]</td></tr>
<tr><td colspan="4">“You guys should probably teach the delivery drivers to not toss packages to dogs. Especially when there are other places to put the packages” [User]</td><td>➡</td><td colspan="4">“Hello [user name], we’re sorry to hear about your delivery experience. Will you please confirm which carrier was assigned here [link]?” [Amazon]</td></tr>
<tr><td>“Just received notification that two packages were delivered. While they were on time and actually came a day early, The driver was too lazy to walk the few steps to put them on the porch and instead set them out in the pouring rain on</td><td>➡</td><td>“We’re sorry to hear about the issues with your deliveries. Could you please confirm the delivery carrier? That information can be found here: [link]. We’re here to help!” [Amazon]</td><td>➡</td><td>“Delivery by Amazon” [User]</td><td>➡</td><td>“When you have time, please send us your order details using this link: [link]. We want to make sure this is reported for you, [user name]” [Amazon]</td><td>➡</td><td>“Amazon.com thank you your excellent customer service department is looking into this ongoing issue” [User]</td><td>Collaborative</td></tr>
</table>

(continued)

TABLE 11.2 Summary of Supportive and Collaborative Response Communication Strategies by Topic (cont.)

Topic	Quote Examples							Strategy
Carelessness by drivers	a bench. Cannot tell you how many times this has happened as well as them throwing packages over my fence at the end of the driveway. I not only have pictures but I have a surveillance camera up as well" **[User]**							Collaborative
	"What's Amazon's policy when one of their delivery drivers hits a customers fence? Watched him do it. And he drives away with out saying anything . . . Happened maybe 5 minutes ago . . ." **[User]**	➡	"Oh no! We certainly don't like to see this, [user name]! When you have a moment, please provide your details here: [link]. Let us know when you've finished, so that we can look into this for you!" **[Amazon]**	➡	"Amazon has already called us on the phone. It's great how the got right on top of it. If I were to damage something at my job and not acknowledge it or let anyone know that needs to know I would be fired immediately if it was found that I was the one to of caused the damage" **[User]**	➡	"Thanks for letting us know. Please reach out if you need further assistance. We're here to help!" **[Amazon]**	

(continued)

TABLE 11.2 Summary of Supportive and Collaborative Response Communication Strategies by Topic (cont.)

Topic	Quote Examples			Strategy
Long delivery time	"Twice in one week your delivery driver has become 'lost' while delivering our packages. And, of course, it's a three ring circus to try to get through to anyone in customer service, much less your delivery department. This is getting VERY old, especially as we have explicit delivery instructions in our prime account" **[User]**	➡	"Hello! We're sorry to hear about the experience you're having with the delivery of your orders, [user name]! To clarify, are all the shipments you're having issues with being elivered by Amazon Logistics? Looking forward to your reply" **[Amazon]**	Supportive
	"I ordered face masks on Feb.26. I received an email said it was shipped on april 8 and money was taken still no masks. Not happy with Amazon and I have prime" **[User]**	➡	"We're sorry about the delivery wait and would like to help! To clarify, have we missed the expected delivery date given in your order confirmation e-mail? You can find this e-mail in your Amazon Message Center here: [link]" **[Amazon]**	
	"Why no estimated delivery times on orders? I could understand if this was the beginning of the pandemic, but what is the reason this far in when the restrictions are being lifted in most states? After being used to such great service from Amazon, this is disappointing!" **[User]**	➡	"Hi [user name], if your item is not in stock you may be able to order but, will be advised at checkout we'll email you when a delivery estimate is known based on the re-supply date of the item from our supplier. In this case you will be emailed as soon as we know. Please see: [link], for more info" **[Amazon]**	
	"I ordered something for same day delivery and I'm 100% sure I won't get it today" **[User]** ➡ "We're quite sorry for any inconvenience! By any chance, were you given a confirmation e-mail with the estimated ➡ "Yes it was supposed to be for today" **[User]** ➡ "We're sorry to hear that you don't have your package as expected. You can find steps to help locate your package ➡ "It came! Sorry!" **[User]** ➡ "Thank you for that update, Jessica! If you ever have any other questions or			Collaborative

(continued)

TABLE 11.2 Summary of Supportive and Collaborative Response Communication Strategies by Topic (cont.)

Topic	Quote Examples							Strategy
			delivery includ-ed?" **[Amazon]**		here [link]. Please keep us updated on how that goes. We'd like to ensure you receive what you've ordered!" **[Amazon]**		concerns, please feel free to reach out to us any time!" **[Amazon]**	
Long delivery time	"I am OK with being patient but I am concerned that UPS isn't scanning in returns now. How long should it take otherwise? I returned some things to UPS a week ago and am wondering what happened to them!" **[User]**	➡	"Hi [user name], We're sorry to hear this. It normally can take up to 14 days to receive your return. Are you able to track the return. If not, you may click here: [link]" **[Amazon]**	➡	"Thank you Amazon, I appreciate all that you are doing right now and I especially appreciate the drivers and employees who are making deliveries from you still possible. I don't mind waiting, I just like to be informed. I know there is a new normal going on right now and I am totally OK with it. Again, thanks for all you do!" **[User]**	➡	"You're welcome, [user name]! Please let us know if there's anything else we can do to assist" **[Amazon]**	**Collaborative**

(continued)

TABLE 11.2 Summary of Supportive and Collaborative Response Communication Strategies by Topic (cont.)

Topic	Quote Examples			Strategy
Mistakes in the order received	"Just terrible having an item sent to you only for it to arrive in a plastic bag and broken! Why am I even paying for Amazon Prime if this is how my orders are going to arrive?" **[User]**	➡	"Thanks for reaching out to us. We're sorry to hear about the trouble [...] It seems as though there is more than one issue going on with your returns. With that said, have you already started the return process for the damaged item that you posted about today?" **[Amazon]**	Supportive
	"I ordered the 7 lb container of the powdered almond milk which cost $199.99 and they sent me 2 small 15 ounce containers, and did not even include a packing slip! They say no refunds on the product, but somebody had better make this right!!!" **[User]**	➡	"Hello, [user name]. We're sorry to hear you received an incorrect item. This is never the experience we aim to provide. Please allow us an opportunity to assist further in real-time by reaching out to us using the following link: [link]" **[Amazon]**	
Scam/Hacking	"Amazon . . . just so you know . . . people are calling me and telling me you are hiring for at home jobs. They hung up on me for refusing to give them my bank information" **[User]**	➡	"We take phishing and spoofing attempts on our customers very seriously. If you receive a correspondence that you think may not be from Amazon, please report it to us. You can learn more here: [link]. Let us know if you have any further questions" **[Amazon]**	
	"Hey amazon is this a scam?" **[User]**	➡	"Hey, [user name]! Thanks for bringing this to our attention. We'll never send unsolicited e-mails that ask you to provide sensitive personal information, and if you find that this is occurring, we'd like to help. You can report these unwanted e-mails here: [link]" **[Amazon]**	
Wrong place of delivery	"Twice in one week your delivery driver has become 'lost' while delivering our packages. And, of course, it's a three ring circus to try to get through to anyone in customer service, much less your delivery department. This is getting VERY old, especially as we have explicit delivery instructions in our prime account" **[User]**	➡	"Hello! We're sorry to hear about the experience you're having with the delivery of your orders, [user name]! To clarify, are all the shipments you're having issues with being elivered by Amazon Logistics? Looking forward to your reply" **[Amazon]**	Supportive
	"My deliveries continue to be delivered to the wrong address, put next to the road and today put in my garbage can. How can we correct this so the deliveries are consistent? Instructions are on my profile. USPS, UPS and FedEx have no issues. Only Amazon" **[User]**	➡	"Hello, [user name]. We're terribly sorry about the delivery issues you've been having and that your packages haven't been arriving as expected. Please provide your contact details and any recently affected orders for us to escalate here: [link]" **[Amazon]**	

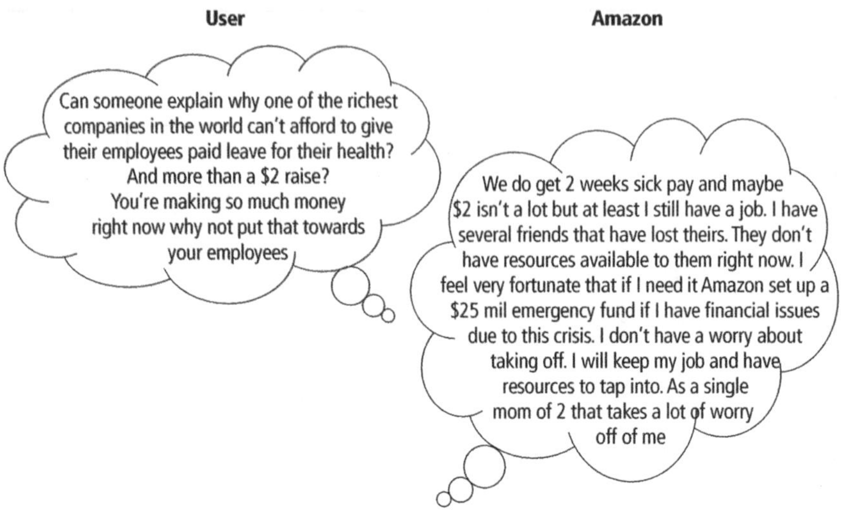

Figure 11.4 Emphatic communication strategy. *Source:* Authors' elaboration.

other words, the person who works at Amazon answers using a "peer conversation," and shares his/her experience at work during the current pandemic. Such strategy is generally found when customers manifest perplexity concerning working or payment conditions at Amazon (see Figure 11.4).

Table 11.3 reports some further examples of interactions as concerns the empathic communication strategy adopted by Amazon.

DISCUSSION

Crisis communication in a social media context represents an increasing body of literature (Cheng, 2018; Fraustino et al., 2017; Veil et al., 2011; Zhao et al., 2018). More systematic studies about how companies could define effective digital communication strategies to react to the various stages of a global emergency as the coronavirus spread are still necessary.

In this chapter, we adopted an explanatory sequential mixed design to investigate and understand the types of communication strategies adopted by organizations during the pandemic crisis underway by looking at the Amazom.com Facebook page. Our study contributes to extend prior research in several ways.

Prior literature extensively discusses the heightened unpredictability of online contexts (Floreddu et al., 2014; Vanbruggen et al., 2010), as customer voices often put at risk organizational reputation (Aula, 2010). Therefore, scholars highlight the importance of making the finest use of social

TABLE 11.3 Summary of Emphatic Response Communication Strategy by Topics

Topic	Quote Examples						
Perplexity about payment conditions	"Can someone explain why one of the richest Company in the world can't afford to give their employees paid leave for their health? And more than a $2 raise? You're making so much money right now why not put that towards your employees..." **[User]**			➡	"We do get 2 weeks sick pay and maybe $2 isn't a lot but at least I still have a job. I have several friends that have lost theirs. They don't have resources available to them right now. I feel very fortunate that if I need it Amazon set up a $25 mil emergency fund if I have financial issues due to this crisis. I don't have to worry about taking off, I will keep my job and have resources to tap into. As a single mom of 2 that takes a lot of worry off of me" **[Amazon]**		
	"How about you share some money with your underpaid and underserved employees" **[User]**	➡	"Brian my pay is just fine. Yes I work the warehouse if you were wondering. I make well over min wage for my state. I am currently making more hourly pay and double for OT as well" **[Amazon]**	➡	"Hope the warehouse employees and other Amazon workers are getting adequate supplies of PPE like face masks and hand sanitizer (and not making you wear the same disposable masks after 1 day, etc.). I've heard stories of the people there getting COVID-19" **[User]**	➡	"Yes I am getting all I need. I wear my own mask to work but there is unlimited masks as needed. Unlimited PPE and unlimited sanitizer supplies to use when i need" **[Amazon]**
Perplexity about working and payment conditions	"Are you motivated to protect your employees? Make your warehouses safer? Pay better wages?" **[User]**	➡	"I'm not gonna say everything is perfect yet, but my FC is actively trying to make sure our employees are safe. A new position called Social Distancing Ambassador was added to my FC, just to	➡	"Amazon.com I work in social media marketing, so I feel confident in saying there is zero chance you've given employees access to your social media accounts to post these 'responses.' Which means, best case	➡	"Confidence in saying something doesn't mean you're right though. If you actually worked in an FC, you'd know. There's a social media program that takes employees (like myself) from the

(continued)

TABLE 11.3 Summary of Emphatic Response Communication Strategy by Topics (continued)

Topic	Quote Examples						
Perplexity about working and payment conditions			remind people to stay away from each other. And I've definitely gotten better pay the last few weeks. $2 raise + double pay overtime" **[Amazon]**		scenario, you've asked real employees to respond to these concerns and posted their answers for them, or worst, you're flat out making them up. Even if you did ask real employees to respond, with 17 million people out of work, they know they're easily replaced and of course are going to respond positively. No one is this excited about a $2/hour raise. Certainly not enough to invoke the 🤑 emoji. An extra $80/week is chump change. How about you, as a company honestly respond to your customers' concerns in good faith" **[User]**		warehouse floor, (2 out of the 4 days we're here a week) and let us respond to customers and tell our experience working here. The best part about it is that it doesn't HAVE to be positive, as long as it's our truth. Oh! Sorry. I didn't know it had to be a certain number to invoke the 🤑 emoji. But once again, if you actually worked in the FC, you'd know ALOT of people are excited about that $2 raise. But not just that, double pay for overtime hours! That's where the 🤑🤑🤑 comes in!" **[Amazon]**
	"Thanks Amazon, been loyal customer for over 10 years, shame you guys are editing the 2 day shipping in some cases and charging more to expedite delivery. The rich get richer, here stories how the employees are treated as well, shame on you" **[User]**			➡	"While I can't really speak to a lot of what you're saying, John, I can tell you that I have been respected and felt protected, as long as I've worked here. Sure, things might have been a wee bit bumpy, while new safety protocols were being put in place concerning COVID19, but I feel they've done a good job over all. I definitely feel safe enough in the FC, to continue coming to work" **[Amazon]**		

(continued)

TABLE 11.3 Summary of Emphatic Response Communication Strategy by Topics (continued)

Topic	Quote Examples				
Perplexity about working conditions	"This is only for the high up employees...Not where I work in the Fulfillment Center...just saying..." **[User]**	➡	"I believe the commercial is simply saying thank you regarding International Women's Day. I work at SAT2 which is also an FC and they're showing their gratitude here as well by passing flowers to all the women here today. We work with a lot of men but we women definitely make our presence known. This is actually one of the first places where I didn't have to worry about male harassment, which is sad when you think about it. Anyway, not trying to be negative at all. Its a thank you to all of us, not just HQ. ☺ ⚓ April, FC Ambassador" **[Amazon]**	➡	"Amazon.com I'm glad you're getting recognition! Women certainly are a vital part of Amazon. It's just that in my FC, there isn't much respect for women's contributions ...But if a man does something, it's big news! It would be nice if our FC would do a little something for the ladies..." **[User]**
	"How about cleaning the FC's and having cleaning supplies for all workers for their stations" **[User]**	➡	"My FC does have cleaning supplies available to wipe down stations. As well as a cleaning crew that is wiping down all stairwell handrails and all other surfaces commonly touched by workers. Sanitizer at the top and bottom of stairwells, sanitizer everywhere. A strict 6 foot social distancing policy with tape on the floors around time clocks so we can easily stay 6 feet apart. Break room tables allowing only one person to sit at. No security screening so there are no lines and social distancing is followed. I feel very safe and am not worried about my health here" **[Amazon]**		

Source: Authors' elaboration.

media tools in managing risk and crisis communication. This aspect comprehends a series of practices to be properly incorporated in social media communication to more effectively engage with public and stakeholders in case of risks or crisis (Veil et al., 2011). By extending prior research, our findings contribute to revealing the different ways through which such practices may be pursued through the design of specific messages and contents published by the company on its Facebook page during a situation of pandemic crisis.

Notably, prior literature emphasizes using social media to ease relationship-building by disseminating and sharing timely and accurate information, thus increasing the organization's trustworthiness and the chance to reach a greater network of individuals (Veil et., 2011). By extending prior research, our analysis reveals how such purposes could be accomplished through company "care-oriented" messages that provide updated information about the ability of his products and services to fulfill the essential needs of the customers during a difficult moment (in our case, the lockdown). In this way, companies improve the positive perceptions that customers may have towards them and increase the opportunity to enlarge their target audience by proposing products or services aligned with the new requests manifested by customers during that particular moment.

Furthermore, literature outlines the importance of providing meaningful communication as concerns the actions taken or recommended by the company in case of risk or crisis, inspiring a sense of control in managing uncertain circumstances (Veil et al., 2011). By extending prior studies, our findings show that "reputation safety-oriented" type of messages, that is, online contents telling how the company is adopting protection and safety measures and protocols at all organizational levels, allow communicating to their stakeholders the efforts made to guarantee the satisfaction of the crucial priorities shared by the general public.

Finally, prior research highlights the need to listen and understand in-depth people's concerns and "humanize" conversations, thus communicating openly and honestly, especially during crises (Veil et al., 2011). By extending prior literature, this work discovers that the design of "emotional closeness-oriented" type of messages allows creating a human contact with customers, demonstrating how the company is close, from a human-psychological perspective to people's problems, sharing the same worries.

In addition to explaining how to make the best use of social media context by "unpacking" the types of messages and contents that firms could publish in their brand's page, this study also contributes to extend literature on crisis communication strategies with a specific focus on the strategies adopted during the pandemic crisis underway.

Particularly, literature on crisis communication strategies generally argues about strategies as instructing information and adjusting information, namely, communication approaches aimed at protecting public safety and informing people about the organization's performance in addressing the situation of crisis (Sturges, 1994). By extending prior literature, we found that, during the pandemic crisis, these informative purposes are accomplished mainly through supportive and collaborative response strategies. When a problem occurs, and the nature of this problem can be traced back to the particular situation of difficulty determined by the pandemic, the company offers prompt support or, alternatively, establishes a highly interactive conversation until solving customer's issue definitely.

Finally, prior research emphasizes reputation repair strategies, which try to lower the negative effects that users' adverse reactions during a crisis can bring about the corporate reputation (Coombs, 2015), for example, by protecting corporate image or inspiring positive feelings (Coombs, 1995, 2014; Coombs et al., 2010). This study contributes to extend prior research, and highlights the empathic communication strategy. Thanks to empathic communication approaches, the company addresses customers' complaints using a "peer tone of conversation." In other words, it does not answer to customers as an abstract entity. Conversely, it addresses people's problems and concerns through the voice of the single worker, who shares his/her personal experiences and feelings at work during the current pandemic.

Managerial Implications

From a managerial perspective, our research findings demonstrate the importance of understanding how firms should build their communication strategies using social media platforms more effectively, especially during challenging times such as a pandemic crisis. Managers need to actively and carefully engage with customers by providing timely responses to each comment in which they manifest concerns, questions, or criticisms towards the company.

More in detail, by employing response communication strategies that offer prompt assistance and support (i.e., supportive and collaborative), managers manage to mitigate customers' negative reactions, and solve their problems quickly. Yet, by adopting more empathic conversations in which they create a deeper relationship with customers, managers can trigger more positive perceptions by the audience, thus increasing corporate reputation.

In summary, this study increases managers' awareness about using social media tools as pivotal real-time supportive tools for customer support and corporate reputation, especially during a pandemic event. On the one hand, they should encourage design contents and messages strictly aligned with the crisis underway. On the other hand, they need to implement appropriate response strategies that enhance customer engagement.

Limitation and Future Research

This study is subject to limitations that could be addressed by future research. Indeed, further attention is needed to increase the understanding of digital communication strategies *versus* pandemic crisis.

For instance, using exploratory research methods, future studies could carry out in-depth interviews with managers to deepen and clarify how firms are addressing their online reputations through social media during the pandemic crisis underway.

Also, this study focuses on a single company and industry, thus our findings have few generalizations to other contexts. Therefore, researchers could extend our analysis to other sectors, and explore whether further digital communication strategies can be identified.

Furthermore, this study analyzes one social media (i.e., Facebook). To improve the transferability of our results and better seize the features of a successful social media communication strategy, future research could extend the analysis to other social media platforms extensively used by firms (e.g., Instagram, YouTube, TikTok, Twitter).

REFERENCES

Allcott, H., & Gentzkow M. (2017). Social media and fake news in the 2016 election. *Journal of Economic Perspectives, 31*(2), 211–236.

Amazon.com. (2020a, January 26). *Wait, who's Alessa? Watch the big game on 02.02.20 to find out what we did #BeforeAlexa* [Attached video] [Status update]. Facebook. https://www.facebook.com/Amazon/posts/10157506956068124

Amazon.com. (2020b, February 12). *Scout, our delivery robot, made a special guest appearance on The Ellen DeGeneres Show yesterday!* [Image attached] [Status update]. Facebook. https://m.facebook.com/Amazon/posts/scout-our-delivery-robot-made-a-special-guest-appearance-on-the-ellen-degeneres-/10157560030308124/?locale=eu_ES

Amazon.com. (2020c, April 1). *We're doing everything we can to keep you protected. From increased cleaning to safer working distances to hand sanitizer stations, your safety is priority one* [Image attached] [Status update]. Facebook. https://www.facebook.com/Amazon/photos/a.10150354146103124/10157717328643124/?comment_id=3010623905654962

Amazon.com. (2020d, April 2). *During these difficult times, we are committed to making Alexa and Amazon Devices more helpful and informative* [Attached image] [Status update]. Facebook. https://www.facebook.com/Amazon/posts/10157722173218124?comment_id=10157768852083124

Amazon.com. (2020e, April 2). *There's hope in togetherness, even when we're apart. Thanks to #believeinrainbows for the powerful reminder to thank all the helpers* [Image attached] [Status update]. Facebook. https://m.facebook.com/Amazon/photos/a.10150354146103124/10157720933303124/?type=3&locale2=ar_AR

Amazon.com. (2020f, April 3). *We're blown away by all the ways you're saying 'thank you' to helpers everywhere. A simple act of kindness can make all the difference. #thanksfordelivering #apartbuttogether* [Attached image] [Status update]. Facebook. https://www.facebook.com/Amazon/posts/10157725981413124

Argenti, P., & Barnes, C. (2009). *Digital strategies for powerful corporate communications.* McGraw-Hill.

Aula, P. (2010). Social media, reputation risk and ambient publicity management. *Strategy and Leadership, 38*(6), 43–49.

Baccarella, C. V., Wagner, T. F., Kietzmann, J. H., & McCarthy, I. P. (2018). Social media? It's serious! Understanding the dark side of social media. *European Management Journal, 36*(4), 431–438.

Baum, T., & Hai, N.T.T. (2020). Hospitality, tourism, human rights and the impact of COVID-19. *International Journal of Contemporary Hospitality Management, 32*(7), 2397–2407.

Cheng, Y. (2018). How social media is changing crisis communication strategies: Evidence from the updated literature. *Journal of Contingencies and Crisis Management, 26*(1), 58–68.

Coombs, W. T. (1995). Choosing the right words: The development of guidelines for the selection of the 'appropriate' crisis response strategies. *Management Communication Quarterly, 8*(4), 447–476.

Coombs, W. T. (2011). *Ongoing crisis communication: Planning, managing and responding* (3rd ed.). SAGE Publications.

Coombs, W. T. (2014). *Ongoing crisis communication: Planning, managing, and responding* (4th ed.). SAGE Publications.

Coombs, W. T. (2015). The value of communication during a crisis: Insights from strategic communication research. *Business Horizons, 58*(2), 141–148.

Coombs, W. T. (2018). *Revising situational crisis communication theory: The influences of social media on crisis communication theory and practice.* In L. Austin & J. Yan (Eds.), *Social media and crisis communication* (p. 21–38). Routledge.

Coombs, W. T., Frandsen, F., Holladay, S. J., & Johansen, W. (2010). Why a concern for apologia and crisis communication? *Corporate Communication: An International Journal, 15*(4), 337–349.

Creswell, J. W., Plano Clark V. L., Gutmann M., & Hanson W. (2003). *Advanced mixed methods research designs.* In A. Tashakkori & C. Teddlie (Eds.), *Handbook on mixed methods in the behavioral and social sciences* (pp. 209–240). SAGE Publications.

Dellarocas, C. (2003). The digitization of word-of-mouth: Promise and challenges of online reputation systems. *Management Science, 49*(10), 1407–1424.

Eisenhardt, K. M., & Graebner, M. E. (2007). Theory building from cases: Opportunities and challenges. *Academy of Management Journal, 50*(1), 25–32.

Falkheimer, J., & Heide, M. (2010). *Crisis communicators in change: From plans to improvisations.* In W. T. Coombs & S. J. Holladay (Eds.), *The handbook of crisis communication* (pp. 511–526). Wiley-Blackwell.

Floreddu, P. B., & Cabiddu, F. (2016). Social media communication strategies. *Journal of Services Marketing, 30*(5), 490–503.

Floreddu, P. B., Cabiddu, F., & Evaristo, R. (2014). *Inside your social media ring: How to optimize online corporate reputation. Business Horizons, 57*(6), 737–745.

Frau, M., Frigau, L., Serpi, S., & Cabiddu, F. (2019, January 17–19). *Value co-destruction: A text-mining-based mixed method study on social media interactions.* 20th International Conference Marketing Trends, Venice, Italy.

Fraustino, J. D., Liu, B. F., & Jin, Y. (2017). *Social media during disasters: A research synthesis and road map.* L. Austin & Y. Jin (Eds.), *Social media and crisis communication* (pp. 283–295). Routledge.

Go, A., Bhayani, R., & Huang, L. (2009). *Twitter sentiment classification using distant supervision* (CS224N Project Report). Stanford.

Hennig-Thurau, T., Malthouse, E. C., Friege, C., Gensler, S., Lobschat, L., Rangaswamy, A., & Skiera, B. (2010). The impact of new media on customer relationships. *Journal of Service Research, 13*(3), 311–330.

Islam, A. N., Laato, S., Talukder, S., & Sutinen, E. (2020). Misinformation sharing and social media fatigue during covid-19: An affordance and cognitive load perspective. *Technological Forecasting and Social Change, 159,* 120201.

Jones, B., Temperley, J., & Lima, A. (2009). Corporate reputation in the era of Web 2.0: The case of Primark. *Journal of Marketing Management, 25*(9), 927–939.

Jurgens, M., & Helsloot, I. (2018). The effect of social media on the dynamics of (self) resilience during disasters: A literature review. *Journal of Contingencies and Crisis Management, 26*(1), 79–88.

Kelleher, T. (2009). Conversational voice, communicated commitment, and public relations outcomes in interactive online communication. *Journal of Communication, 59*(1), 172–188.

Kietzmann, J. H., Hermkens, K., McCarthy, I. P., & Silvestre, B. S. (2011). Social media? Get serious! Understanding the functional building blocks of social media. *Business horizons, 54*(3), 241–251.

Levenson, J. C., Shensa, A., Sidani, J. E., Colditz, J. B., & Primack, B. A. (2016). The association between social media use and sleep disturbance among young adults. *Preventive Medicine, 85,* 36–41.

Liu, B. F., Austin, L., & Jin, Y. (2012). How publics respond to crisis com munication strategies: The interplay of information form and source. *Public Relations Review, 37*(4), 345–353.

Marken, G.A. (2007). 'Social media . . . the hunted can become the hunter.' *Public Relations Quarterly, 52*(4), 9–12.

Meyer, D., Hornik, K., & Feinerer, I. (2008). Text mining infrastructure in R. *Journal of statistical software, 25*(5), 1–54.

Miles, M. B., & Huberman, A. M. (1994). *Qualitative data analysis: An expanded sourcebook.* SAGE Publications.

Mirbabaie, M., Bunker, D., Stieglitz, S., Marx, J., & Ehnis, C. (2020). Social media in times of crisis: Learning from Hurricane Harvey for the coronavirus disease 2019 pandemic response. *Journal of Information Technology, 35*(3), 1–19.

Moi L., Cannas R., Frau M., & Cabiddu F. (2018a). Capturing customer emotions and experiences to enhance value co-creation: The Ichnusa online brand community. *Sinergie, 36*(106), 157–178.

Moi L., Frau M., & Cabiddu F. (2018b). Exploring the role of NVivo software in marketing research. *Mercati & Competitività, 4*(22), 65–86.

Selivanov, D., & Wang, Q. (2018). *Text2vec: Modern text mining framework for r.* CRAN. https://CRAN.R-project.org/package=text2vec

Sturges, D. L. (1994) Communicating through crisis: A strategy for organizational survival. *Management Communication Quarterly, 7*(3), 297–316.

Sweetser, K. D., & Metzgar, E. (2007). Communicating during crisis: Use of blogs as a relationship management tool. *Public Relations Review, 33*(3), 340–342.

Valentini, C. (2015). Is using social media "good" for the public relations profession? A critical reflection. *Public Relations Review, 41*(2), 170–177.

Van Noort, G., & Willemsen, L. M. (2012). Online damage control: The effects of proactive versus reactive webcare interventions in consumer-generated and brand-generated platforms. *Journal of interactive marketing, 26*(3), 131–140.

Vanbruggen, G. H., Antia, K. D., Jap, S. D., Reinartz, W. J., & Pallas, F. (2010). Managing marketing channel multiplicity. *Journal of Service Research, 13*(3), 331–340.

Veil, S. R., Buehner, T., & Palenchar, M. J. (2011). A work-in-process literature review: Incorporating social media in risk and crisis communication. *Journal of Contingencies and Crisis Management, 19*(2), 110–122.

Walwema, J. (2021). The WHO health alert: Communicating a global pandemic with WhatsApp. *Journal of Business and Technical Communication, 35*(1), 35–40. https://doi.org/10.1177/1050651920958507

Ye, L., & Ki, E.-J. (2018). Impact of message convergence on organizational reputation: An Examination of organizational crisis communication on Facebook. *Corporate Reputation Review, 21*(1), 1–8.

Zhao, H., Falkheimer, J., & Heide, M. (2017). Revisiting a social constructionist approach to crisis communication: Investigating contemporary crises in China. *International Journal of Strategic Communication, 11*(5), 364–378.

Zhao, X., Zhan, M., & Wong, C.-W. (2018). Segmenting and understanding publics in a social media information sharing network: An interactional and dynamic approach. *International Journal of Strategic Communication, 12*(1), 25–45.

Zheng, Y., Goh, E, & Wen, J. (2020). The effects of misleading media reports about COVID19 on Chinese tourists' mental health: A perspective article. *Anatolia, 31*(2), 337–340.

CHAPTER 12

COVID-19 CRISIS

Chaos and Opportunities for Newer Organizational Configurations for Multinational Oil Enterprises

Riad A. Ajami
Wright State University

Homa Karimi
Journal of Asia-Pacific Business

Rachel E. Sturm
Wright State University

Berkwood Farmer
Wright State University

The COVID-19 crisis is one of the most severe global health care calamities of this century that is having an impact on global society, markets, and organizations. It is also an economic challenge. The GDP growth rates across various markets and countries, from China to the United States to Latin

Crisis, Chaos, and Organizations, pages 309–320

America, the eurozone, emerging markets and economies, including the oil producers have declined significantly and this decline may carry forward into the year 2021. The global lockdown in Organisation for Economic Co-operation and Development (OECD) countries and emerging economies may not be remembered only as a global healthcare disaster but also as an economic catastrophe that impacted global markets in various sectors, and particularly devastated the global oil industry.

The growing globalization we have witnessed during the last 5 decades has slowed down and will reshape economic links among various players. Market interdependencies are likely to be altered, and strategic alliances could present themselves as a way to enhance and create newer linkages that would allow us to overcome some of the disadvantages of COVID-19.

Corporate linkages and markets may not return to their ways of pre-COVID-19 but could present us with opportunities to enhance our future global supply chain linkages. Rather than restoring yesterday's economic links, corporations and governments must learn to adapt to the new reality paradigm and must embrace the current and long-lasting changes to various industries.

The lockdown severely impacted the job market, the transportation sector, and the need for petroleum products. The global oil industry has a vertically integrated structure from exploration to oil production to refinery and, ultimately, delivery of oil products at the gas pump. Equally, the petrochemical industry is also dependent on a viable oil industry. The structure of the global oil industry is likely to change and the positioning and sustainability of global oil firms, both state-owned enterprises (such as Saudi Aramco) and publicly traded (i.e., ExxonMobil and Shell, among others) could demand newer global configurations in this value-added chain.

State-owned global producers in the oil industry have massive oil endowments and production capabilities. Of the largest oil-producing firms in the world, the top ones are state-owned and domiciled in non-OECD countries. The largest, Saudi Aramco, has a daily output exceeding 11 million barrels (pre-COVID-19 crisis) and sits on an estimated 16% of global oil reserves. In contrast, the daily output of the largest publicly traded OECD oil companies, Exxon, Shell, and BP is equal to that of Saudi Aramco.

The state-owned oil companies receive significant resources from their governments, and have somewhat significant oil supplies with an average cost of production at about $5/barrel. Moreover, they accept lower rates of return on their invested capital while publicly traded firms must compete for risk capital for high rates of return in an attempt to meet the demands of their stockholders and other stakeholders. Most importantly, the state-owned enterprises are also able to enter newer markets that used to be the domain of the United States and other OECD oil multinationals.

The viability of OECD-based, publicly traded oil companies is vital for market stability in a precarious oil market where demand is high in OECD countries, but oil endowment and production are low. The Middle East and North Africa hold over 60% of global oil reserves (BP Statistical Review of Energy, 2020), while the U.S. oil reserve endowment is estimated to be less than 10% of global endowments, including the fracking sector. Current U.S. daily production, including fracking, places the United States corporate oil sector as the top oil producer, with an estimated daily production exceeding 13 million barrels daily (mbd; U.S. Energy Information Administration, 2018), while U.S. daily consumption was estimated, prior to COVID-19 to exceed 19 mbd, thus making the U.S. oil companies both top producers and top importers.

In a global oil market of 100 mbd, prior to the coronavirus, the Organization of Oil Producing and Exporting Countries (OPEC) oil producers accounted for 36 mbd, according to the BP Statistical Review of World Energy 2019. Russia, a non-OPEC member, is a major oil producer, with an estimated daily output of 8.5 million barrels. The oil industry is an excellent example of an oligopolistic market. Royal Dutch Shell and Saudi Aramco, had nearly 400 million dollars in sales revenue in 2019. Table 12.1 shows the TOP 10 list of oil companies' income.

Oil is an undifferentiated commodity with variable costs of production from less than $10/barrel for Middle Eastern oil producers to an average cost for U.S. frackers estimated at $28/barrel. The overall price range for a barrel of oil following the pandemic is likely to settle at a level between $70 and $90/bbl for Brent overall ($62/bbl was the price prior to COVID-19

TABLE 12.1 Oil and Gas 50 2020. Brand Value Ranking League Table

Ranking	Name	Country	Income
1	Shell	Netherlands	$47b
2	Saudi Aramco	Saudi Arabia	$46b
3	PetroChina	China	$38b
4	Sinopec	China	$33b
5	BP	UK	$23b
6	Total	France	$23b
7	Chevron	United States	$18b
8	ExxonMobil	United States	$15b
9	Petronas	Malaysia	$15b
10	ADNOC	Abu Dhabi	$11b

Source: Brandirectory

in 2020). Oil prices per barrel have ranged from a low of $10/bbl to a high of $145/bbl (oecd.org/iea, 2019). Higher oil prices overall benefit the oil producers and reduce consumption, while lower oil prices negatively impact the oil producers, both OPEC firms and publicly traded oil companies. Moreover, an oil price lower than $55/bbl significantly impacts the U.S. fracking companies, thus, the importance of oil price stability for a functioning and orderly market for oil and, particularly, the U.S. oil market.

Following the coronavirus and the lockdown, demand for oil has been reduced by an estimated 30 mbd. A reduced GDP growth rate and a higher level of unemployment are behind this reduction in oil consumption. The global pandemic is creating a new paradigm for organizational competitiveness and sustainability. This is likely to impact the structure of the oil industry and create significant challenges for global enterprise configurations for both publicly traded OECD oil companies and state-owned oil companies.

In today's world of global economic challenges, opportunities, and realism, newer organizational linkages and configurations could lead to sustainability in industry, particularly the oil industry. In order for resource deployment and capabilities to make sense, organizational decisions and configurations must be cost effective. The forces driving globalization were technological advances and innovation in information technology. The world was on its way to becoming a transnational market for goods, capital, and economic services prior to the COVID-19 crisis. The coronavirus has altered the international markets' configurations of assets and capabilities.

The newly fractured economy has altered established global supply chains that benefited both global producers and consumers. A reconfigured, seamless global economy should allow for a better fit for both customers and suppliers. Through technological linkages and configurations, these companies could allow enterprises to capture economies of scale and scope, and address organizational efficiencies and effectiveness. Table 12.2 maps out the differences between multinational and transnational corporate strategic orientations and assets and capabilities.

TABLE 12.2 Corporate Strategic Orientation and Assets and Capabilities

MNC Type	Strategic Orientation	Assets and Capabilities
Multinational	Building flexibility to respond to national differences through strong, resourceful, and entrepreneurial national operations	Decentralization and rational self-efficiency
Transnational	Developing global efficiency, flexibility, and worldwide learning capability simultaneously	Dispersion, interdependence, and specialization

Source: Adapted from Barlett & Ghoshal, 2003 and Ajami & Goddard, 2018

THE GLOBAL OIL INDUSTRY

The unique structure of global oil organizations reflects the following. The share of domestic consumption of oil within the oil producing countries in OPEC is relatively small. Table 12.3 indicates that the majority of the oil producing enterprises in OPEC produce far more than they consume. For example, while Saudi Arabia is the largest oil producer in OPEC at over 11 mbd, it only consumes less than 4 mbd and must sell the surplus oil to global consumers in China, today the largest oil importer, as well as other OECD markets and in emerging markets. The initial number of firms in this oligopolistic oil industry is small, and creates a favorable situation for cross-organizational alliances between state-owned oil firms (i.e., Aramco, among others) and publicly traded companies (i.e., Exxon, among others). The publicly traded firms in OECD countries have limited oil reserves but are present with retail outlets in the majority of oil-consuming markets. The state-owned companies have significant reserves and production capabilities but a limited presence in the largest oil-consuming countries as well as lesser refining capabilities. Thus, strategic alliances between state-owned oil companies and publicly traded oil firms present an opportunity to have a semblance of balance in the market from production to retail and to stabilize oil prices and allow for organizational sustainability of both state-owned oil companies and publicly traded firms (Ajami, 2004).

Transnational organizational alliances can capture economies of scale and scope in asset configurations and capabilities. Strategic alliances could allow for sustainable enterprises and the nurturing of newer and positive sustainable structures (Lubin & Esty, 2010). In these forms of positive organization, unconventional practices are emerging to allow successful

TABLE 12.3 Share of Domestic Consumption in OPEC Countries 2018

	Thousand Barrels Daily, 2018	
Country	**Total Oil Production MBD**	**Consumption MBD**
Saudi Arabia	11.08	3.90
Kuwait	2.93	0.50
Iraq	4.48	0.80
Iran	4.67	1.82
Venezuela	1.60	0.51
Nigeria	1.50	0.27
Libya	1.00	0.31

Source: U.S. Energy Information Administration (USEIA, 2018)

organizations to serve local, regional, and global markets. The challenge today is to also capture the sustainability premiums that go beyond serving local markets to become efficient and to serve transnational markets, which would enable firms to become both winning and sustainable organizations in terms of efficiency and effectiveness.

RESOURCE-BASED VIEWS, TRANSACTION COSTS, AND STRATEGIC ALLIANCES

The resource-based view of the firm (RBV) suggests and indicates that assets, capabilities, and organizational processes, if aligned properly within the firm and across various corporate players within the industry, can improve efficiency and effectiveness (Barney, 1991). Chisholm and Nielsen (2009) suggest that intangible resources in addition to tangible ones, if properly exploited, can create competitive advantages. The transaction cost analysis overview suggests also that joint ventures and multinational corporate alliances can create opportunities to execute transaction costs more efficiently (Adler & Scherer, 1999). Moreover, Jones and Hill (1988) indicated that in an oligopoly, particularly in the oil industry, said specificity can lead to comparative advantages, and when these cross-corporate activities are internalized they can lead to lower costs and provide for additional advantages. Core competencies and resources that are replicable when shared in alliances could lead to performance improvement and competitive advantages.

The resource-based view as well as the transaction-cost analysis of the firm both suggest that exploiting resources and capabilities across firm members could lead to competitive advantage, enhanced capabilities, and long-term performance improvement (Amit & Schoemaker, 1993; Barney, 1991; Eisenhardt & Martin, 2000). Newbert (2008) indicates that rare resources and capabilities, when exploited, can enhance capabilities. Finally, Conner (2002) indicates that strategic success through linkages to acquire resources across firms could lead to corporate improvement and could sustain competitive advantages if these rare resources are applied correctly (Kraaijenbrink et al., 2010).

Strategic alliances are assumed to design a strategic link, which could change incentive in the output market that could serve the producer and consumers domestically and internationally, specifically, (a) when state-owned oil firms' share of the domestic consumption of their output is small; (b) when the product is similar or identical as is the case in the crude oil market; and (c) when the initial number of firms in the industry, whether state-owned or publicly traded are limited and constitute an oligopoly (Morasch, 2000).

Strategic alliances between state-owned and publicly traded firms would allow each participant to play to their strength and to minimize their weaknesses. Moreover, in an oligopolistic market, the high cost of exploration and development of oil fields can allow for cost reduction across the global oil industry. Strategic alliances can improve the capital base of the participants in the industry and will improve product distribution and reduce the risks even when organizational and cross-cultural conflicts are present. Strategic alliances could provide for both improved scale and scope and stability in oil output and oil prices and will provide for benefits to distributors and consumers as well as the oil producers.

Successful business alliances are a significant strategic element in many industries, but too many strategic alliances fail to meet their partners' aspirations. The knowledgeable and purposeful choice of alliance cohorts is an essential element in building successful alliances. This requires a strategic management-based industry and partner selection method and a new dynamic partner selection instrument for evaluating target industries.

The alliance of Cosan and Shell in the Brazilian fuel market is a sample strategic alliance showing how new markets can be established through sharing of core competencies locally. The sharing of competencies and firm growth are natural consequences of the alliance.

THE EDGEWORTH FRAMEWORK AND ROLE OF ALLIANCES

The Edgeworth Box economic analysis framework will be used to empirically map out the exchanges in benefits for a sustainable production and consumption international oil market allocating the benefits in oil production and consumption capabilities between publicly traded and state-owned multinational oil companies (Ruby, 2020). The conceptual and theoretical constructs behind the Edgeworth exchange indicate that two organizational players could come into trade-production linkages as long as they have two distinct capabilities to exchange with each other.

The Edgeworth Box conceptual framework allows us to study the oil industry in terms of oil reserve capabilities being exchanged to access consumer markets. Since OECD countries, and particularly the United States in the amount of oil reserves, is proportionately lower when compared to the consumption needs of the United States, this will reap a profitable and strategically successful interaction between the OPEC oil producing companies and publicly traded global oil companies. The United States is the leading consumer of petroleum and securing oil resources to supply the U.S. market is in the best interest of the U.S. oil firms, and, at the same time, will benefit state-owned oil companies in OPEC, allowing them to sell their additional output and secure entry to the largest oil-consuming markets. The U.S. oil consumption is much larger than U.S. oil endowments as well as U.S. product capabilities. At the same time, the state-owned oil companies' oil endowments and production capabilities is larger than what the local oil consumption of the oil producing states.

The United States remains the largest consumer of petroleum products, while OPEC oil companies are the leading oil reserve holders. The analysis of the Edgeworth box exchange will show that both the United States and the oil producers can benefit through the process of exchange, giving each partner in this exchange what they need and providing to the other what they desperately need.

Figure 12.1 shows indifference curves to explain the trading patterns of two partners, an oil-producing entity (OPEC) and another with a relatively large oil consumption market (U.S.). In this chart, "O" represents the point of origin, while "W" indicates the point of initial endowment for all commodities, in this case oil consumption and oil reserves.

As these initial indifference curves cross each other they create an oval space between them. This space of negotiation (see Figure 12.2) represents any trading activities taking place between U.S. companies and state-owned OPEC firms. In fact, any trade occurring within this area is thought to be of benefit to one or both of the entities. As long as this result takes place, the two entities continue to have incentives to engage in trade and/or exchange their distinct commodity with each other.

According to Figure 12.2, the point labeled "US1" is the initial trading position, while "US2" signifies the ending position after trading has taken place. After a trade has taken place, both partners have moved to point "R," which in this case means that the United States' position has improved without causing harm to the OPEC firms' interests. The process that places one or both of the parties into the space of negotiation is known as a Pareto Improvement.

However, a better outcome exists where both partners can be made better off simultaneously. This outcome is called Pareto optimality. While

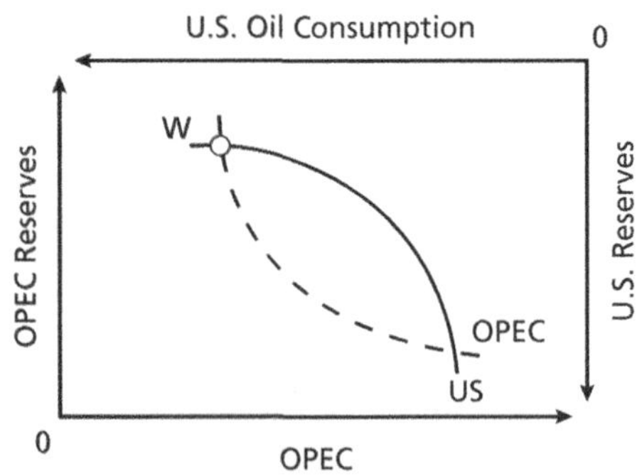

Figure 12.1 U.S. and OPEC oil consumption and reserves.

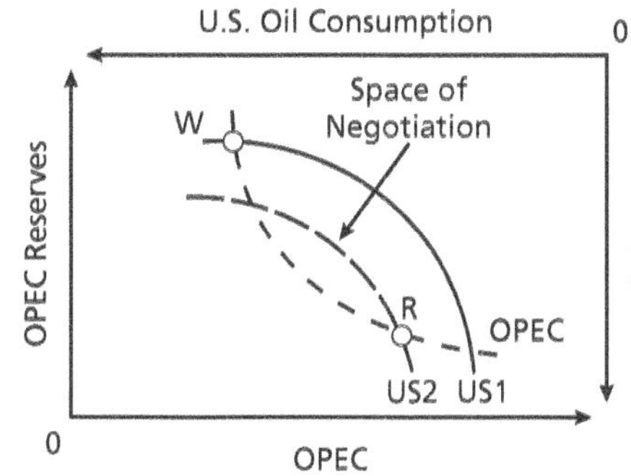

Figure 12.2 U.S. and OPEC oil consumption and reserves showing space of negotiation.

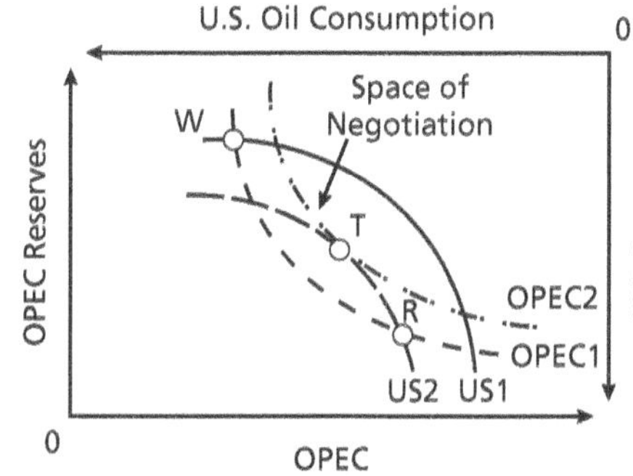

Figure 12.3 U.S. and OPEC Pareto optimality.

examining the indifference curves in an Edgeworth exchange box, a Pareto optimal point (where it is impossible to benefit one partner without benefiting the other) lies within the space of negotiation (or opportunity). However, the shift in the two partners; indifference curves from their initial point, one moving right while the other moves left, causes the two curves to touch once and thus creates a tangency point. When a situation exists where the indifference curve of entity A touches the indifference curve of entity B, this represents a condition (once again) of Pareto optimality (see point "T," Figure 12.3), a point where trade can benefit both entities at the same time.

CONCLUSION

COVID-19 is likely to impact organizational structures and make cross-country alliances in the international oil industry desirable; whereby, each organizational participant can be encouraged to leverage its most valuable assets and exchanges of resources and capabilities to generate revenue for both state-owned oil organizational entities, as well as the publicly traded multinational organizations. Leading Fortune 500 OECD oil firms are spending less money on oil exploration. Exxon is a prime example. The slogan, "Beyond Petroleum" by the British oil giant BP is another indication that these oil companies are leveraging their capabilities and endowments to focus on their future sustainability by doing what they can do best, primarily, having significant outlets in OECD markets, as well as technological endowments and capabilities that they can offer to state-owned oil firms from the Middle East and elsewhere. The OPEC Middle East oil producers can also focus on their capabilities, producing a barrel of oil for less than $10.00.

Multinational firms, regardless of nationality, straddle diverse economies and boundaries. The questions of accountability, legitimacy, and sustainability become particularly touchy. The corporate argument that these entities seek to be good citizens in all the countries and markets in which they operate will not always suffice in a global context. The recent sentiments behind rising protectionism and mercantilism in the American economy do not differ fundamentally from the economic nationalism of others in emerging markets, oil producers, nor disadvantaged communities in industrialized countries.

Protectionist sentiments in the United States are not unlike Indian, Chinese, Nigerian, Saudi, and other national schemes being proposed in many markets as well as non-market economies protecting their local and national interests. Today the distribution of both social and financial costs, as well as the benefits from corporate institutions are relatively broad and transnational. Multinational corporations now confront a more centrist critique in the countries where they operate.

Powerful and seemingly inexorable technological forces and change have pushed the world along the path of economic interdependence, while the desire for national control and autonomy remains strong in all societies. This imbalance can be expressed in terms of inherent conflicts between a growing range of stakeholders' interests, which must be negotiated through the firm's governance, structure, and mechanism. Multinational firms cannot merely think of themselves as profit-seeking institutions without any responsibilities to their other stakeholders. Chandler (1977) argues that companies are simply a "mechanism" within a market context, "the artisans, not the architects of the world." The ambitious nature of the multinational firms as asserted by critics and advocates alike, makes it difficult to retain a sensible and essential distinction between artisanship and architect. A workable system with the proper architectural strategic linkages will govern the multinational firms of the future if they are to remain sustainable within a framework of global accountability.

The global oil industry, regardless of its future configuration, must address the emphasis on climate change. India, China (the Number 1 carbon emitter), and Europe have committed to reduce carbon emissions. The United States, being the second-largest carbon emitter, is returning to the Paris Climate Accord. President Biden has suggested a 1.7 trillion dollar green package and appointed a new energy czar. The Chinese and the Europeans have similar financial commitments to that of the United States. Equally, the United Kingdom has committed itself to become the financial center of green finance.

The Middle East OPEC oil producers, sitting on the largest oil endowments, have recently reached for cooperation with Israel in pursuit of peace. The Israeli economy is committed also to green energy and reliance on solar technology, wanting to become the lead solar energy producer by 2030. That suggests further challenges to the current structure of the global oil industry. In addition to advances in solar energy, the global economy is moving to replacing gas-powered vehicles with electric ones somewhere between 2030 and 2050. This could result in fewer oil firms. Moreover, OPEC is a cartel, and like all cartels, it has built into its structure a potential for future instability. OPEC currently supplies and will continue to supply over 1/3 of global oil production, and its fractious membership will continue to find areas of disagreement. Add to that internal level of difficulties, its relationship with Russia, the third-largest oil producer, is equally problematic, and its future as a cohesive cartel is, at best, tentative.

The future organizational configuration for international firms in the global oil industry is going to reflect a networked configuration, where ownership and control are diffused. COVID-19 has impacted our global economy and has altered our views and conceptualizations of organizational configurations. While this is true for many sectors, in the global economy, it certainly is altering the future multinational oil firm.

ACKNOWLEDGMENTS

I would like to thank my colleagues for insightful comments regarding the content of this research, in particular, Dr. Kamel Abdullah, formerly of The Ohio State University and Otterbein University. Thanks are also due to Dimeter Gerensky, formerly of the University of North Carolina and G. Jason Goddard of Wake Forest University.

I also would like to thank the supporting team of the Center for Global Business at Wright State University: Susan E. Meindl of the *Journal of Asia-Pacific Business.*

REFERENCES

Adler, T. R., & Scherer, R. F. (1999). A multivariate investigation of transaction cost analysis dimensions: Do contract types differ? *Journal of Applied Business Research, 15*(3), 65–80. https://doi.org/10.19030/jabr.v15i3.5673

Ajami, R. (2004, August 18). Exxon–Aramco? *The Wall Street Journal.* https://www.wsj.com/articles/SB109278404471694225

Ajami, R., & Goddard, G. J. (2018). *Global business: Competitiveness and sustainability.* Routledge.

Amit, R., & Schoemaker, P. (1993). Strategic assets and organizational rent. *Strategic Management Journal, 14*(1), 33–46.

Barney, J. (1991). Firm resources and sustained competitive advantage. *Journal of Management, 17*(1), 99–120. https://doi.org/10.1177%2F014920639101700108

Bartlett, C. A., & Ghoshal, S. (1991). *Managing across borders: The transnational solution.* Harvard Business School Press.

Brandirectory. (2020). *Oil and Gas 50 2020.* https://brandirectory.com/rankings/oil-and-gas/2020

BP Statistical Review of World Energy. (2020). https://www.bp.com/en/global/corporate/energy-economics/statistical-review-of-world-energy.html

Chandler, A. D., Jr. (1977) *The visible hand: The managerial revolution in American business.* Belknap Press.

Chisholm, A. S., & Nielsen K. (2009). Social capital and the resource-based view of the firm. *International Studies of Management and Organization, 39*(2), 7–32. https://doi.org/10.2753/IMO0020-8825390201

Conner, T. (2002). The resource-based view of strategy and its value to practising managers. *Briefings in Entrepreneurial Finance, 11*(6), 307–316.

Eisenhardt, K., & Martin, J. (2000). Dynamic capabilities: What are they? *Strategic Management Journal, 21*(10/11), 1105–1121.

Jones, G., & Hill, C. (1988). Transaction cost analysis of strategy-structure choice. *Strategic Management Journal, 9*(2), 159–172. https://doi.org/10.1002/smj.4250090206

Kraaijenbrink, J., Spender, J.-C., & Groen A. J. (2010). The resource-based view: A review and assessment of its critiques. *Journal of Management, 36*(1), 349–372.

Lubin, D. A., & Esty, D. C. (2010, May). The sustainability imperative. *Harvard Business Review.* https://hbr.org/2010/05/the-sustainability-imperative

Morasch, K. (2000). Strategic alliances: A substitute for strategic trade policy?" *Journal of International Economics, 52*(1), 37–67.

Newbert, S. (2008). Value, rareness, competitive advantage, and performance: A conceptual-level empirical investigation of the resource-based view of the firm. *Strategic Management Review, 29*(7), 745–768. https://doi.org/10.1002/smj.686

Organisation for Economic Cooperation and Development International Energy Agency. (2019). oecd.org/iea/

Ruby, D. A. (2020). *The Edgeworth Box and Exchange* [Online]. http://www.digitaleconomist.org/microeconomics/edgeworth_box.html

ABOUT THE CONTRIBUTORS

Riad A. Ajami is professor of international business and director, Center for Global Business at Wright State University. Professor Ajami previously held the position of professor of international business (with tenure) at the Fisher College of Business at The Ohio State University, Charles A. Hayes Distinguished Professor of Business and director, Center for Global Business at the University of North Carolina, Greensboro (UNCG), and Benjamin Forman Chair Professor of International Business at the Rochester Institute of Technology. He has had visiting appointments as the Dr. M. Lee Pearce Distinguished Professor of International Business, School of International Studies at the University of Miami; School of Business Administration at the University of California, Berkeley; the Wharton School, University of Pennsylvania; and the Harvard Center for International Affairs at Harvard University; Hautes Etudes Commercials—HEC (Grande Ecole of Management), France; and a distinguished faculty affiliate at Audencia (School of Management), France. Dr. Ajami received his PhD from Pennsylvania State University in International Business, Strategic Management and Oil Economics. Currently, Dr. Ajami is the editor in chief of the *Journal of Asia-Pacific Business* and serves as an editorial board member of some other leading international, academic business journals. Dr. Ajami has also co-authored *Global Business: Competitiveness and Sustainability* (Routledge, 2018), *International Business: A Course on the Essentials, 3rd edition,* (M. E. Sharpe, 2014); *The Psychology of Marketing: Cross-Cultural Perspectives* (Gower Publishing, 2010), *Customer Relationship Management: A Global Perspective* (Gower Publishing, 2008), *The Global Enterprise: Entrepreneurship and Value*

Crisis, Chaos, and Organizations, pages 321–332

Creation (2007, The Haworth Press), *Globalization, Management Control and Ideology* (editor, DJØF Publishing, 2005), and *Arab Response to the Multinationals* (Praeger Publishers, 1979). He has had articles published in *The Wall Street Journal, Journal of International Business Studies, Management International Review, Strategic Management Journal, Journal of International Management,* and other leading international, academic journals. Professor Ajami has appeared on national television and radio.

Ignacio L. Azcarate is a senior at the University of Central Florida (UCF) completing a bachelor of science in psychology with a track in industrial and organizational psychology and a minor in cognitive sciences. Ignacio is currently a lab manager of the Stressful Events and Experiences research group as well as a member of UCF's Undergraduate Research Council.

Francesca Cabiddu is a full professor of management at the University of Cagliari (Italy). Her research expertise is in marketing and the use of IT to support customer service and engagement in the services sector. Her research has appeared in *Annals of Tourism Research, Business Horizon, The Service Industries Journal, Industrial Marketing Management, Journal of Service Research, Journal of Sustainable Tourism,* as well as other academic and applied journals. She currently serves on the editorial review boards of different international journals: *Tourism Management, Marketing Theory, Journal of Marketing Theory and Practice, Journal of Service Research,* among others. She has also served as guest editor of a special issue of the journal *Sustainability.*

Susan R. Cannon, PhD, interdisciplinary scholar-practitioner, author, executive master coach, and futurist brings 30+ years of experience in innovation, learning, and change in human systems. She is a partner at Vollett Executive Coaching, an innovation focused coaching and organizational consulting firm, professor of organizational development and leadership at Fielding Graduate University in Santa Barbara, and recently a chapter lead author for *Leadership 2050: Critical Challenges, Key Contexts and Emerging Trends* (Emerald Publishing, 2015). Susan is also a pioneer in women's leadership development and co-author of a Nautilus Book Awards gold medal recipient for *The Way of The Mysterial Woman: Upgrading How You Live Love and Lead* (She Writes Press, 2016). Her work history spans engineering and senior executive positions, historic global change projects including development initiatives in the Soviet Far East during the Cold War, multiple Association of Washington Businesses awards, and patents in the semiconductor field. Susan received a BS degree in engineering physics from Texas Tech University, an MS degree in chemical engineering from Purdue University, and a PhD degree in integral studies with a concentration in transformative learning and change in human systems from the California Institute of Integral Studies in San Francisco.

Marc Cubrich, MA, is an analyst on the assessment design and development team at Modern Hire. Marc obtained his master's degree in Industrial-Organizational psychology from the University of Akron where he is currently a PhD candidate. His research interests include personnel selection, feedback seeking, cultural values, and issues relating to diversity, equity, and inclusion in the workplace. He has authored several book chapters and his work has appeared in journals such as *Computers in Human Behavior* and *Industrial and Organizational Psychology: Perspectives on Science and Practice.*

Michael DiStaso, MS, is a doctoral candidate in the University of Central Florida's industrial and organizational psychology program. His research concerns employees' cognitive and behavioral reactions to experiencing and anticipating stressful events. He directs the psychology department's Stressful Events and Experiences (SEE) research group. His work has been published in outlets such as *Journal of Occupational Health Psychology* and *Group & Organization Management.*

Dennis Doverspike, PhD, ABPP, is president of Doverspike Consulting LLC, also doing business as HR Litehouse. He is a People Scientist, certified as a specialist in industrial-organizational psychology and in organizational and business consulting psychology by the American Board of Professional Psychology (ABPP), and a licensed psychologist in the state of Ohio. Dr. Doverspike has over 40 years of experience working with consulting firms and with public and private sector organizations.

Berkwood M. Farmer, PhD, received his degree in economics from North Carolina State University in 1969. He was a faculty member at the United States Military Academy (West Point) from 1968–1971; University of Richmond from 1971–1974; dean, Longwood University College of Business from 1991–2001; dean, Wright State University College of Business from 2001–2013; full-time economics professor in Economics Department, Wright State University, 2013 to present. He was chief agricultural economist for the Commonwealth of Virginia from 1975–1991. During this time, he was a member of the Governor's Council of Economic Advisors for 8 years; was a founding director of a bank in Virginia and later was a member of the board of directors for Virginia Region BB&T. He has published in numerous referred journals that focus on agricultural policy, economic development, and accreditation of AACSB business colleges. Recently, his research focus has been in the areas of business supply chains and education technology. For more than 20 years, he was very active with AACSB International (professional accrediting body for business schools) as a member and chair of numerous peer review teams.

Kristin A. Horan, PhD, received her PhD in psychology from Bowling Green State University in 2018. She is an assistant professor in the industrial and organizational psychology program at the University of Central Florida. Her research centers on improving the design, implementation, and evaluations of interventions to improve employee safety, health, and well-being, particularly for vulnerable occupations and populations. She also researches the relationship between work and health behaviors. She has published in journals such as *Journal of Organizational Behavior, Group & Organization Management, Stress & Health,* and *Occupational Health Science* and serves as an editorial board member of *Stress & Health.*

Dr. Laura Hyatt is a professor and chair of doctoral leadership studies in the Graduate School of Education at Pepperdine University and also serves as executive director of academic affairs. She is an associate of an international think tank, participated as an advisor to the Office of the Assistant Secretary for Planning and Evaluation at the Department of Health and Human Services in Washington, DC, and was appointed to a White House Policy Conference by the president of the United States. Prior to teaching, she was vice president of education for a production company and part of a collaborative effort that won several awards in the entertainment industry. Dr. Hyatt has published books, book chapters, and journal articles and serves on editorial boards for peer-reviewed journals. Dr. Hyatt has received recognition and grants for her research, which focuses on the intersections of learning, neuroscience, change, and sensemaking created by our convergent stories as individuals, organizations, and communities.

Homa Aniya Karimi is currently assistant editor of the peer-reviewed *Journal of Asia-Pacific Business,* published by Taylor & Francis. She also was a research and teaching assistant in the Raj Soin College of Business at Wright State University, Center for Global Business, where she received her MBA with distinction. She holds a master's degree in industrial engineering and systems management, as well as a BS of electronic technology engineering with distinction from Arak University, Iran. She has had professional work experience in environmental economic analysis as well as industry strategic analysis. She is a co-author for three peer-reviewed journal articles in *International Journal of Business Management and Commerce* and *The Journal of Applied, Science, Engineering, and Technology.* She is also interested in pursuing a PhD in the STEM area.

Chelsea A. LeNoble, PhD, is an assistant professor of industrial/organizational psychology at Embry-Riddle Aeronautical University. Her research program focuses on the individual, team-level, and organizational factors related to employee engagement, resilience, and recovery from work stress. Dr. LeNoble earned her PhD in industrial/organizational psychology from Florida Institute of Technology. After graduating, she completed a 2.5-year postdoctoral fellowship at Clemson University and Prisma Health in Greenville, SC.

Jennifer McLean, MA, is a student advocate bringing over 19 years of educational experience to the North Carolina Community College System Office as the associate director of student support services. She received her master's degree in community counseling at Appalachian State University and is a current doctoral student in the educational leadership program at Appalachian State University. Her experience includes working with a public 4-year university, community colleges and a non-profit agency centered on work for marginalized populations. Ms. McLean previously worked as the director of TRIO Programs, a grant awarded through the U.S. Department of Education, at Johnston Community College and Robeson Community College.

Dr. Ruth Middleton House helps organizations, teams, and individuals navigate dangerous intersections: situations that put people in-between, in crisis, and in overload all at the same time. First, she helps them change the rhythms in their organizations and in their lives to minimize the risk and maximize the opportunity. Then she helps them travel through the dangerous space, grow as a result of this travel, and—in some cases—be transformed by it. She is president of Middleton-House & Company and an experienced educator, consultant, author, and public speaker. At Fielding Graduate University, University of the Virgin Islands, and Keller Graduate School of Management, she has taught Strategies for Complex Change, Leadership Theory and Practice, Managing Organizational Change, and Group Process. As a consultant she specializes in troubleshooting high risk, high-conflict, high-visibility projects. She has written several books, including *The Human Side of Project Management* (Addison-Wesley, 1988) and *It's Time to Change the Way You Change* (Middleton-House, 2005) and she is a frequent contributor to *The Georgia Engineer.* She is an in-demand public speaker on such topics as Crisis Decision-Making, Managing the Unexpected, and Caught in the Middle of Change. Dr. House earned an MA in counseling psychology from The University of Alabama and an EdD in organization development from the University of Georgia.

Ludovica Moi is a postdoctoral research fellow at the University of Cagliari (Italy), where she has obtained her PhD in economics and business awarded with the Doctor Europaeus label. As part of the Erasmus PlaceDoc program, she was a visiting scholar at Universidad Carlos III de Madrid (Spain) between October 2017–June 2018. Her research interests focus on marketing capabilities, digital technologies, dynamic capabilities, and agile marketing capabilities. Current projects investigate agile and lean models for entrepreneurship. She has published in peer-reviewed journals such as

Journal of Management and Governance, International Journal of Marketing Studies, SINERGE, among others. She has also co-authored book chapters and conference proceedings, including the *Academy of Management Annual Meeting, ITAIS,* and *SINERGIE-SIMA* conference.

Jenifer Neale, EdD, received her degree from the University of South Florida in 2011. She is currently an adjunct professor with both Florida Southern College and National Louis University. She was co-author on a chapter in *Leading Schools in Challenging Times: Eye to the Future* (Information Age Publishing, 2006). This chapter focused on managing systems of instruction leadership, published in 2016. Dr. Neale has been employed with Hillsborough County Public Schools in Tampa, Florida for over 30 years, and has served in a variety of capacities including classroom teacher, site administrator, and currently district-level administrator. Her research interests include educational leadership, the use of language, power dynamics, historical implications, achievement gaps, and organizational culture.

Col. (ret) Paul H. Nelson, MD, MPH, received his bachelor's degree and commissioning from the University of Mississippi in 1989, and went on to receive his medical diploma from the Uniformed Services University (USU) School of Medicine in 1993. Boarded in family medicine and aerospace medicine, Dr. Nelson recently retired from the Air Force after 31 years in October, 2020 after serving in a variety of operational tours. His military career culminated over the past 5 years in service as the surgeon general's chair to the Air University, serving as the senior medical officer assigned to the Air Force's leadership and development institution. In this last role, he has worked, researched and taught in the areas of individual and organizational resiliency and effectiveness, disruptive innovation and organizational change within a bureaucracy, strategic messaging, bridging the mil-civ divide through partnership, veteran and military family issues, and youth outreach, paying the blessings of service forward to a new generation. Over the year prior to retirement, he has worked collaboratively with a cross-functional, multidisciplinary team including partners at the McCrary Institute at Auburn University to develop national solutions for the current COVID national response. Since retirement, he and his wife of 30 years have co-founded Mission-Next, LLC to continue their community service commitment by working with cool people to do good things that matter for others.

Robert A. Norton, PhD, is professor of veterinary infectious diseases, biosecurity, and public health at Auburn University. Dr. Norton received his PhD from the University of Arkansas and has 35 years of experience in veterinary infectious diseases, national security, bioterrorism and agroterrorism detection and defense. A veterinary microbiologist by training, Dr. Norton served in multiple commands within the U.S. Army, his last assignment being at the U.S. Army Medical Research Institute of Infectious Diseases (USAMRIID) at Fort Detrick, Maryland. He now serves as the chair of the Biosecurity and Food Defense Working Group in the Auburn University Foods System Institute (AUFSI) and the National Security Programs coordinator for The Futures Laboratory, an Auburn outreach effort to Army, Air Force, and U.S. Special Operations Command (USSOCOM). Dr. Norton is the founder and former director of the Auburn OSINT (AU-OSINT) Laboratory, where he currently serves as coordinator of National Security Projects. He also served as the 2019–2020 fellow in the Air Force Surgeon General's Visiting Scholar Program. His long-term research interests include biological weapons defense, One Health/Public Health, food and agriculture systems defense, open source intelligence, technical intelligence (CBRNE/weapons systems), red teaming, and critical infrastructure protection. Dr. Norton currently serves as the senior faculty advisor to the Auburn University COVID Resource Center.

Genevieve Oswald is an entrepreneur, community leader, writer, public speaker, academic research assistant, and certified yoga teacher specializing in yoga philosophy. Genevieve currently operates her third successful business venture in Taos, New Mexico where she also serves as the president of Downtown Taos Mainstreet. As a long-term research assistant to Dr. Theodore Wiard, Genevieve assimilates leadership theory in practice in her entrepreneurial pursuits. Genevieve holds multiple yoga certifications and for more than a decade teaches classes focusing on the power of yoga philosophy in practice to enhance the quality of a person's life. Genevieve speaks publicly and writes professionally about yoga's transformative powers.

Alexandra Petruzzelli is a doctoral candidate in the industrial-organizational psychology program at the University of Akron where her research focuses on employee voice, teamwork, and innovation. She earned her BS in psychology from the University of Central Florida and her MA in industrial-organizational psychology from the University of Akron. Allie is currently a consultant with APT*Metrics*. In her current role, she primarily provides consulting services in the talent acquisition practice area of APT*Metrics* for Fortune® 100 clients across a range of industries. Prior to this, Allie worked as a consultant with the Center for Organizational Research at the University of Akron where she developed selection assessments, competency models, and organizational surveys.

Zoe L. Politis, BS, is a current graduate student in the University of Central Florida's (UCF) Industrial and Organizational Psychology Master's program. She currently holds a role as a graduate research assistant. She received her bachelor's degree in psychology with a track in industrial and organizational psychology and a certificate in human resources from UCF.

Mary J. Goggins Selke, PhD, received her doctoral degree in educational administration and supervision from Marquette University in 1992. She was a faculty member at the University of Northern Iowa from 1992 to 1999, where she was tenured in 1998, and chair of the Education Department at Elmhurst University from 2000 to 2005. She is currently a senior dissertation faculty member in the College of Doctoral Studies at Grand Canyon University. Dr. Selke has published in journals such as *Action in Teacher Education, Critical Issues in Teacher Education, European Journal of Teacher Education, and Success in High-Need Schools.* Book chapters and books include *Rubric assessment goes to college: Objective, comprehensive evaluation of student work* (Roman and Littlefield, 2013). Professional service commitments encompass founding and chairing the SIG for Educational Leadership and serving as team leader of the Induction System for New Professors, both for the national Association of Teacher Educators. A professional focus on graduate teaching, graduate program design and implementation, induction and mentoring, and post-secondary applications of rubric assessment has resulted in an extensive record of teaching and applied research, publications, presentations, consulting, and grant writing.

Simone Serpi has obtained his master's degree in management at the University of Cagliari (Italy). His research thesis focused on understanding how the negative emotions impact the value co-destruction process in a social media context. Currently he is a management consultant in a multinational consulting company operating worldwide. He has co-authored conference proceedings including the *International Marketing Trends Conference 2019.*

Lisa Cuevas Shaw is a senior executive, consultant, and educator with more than 20 years of progressive leadership, strategy and business development, and operations experience across academic, educational, and professional publishing, digital products, programs, and services. Ms. Cuevas Shaw is currently completing her PhD in global leadership and change in Pepperdine University's Graduate School of Education and Psychology. She is exploring leadership theory with regard to the future of scholarly and educational publishing, including digital transformation; the democratization of knowledge; the process of knowledge acquisition and sensemaking in the new information era; and transformative leadership among knowledge professionals. Her current research applies systems theory, complexity theory, and sensemaking to the open science movement, exploring new connections across the literature that offer retrospective and future-oriented insights for leaders in this and related innovation spaces.

Mindy Shoss, PhD, is an associate professor of psychology at the University of Central Florida and honorary fellow of Australian Catholic University. Her research involves workplace stress, job insecurity, economic recessions, worker adaptability, and worker misbehavior. Her work has appeared in top outlets, such as *Journal of Applied Psychology, Organizational Behavior and Human Decision Processes, Journal of Organizational Behavior,* and *Human Resource Management Review.* She is associate editor of *Group & Organization Management* and guest editor of *Journal of Occupational Health Psychology* submissions on the COVID-19 crisis. She also serves on the editorial boards of *Journal of Applied Psychology, Journal of Occupational Health Psychology, Journal of Organizational Behavior, Journal of Business and Psychology, Stress and Health, Occupational Health Science,* and *Journal of Vocational Behavior.*

Ketaki Sodhi, MA, is a doctoral candidate in industrial and organizational psychology at the University of Akron. Her research focuses on the intersection of technology, teamwork, and inclusive talent management. She is currently a part of Microsoft's people analytics function leading employee listening in the internal mobility space. Prior to this, she was part of the succession, performance, and assessment team within Global Talent Management at Johnson & Johnson. She has also served as a consultant and led the operational management of the Center for Organizational Research, an in-house consulting group at the University of Akron.

Bert Spector received a PhD in American history from the University of Missouri–Columbia. He is currently an associate professor of international business and strategy at Northeastern University's D'Amore-McKim School of Business. He has published in numerous journals, including the *Harvard Business Review,* the *Sloan Management Review, Human Resource Management, Organization, Advances in Global Leadership, Management and Organizational History, Journal of Management History, Journal of Contingencies and Crisis Management,* and *Leadership.* He currently serves on the editorial board of *Leadership.* He has published in journals such as the *Journal of Applied Psychology, Journal of Vocational Behavior, Journal of Applied Behavioral Sciences,* and *Human Relations.* He has published nine books, including his recent *Constructing Crisis: Leaders, Crisis, and Claims of Urgency* (Cambridge University Press, 2019) and *Discourse on Leadership: A Critical Appraisal* (2016, Cambridge Uniersity Press). He is a frequent contributor to *The Conversation* and Cambridge University Press' *FifteenEightyFour* blog.

Rachel E. Sturm, PhD, received her degree from the University of Houston in 2014. She joined the Raj Soin College of Business at Wright State University soon after and became an associate professor with tenure in 2017. She earned the 2016 university-wide Presidential Award for Early Career Achievement for excellence in research, teaching, and service. She has also been honored three times with the Outstanding Teacher Award for the Department of Management and International Business and received the 2020 MBA Excellence in Teaching Award for the Raj Soin College of Business. She is an active researcher in the areas of leadership, character, power, and self-other agreement. Her research has been published in journals such as the *Harvard Business Review, Journal of Management, Journal of Organizational Behavior,* and *The Leadership Quarterly.* Her research has earned numerous media mentions and accolades including the 2020 Scholarly Impact Award at the *Journal of Management.* She is also on the editorial board at *The Leadership Quarterly,* and has presented her research both nationally and internationally at conferences. In addition, she has consulted with several organizations on the topic of leadership and plans on becoming a certified professional coach.

Daniel J. Svyantek, PhD, received his degree from the University of Houston in 1987. He was a faculty member in the industrial/organizational psychology PhD program at The University of Akron from 1987 to 2003. He is currently a full professor in the Psychology Department of Auburn University. He has served as the program director of the industrial/ organizational psychology PhD program from 2003 to 2008 and as chair of the Auburn University Psychology Department from 2008 to 2014. He has published in journals such as the *Journal of Applied Psychology, Journal of Vocational Behavior, Journal of Applied Behavioral Sciences,* and *Human Relations.* He has served as associate editor of *Management Decision,* editor of the journal *Organizational Analysis,* and is currently series editor for the annual series, *Research in Organizational Sciences* (Information Age Publishing). He has consulted with several organizations on organizational change projects in the areas of problem solving, compensation systems and implementing work teams. He is particularly interested in the development of new evaluation methods for assessing the practical value of applied research within applied contexts. In addition, his research interest areas include person-organization fit issues and the role of organizational culture and climate as the context for the expression of individual behavior in organizations.

Martina Svyantek, PhD, completed an individualized, interdisciplinary doctorate from Virginia Tech. She served in the Accessible Technologies group at Virginia Tech for 3 years before starting as the assistive technology specialist at the University of Virginia in 2021. She has published in the *International Journal of ePortfolio* and the *Journal of Engineering Education.* Her research interests within critical disability studies focus on accessibility and institutional policy within higher education.

Carrol Warren, EdD, is a faculty scholar with the Belk Center for Community College Leadership and Research at North Carolina State University. Warren's role as a faculty scholar focuses on the development of stakeholder relationships, the executive mentorship program for EdD students, and other special projects connecting the work of the center to the success of doctoral students. In addition to administrative duties, Carrol teaches graduate courses in the EdD program focusing on topics including organizational change, program planning and evaluation, and workplace ethics. Prior to serving graduate students at NC State University, Warren devoted 15 years of service to North Carolina community colleges. Aside from teaching, Carrol provides consulting services to organizations. Warren values collaborating with others on projects related to distance education, underserved populations, and student success.

Greg S. Weaver is an associate professor and interdepartmental graduate program co-director (Sociology) at Auburn University. He is also director of the AU Open Source Intelligence Laboratory. His research and teaching interests include lethal violence, substance use, and research methods. He is co-author of *The Sociology of American Drug Use* (Oxford University Press, 2014). Dr. Weaver is a former probation officer with the Florida Department of Corrections, and since 2009 he has been a member of the reserve unit of the Lee County (AL) Sheriff's Office. In 2010 he completed the Jefferson County Sheriff's Office Law Enforcement Academy. He is past president of the Homicide Research Working Group and currently serves as president of the Alabama Sheriff's Reserve Association.

Theodore J. Wiard, EdD, received his degree from Grand Canyon University in 2018 in organizational leadership with an emphasis in organizational development. In 2001, he became the co-founder of Golden Willow Retreat, an emotional healing sanctuary focused on grief and loss, and Golden Willow Counseling in 2017, a behavioral health agency. He is the director of both agencies, which are located in New Mexico. In addition to directing these organizations, he has a private therapy practice. He is a New Mexico licensed professional clinical counselor, a certified grief counselor, and a New Mexico certified school teacher. He is presently the director of the trauma, grief, and renewal program at Southwestern College & New Earth Institute. He is the co-author of *Witnessing Ted: The Journey to Potential through Grief and Loss* (CreateSpace Independent Publishing Platform, 2011). He is a columnist for the *Taos News* and the *Los Alamos Daily Post.* He has been a public speaker and a consultant on topics pertaining to emotional healing focused on loss, trauma, and grief as well as organizational leadership behaviors pertaining to change and transition. He is particularly interested in organizational leadership related to emotional healing and its impact on individuals, families, communities, and emotional health within an organization.

Rua M. Williams, PhD, received their doctorate in human centered computing from the University of Florida in 2020. They are currently an assistant professor in the user experience design program of the Computer Graphics and Technology Department at Purdue University. They are a scholar of critical disability studies and science and technology studies, with publications in the *Canadian Journal of Disability Studies and Techne,* a journal of research in philosophy and technology. Their research explores interactions between technology design, research practices, and disability justice.

Printed and bound by CPI Group (UK) Ltd, Croydon, CR0 4YY
16/09/2026
14963133-0001